OTHER PEOPLE'S WARS

THE US MILITARY AND THE CHALLENGE OF LEARNING FROM FOREIGN CONFLICTS

Brent L. Sterling

Georgetown University Press
Washington, DC

Library of Congress Cataloging-in-Publication Data

Names: Sterling, Brent L., author.
Title: Other people's wars : the US military and the challenge of learning from
    foreign conflicts / Brent L. Sterling.
Other titles: US military and the challenge of learning from foreign conflicts
Description: Washington, DC : Georgetown University Press, [2021] | Includes
    bibliographical references and index.
Identifiers: LCCN 2020016389 | ISBN 9781647120597 (hardcover) |
    ISBN 9781647120603 (paperback) | ISBN 9781647120610 (ebook)
Subjects: LCSH: Military observers—United States—Case studies. | Military
    education—United States—History—19th century. | Military education—United
    States—History—20th century. | Military art and science—United States—
    History—19th century. | Military art and science—United States—History—20th
    century. | Crimean War, 1853–1856. | Russo-Japanese War, 1904–1905. | Spain—
    History—Civil War, 1936–1939. | Israel-Arab War, 1973.
Classification: LCC U267.5 .S84 2021 | DDC 355.4/80973—dc23
LC record available at https://lccn.loc.gov/2020016389

♾ This book is printed on acid-free paper meeting the requirements of the American National Standard for Permanence in Paper for Printed Library Materials.

22 21   9 8 7 6 5 4 3 2 First printing

Printed in the United States of America

Cover design by Jeremy John Parker
Interior design by Paul Hotvedt, Blue Heron
Cover image by Fujitarō Hibino, May 1904, *Japanese and Russian Soldiers in Fierce
Battle at Chiu-tien-Ch'eng, Manchuria the Battle of Yalu River.* Library of Congress
Prints and Photographs Division.

OTHER PEOPLE'S WARS

Related Titles of Interest from Georgetown University Press

Do Good Fences Make Good Neighbors? What History Teaches Us about Strategic Barriers and International Security
by Brent L. Sterling

Israel's Long War with Hezbollah: Military Innovation and Adaptation Under Fire
by Raphael D. Marcus

The Marines, Counterinsurgency, and Strategic Culture: Lessons Learned and Lost in America's Wars
by Jeannie L. Johnson

The New Counterinsurgency Era: Transforming the US Military for Modern Wars
by David H. Ucko

A Revolution in Military Adaptation: The US Army in the Iraq War
by Chad C. Serena

To Joe Lepgold,
scholar, colleague, teacher, and friend,
who passed along the great importance of
learning and sharing that knowledge.

CONTENTS

MAPS

ACKNOWLEDGMENTS

This project evolved considerably over nearly a decade from the original idea to the final product. I am grateful for the assistance of colleagues in helping me navigate this process, which resulted in a much better book. Dan Byman, Steve Ward, and Ken Pollack provided constructive comments throughout the effort, including after reading the entire manuscript. In particular, I want to express my deep gratitude to Ken Pollack, who has been an invaluable sounding board to hash out conceptual and structural issues as well as a constant source of enthusiasm for the subject's import. I also want to thank the anonymous reviewers for Georgetown University Press; their thought-provoking responses abetted improving the introduction and conclusion. As with my previous book, longtime friend Beth Pincus contributed her keen eye for language and clarity to make the work more readable. Finally, I want to recognize Sandra Llewellyn, who arranged the logistics for my travel across the globe to key battlefields for all the cases covered. Visiting these locations not only facilitated insights into the combat and potential lessons, but the trips served as a source of inspiration for carrying out the study.

Researching the US military across 120 years has proven an immense task but one I completed due to the generous assistance of librarians and archivists. The twenty-first-century scholar profits greatly from being able to access electronically voluminous information including primary documents. I want to communicate my appreciation to everyone who makes that possible, saving much time and expense for not having to travel to dispersed information repositories. In the collection of such material, I benefited considerably from the labor of the reference librarians at Georgetown University's Lauinger Library. Additionally, I want to convey my indebtedness to personnel at the US Army Heritage and Education Center at Carlisle Barracks, who provided valuable aid during multiple trips to examine and photograph documents in the service archives. Maj. Zach Alessi-Friedlander (USA) kindly supplied me with useful guidance and documents on lessons learned from the Yom Kippur War.

For the second time, I've been fortunate to have Don Jacobs as my acquisitions editor. His hard work and wise suggestions have markedly improved the manuscript. I am grateful to everyone at Georgetown University Press for their contributions to the process. No war-related publication would be complete without maps, and I want to acknowledge Chris Robinson for his skilled cartography. I take full responsibility for any remaining errors.

Finally, I want to thank my family and friends for their sustained and strong support. After many years listening to stories about lessons from far-off battles, I know they are eager for the transition to my next project, which will result in an entirely new set of anecdotes to bore them.

ABBREVIATIONS

AA	antiaircraft
AAA	antiaircraft artillery
AAH	advanced attack helicopter
ACTS	Air Corps Tactical School
AEF	American Expeditionary Force
ATGM	antitank guided missile
AWACS	airborne warning and control system
AWC	Army War College
BMP	Boyevaya Mashina Pekhoty
CAS	close air support
CBR	chemical, biological, and radiological
CEWI	Combat Electronic Warfare Intelligence
CGSS	Command and General Staff School
CSA	Confederate States of America
CW	chemical warfare
DOD	Department of Defense
DOTMLPF-P	doctrine, organization, training, materiel, leadership, personnel, facilities, and policy
DRS	division restructuring study
ECM	electronic countermeasures
EW	electronic warfare
FSR	*Field Service Regulations*
GSSC	General Service and Staff College
HIFV	heavy infantry fighting vehicle
IAD	integrated air defenses
IAF	Israeli Air Force
IDF	Israeli Defense Forces
IDR	*Infantry Drill Regulations*
IFV	infantry fighting vehicle
JCS	Joint Chiefs of Staff
JLLP	Joint Lessons Learned Program
JSTARS	joint surveillance target attack radar system
LGB	laser-guided bomb

LWF	lightweight fighter
MICV	mechanized infantry combat vehicle
MID	Military Intelligence Directorate
MLRS	multiple launch rocket system
NTC	National Training Center
ONI	Office of Naval Intelligence
OSD	Office of the Secretary of Defense
PELSS	Precision Emitter Location Strike System
PGM	precision-guided munition
R&D	research and development
SAM	surface-to-air missile
SAM-D	surface-to-air missile development
SEAD	suppression of enemy air defense
SHORAD	short-range air defense missile
SRSG	Special Readiness Study Group
TAC	Tactical Air Command
TOW	tube-launched, optically tracked, wire-guided
TRADOC	US Army Training and Doctrine Command
USAF	US Air Force
USMOST	US Military Operations Survey Team
WSEG	Weapons Systems Evaluation Group

INTRODUCTION

> Happily we may profit by the experience of others without suffering
> the evils that attend the practical solution of such problems.
> —*Secretary of War Jefferson Davis*

On Thursday, April 5, 1855, three highly regarded soldiers (Maj. Richard Delafield, Maj. Alfred Mordecai, and Capt. George McClellan) entered the War Department building, located just northwest of the White House, to be briefed on their unprecedented mission. Awaiting them was Jefferson Davis, whose heroic exploits as commander of the 1st Mississippi Rifles in the Mexican-American War had propelled him to prominence and his current office. Victory in that conflict less than ten years earlier instilled a healthy confidence in the US officer corps about its ability to meet defense challenges. Davis, not wanting the army to rest on its laurels, dispatched this trio—subsequently known as the Delafield Commission—to observe the ongoing combat between three of Europe's leading military powers. Physical distance combined with diplomatic obstacles meant they disappointingly did not reach the Crimean Peninsula until just after the British and French captured Sebastopol. Still, when the weary soldiers sat down again with the secretary thirteen months after that initial meeting, the commissioners possessed a wealth of information. For example, the group documented the outstanding performance of the new French 12-pound field artillery piece, the failure of the much-touted British Lancaster 68-pound rifled artillery gun, and the increased power projection capabilities of modern militaries.

Davis and other American decision-makers had to assess whether these findings were accurate lessons about contemporary war and whether they should be applied by the US Army. The answers were mixed. The service eagerly embraced the French 12-pounder, which provided excellent support as the primary field gun for both the US Army and Confederate Army in the Civil War. Information on the Lancaster gun's failing imbued War Department leaders with confidence in the continuing viability of masonry fortifications, but such works proved highly vulnerable from April 1862 with the introduction of effective rifled artillery. The US government largely ignored as irrelevant the overarching lessons about the expanded scale of war and power projection potential, contributing to the chaotic scramble at the outset of the internecine American fight and potential danger if the British and French allied with the Confederacy.

Although widespread belief exists in the military ranks that "victory smiles upon those who anticipate the changes in the character of war, not upon those who wait to adapt themselves after the changes occur," soldiers, sailors, marines, and aviators struggle with foreseeing shifts in combat dynamics and fear errant choices.[1] Based on their experience, imagination, and study of highly regarded foreign armed forces, officers devise or copy new weapons, alternative organizational structures, modified training regimes, and innovative tactical and operational concepts. Before introducing such reforms, the services attempt to validate their merit through experiments, field trials, and war games. Truthful evaluations require realism and rigor, but satisfying those conditions is difficult for cultural, informational, fiscal, and safety reasons. Even when evidence supports proposed measures, reluctance often exists to initiate major adjustments. As Stephen Rosen opines, military organizations are large bureaucracies, and "almost everything we know in theory about large bureaucracies suggests not only that they are hard to change, but that they are *designed not to change.*"[2] As a result, battle-tested practices usually act as a "cognitive anchor" long after the war in which they occurred.[3] Unsurprisingly, militaries tend to struggle at the outset of conflicts. Given the difficulty in prewar preparation, some military historians stress the importance of adaptability after fighting commences.[4] To enable such intrawar changes, the US and other militaries have developed robust programs to learn from their combat experiences.[5]

Yet proficiency at adaptability does not eliminate the significance of prewar preparation. Even historians stressing such learning acknowledge that taking advantage of new data is heavily dependent on the soundness of the service's prewar foundation. Moreover, at times the gap between opposing forces is so great that the opening campaign proves determinative, rendering adaptability irrelevant. Plus, a credible standing military capability has critical importance for states' abilities to deter aggression and thus avoid war. The very term *war game* (*Kriegsspiel*) reflects the desire to discern deficiencies without actual combat. Unfortunately, informational benefits of such simulations do not match the data provided by actual combat. Officials have even suggested manufacturing modest military action purely for knowledge acquisition. For example, Assistant Secretary of the Navy Theodore Roosevelt advocated in late 1897 for a Cuban landing, "if only for the sake of learning from our own blunders."[6] Such provocative behavior, however, rarely if ever occurs in modern times.

The best potential source of battlefield knowledge outside of one's own combat is other people's wars, but learning from such events is challenging. For an army that had been at peace for many years, German military theorist Carl von Clausewitz recommended that some officers "should be sent to observe operations and learn what war is like."[7] Whether or not armed forces have recent fighting experience, as William McBride notes, "other people's wars have been touchstones for modern military professionals."[8] Even conflicts between smaller, less powerful nations have potential for revealing the effects of new technology, tactics, or systems. Andrew Krepinevich characterizes such battles as "precursor wars," the neglect of which imperils major powers existing in an unstable security environment.[9] Nevertheless, the extent to which attempts at learning from these events has led to better preparedness is an open question. The idiosyncratic nature and investigatory difficulty of foreign wars complicates accurately capturing what happened. Historian Robert Citino pessimistically writes that external conflict examination since its nineteenth-century origin has proven "a highly problematic venture, one that resists any kind of scientific or objective standards."[10] Even with accurate data, doubt exists to its relevancy. President Theodore Roosevelt cautioned the US Army chief of staff after the Russo-Japanese War against following in "servile fashion" the victorious Japanese because "not all of the things they have done have been wise, and some of the wise things they have done are not wise for us."[11] Sound advice, but such guidance is prone to abuse if findings suggest the need for bureaucratically or culturally unappealing changes.

We need to better understand the dynamics of learning from foreign wars to avoid recurring pitfalls and maximize their utility. This subject has been neglected in contrast to an extensive literature examining learning from one's own experiences. Previous works have consisted of either single case histories (e.g., Greenwood, Juntunen, Moten[12]) or investigations of multiple experiences from a single war or era (e.g., Luvaas, O'Connor, Vacca[13]). These studies yield insights about the practical challenges involved in such efforts and some ability to consider the relative merit of contrasting approaches. They, however, preclude discovery of recurring obstacles and enablers of success across different periods and contexts. The potential to obtain such understanding exists from an exploration of multiple attempts by a single military over an extended period as it developed institutionally and as the nature of war evolved. Completing such an investigation involves answering a series of distinct but related questions. How did the service attempt to discover what happened? What types of lessons were identified and what were missed? When, why, and how did the service apply its findings? What accounts for the resistance to using such information, and was such pushback appropriate? Why did implementation at times improve effectiveness but in other cases prove counterproductive in preparing for future war? How do the dynamics of such learning efforts differ from attempts to benefit from one's own experiences? To answer these questions, I conduct an inductive investigation through a series of in-depth case studies.

The work, however, has been informed by three interrelated literatures that address aspects of learning and military change. The first and most developed area attempts to understand why militaries innovate—why they initiate significant reforms that produce improved battlefield performance.[14] One school of thought stresses the role of external (civilian) pressure, often in cooperation with maverick officers, in overcoming an institutional reluctance to adjust.[15] Yet the frequent failure of even highly motivated civilians to achieve their desired objective has led others to place the primary onus for innovation within militaries. A range of distinct explanations exist for such internally directed change, including the armed forces' position in the governing process, interservice competition for scarce reasons, and intraservice dynamics.[16] For intraservice dynamics, improvement results when proponents of a new "theory of victory," especially senior officers, successfully combine collected evidence with internal politics to prevail over status-quo-preferring forces.[17] Scholars have increasingly stressed the role of organizational culture as a factor in promoting or frustrating change, given its effects on the collection, evaluation, communication, and embrace of new knowledge.[18] No theoretical reason exists to dismiss or give an a priori preference to any of these explanations when considering the influence of combat lessons from a foreign war. Given the relatively limited and hard to acquire data compared to that available from one's own experiences, one might expect the increased need for external pressure to "learn" from a foreign war. Yet findings from such conflicts, especially those of modest political significance, are likely to be of much greater interest to military audiences, fueling inter- and intraservice battles over how best to react.

For insights into the process by which militaries assess the desirability and practicality of responding to external cues, the literature on the diffusion of military power is instructive.[19] This subfield focuses not on the initial innovation but the transfer of that knowledge throughout the international system. Whereas neorealists expect competition between states to precipitate uniform diffusion, these scholars stress that it "varies with the social, cultural, organizational, and political context."[20] Researchers have identified a number of reasons why nations embrace or reject major military innovations including cost requirements, degree of organizational decentralization (veto points), ability to experiment, breadth of organizational focus (mission), and compatibility (perceived fit of innovation with organizational culture, values, and needs). This literature also makes clear that rather than a binary adopt / not adopt decision, militaries pursue a range of responses—copy, selectively emulate (modify for different circumstances), counter, neglect (due to low priority), or reject. Despite the relevance of the diffusion research, some notable differences exist. First, their unit of investigation is a development (e.g., a major military innovation) compared to an event (e.g., a foreign war) with potentially many meaningful lessons (big and small) on a wide range of topics. Second, diffusion scholars' interest begins only when the international community has sufficient data—a demonstration point— about an innovation's effectiveness, unlike foreign-war investigators.

The literature on organizational learning and knowledge management provides insights about the collection of information as well as the understanding of what militaries do with that data.[21] Scholars in this field point out that lesson drawing

4

begins with individuals either through experience (hands-on) or reflection (reading, listening, thinking). For these discoveries to be beneficial, the organization must have structures and processes to transition such findings into institutional learning via knowledge acquisition, analysis, dissemination, and absorption stages. Achievement of this goal requires satisfying three conditions, as Janine Davidson explains: "There must be clarity and consensus regarding the events that occurred (what happened or what is happening), what those events mean (why this matters to our organization), and what the proper course of action should be (what should be done about it)."[22] Research has shown that certain factors enhance military learning such as information flow (horizontal as well as vertical), commitment to rigorous experimentation, openness to disruptive data, and a collective problem-solving mentality. Moreover, leadership plays a significant role in strongly hierarchical organizations such as the uniformed services, either facilitating or impeding knowledge growth. Finally, lesson drawing needs to be prospective, considering whether what is successfully done today will improve conditions in the future. This task is particularly difficult but essential for militaries, which are engaged in dynamic and obscure competition with adversaries simultaneously adjusting.

The US military has attempted to apply these insights in developing an increasingly sophisticated program to learn from its own experiences. Such learning largely occurs from the bottom up as frontline units discover deficiencies with the status quo from combat and even exercises. Cases studies documenting this process have prompted criticism of the aforementioned innovation theories for disproportionately weighting top-down change mechanics.[23] While scholars have explored more integrative models, militaries have attempted to improve the collection and use of bottom-up inputs.[24] Struggles in Afghanistan and Iraq reinforced for the US services the benefit from becoming more effective learning organizations.[25] For one's own experiences, soldiers, sailors, aviators, and marines are present at the information source, but effective collection of information on a foreign conflict requires a dedicated effort initiated by the leadership. Thus, learning from other people's wars is largely a top-down process. Moreover, the assessment and reaction to findings occurs in distinct decision contexts. During war, a necessary delegation of authority to the tactical level abets rapidly translating battlefield discoveries of best practices and issues needing resolution into improved performance. In peacetime, when considering lessons from foreign wars, military organizations revert to their strongly hierarchical nature and display reluctance to accept findings that diverge from the sentiment of the service's leadership and organizational culture.

While these contextual differences will likely lead to distinct approaches for maximizing learning, shared core elements of the tasks allow taking advantage of the well-established definitions used by the US military for its own experiential learning when characterizing key terminology for the investigation of foreign wars. Beginning in the late 1980s, after a long failure to delineate terms, especially "lessons learned," the army issued formal definitions as a part of the effort to standardize and enhance learning from its own experiences.[26] The US military has refined this terminology through several generations of guidance over the last thirty years.[27] As a result, the current versions clearly and accurately depict the basic process elements, so I use them in this study. Of course, participants in the pre-1980s cases did not possess such clarification and at times used words, especially *learning*, in different ways. Such a tendency does not present a difficulty as long as I maintain consistency in what is actually occurring. The process begins at the information-gathering stage with the collection of observations, insights, and lessons. The most recent Army Lessons Learned Program guidance defines an observation as "a statement of the conditions experienced or observed with recommended changes to improve performance" and a lesson as "a potential solution to a problem experienced as a result of an observation."[28] Importantly, this document conveys the value of both positive (evidence supporting sustainment) as well as negative (evidence of need for improvement or change) data.[29]

Most critically, what is a "lesson learned"? Scholars and practitioners appropriately differentiate between drawing a lesson and learning a lesson.[30] The latter requires "application" of the former. What is meant by application, however, is a source of disagreement. Some commentators limit learning to organizational action.[31] Typifying many commentators, Robert Foley, Stuart Griffin, and Helen McCartney contend that "only when positive change has been made can a lesson really be said to have been learned."[32] Similarly, the most recent Joint Chiefs of Staff Joint Lessons Learned Program (JLLP) guidance characterizes a lesson learned as "an operationalized resolved issue or best practice that resulted in behavioral change and improved operations or activities."[33] Beneficial impacts can occur across the full spectrum of doctrine, organization, training, materiel, leadership, personnel, facilities, and policy (DOTMLPF-P), but decision-makers attach particular attention to the first four subjects.[34] Yet the requirement of adjustment for "learning" to take place omits two valuable uses of collected information. First, consideration of other people's mistakes can prevent adoption of harmful changes previously under consideration by revealing what not to do. Second, findings may indicate the continuing viability of existing DOTMLPF-P. As the 2005 version of the JLLP guidance states, "a lesson learned also results from evaluation or observation of a positive finding that did not necessarily require corrective action other than sustainment."[35] Such effects should not be dismissed as of trivial importance given doubt about status quo methods and techniques the more time passes from a prior war and the emergence of alternative approaches and new technology.

As I noted, consideration of a single military's efforts to learn lessons from foreign wars offers an unexplored way to identify recurring challenges and issues as well as potentially ameliorating measures in this nuanced multistage process. Although a half dozen militaries qualify as potential candidates, I selected the US armed forces given the varied environments in which it has conducted such investigations and the relative availability of information. My initial thought was to examine a combination of conventional wars and counterinsurgencies, but I decided to concentrate on the former because extended US operations in Afghanistan and Iraq over the last twenty years have prompted numerous studies of prior counterinsurgency efforts (e.g., the British in Malaya; the French in Algeria) and their impact on the US Army.[36] Rather than rehash this terrain, I consider learning from four conventional wars between the 1850s and 1970s. During this span, the active army transitioned from a small, decentralized fifteen-thousand-man force with minimal investigative capability to a large, complex, nearly eight-hundred-thousand-man institution with expansive analytical and educational components. Given that most research on this subject has focused on ground forces, I also consider how either the US Navy or US Army Air Corps / Air Force responded to each conflict.

The study begins with the Crimean War (1854–56). The army's Delafield Commission marked the first major American attempt to observe a foreign war, occurring only a half decade before the US Civil War. The navy conducted no formal fact-finding assessment, but key US sailors sought insights at a time of rapidly evolving technology. The Russo-Japanese War (1904–5) offers a case of strong interest for the army and navy, both undergoing substantial institutional development and facing notable technological changes. Thirty years later, after significant post–World War I improvements to the tank and aircraft, the army leadership appreciated the potential of the Spanish Civil War (1936–39) to yield valuable information about the evolution of modern war. This case technically involves only the army, but the Army Air Corps operated with considerable autonomy and possessed a sharply divergent perspective on the Iberian struggle. Finally, the Yom Kippur War (October 1973) warrants inclusion as the most extensive—by far—American foreign-war investigation. As the army and air force transitioned from a focus on the Vietnam War to the Soviet threat in Central Europe, US officers regarded the intense, lethal Arab–Israeli fighting as almost a proxy for combat with the Russians.

Each case study starts by considering the way in which the services collected data. Then, I identify what information each institution obtained and what it missed and why. Subsequently, I explore efforts to apply findings, especially to doctrine, organization, training, and materiel. Some applications involve maintaining the status quo, but most are adjustments, either innovations (transformative changes) or adaptations (incremental changes). Whereas military change scholars have long focused on innovation, they have increasingly appreciated that adaptation is not less significant in facilitating preparedness.[37] Although apportioning responsibility for multicausal actions is an admittedly hard task, understanding organizational learning is not possible without careful assessment of how a service "used" the data. The skewed emphasis on the discovery phase in previous studies of foreign-war investigations has, I believe, accounted for an excessive dismissiveness of findings' impact as commentators look for the rare instances in which a lesson provides the sole impetus for change. Such a perspective neglects the often-meaningful contribution of insights in shifting the balance of argument in ongoing debates. This impact reflects what scholars describe as key for organizational learning—how to integrate acquired knowledge into existing knowledge to facilitate superior understanding and improved practices.[38]

The subsequent case studies reveal that applied findings from foreign wars benefited the US services in three basic ways: instrumentally, instructionally, and inspirationally. That is, the combat (1) generated compelling evidence used to overcome resistance from military and/or civilian officials to doing what had already been recognized as necessary by a group of officers, a force subcomponent, or even the entire service; (2) provided insights on how to better prepare for and conduct martial affairs; and (3) sparked recognition or increased appreciation of battlefield challenges requiring resolution and even at times fueled imaginative responses. Although the US military's learning capacity and performance generally improved (except for the Spanish Civil War case), recurring pitfalls in both the discovery (e.g., allowing preexisting preferences to corrupt interpretations of what happened) and application (e.g., embracing cues that rapidly became obsolete) stages impeded performance.

The book's conclusion lays out the most problematic hazards for learning lessons and considers how best to overcome or minimize their impact. Looking for practical benefits from investigations of other people's wars, the US military, especially the army, has tended toward rapidly drawing preliminary findings and seeking hard (quantitative) data to support such insights. While producing some notable benefits, this orientation problematically discourages attention to operational and strategic elements and dangerously promotes static, not dynamic, learning. A more effective approach requires broadening both the investigative scope and perceived applicability of findings. That is, rather than a tasking-driven exploration of subjects deemed highly relevant to the service mission, the endeavor needs to encompass as full a history as possible and respond to cues in areas of potential, not just current, relevance. Such a perspective protects against mistaken presumptions about what will be germane, especially since salient areas of warfare not regarded as relevant today are almost always less well understood and thus where the institution would gain the most from applying foreign-war information. To best contribute to military preparedness, lessons learned should not only strengthen core competencies but also enhance adaptability given the likelihood of the next war occurring in an unanticipated manner. As a part of this effort, the armed forces must consider not only a foreign war's combat but also what other militaries identified as lessons from the conflict and their application of that information. How I arrive at this somewhat contrarian perspective in favor of a broadened effort requires returning to 1855 and considering that and subsequent American experiences.

NOTES

Epigraph: Jefferson Davis, *Report of the Secretary of War*, December 4, 1854 (Washington, DC: A.O.P. Nicholson, 1854), 19.

1. Giulio Douhet, *The Command of the Air*, ed. Joseph Harahan and Richard Kohn (Tuscaloosa: University of Alabama, 2009), 30.

2. Stephen Peter Rosen, *Winning the Next War: Innovation and the Modern Military* (Ithaca, NY: Cornell University Press, 1991), 2; emphasis original.

3. Thomas Mahnken, *Uncovering Ways of War: US Intelligence and Foreign Military Innovation, 1918–1941* (Ithaca, NY: Cornell University Press, 2009), 9; and James Russell, *Innovation, Transformation, and War: Counterinsurgency Operations in Anbar and Ninewa Provinces, Iraq, 2005–2007* (Stanford, CA: Stanford University Press, 2011), 25.

4. Russell Hart, *Clash of Arms: How the Allies Won in Normandy* (Norman: University of Oklahoma Press, 2004), 9; Michael Howard, "Military Science in an Age of Peace," *RUSI Quarterly* 119, no. 1 (1974): 7; and Allan Millett and Williamson Murray, "Lessons of War," *National Interest*, no. 14 (Winter 1988–89): 86.

5. Tom Dyson, *Organizational Learning and the Modern Army: A New Model for Lessons-Learned Processes* (London: Routledge, 2020); Robert Foley, Stuart Griffin, and Helen McCartney, "'Transformation in Contact': Learning the Lessons of Modern War," *International Affairs* 87, no. 2 (2011): 253–70; and Jon Thomas and Douglas Shultz, "Lessons about Lessons: Growing the Joint Lessons Learned Program," *Joint Forces Quarterly* 79, no. 4 (October 2015): 113–19.

6. Theodore Roosevelt to William W. Kimball, November 19, 1897, in *The Letters of Theodore Roosevelt, The Years of Preparation: 1868–1898*, ed. Elting Morison (Cambridge, MA: Harvard University Press, 1951), 717.

7. Carl von Clausewitz, *On War*, book 1, chap. 8, ed. and trans. Michael Howard and Peter Paret (Princeton, NJ: Princeton University Press, 1984), 122.

8. William McBride, *Technological Change and the United States Navy, 1865–1945* (Baltimore: Johns Hopkins University Press, 2000), 237. For a recent attempt to benefit from both direct experience and foreign fighting, see Thomas Mahnken, ed. *Learning the Lessons of Modern War* (Stanford, CA: Stanford University Press, 2020).

9. Andrew Krepinevich, "Cavalry to Computer: The Pattern of Military Revolutions," *National Interest*, no. 37 (Fall 1994): 40–41.

10. Robert Citino, *Blitzkrieg to Desert Storm: The Evolution of Operational Warfare* (Lawrence: University Press of Kansas, 2004), 82.

11. Theodore Roosevelt to Adna Chaffee, July 3, 1905, in *The Letters of Theodore Roosevelt, The Square Deal: 1903–1905*, ed. Elting Morison (Cambridge, MA: Harvard University Press, 1951), 1261.

12. John Greenwood, "The American Military Observers of the Russo-Japanese War, 1904–1905" (PhD diss., Kansas State University, 1971); Kim Juntunen, "US Army Attachés and the Spanish Civil War, 1936–1939: Gathering of Technical and Tactical Intelligence" (Master's thesis, Temple University, May 1990); and Matthew Moten, *The Delafield Commission and the American Military Profession* (College Station: Texas A&M University Press, 2000).

13. Jay Luvaas, *The Military Legacy of the Civil War: The European Inheritance* (Lawrence: University Press of Kansas, 1988); Maureen P. O'Connor, "In the Eye of the Beholder: Western Military Observers from Buena Vista to Plevna" (PhD diss., Harvard University, 1996); and William Vacca, "Learning about Military Effectiveness: Examining Theories of Learning during the Russo-Japanese War" (PhD diss., Rutgers University, 2009).

14. For a classic review of this literature, see Adam Grissom, "The Future of Military Innovation Studies," *Journal of Strategic Studies* 29, no. 5 (2006): 905–34; for a recent update, see Dyson, *Organizational Learning and the Modern Army*, 51–69.

15. For example, see Barry Posen, *Sources of Military Doctrine: France, Britain, and Germany between the Wars* (Ithaca, NY: Cornell University Press, 1984).

16. For example, see Rosen, *Winning the Next War*; Deborah Avant, *Political Institutions and Military Change: Lessons from Peripheral Wars* (Ithaca, NY: Cornell University Press, 1994); and Elizabeth Kier, *Imagining War: French and British Military Doctrine between the Wars* (Princeton, NJ: Princeton University Press, 1997).

17. Grissom, "Future of Military Innovation Studies," 919.

18. Dyson, *Organizational Learning and the Modern Army*, 55–59; Eric Sangar, "The Pitfalls of Learning from Historical Experience: The British Army's Debate on Useful Lessons for the War in Afghanistan," *Contemporary Security Policy* 37, no. 2 (2016): 223–24, 230–31; Robert Foley, "Dumb Donkeys or Cunning Foxes? Learning in the British and German Armies during the Great War," *International Affairs* 90, no. 2 (March 2014): 296–97; and Raphael Marcus, "Military Innovation and Tactical Adaptation in the Israel–Hizbollah Conflict: The Institutionalization of Lesson-Learning in the IDF," *Journal of Strategic Studies* 38, no. 4 (2015): 502–4.

19. Leslie Eliason and Emily Goldman, "Theoretical and Comparative Perspectives on Innovation and Diffusion," in *The Diffusion of Military Technology and Ideas*, ed. Emily Goldman and Leslie Eliason (Stanford, CA: Stanford University Press, 2003), 3–30; Michael Horowitz, *The Diffusion of Military Power: Causes and Consequences for International Politics* (Princeton, NJ: Princeton University Press, 2010); Emily Goldman and Richard Andres, "Systemic Effects of Military Innovation and Diffusion," *Security Studies* 8, no. 4 (Summer 1999): 79–125; and Fabrizio Coticchia and Francesco Niccolò Moro, "Learning from Others? Emulation and Change in the Italian Armed Forces since 2001," *Armed Forces & Society* 42, no. 4 (January 2016): 696–718.

20. Goldman and Andres, "Systemic Effects," 93.

21. Janine Davidson, *Lifting the Fog of Peace: How Americans Learned to Fight Modern War* (Ann Arbor: University of Michigan Press, 2010), 3–28; Dyson, *Organizational Learning and the*

Modern Army, 21–42, 246; Richard Rose, "What Is Lesson-Drawing?," *Journal of Public Policy* 11, no. 1 (January–March 1991): 3–30; Peter Senge, *The Fifth Discipline: The Art and Practice of the Learning Organization* (New York: Doubleday, 1990); Steven Mains and Gil Ad Ariely, "Learning while Fighting: Operational Knowledge Management That Makes a Difference," *Prism* 2, no. 3 (2011): 173–74; and Anthony Dibella, "Can the Army Become a *Learning Organization?* A Question Reexamined," *Joint Forces Quarterly* 56, no. 1 (2010): 121–22.

22. Davidson, *Lifting the Fog of Peace*, 23.

23. Russell, *Innovation, Transformation, and War*, 23–27, 35; Dyson, *Organizational Learning and the Modern Army*, 23–25; and Grissom, "Future of Military Innovation Studies," 905, 920–24.

24. Grissom, "Future of Military Innovation Studies," 926n105; Marcus, "Military Innovation and Tactical Adaptation," 501–3, 523–25; and Foley, "Dumb Donkeys or Cunning Foxes?," 5–22; and Dyson, *Organizational Learning and the Modern Army*, 66–67.

25. Foley, Griffin, and McCartney, "'Transformation in Contact'," 266; Davidson, *Lifting the Fog of Peace*, 23; Dyson, *Organizational Learning and the Modern Army*, 4; and Mains and Ariely, "Learning while Fighting," 168.

26. US Army Regulation (AR) 11-33, Army Lessons Learned Program (ALLP): System Development and Application, October 10, 1989, p. 10, http://www.citeseerx.ist.psu.edu; and Dennis Vetock, *Lessons Learned: A History of US Army Lesson Learning* (Carlisle Barracks, PA: US Army Military History Institute, 1988), 2.

27. For the most recent versions, see US Chairman of the Joint Chiefs of Staff Manual (CJCSM) 3150.25B, Joint Lessons Learned Program (JLLP), October 12, 2018, http://www.jcs.mil; and AR 11-33, ALLP, June 14, 2017, http://www.armypubs.army.mil.

28. AR 11-33, ALLP, June 14, 2017, p. 22.

29. AR 11-33, ALLP, June 14, 2017, p. 1.

30. AR 11-33, ALLP, June 14, 2017, p. 9; and CJCSM 3150.25B, JLLP, October 12, 2018; Vetock, *Lessons Learned*, 2; Dyson, *Organizational Learning and the Modern Army*, 17–42; Sergio Catignani, "Coping with Knowledge: Organizational Learning in the British Army?," *Journal of Strategic Studies* 37, no. 1 (2014): 31–32, 39, 48.

31. Eliason and Goldman, "Theoretical and Comparative Perspectives," 12.

32. Foley, Griffin, and McCartney, "'Transformation in Contact'," 268.

33. CSJSM 3150.25B, JLLP, October 12, 2018, p. GL-8.

34. Jeffrey Isaacson, Christopher Layne, and John Arquilla, *Predicting Military Innovation* (Santa Monica, CA: RAND, 1999), 8; Russell, *Innovation, Transformation, and War*, 26–28, 205; CSJSM 3150.25B, JLLP, October 12, 2018, p. B-3; and Grissom, "Future of Military Innovation Studies," 913–14, 919.

35. Quoted in Foley, Griffin, and McCartney, "'Transformation in Contact'," 258n28.

36. For examples, see John Nagl, *Learning to Eat Soup with a Knife: Counterinsurgency Lessons from Malaya and Vietnam* (Chicago: University of Chicago Press, 2005); David Ucko, *The New Counterinsurgency Era: Transforming the US Military for Modern Wars* (Washington, DC: Georgetown University Press, 2009); Grant Vaughn, "Counterinsurgency Lessons Learned from the French-Algeria War Applied to the Current Afghanistan War" (Master's thesis, Marine Corps

Command and Staff College, April 2010); and Winston Marbella, "Hearts and Minds: Its Evolution and Relevance to Counterinsurgency Campaigns" (Master's thesis, Army Command and General Staff College, October 2010).

37. Theo Farrell, "Improving in War: Military Adaptation and the British in Helmand Province, Afghanistan, 2006–2009," *Journal of Strategic Studies* 33, no.4 (2010): 567–94. Dibella, "Can the Army Become a *Learning Organization?*," 119–20; Foley, "Dumb Donkeys or Cunning Foxes?," 4; and Marcus, "Military Innovation and Tactical Adaptation," 503.

38. Dyson, *Organizational Learning and the Modern Army*, 19–20, 30–37; Coticchia and Moro, "Learning from Others?," 5, 13; and Sangar, "Pitfalls of Learning," 231–32, 239.

CHAPTER 1

THE CRIMEAN WAR
Partial but Precedent-Setting Probe

The contest that commenced, in 1854, between the principled
military and naval powers of Europe, gave rise, during its progress,
to the belief that the art of war had undergone some material
changes since the days of Napoleon and Wellington.
—*Maj. Richard Delafield, USA*

The Crimean War, the first major conflict between European great powers since the
Napoleonic era, generated considerable attention in the United States. Diplomats and
politicians weighed the foreign policy implications while a curious public devoured
unprecedented coverage from far-off battlefields. The most interested Americans
were those in the business of war. Reflective of this last group, Cdr. David Farragut,
USN, requested in April 1854 appointment to any commission or command sent to
the deployed English and French fleets "with a view to ascertaining whether in the
outfits and preparations for war they possess any advantages over our ships of war,
and if so, in what they consist."[1] Although duty necessitated that Farragut follow
events from California, his foster brother and future fellow admiral Lt. David Dixon
Porter reached the Crimean theater in late 1855. Secretary of War Jefferson Davis, an
inquisitive military reformer, would undoubtedly have leaped at a similar chance. His
position precluded such a journey, leaving him to scrutinize battlefield reports and
track fighting forces on a large map in his office.[2] More importantly, Davis convinced
President Franklin Pierce to approve an unprecedented visit by an American military
commission to a theater of war.[3] This chapter explores the US Army and US Navy
efforts to learn from this largely forgotten but militarily significant struggle, which
included the battlefield introduction of significant technologies (e.g., rifled cannon,
submarine mines, armored warships). These initial endeavors serve as a benchmark
against which to judge subsequent American attempts at learning from foreign wars.

HOW DID THE AMERICANS ATTEMPT TO IDENTIFY LESSONS?

US officials discovered information about what many at the time called the Russian War in four basic ways: newspapers, combatant data relayed by Americans in Europe, firsthand accounts of US observers, and postconflict studies. The telegraph and the dedicated war correspondent combined for unprecedented reportage as "major newspapers throughout the country carried hundreds of articles" about the conflict.[4] Soldiers, even those garrisoned at isolated frontier posts that usually had to wait a month for newspapers, closely reviewed the latest dispatches.[5] Yet, as Jay Luvaas points out, these articles lacked desired technical data as "most war correspondents were not military men, and, like the majority of their readers, they were concerned primarily with general conditions and broad issues."[6] Moreover, news stories often contradicted each other. For example, Cdr. John Dahlgren, USN, the service's foremost ordnance expert, complained that statements about the much-anticipated combat debut of the Lancaster gun (a British rifled, muzzle-loading cannon that fired a 68-pound shell) varied "so widely that it is difficult to understand that they were speaking of one and the same operation."[7]

More detailed and accurate information potentially could be obtained from the combatants. In an era that preceded military attachés, US diplomats as well as other Americans residing abroad relayed relevant conversations and gathered documents to the best of their ability.[8] For example, a friend of Secretary Davis in London forwarded to him reports on artillery and logistics in the Crimea. Although helpful, such works suffered from participant bias, removal of sensitive information, and efforts to cast home forces in a positive light. Dahlgren noted that the official French, English, and Russian accounts of the October 1854 Sebastopol naval battle were "altogether wanting in those technical minutiae that the professional inquirer needs."[9] None of the other American sources (e.g., doctors volunteering with the Russian army, entrepreneurs seeking weapons contracts) provided data of much value.

American officers regarded direct observation by their own kind as vastly superior to the preceding methods. Since 1815 the army had periodically dispatched soldiers to study at European military schools, collect data, and conduct broad-based examinations of the latest military technology and practice.[10] As secretary of war, Davis was particularly supportive of such efforts. Possessing a rare combination of military experience, political adroitness, and openness to new ideas, the Mississippian in 1853 had reluctantly left his position as chairman of the Senate Committee on Military Affairs.[11] His close relationship with President Pierce, a fellow Mexican War veteran who ardently lobbied Davis to join the administration, proved a valuable resource. Robert Utley characterizes him as the "ablest and best-qualified secretary of war in the nineteenth century."[12] Matthew Moten adds that while Davis "had shown a capacity for original thought, he was eager to learn from others."[13] Secretary Davis recognized that the Anglo-French failure to capture Sebastopol before the first winter created an opportunity for American observation of the fighting. He first contemplated establishing a commission in December 1854 or early 1855, but its belated formation that spring possibly resulted from a delay in obtaining President Pierce's approval.[14]

For this mission, Davis chose three well-regarded officers after his friend Col. Joseph Mansfield and possibly Lt. Col. Robert E. Lee rejected participation.[15] Maj. Richard Delafield, superintendent of New York harbor defenses and a member of the Board of Engineers, led the delegation and focused on fortifications. Moten, author of the most authoritative account of the commission, notes that "observing a war that had degenerated into a siege of a port city was an excellent assignment for a man of his talents."[16] Davis tapped Maj. Alfred Mordecai, commandant of the Washington arsenal and a long-standing member of the Ordnance Board, to cover artillery and small arms. A relentless data collector and excellent scientist, Moten points out that "no officer in the army was better qualified to investigate the technical aspects of foreign weaponry."[17] Much younger and recently transferred from the Corps of Engineers to the Cavalry, Capt. George McClellan would be the third member with primary responsibility for infantry and especially cavalry insights. The extremely ambitious McClellan, the only participant with combat experience, had previously undertaken sensitive missions for Davis.

In meeting with the commissioners before their April 11, 1855, departure, the secretary identified eleven areas "to which it is particularly desirable to direct your attention."[18] Topics of interest ranged from the latest on weapons and fortifications to logistics and field medicine, but the trio had the latitude to explore what they deemed noteworthy. Although responsible for investigating military developments throughout Europe, Davis urged the commissioners to "proceed as soon as possible to the theatre of war in the Crimea, for the purpose of observing the active operations in that quarter."[19] He also wanted the trio, if possible, to visit the Baltic theater before their expected November 1855 return. Davis, however, had not obtained permission for battlefield visits, only writing the relevant US ambassadors to give as much assistance as possible. Unfortunately, only six months earlier the US representatives to France and Great Britain had played key roles in the Ostend Manifesto as part of an unabashed US effort to annex Cuba, alienating their host governments and exacerbating the difficulty of obtaining clearance for Crimean travel.

Nevertheless, Delafield, Mordecai, and McClellan enthusiastically headed for Great Britain with the intention of visiting the Allied side first.[20] While in England, they explored military facilities and warships, observed weapon demonstrations, and received a valuable war account from the recently returned Lt. Gen. John Burgoyne. Despite crises still periodically threatening a third US–UK war, the British government provided introductory letters to its land and naval commanders in the Crimean theater. Disappointment, however, soon followed when the French government proved uncooperative, making approval of a frontline visit conditional on the Americans not subsequently traveling to the Russian side. Given the French Army's historically close relationship with the US Army and the latter's accommodation of a French military observer (the Marquis de Radepont) during the Mexican-American War, the attitude in Paris frustrated the delegation. Its persistence prompted the commissioners to adopt something of an anti-French bias.

After three weeks idling in France, the Americans departed for Russia in the hopes of obtaining access to the Crimean defenders.[21] Reflecting the tsar's desire to ally with the United States, the Russians openly welcomed the group with tours of military forces, arsenals, and some key fortifications. Still, Alexander II, who had become ruler only that March, would not grant permission to enter the Crimean Peninsula, citing the local commander's opposition to neutral observers. Blocked by both sides from the war zone, Mordecai complained in June 1855 that "since we left England we have been much less informed of the Events & details of the war than we were at home."[22] The failure of a major June 1855 assault on Sebastopol prompted the Americans to believe they could visit Prussia before heading toward the Crimea in the hope of gaining clearance. Their assessment would be mistaken as news reached the group in Prussia on September 8 that the Allies had finally captured Sebastopol. The dismayed commissioners hurried to the war zone, reaching Constantinople in nine days and after a twenty-day wait, receiving British approval for passage to Balaclava.

The Americans arrived in the Crimea on October 8, 1855.[23] Although frustrated about missing active combat, the group obtained valuable information as "they toured the battlefields daily and seem to have worked harder during this part of their trip than at any other time."[24] In particular, the commissioners benefited from exploring the captured Russian fortifications that had enabled the protracted defense and the British siege works used to defeat them. The French, however, continued to be obstructionist, and the Russians would not allow the Americans access to their new positions. Given that opposing forces now occupied opposite sides of the harbor, "the siege of Sebastopol and the artillery duel—the war's salient novel characteristic—were still ongoing," offering a glimpse of the action.[25] After three weeks of investigation, including trips to the Alma and Inkerman battlefields, the delegation headed for Constantinople to explore support operations. From the Ottoman capital, Delafield wrote Davis that "it is believed that as a general rule, the information contemplated in our instructions has been procured to a useful extent."[26] The secretary closely examined this letter and another twenty-plus updates that provided preliminary observations.[27] Two months after Davis wrote how "anxious" he was for their overdue return, the three weary travelers arrived in New York City on April 29, 1856.[28]

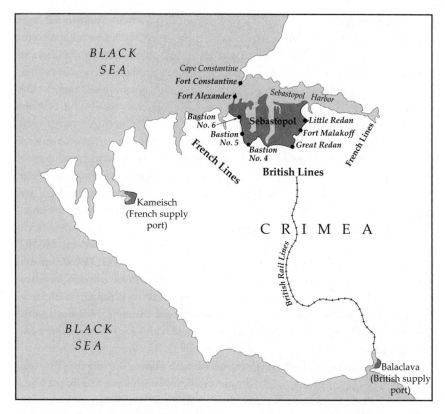

Map 1.1 Southwestern Crimean Peninsula

Given the importance he attached to the effort, Davis unsurprisingly met with the commissioners only four days later.[29] Whereas Delafield, McClellan, and especially Mordecai had at one time feared their mission would be a much-criticized failure, this session confirmed prior correspondence that "their views had enormous potential to influence the army's future."[30] Yet, although Davis "made clear that he desired their reports to be printed as soon as possible," decisions by both him and the commission delayed their completion and diminished the quality. In mid-May Delafield reported to Davis that each member planned to write a separate account on his particular areas of investigation. Besides avoiding the potentially painful effort to reconcile views, this approach allowed the three to write in different cities. The secretary initially pushed back, but he capitulated likely because of a desire for Delafield and Mordecai to perform other duties. Wanting to revise the army's General Regulations (1847) before leaving office, Davis tasked the capable Mordecai with this assignment. Mordecai's participation on the Delafield Commission almost certainly contributed to his selection given that, as Michael Bonura points out, "the 1857 regulations had

17

more of a battlefield focus . . . in a War Department that wanted to refocus the army regulations on European-style warfare and decisive battle."[31] Meanwhile, problems at West Point prompted Delafield's reappointment as superintendent, a position he held from 1838 to 1845. In his 1856 Annual Report, the secretary lamented the "necessity" of these actions.[32] As a result, McClellan's rapidly completed report, published in early 1857, would be the only one available internally before mid-1858 and the only one published before mid-1860.

Still, findings about the Crimean War reached key audiences.[33] The secretary of war referenced lessons in every annual report in the mid-1850s, as did some supplementary statements by the commanding general and bureau chiefs. In particular, Davis's 1856 Annual Report, the first after the observers returned, "reveals how greatly the commission's work had influenced him."[34] To facilitate its composition, the secretary had received from Delafield a thirty-two-page "general outline" envisioned for his final report as well as input from McClellan and Mordecai. McClellan's work received considerable attention, exemplified by Dennis Hart Mahan and Maj. William Hardee incorporating parts into their West Point courses. Mordecai and Delafield had ample opportunity earlier to transmit their primary insights to core army bodies. Mordecai was now the most important member of the influential Ordnance Board, while the well-connected Delafield was the service's leading advocate for coastal fortifications.

Postwar examinations built on the commissioners' efforts. Writing that "the Russian retreat to the north side [of Sebastopol] and the French assault upon the Malakoff must each be regarded as a masterpiece of its kind," McClellan recommended they receive "the closest study."[35] Focusing on naval assaults of coastal fortifications, Delafield asserted that "it is the bounden duty of the officers of our army and navy to study this branch of the art of war."[36] Younger officers such as Capt. John Gibbon and 1st Lt. Cadmus Wilcox attempted to extrapolate from this experience.[37] In 1858 the influential professor Mahan commenced a major revision of his text *Permanent Fortifications*, weighing evidence from the recent conflict.[38] In his second edition of *Elements of Military Art and Science* (1859), retired captain and highly respected defense intellectual Henry Halleck also addressed activity, especially field engineering, which had "received its greatest development and most brilliant application in the Crimean War, particularly in the siege of Sebastopol."[39]

The navy undertook no effort like the Delafield Commission. Secretary of the Navy James Dobbin had good reason to reject Farragut's request given the latter's import in establishment of the West Coast's first naval yard, but he initiated no search to find a substitute or create an investigatory body.[40] Dobbin may have been "a godfather of modern American sea power," but he lacked Davis's commitment to learn from the Crimean War.[41] The decision stemmed not only from differences between the secretaries but from the navy's operating context. Usually forward-deployed sailors frequently interacted with their European counterparts, diminishing the incentive for an extraordinary wartime initiative. For example, Capt. Samuel Du Pont and Cdr. Andrew Foote, among other American naval officers, spent time in the late 1850s with British and French forces attacking Chinese barrier forts during the Taiping Rebellion.[42] Over the previous four decades, American sailors had undertaken far less exploratory European trips than their army counterparts, with most such efforts involving naval ordnance experts.[43]

Still, the navy had indirect and idiosyncratic opportunities to obtain combat insights.[44] In 1854 Dobbin sent engineer-in-chief Daniel Martin and Lieutenant Walker to Europe to examine the latest technological developments (e.g., steam machinery, screw propellers) before choosing among submitted proposals for the six newly funded *Merrimack*-class frigates.[45] Neither Martin nor Walker apparently ventured to war zones, but the USS *Cumberland*, flagship of the Mediterranean squadron, observed British and French vessels' initial preparations.[46] Most notably, the aforementioned Porter, one of the service's most talented officers, reached Sebastopol just after its capture. He had been dispatched, with army captain Henry Wayne, to the Middle East to acquire camels as part of a War Department experiment on whether this beast of burden could ease frontier supply difficulties.[47] Porter journeyed to the Crimean Peninsula ostensibly to collect data on the use of camels, but the inquisitive officer also visited the Malakoff fortification, inspected the innovative French ironclad floating battery (even making a model), and investigated improved British / French underwater explosives. The lieutenant relayed his findings to the Navy Department in lengthy reports. Dahlgren also believed "there is much to be gleaned from the incidents of this war."[48] His seminal 1856 work, *Shell and Shell Guns*, concludes with a 125-page examination of the Crimean War's maritime component. A need to rely heavily on official accounts for the facts that underlay his analysis, however, prompted Dahlgren to warn that "the actors in the eventful drama are too recently from its thrilling scenes to be inclined to the sober duties of the chronicler."[49] Still, the navy captain likely benefited from a friendship with Mordecai in drawing his assessment. What Dahlgren learned is a part of the next section, but his study represents the primary US naval appraisal of the conflict.

WHAT LESSONS DID THE AMERICANS IDENTIFY?

Less than five years after the Delafield Commission returned, the US Civil War commenced in Charleston's harbor. It is helpful to review the critical military features of that existential struggle to facilitate consideration of what study of the Crimean War could have revealed to enable better preparedness. The opposing sides organized, maintained, maneuvered, and fought armies far larger than any prior American force. With the standard infantry weapon being a rifled musket, soldiers inflicted much more lethal fire, especially when defending. While improved field artillery added to the destructiveness of battle, larger rifled guns rendered heretofore strong masonry fortifications highly vulnerable. Such works were most expeditiously overcome by army–navy cooperation, which, when employed, facilitated the US military outmaneuvering and defeating Confederate forces. Steam propulsion, armor protection, and enhanced armament enabled the US Navy to isolate the Confederate States of America by closing its primary ports.

Some of these key Civil War elements echoed Crimean combat, while others entailed significant departures. Combatants in the earlier conflict demonstrated the increased scale of war, potential for moving significantly larger forces, value of army–navy cooperation, utility of railroads and telegraph, and availability of better field artillery. The fighting also showed the naval benefits from improved armament, armor, and propulsion for blocking enemy ports. Yet study of the Crimean War would not have led one to expect the essential obsolescence of masonry fortification because the employed rifled artillery performed poorly. Moreover, although elite troops possessed rifled muskets, most soldiers did not have such arms, preventing the generation of clear lessons about their lethal impact.

The subsequent discussion of what the US military discovered from the Crimean War primarily reflects the Delafield Commission's findings but includes inputs from other contemporary commentators. Before commencing this discussion, a few caveats regarding the delegation's information. First, I focus on war-related topics, but drawing a sharp distinction between their Crimean War and non-Crimean findings is sometimes not possible. Second, the delayed completion and publication of two of the three commissioners' reports resulted in their correspondence and oral discussions playing a critical role in information transmission. The passage of years between the Delafield Commission's return and the final published accounts created a possibility of insights being influenced by subsequent events. This development may have happened minimally, but evidence is lacking of a lesson being significantly altered, so I use material from the published reports when discussing the findings and their application in the late 1850s.

Enlightening Lessons

Unprecedented scale of warfare and ability to project power. Although the Delafield Commission "provided no sweeping synthesis of the war's lessons," its members identified two overarching themes.[50] First, increasing industrialization facilitated violence on an unprecedented scale, far beyond the US military's prior

experience or preparation. They characterized this quantitative change as more salient than any identified qualitative shift in weapons or tactics. Given that the battle
for Sebastopol essentially became an artillery duel, the Americans not surprisingly
focused on that aspect. They noted by October 1855 that the ruined port had absorbed 2.4 million rounds of "shot and shell" from an Allied arsenal of 2,500 guns.
Second, the British and French militaries demonstrated the enormous power projection capability of steam-powered navies with potentially grave consequences for US
security. Allied navies landed sizable armies on the Crimean Peninsula at Europtria,
from which they rapidly fought their way fifty miles south to Sebastopol (and likely
would have immediately captured it under better leadership). Davis warned in his
1856 Annual Report that "remoteness from the great naval powers of the world can,
therefore, no longer be considered as giving to our commercial cities immunity from
the danger of a sudden descent."[51]

Benefit from army–navy cooperation. The Americans stressed that the conflict
reinforced the timeless lesson of soldier–sailor teamwork, which greatly enhanced
combat effectiveness, especially when attacking coastal fortifications.[52] Although Sebastopol's strong shore works stymied the British and French navies, US analysts
highlighted that the Allies obtained victory by overcoming the weaker landside defenses. After cautioning that purely naval action on coastal works was unlikely to
succeed, Dahlgren argued that "the issue assumed a totally different aspect when
connected with an assault by land."[53] Likewise, Delafield emphasized that "harbor
defenses were of no value without being properly protected in the rear."[54] He added
that the Russians staved off defeat for almost a year by rapidly redeploying a large
army and naval guns, but the US lacked such resources with which to erect effective temporary land defenses. Evolving Allied wartime practice suggested future
operations would involve joint land–sea advances. Commentators added that the
increased mobility of armies transported by steam-powered ships enhanced this lesson's significance.

Value of torpedo mines. One clear positive for defenders was the effective Russian
use of "torpedo mines."[55] Inventors, such as Samuel Colt, had long failed to interest
US soldiers and sailors in mines. The besieged Russians, benefiting from Immanuel
Nobel's design, employed large numbers of submerged, moored contact (as well
as electrically controlled) devices to protect naval bases and strategic waterways.
Inadequate charges diminished physical destruction, but they prompted considerable caution among Allied naval captains after four vessels detonated explosives at
Kronstadt early in the war. Although noting their impact, Delafield provided limited
details as the Russians treated the mines as a tightly guarded secret. I found no American commentary on the unprecedented British minesweeping effort.

Floating battery—impressive debut. The British and French introduced innovative warships, especially the "floating battery," that enhanced their ability to attack coastal fortifications.[56] The concept—combining powerful steam engines, shallow draft, large guns, and iron plating—had existed for many years, but navies ignored these unconventional, inelegant-looking vessels until the Allies adopted them out of necessity. After observing their construction in England, the Delafield Commission sent Davis a special report in May 1855.[57] During their combat debut four months later, French floating batteries advanced much closer than the rest of the fleet, each receiving at least forty hits without suffering significant damage and contributing significantly to the rapid fall of Fort Kinburn. Leading British war correspondent William Howard Russell declared that "the success of the experiment (iron-cased batteries) is complete," but American reports, although positive, were not so definitive.[58] Porter found the French ship he visited quite impressive, while Delafield warned that floating batteries "can cross the Atlantic."[59] US commentators pointed out that their steam power and shallow draft enabled attacking from unanticipated directions. The reserved Dahlgren found them formidable and requiring countermeasures but cautioned that assessing their value requires "further confirmation of their asserted invulnerability," especially given his expectation of coastal fortifications employing heavier cannon.[60] Delafield and Dahlgren added that small mortar vessels, which also could cross the Atlantic, presented difficult targets for Russian gunners while inflicting meaningful damage.

Superior new French 12-pound gun. For ground forces, the performance of one weapon stood out—the new French light, 12-pound smoothbore gun.[61] Although the scientist-soldier Mordecai unemotionally documented weapons ranging from small arms to monster siege guns, even he expressed enthusiasm for this armament based on its contribution to operations at Sebastopol. The ordnance expert explained that the versatile field gun was both lighter and more durable than its predecessors, could be employed as a cannon or howitzer, and fired all ammunition types, greatly simplifying logistics. Delafield added that its outstanding battlefield performance ("a material change" for field guns) had prompted other European powers to rush into production versions of the French piece.[62] Still, the judicious Mordecai cautioned it "may be doubted . . . whether the experience of the Russian war was sufficient to establish the efficacy of these pieces for all the service that may be required of field artillery."[63]

Utility of iron gun carriages. Even though the commissioners disagreed somewhat on lessons regarding larger garrison and siege artillery, as will be discussed, they seized on a small but valuable support innovation. The Europeans, who, like the Americans, suffered from rotted and warped wooden ordnance carriages, shifted to iron alternatives.[64] In particular, they found that the wrought iron used by the Russians proved more durable than the initial British and French preference for cast iron.

Need for greater logistical support. Finally, although less interesting than weapons or fortifications, the Americans noted that the expanded scale of siege trains and expeditionary forces required far greater management and support.[65] For the British, the challenge had proven too demanding in the first Crimean winter, resulting in such atrocious losses through deprivation and disease that newspaper accounts of this misery led to the Aberdeen government's collapse. Their logistics improved significantly by the second winter, when the French had a much harder time. As indicated by support-related questions composing almost half of the subjects with which Davis explicitly tasked the Delafield Commission, this area was important to the War Department. The commissioners related how railroads assisted British and French advancement of men and materiel from the disembarkation ports to the frontline. Praising this innovative and necessary effort, Delafield remarked that for the first time railroads had been employed "in *presence of an enemy.*"[66] With regard to the care and feeding of soldiers, Delafield's report was "encyclopedic in scope," including medical and camp equipment.[67] When first arriving in England, the Americans heard about long-lasting dehydrated food that had been developed for the field armies and supplied the War Department with a sample. Delafield would later add that widespread use of such "prepared food" by both sides proved its value.[68]

Misleading Lessons

Masonry coastal fortifications remain stout. While the preceding observations conveyed helpful information, US officials with equal diligence and confidence relayed other findings that, although accurate, would not be in the near future. Most notably, the Americans viewed the conflict as indicating that strengthening masonry coastal fortifications represented the best response to the aforementioned increased threat from expeditionary forces. Given that the continuing effectiveness of stone and brick works in light of new gun technology had been a hotly debated subject in the prewar years, policymakers not surprisingly looked to the conflict for guidance.[69] Noting that the danger the US had risked from neglect of coastal fortification, Delafield highlighted "the severe test to which these casemated defenses were subjected in proof of their efficiency and reliability."[70] Army chief engineer Col. Joseph Totten added that the failure of British and French attacks on Russian works illustrated that well-constructed strongholds can resist the greatest expeditions, although not improvised structures.[71] Similarly, McClellan stressed that Crimean War operations showed the value of a "wise" and "proper" permanent fortification system.[72]

In his December 1856 Annual Report, Davis, after discussions with the returned commissioners, declared that the war's combat appeared to show "conclusively that properly constructed fortifications are a sure reliance against the most formidable fleets."[73] Navy Secretary Dobbin, in his annual report that same month, acknowledged that "recent developments in the late European wars will hardly encourage such [naval] assaults to be often undertaken."[74] After weighing the fighting, Dahlgren judged that "the introduction of heavy shells is more advantageous to the fort than to the ship" and noted how naval gunnery struggled against elevated fortifications such as at Cape Constantine.[75] He added the critical caveat that "works which are less complete in all respects, cannot, however, be assumed as impregnable."[76]

Rifled artillery ineffective. Information on the rifled artillery's disappointing performance boosted the lesson of masonry fortifications' resiliency.[77] Davis had explicitly tasked the commissioners to evaluate the performance of long-range, rifled guns. The much-hyped British Lancaster greatly increased artillery range, but Delafield and Mordecai reported that it proved wildly inaccurate and fragile. Dahlgren simply stated that the conflict attested to "its entire failure in service."[78] Given poor results at Sebastopol and Bomarsund, use of the Lancasters diminished as the war progressed and the Admiralty dropped plans to put them on warships. Beyond this weapon, Mordecai reported that "no cannon of extraordinary caliber or range, no breech-loading guns, no rifled cannon, (except the Lancaster gun,) were put to the test of actual service."[79] The Americans did at least qualify this overarching finding by noting that the Europeans would continue to develop rifled artillery and urging the US Army and US Navy to do likewise. Delafield observed that the increased range of British and French nonrifled naval shell guns meant it was "necessary to carry the defenses of any point at least 7,000 yards in advance of it."[80] Thus, he pointed out the value of detached outer works and use of long-range weapons in coastal fortifications. Dahlgren and Delafield reported that the fighting demonstrated, as the former wrote, that "the new motor [steam propulsion] is entirely adverse to the fort."[81] The Americans explained that the elimination of sails and masts significantly reduced targets, while crippled vessels, unless catastrophically damaged in the engine space, moved expeditiously out of danger. Most significantly, naval commanders could now orchestrate attacks with far greater precision, each ship in its place.

Missed Lessons

Command-and-control challenges. Despite not arriving until after the crux of the fighting concluded, the salient information neglected by the commissioners was mostly due to a lack of interest. The most legitimate complaint rests on a failure to appreciate the increased command-and-control difficulties resulting from the greater scale and mobility of forces. The Americans appreciated the transformational role of the England-to-Crimea telegraph.[82] Not surprisingly, Delafield judged it "was so far unquestionably useful" when communicating army needs home, but "its advantage was somewhat questionable" when carrying government orders to commanders.[83] He added that the British also effectively used telegraph lines to send messages between the forward trenches, headquarters, and depots. The increased information flow enhanced situational awareness, but effective management required more than communication. J. D. Hittle emphasizes that, with the conflict's overwhelming demands, "it became unmistakably apparent that British staff organization was not capable of coping with war requirements."[84] Mordecai believed that the British Army's response of establishing a "chief of the staff" office best explained its army's improved management after the first winter.[85] This insight aside, the Americans displayed little interest in staff operations—a critical task that would bedevil large American field forces during the Civil War. The absence of any American observer with significant staff experience likely contributed to this neglect.

Cavalry concerns. Given that the war's infamous Charge of the Light Brigade indicated the horse's diminishing role in battle and a Davis-directed emphasis on obtaining cavalry lessons, the Americans could also be charged with failure in this area.[86] Understandably, the combat use of horse soldiers on the battlefield á la the British during the Battle of Balaclava was not the way US cavalry had been historically employed and thus was of minimal interest. Rather, commissioner attempts to identify best practices regarding equipment, training, and organization came more from their travels across the continent than Crimean fighting (e.g., superiority of a Hungarian saddle; preference for breach-loading guns). Despite Russian regular officers' criticism of the Cossacks, McClellan and Mordecai praised them as ideal light cavalry. McClellan argued that their intelligence, mobility, endurance, and reliability fit well with the reconnaissance, escort, and messaging missions relevant on the American frontier. Desiring "applicable" lessons, even at the cost of accuracy, left McClellan particularly susceptible to being swayed by both foreigners (e.g., Russians) and friends at home (e.g., Lt. Col. Joseph Johnston).

Unclear Lessons

Rifled muskets' impact. Much of the modern criticism about the US military's battlefield ignorance at the outset of the Civil War comes from a mistaken belief that the Crimean War clearly signaled the increased range and lethality of small arms and need to modify infantry tactics accordingly. With the US infantry in the process of transitioning from smoothbore to rifled muskets and rewriting what then passed for doctrine, the Crimean War's timing seemed fortuitous. Alas, it did not provide conclusive data on hotly debated questions about this weapon.[87] As an ordnance expert, Mordecai concentrated on the relative performance of gun types, while McClellan emphasized Russian "valor and discipline" and French fencing, gymnastic, and marksmanship training. Assessing the tactical implications of rifled muskets would have been difficult even if the observers had focused on the subject given the surprisingly limited use of this weapon. Essentially only British and French light infantry units and other elite elements on both sides fielded these guns, with most soldiers equipped with smoothbore muskets. As a result, fighting usually occurred at close range. Thus, Mordecai reported that the combat "did not allow of a full trial of the effect of the new arms, and of their influence on the tactics of armies."[88]

Although the absence of widespread use of rifled muskets precluded an overarching assessment, these weapons' limited employment generated some salient observations about their danger and how to counteract them. Mordecai noted that the Sebastopol siege "served to develop the importance of these arms of long range [rifled guns], as an auxiliary, in both the attack and defense of places."[89] Facilitating the use of and protection from rifles, pits dug out from the ground had been increasingly employed by the Russians in front of their Sebastopol works. McClellan explained that they "contributed very materially towards impeding the progress" of advancing British and French troops.[90] The Americans characterized these obstacles, which ranged from single-person positions to small lunettes holding ten to twenty men, as a part of the "grander scale of entrenchments" dug by troops to protect themselves from the battlefield's increasing lethality.[91] Some historians interpret the discussion of rifle pits or, more generally, field fortifications as indicative of a revised tactical outlook. For example, Edward Hagerman sees in McClellan's report an appreciation that rifled muskets shifted the tactical balance away from open frontal assault, yet, as Wayne Hsieh points out, he "made no comments on any perceived increase in defensive firepower created by the rifle-musket's increased accuracy."[92] The demonstrated danger from the increased range of rifled muskets prompted Mordecai to recommend for the field artillery "spherical case shot [antipersonnel round] as one of the most effectual means of defense."[93]

Earthworks utility. For some issues, the difficulty was not a lack of available data but divergence on how to interpret its meaning. This case offers two examples of this challenge related to explaining Sebastopol's extended survival and ultimate capitulation. First, American commentators disagreed on the value of the landside earthworks that stymied the British and French for almost a year.[94] Some commentators—critics of masonry fortifications such as 1st Lt. James St. Clair Morton and

Capt. Edward Hunt—exclaimed that the punishment absorbed by earthworks demonstrated their superiority.[95] Delafield praised their designer (the esteemed Russian engineer Eduard Totleben), but he questioned their utility, at least for the United States, given that the Sebastopol defenses required a large Russian army and relocated naval guns. McClellan also strongly supported the traditional engineering view, arguing that "the plain truth is that these defences were simple temporary fortifications of rather greater dimensions than usual, and that not a single new principle of engineering was there developed."[96] Ultimately, the commissioners stressed that Allied mistakes (e.g., divided councils, lack of intelligence, poor preparations) were primarily responsible for their lengthy struggle to overcome these landside defenses.

Monster gun merit. Allied extensive use of large-caliber "monster guns" contributed materially to the seizure of Sebastopol, but a difference of opinion emerged among the Americans over the basic lesson.[97] The commissioners found that the most damaging pieces were large mortars, of which the French alone employed over 350 at least eight inches in diameter. Thus, Delafield concluded that the US Army should "lose no time in substituting the like for the 24 and 32-pounders, on which we at this moment must mainly rely."[98] Yet Mordecai emphasized the limitations of the so-called monster guns (e.g., cost, limited mobility, and barrel fragility).[99] For Moten, the contrasting perspectives of the two main commentators (Mordecai and Delafield) on this subject "perfectly illustrates the army's highly developed branch loyalties."[100]

HOW DID THE ARMY APPLY ITS FINDINGS?

The Americans identified a wide range of lessons, as articulated in the preceding section, but these findings received limited application. Why? Despite the secretary of war's enthusiasm for this project, the second half of the 1850s was not a favorable context for using such information.[101] Above all, conservative and ineffectual army leadership proved a hindrance. Davis found the War Department's eight independent staff bureaus (e.g., ordnance, quartermaster) "ingrown, parochial, conservative, resistant to change, jealous of their prerogatives, headed by aging but solidly entrenched and politically powerful chiefs."[102] His attempt to gain control over these politically well-connected entities failed. Maj. Gen. (Bvt. Lt. Gen.) Winfield Scott, who zealously guarded his domain as commanding general and possessed an extremely conflictual relationship with the secretary, complicated reform efforts. After Davis returned to the Senate in early 1857, his incompetent successor (John Floyd) further diminished the prospects for applying lessons. As Brent Nosworthy laments, with this transition, "indolence, myopia, and corruption replaced open-mindedness, pragmatism, and a sense of intellectual adventure as guiding traits at the highest level of the War Department."[103]

The vast physical expansion of the United States in the previous decade and growing threats in the West greatly exacerbated the defense challenge.[104] In his 1853 Annual Report, Davis warned that the increasing danger of Indian attacks resulting from westward population movement necessitated 80 percent of the army being deployed or in the process of deploying to frontier posts.[105] The gross insufficiency of its less than eleven thousand soldiers enabled the secretary to convince Congress to bolster recruitment with increased pay and to add four regiments (two infantry and two cavalry). Still, trouble out West in the mid- and late-1850s including hostile Indians, rebellious Mormons, and sectional-fighting Kansans left the small force (15,800 men) heavily engaged. Lacking adequate infantry, Secretary Floyd employed most troops without regard to their specialty, harming efforts to develop expertise. Although the army's budget grew significantly in the second half of the decade, the four new regiments, the 30 percent pay increase, and operations in the West absorbed most of this increase.[106]

Despite an avowed interest in the Crimean War, officers exhibited limited enthusiasm for adopting its lessons.[107] William Skelton points out that by the mid-1850s, with West Point graduates composing 75 percent of the officer corps, the US Army had "surely one of the world's best-educated military elites" and prioritized European-style conventional warfare despite past efforts by some notable soldiers such as major generals Alexander Macomb and Edmund Gaines to promote more attention to the frontier.[108] Thus, the thankless and tough Indian problem was "almost totally neglected by West Point, the schools of practice, and professional boards."[109] The US Military Academy in particular had importance because, as Moten stresses, it was "the only place where formal study occurred in the army."[110] After the Mexican-American War, Professor Mahan helped initiate the Napoleon Club to examine the French emperor's campaigns because he worried that "ignorance and self-presumption from past successes" would claim the Americans as it did the Prussians in 1806.[111] Such a concern was not without foundation as the dominant victory a decade earlier contributed, as Hsieh relates, to officers' strong belief in their "ability to master and guide further military change in the United States."[112] Skelton adds that West Point's engineering focus resulted in officers who tended "to be intellectually shallow and relatively ineffective in unstructured situations that require independent, creative thought."[113] Critically, Congress's refusal to establish a pension for military service exacerbated the army's natural conservatism as older soldiers rarely retired and seniority determined promotion.

Despite a Davis-led effort to expand US officers' horizons, the Americans continued to regard the French Army as the premier source of military knowledge.[114]

Delafield averred at the end of his report that US soldiers should cease our "custom of looking to France alone for military information," observing that the other European armies in some things provided "information quite as valuable as that derived from France."[115] Yet even officials who recognized the merit of this advice struggled to follow it. The secretary himself continued to regard, as a biographer notes, "the French army the best in the world and French military thought the most advanced."[116] Likewise, Mahan, despite stressing to cadets in his seminal West Point course to adopt the best methods from each army, drew heavily on French military examples. Commandant Hardee wrested control of the "Strategy of War" course from Mahan because of philosophical differences, but this former student at the French cavalry school shared his high regard for the French Army. In an investigation of this subject, Bonura identifies the 1848–65 era as "the high-water mark for explicit recognition of the importance of the French influence on American warfare."[117]

While both enlightening and misleading lessons received some embrace, American officials did not act on most cues given a sense of their irrelevance or at least low priority. As William Cooper observes, information by the Delafield Commission "constituted an important installment" for modernizing the army, but it was not a unified "plan of action dictating immediate change."[118] This section lays out the resultant varied outcomes—beneficial and counterproductive applications, neglected uses of information, and, finally, circumstances where the data did not facilitate a decision despite the hopes of uncertain officials. As noted in the introduction, lessons from a foreign war contribute in three basic ways—instrumentally (abetting accomplishment of already recognized needs), instructionally (guiding what to do or not to do), and inspirationally (prompting attention to revealed issues in need of resolution). In this case, influence essentially occurred via instructional and instrumental effects.

Beneficial Applications

Enthusiastic adoption of 12-pound Napoleon gun. The field artillery benefited the most from study of the Crimean War, which revealed a clearly superior weapon.[119] Although this branch had gained a lofty reputation during the Mexican-American War, the army subsequently focused on coastal artillery. The field artillery's limited utility against Indians prompted an infantry-deficient War Department to employ gunners frequently as foot soldiers. Amid such neglect, Delafield and Mordecai returned extolling the French 12-pound light cannon-howitzer. Yet neither Davis nor Ordnance chief Col. Henry Craig included it on the packed agenda of the Ordnance Board's first session after the Crimean War. Rather, it was apparently Mordecai's own initiative that prompted that meeting to recommend construction of several copies for field trials. This act highlights the potentially critical role of personal agency in applying lessons, a factor repeated in the subsequent case studies. Enthusiasm for the field piece rapidly grew, but the Ordnance Board modified the design (e.g., shortened barrel) to optimize it for American needs. Tests, commencing in May 1857, affirmed the gun's attributes.

The army soon adopted it as the light, 12-pound gun (model 1857), more commonly known in the United States as the Napoleon (after the French emperor Napoleon III).[120] Artillery officers embraced the relatively lightweight weapon that had the mobility of a 6-pounder but the range and firepower of a 12-pounder. Given its versatility, the War Department intended it to replace three field pieces—6- and 12-pound cannons and the 12-pound howitzer. The always cautious Mordecai expressed some concern about this amalgamation of roles in one gun, but Ordnance chief Craig and others seized on the opportunity for a logistics-easing simplification of the US field artillery system. Contemporary commentators, such as anonymous R.E.C. and Gibbon, endorsed Mordecai's lesson on using spherical case shot to counter infantry armed with rifled muskets. Ordnance Board members agreed, successfully recommending in April 1859 an increase in the number of antipersonnel rounds in ammunition chests. Large-scale production of Napoleons would not occur until the outbreak of the Civil War, during which the reliable and effective gun was the most used artillery piece by both sides. Historians regard the gun's adoption as the Delafield Commission's most tangible benefit.

Transition to wrought iron gun carriages. The coastal artillery benefited from adoption of a modest but instructive Crimean War finding—the superiority of wrought iron gun carriages.[121] Intrigued by Delafield and Mordecai's information on this subject, Davis added it to the agenda for the October 1856 Ordnance Board. Mordecai's supportive presence likely ensured concurrence from the rest of the body, but understandably it still ordered experiments before giving a final endorsement. These trial carriages demonstrated improved performance and durability, although their construction and further testing delayed acceptance. Finally, in his December 1859 Annual Report, Secretary Floyd observed that "models of wrought iron seacoast and garrison carriages have accordingly been adopted, and iron will be used in their fabrication hereafter."[122] Despite not being a high-profile change, iron carriages represented a meaningful improvement that Davis appropriately "took great pride" in having facilitated.[123] Yet even with observers' effusive praise and successful testing leading to the wrought iron carriage's complete embrace, wooden variants remained primarily in use at the start of the Civil War as their replacement was not a high priority. This effort exemplifies the inevitable time required for militaries to respond to even clear and strong cues unless revealing a perceived urgent deficiency.

Counterproductive Applications

Maintained faith in masonry fortifications. While wrought iron gun carriages represented a positive change for coastal defense works, embrace of these fortifications' continuing viability demonstrates the danger from applying a finding that would not long remain valid.[124] Actually, the three primary findings identified by the Delafield Commission—increasing scale of war, expanding power projection capability, and continuing strength of coastal fortifications against naval aggression—encouraged upgrading such works. The so-called Third System of coastal defenses dated to 1821, with structures ranging from large masonry (stone and brick) complexes to stand-alone, small-gun batteries that would be manned during crises. Progress had been gradual given a lack of engineers, limited funds, rising costs, expanding requirements, and increasing concern about their effectiveness. In 1851 congressional opponents blocked spending, condemning these works as worthless pork-barrel projects given improvements in armament technology. Proponents, led by longtime chief engineer Totten, fought back, getting construction funding restored in 1853. Although many fortifications had been built, they were severely deficient in artillery and personnel.

Exemplifying the potential instrumental as well as instructional influence of a foreign conflict lesson, fortification advocates repeatedly cited the Crimean War experience when campaigning for increased funding.[125] For example, in his 1856 Annual Report, Davis noted the lesson in urging "liberal and regular grants" as important seaports lacked adequate protection and "such preparation requires time for its accomplishment."[126] The following year in his first annual report, Secretary Floyd echoed that the recent combat had shown coastal fortifications were "now very justly esteemed the cheapest and far the most effectual means of defense for every important commercial point."[127] Senior army engineers Totten and Delafield highlighted the Russian experience in calling for more money for coastal works as well as garrison armaments. Maj. John Barnard frequently referenced the Crimean War in his 1859 work urging completion of New York City's defenses.[128]

Yet, as noted in the prior section, some younger engineering officers rejected this lesson.[129] Barnard composed his book as a rebuttal to 1st Lt. James St. Clair Morton's opposition to the standard approach. Like Hunt, Morton believed that the performance of British and French siege guns revealed the increasing vulnerability of masonry fortifications and urged construction of more resistant earthworks or at least an earthen outer layer. Employing other noted Crimean War insights, Morton advocated for protecting the leading US metropolis with "a series of bastioned redoubts in key positions, connected by earthen embankments, and the development of floating batteries."[130] This intelligent and brash officer had supporters including Secretary Floyd, who facilitated publication of his works. As Mahan's assistant in the mid-1850s, Morton boldly and rashly challenged the renowned professor's fitness for fortification instruction. Mahan, however, successfully countered this attack in a December 1858 court martial, with McClellan serving as star witness based on his Delafield Commission experience.

More constraining for the army and Corps of Engineers leadership was the strong competition for limited dollars that resulted in the service initiating few new projects.[131] The most notable effort was a fort on Ship Island off the Mississippi coast to safeguard the inner coastal waterway approach to New Orleans.[132] Congressional authorization after many years of failed advocacy may well have been attributable to the recent conflict's illustration of the danger from "light-draught war steamers," as Davis noted in his 1855 Annual Report, although definitive evidence is lacking.[133] Similarly, praise of outer works by Delafield and others may have prompted or contributed to the army's decision to build a water battery downstream from Fort Jackson, the key position protecting New Orleans.

Neglect of rifled artillery. The poor Crimean performance of the 68-pound Lancaster rifled cannon not only undergirded army confidence in masonry fortifications but contributed to a much-criticized failure to prioritize development of such a weapon.[134] The Ordnance Board considered rifled artillery in early 1855, but it concluded insufficient information existed to assess their value. The body recommended conducting additional experiments and gaining insight into European actions, especially from the Crimean War. Although Mordecai favored their development based on potential and European investment, he had accurately documented the Lancaster gun's poor wartime performance, which demonstrated continuing difficulties with such weapons. While the Europeans redoubled efforts to overcome technical challenges, the lack of a clear requirement for the US Army enabled War Department neglect for the rest of the decade. The army's conservative orientation may well have meant the same outcome without the Crimean War data, but it played a counterproductive role in parrying progressive forces. Ultimately, West Point foundry superintendent Robert Parrott developed an accurate, albeit initially fragile, rifled gun in 1860–61 that had great impact early in the Civil War.

Ignored Lessons

Rejected relevance of command-and-control/support insights. The army did not respond to some findings. Ignoring such cues should not automatically be deemed a failure as the information may not be germane for the US force, given its culture, resources, or mission. Improving support operations had been a driving concern for Davis, as evidenced by the commissioners' tasking, but the army initially derived modest benefit from the collected data. Reporting on the improvement produced by the British adoption of a chief of staff sparked no action from US officials. Even if the commissioners had captured available lessons about the type of staff needed to deploy, maintain, and maneuver such large forces, they would likely have been ignored given the pre–Civil War army's expectation of small-scale actions.[135] Still, this failure was a missed opportunity as staff capacity proved grossly inadequate for the hugely expanded forces at the beginning of the internecine struggle. While army leaders used the Crimean War's illustration of increased naval-based power projection capabilities to lend support for its campaign to extend the railroad to California, the unprecedented tactical use of railroads to move materiel generated little attention.[136] For evolving technologies such as the telegraph and railroads, US officials acknowledged their value and developed capabilities without appreciating their dynamic impact on operations and the security requirements, which would be so amply demonstrated in the Civil War. Data about the care and feeding of soldiers prompted modest action until the start of the Civil War. For example, although the United States "introduced" dehydrated food in 1857 after testing the sample sent by Delafield, the army made little use of it.[137] Interest in Crimean-derived support information grew sharply with the Civil War's commencement. Indicative of this changed perspective, Col. James Henry Carleton, commanding a large column across the Southwest United States, found his concerns about the daunting administrative tasks eased after consulting the Delafield Commission reports.[138]

Negligible change from cavalry findings. Cavalry represents another area where findings had limited impact, with the notable exception of a McClellan discovery unrelated to the Crimean War.[139] Writing in late 1856 that the "experience of our army is comparatively small in Cavalry service," Davis particularly hoped that the Delafield Commission's insights would be helpful for that branch.[140] The 1855 formation of two new cavalry regiments reflected a growing appreciation of their utility against Indians, but the secretary added that the cavalry must also "be prepared for the contingency of operations against a civilized foe."[141] Thus, McClellan's observations in this area—albeit not generally from the conflict—had great potential for influence. Frustration with the lack of rapid response to his recommendations contributed to McClellan's January 1857 resignation. Rather, the secretary selected Carleton, then a captain, to review the information and evaluate the suggestions' merit in early 1857. In the introduction of Col. Phillip St. George Cooke's late 1850s cavalry tactical manual, he cited the "able work of Captain Geo. B. McClellan . . . by which I have been much assisted."[142] Yet McClellan's observations, such as the uselessness of heavy cavalry and tactical benefits of a single rank, reflected US Army conventional wisdom. His most enthusiastic conclusion—the benefit of native light cavalry like the Cossacks—proved problematic. Carleton explored this idea, but he, like army leaders, did not see any suitable, skilled, and committed Indian tribes available to fill the native role. The contribution to the cavalry from the Delafield Commission was essentially a Hungarian saddle, an excellent model that would remain in use until the horse cavalry's mid-twentieth-century demise. This disappointing outcome was fully justified given that most observations did not fit with American culture, resources, and requirements.

Divergent Information and Interpretations

Dispute over monster guns prevents action. Disagreement between senior officials and some junior officers (e.g., over the relative utility of masonry and earthen fortifications) did not prevent the service from seeking to apply "lessons," but disagreement among influential actors inhibited action. Although agreement existed on the Crimea War highlighting the already-appreciated deficiency of weapons at US coastal defense works, the Delafield–Mordecai split on the proper lessons regarding garrison artillery precluded addressing this requirement.[143] Chief Engineer Totten embraced Delafield's recommendation for adopting so-called monster guns, and a similarly inclined Davis solicited the input of the October 1856 Ordnance Board. This body, with Mordecai exerting decisive influence, highlighted ballistic and reliability issues. Davis remained sympathetic to Delafield's perspective, but the Ordnance Board's position held sway before the Civil War. Instead, it recommended upgrades to the core coastal batteries—8-inch and 10-inch Columbiads (smoothbore, muzzle-loading cannon). The Ordnance Board's rejection of monster guns had in part been based on rifled artillery's potential, but, as noted, evidence from the Crimean War demonstrated the current deficiency of this weapon type. In essence, conflict data assisted opponents of both rifled artillery and large, smoothbore guns to undermine pursuit of the alternative.

Limited rifled musket use does not alter infantry views. Insufficient information on the implications of rifled musket use meant that the Crimean War had little impact on the army's underway transition to this weapon as the infantry's standard arm.[144] Believing that the adoption of rifled muskets necessitated revised infantry tactics, the secretary assigned the then-captain Hardee to produce a manual specifically for rifle-equipped light infantry. Hardee borrowed heavily from the French light infantry guidance, which stressed maneuver, speed, and use of skirmishers. Davis did not rush completion of the manual to allow time for experimentation and consideration of the Crimean War combat.[145] Yet, after West Point cadets tested the new approach successfully, the secretary decided to accept it as *Rifle and Light Infantry Tactics* on March 29, 1855 (a few weeks before the Delafield Commission even departed). Shortly thereafter, the army adopted the .58-caliber Springfield rifle (US Model 1855), a refined version of the French Minié rifle, as the foot soldier's primary weapon. As Nosworthy points out, the commissioners' expectation that all the major European armies would soon adopt the rifled musket simply "lent credence to the decision of the American army to do the same."[146] In his 1856 Annual Report, the secretary asserted the need to convert all old smoothbore muskets into rifles, despite the cost.[147] In late February 1857, a week before Davis left office, the War Department "ordered all foot soldiers to be regularly exercised in Hardee's tactics."[148]

Although it introduced greater movement and flexibility, this guidance did not represent a major departure in combat doctrine, and Crimean War fighting did not indicate to the Americans a fundamental need for change.[149] Observations, like the discussion of the utility of rifle pits at Sebastopol, showed some awareness of the evolving battlefield, but the conflict did not provide a clear demonstration of how the rifle's lethality necessitated revising tactics. Thomas Greiss claims that Mahan was aware by this time that rifled arms would require a drastically altered approach, yet "it went against his cautious nature to trumpet in print that assault tactics were all wrong unless there was solid evidence to the contrary."[150] The historian adds that, for Mahan, understandably given the limited data, "the Crimean War was not alone sufficient indication to him."[151] Once Davis left office, the meaning of the Crimean War became part of the "battlefield" over infantry tactics between progressives and traditionalists. Insightful soldiers, such as Wilcox and Capt. Henry Heth, stressed the need for mobility and skirmishers, citing recent European experiences. Yet, as Nosworthy points out, "Jomini's retrogressive effort to intertwine Napoleonic concepts within a linear framework appealed to the more conservative sensibilities of the new Buchanan administration."[152] Many US officers initially resisted the French Army's retreat from the rifled musket being a transformational weapon, but celebrated bayonet charges during the 1859 Franco-Austrian War converted most to this view. In contrast to the inconclusive Crimean War experience, evidence in this latter conflict seemed to provide a clear signal—albeit a faulty one.

HOW DID THE NAVY APPLY THE FINDINGS?

Given that the navy undertook no institutional effort to collect information about the Crimean War, it unsurprisingly displayed even less interest than the army in applying data from the European struggle. Secretary Dobbin in April 1854 took advantage of the war's outbreak and enhanced threat perception to help secure congressional funding for six long-sought screw-propelled, steam-powered frigates (the *Merrimack*-class).[153] Beyond the war's instrumental value, one might have expected a more thorough consideration of and reaction to the experience given it was the first combat test for several key naval technologies. At the time, debates existed among American sailors and the maritime community over the relative value of steam propulsion, best type and size of guns, and the potential value and practicality of greater ship protection. The opportunity to consider these issues in the context of a major conflict explains the attraction of inquisitive sailors such as Dahlgren, Farragut, and Porter to the Crimean War.

The conservative outlook of senior sailors, however, created a hostile environment for progressives.[154] Dobbin's reform efforts occurred in a decentralized department in which the bureau chiefs and squadron commanders exerted significant influence. As Paul Lewis observes, "the older, senior officers had no desire to change the status quo, and actively discouraged technical innovations and the application of new inventions."[155] Dobbin removed more than two hundred officers as unfit for duty, but Congress restored more than half of them to active status. Management of the challenging Navy Department declined after Isaac Toucey ("one of the worst secretaries in American naval history") took over at the outset of the Buchanan administration.[156] Congressional funding constraints exacerbated conservatism as the navy's budget bottomed out in 1857, with only modest growth the rest of the decade.[157] This state of affairs frustrated innovators such as Dahlgren, who exclaimed that "the navy of the United States, if not superior in numbers, *must be superior in all else.*"[158]

Faced with a demanding set of missions and limited resources, navy leaders focused on what they believed was relevant and doable.[159] Dahlgren, in an 1850 paper, laid out a widely accepted view of the service's core objectives—defend the US coastline, protect American commerce, and keep open sea lines of communication. The acquisition of Texas, Oregon, and California complicated safeguarding the US coastline, while America's ever-expanding trade increased the need for a global naval presence. Prioritizing the "doable" commerce protection mission, the navy acquired a fleet of smaller ships—frigates, sloops, and brigs. Secretary Toucey displayed a blasé attitude about the potential danger from the larger and more capable British and French navies, arguing, "it is universally admitted to be inexpedient to endeavor to compete with other great commercial powers in the magnitude of their naval preparations."[160] Such an attitude greatly diminished the perceived need to react to events from the Crimean War and may have actually encouraged downplaying its lessons that could call into question the existing fleet's worthiness.

Beneficial Applications

Deployment of Dahlgren guns. The navy attempted to take advantage of findings that fit with its core activities. Most notably, it embraced lessons that supported the service's effort to remain competitive in its one field of excellence—ordnance.[161] The 1844 explosion of a new shell gun on the *Princeton*, killing the secretaries of navy and state, among others, provided a significant impetus for more rigorous ordnance development. As a part of this process, the innovative Dahlgren eventually produced an outstanding cast iron, muzzle-loading, smoothbore 9-inch gun. Yet the merit of employing such large, powerful weapons versus arming warships with more numerous, smaller calibers remained a source of contention within the US Navy when the Crimean War commenced. Using data from that conflict to illustrate the superiority of the big-gun approach, Dahlgren and his supporters convinced the department to arm its new frigates with these weapons. In the fall of 1856 the *Merrimack*, with its Dahlgren guns, deployed to Europe, creating considerable excitement among naval communities. By 1858 Dahlgren guns had become widely popular with 9- or 11-inch variants placed on all new ships. Unfortunately, as Robert Schneller points out, "while Dahlgren was stumping to institutionalize his gun, Europeans [undeterred by the Lancaster's poor performance] were striving to perfect rifled cannon."[162] The conservative US Navy would not begin to develop rifled guns until 1859, by which time the British and French had achieved significant advances.

Assignment of dedicated gunnery sloop. Crimean War fighting prompted not only adoption of larger ordnance but also appreciation of the need for better shooting.[163] At the time the US Navy had no standard gunnery drill, with variance often existing not only between warships but even between divisions on the same warship. Although new technologies (e.g., elevating sights, efficient percussion systems) had enhanced the accuracy of naval fire, British and French combat shooting had been very uneven, reinforcing for Dahlgren the importance of marksmanship. The overwhelming evidence for this conclusion led him to press for action even before the conflict ended. Secretary Dobbin responded by assigning him a sloop "devoted exclusively to gunnery practice," following the British precedent.[164] Dahlgren initiated a program to train enough ordnance specialists so that at least one would be assigned to every warship. Embracing the need for better gunnery skills was a valuable lesson learned but one that fit easily within the navy's culture. This successful application provides another example of the critical role often provided by personal agency as Dahlgren, like Mordecai, identified a key finding and facilitated the necessary change.

Bolstered sloop acquisition. Finally, the navy employed Crimean findings relating to the utility of small, quick warship types that fit with its perceived mission requirements.[165] The effectiveness of heavy shell weapons prompted the removal of the frigate *Cumberland*'s deck and quarter galleys to transform it into a one-gun-deck fast corvette.[166] More significantly, Dobbin pressed for constructing new steam-powered sloops, noting that "vessels of this size have attracted much consideration and acquired much character during the recent conflicts in Europe."[167] Toucey continued this push after becoming secretary, which in March 1857 resulted in approval of five *Hartford*-class steam-powered sloops. The following year Congress funded even smaller sloops with shallower drafts to conduct coastal and river operations.

Ignored Lessons

Neglect of the floating battery. The navy, however, ignored some salient findings, as the Civil War would reveal. This neglect is most evident with regard to the floating battery.[168] While the aforementioned Battle of Kinburn sparked the British and French to embark on major building campaigns (the "first ironclad race"), the US Navy did not even construct a test ship. Lewis claims that Porter's model of a floating battery and voluminous notes "aroused considerable interest" in the Navy Department, but other historians found his reports from the Crimea ignored.[169] Donald Canney persuasively posits that the navy's lack of interest in floating batteries reflected their seeming incompatibility with duty on foreign stations and a related priority on speed in warship design. For naval observers of the Crimean War, speed stood as a tertiary consideration, with shell guns necessitating armor for warship protection and the addition of such defenses requiring larger, heavier guns. The above-discussed classes acquired in the late 1850s proved useful in the Civil War, but Jack Greene and Alessandro Massignani stress that the US Navy would have been at a considerable disadvantage if British and French fleets had entered the conflict in its early years.[170]

Dismissal of mine relevance. Similarly, Russia's demonstration of the potential danger from "torpedoes" (submerged mines) did not cause either the navy or the army to initiate meaningful development of mine or mine-countermeasure capabilities.[171] American sailors had long shown disdain for this subject, which was anathema to the seafaring culture. Now, however, the Navy Department possessed evidence of how problematic mines could be for operations, especially assaulting ports. As with the floating battery, the low expectation for conducting such attacks meant this weapon could be treated as of negligible importance. Further diminishing interest was the designation of mines as a component of coastal defense under army control. Yet conversations with British ship captains who fought in the Crimean War should have disabused American sailors of their blasé attitude. The navy was unprepared for this challenge during the Civil War, after which then army chief engineer Delafield identified the mine's value as one of that war's primary lessons.[172] The navy's neglect of mine warfare after the Crimean War was emblematic of a tendency to ignore disruptive lessons whose implementation entailed unappealing consequences for essentially surface warfare officers.

HOW DID THE FINDINGS IMPACT CIVIL WAR DECISION-MAKING?

As tension escalated over Fort Sumter in early 1861, insights from the Crimean War suddenly resonated with officials from both sides.[173] In lobbying for a resupply mission of the isolated garrison, Gustavus Vasa Fox, soon to be the Navy Department's assistant secretary, informed President Abraham Lincoln that the actions in that prior conflict and other recent experiences had shown that steamships could pass land-based guns. While Lincoln moved to bolster Maj. Robert Anderson's small force, the South Carolinians, inspired by the floating batteries used against Russia, constructed a one-hundred-foot towed variant (lacking the resources for steam propulsion). Although it inflicted limited damage despite firing several hundred rounds, the "vessel" proved impervious to counterfire, while mortars, as at Sebastopol, had a major impact before Anderson's capitulation.

As the United States and Confederate States of America (CSA) scrambled to establish forces of a scale and complexity unprecedented in North America, the Delafield Commission reports offered "a comprehensive introduction to contemporary military science" and "the most current evaluation of military operations."[174] Mordecai's volume served, for both sides, as "a sourcebook on artillery and small arms during the Civil War."[175] The potential benefit to Southerners of Delafield's engineering data prompted the federal government to try to halt his report's distribution. The indisputable interest in these documents and signature examples of their use, however, does not prove they had widespread influence. As Nosworthy observes, "unfortunately, it is not possible to determine who had access to these works and the extent to which they were actually read."[176] For example, we know that in June 1861, shortly after taking command of 21st Illinois regiment, Col. Ulysses Grant asked his wife, "If you have an opportunity I wish you would send me McClellands report of battles in the Crimea."[177] Did he receive it? If so, did he review it and did it contribute to his rapid emergence as the Union's best general?

For the Southern leadership facing the challenge of defending against an adversary possessing an enormous resource advantage, lessons from the Russian experience in an analogous context seemed applicable.[178] The CSA government attached considerable faith to the defensive strength of coastal and riparian fortifications that had been so effective in the Crimean War. For example, in April 1862 CSA president Jefferson Davis assured the governor of Louisiana that works south of New Orleans would block any naval force attempting to ascend the Mississippi River.[179] Although preferring masonry fortifications as signaled by their interpretation of the previous conflict's lessons, a lack of time necessitated that they construct in key areas without prior structures earthen parapets reinforced by logs, as the Russians had done at Sebastopol. With the geographically well-protected port of Wilmington, North Carolina, needing defenses, Col. William Lamb modeled Fort Fisher's large sand curtains on the Russian positions that had guarded Sebastopol's southern side. That Lamb could erect only earthworks proved fortuitous, given that such defenses were far better at absorbing bombardments than stone and brick structures.

To buttress coastal fortifications and offset its lack of warships, the CSA embraced two Crimean War innovations ignored by the antebellum US military—floating batteries and mines. Whereas in the prior conflict ironclads had been introduced to attack Russian coastal fortifications, the Confederates attempted to use them to prevent US warships from maintaining station off key ports.[180] The transformation of the mid-1850s steam frigate *Merrimack* into the powerful ironclad *Virginia* marked the centerpiece of this effort. Although inconclusive, its March 1862 battle with the *Monitor* at Hampton Roads precipitated *"Monitor* fever," with both sides rushing to build more ironclads, a competition that the far-better-resourced North won decisively. Union warships emerged unscathed from their first encounter with torpedoes (maritime mines) on July 7, 1861, but Confederate officials appreciated their potential and established the Submarine Battery Service and Torpedo Bureau to set up stations at key ports.[181] Despite qualitative and quantitative deficiencies, the presence of mines exerted a significant deterrent on cautious Union naval commanders. For example, Dahlgren, in charge of the mid-1863 assault on Charleston, South Carolina, hesitated, arguing that the underwater defenses "would have to be removed before his ships could pass into the harbor without undue risk."[182] The US Navy's failure to study British mine-countermeasure efforts in the Crimean War resulted in its sailors initially being reduced to trying to explode sea mines with small-arms fire. Confederate mines improved over time, ultimately sinking twenty-nine Union warships and damaging fourteen more. The toll claimed by these devices helps account for the acclaim garnered by Farragut, who reputedly declared "damn the torpedoes" and advanced forward to close the Mobile, Alabama, harbor in August 1864.

In attempting to isolate and defeat the Confederacy, the US Navy drew on insights from the Anglo-French experience in the Crimean War as well as their own history off Mexico and China.[183] For example, after overcoming the heavily fortified Port Royal Sound, South Carolina, in November 1861, Flag Officer Du Pont wrote that the British attacks at Odessa and Sebastopol underlay his approach. With blockading squadrons needing continuous repairs, Du Pont urged the Navy Department to modify some vessels to function as floating machine shops, as done by the Allied navies during the Crimean and Chinese wars. Fifteen months later, he relayed the value of the squadron's floating machine shop in keeping warships on station. Early in the war the US Navy achieved success in the western theater, where the highly capable Farragut and Porter directed operations in accord with Crimean War best practices. Findings from the earlier conflict influenced their plan to overcome the Mississippi River fortifications south of New Orleans. In particular, Porter pressed Farragut to employ mortar boats, "citing his experience at Kinburn."[184] These warships played a valuable role in the fleet's advance past the works, which prompted a Confederate withdrawal from the South's largest city. The result was a shocking and problematic development for Davis, who, as noted, had only recently reassured the Louisiana governor that such an outcome was not possible.

Unfortunately for Davis and the Confederacy, masonry fortifications were proving far more vulnerable than expected (at least by senior army engineers and War Department officials).[185] It was true that the under-resourced Southerners struggled to arm and man their works properly, a requirement reiterated by students of the Crimean War. Yet, whereas the rifled Lancaster guns had failed in the Crimean War, a half decade later the US Army's Parrott guns proved lethal for brick and stone structures, especially when combined with heavy mortars. Illustrating this new reality, gunners quickly overwhelmed Fort Pulaski, guarding the entrance to the Savannah River. As a result, Angus Konstam argues that "in effect, on April 12 1862, all of the Third System coastal forts in the United States were rendered obsolete."[186] The survival of Charleston and Mobile until late in the war counters that exaggerated claim, but he is basically correct.

The survival of some ports, especially Charleston, reflected the incomplete adherence to another Crimean War lesson—the need for joint ground and sea assaults against coastal fortifications.[187] Demonstrating the benefit on interservice cooperation, Foote, Farragut, and Porter partnered effectively with Grant and William T. Sherman along the western theater's key rivers to produce important victories. Charleston's continued resistance vexed Union leaders, but Assistant Secretary Fox exacerbated the difficulty of its capture by pushing for a purely naval action. Du Pont, the local commander, referenced Allied experiences at Sebastopol and Kronstadt in expressing his pessimism about attacking the Confederacy's most heavily fortified port. The defenses' proximity to Charleston meant that the US Navy had to defeat them directly rather than pass by as occurred below New Orleans. The April 7, 1863, operation proved a great disappointment, with warships, including nine ironclads, suffering heavy damage while inflicting little harm. Lincoln and Navy Secretary Gideon Welles, who had invested heavily in ironclads, concluded the failed attack revealed less about the limitations of this vessel type than Du Pont, whom they replaced with Dahlgren. A second attack (July 1863) incorporated army units that captured outer forts, but Dahlgren, as noted, proved unwilling to advance as long as mines and other obstacles guarded the channel, ensuring that Charleston remained in Confederate hands until late in the war. Fort Fisher, which also held out until early 1865, finally "was doomed from the moment Navy Secretary Gideon Welles concocted the grand scheme for '*a conjoint* [army–navy] *attack upon Wilmington.*'"[188] Rather than serving as a model for future operations, the requirement for army–navy cooperation to capture strong coastal positions, Kenneth Hagan points out, "was an unpleasant lesson to contemplate."[189] Instead, American naval officers after the Civil War focused "on the apparent promise for the future revealed in the short happy life of the C.S.S. *Alabama*, the greatest American commerce raider of all time."[190]

Recognizing that simply waiting for the blockade to have effect was strategically dangerous and politically untenable, Lincoln commenced ground operations as soon as possible. Union success in the western theater contributed greatly, if not primarily, to victory, but as the Crimean War essentially became a struggle for Sebastopol, leaders early in the war believed control of Richmond, Virginia, would be determinative. Given this seeming parallel, the specter of that Crimean port appears to have influenced decision-makers on both sides.[191] In 1861 McClellan rapidly ascended to become commander of the Army of the Potomac and general-in-chief of all field armies. Stephen Sears observes that McClellan's service on the Delafield Commission, "more than any other, firmly fixed his reputation as an expert on the art of war."[192] The Union commander seized on two lessons from the analogous Anglo-French experience—Russia's inaccessibility complicated victory, and the Allies' ability to move ground forces by sea critically contributed to their ultimate success. In proposing an amphibious landing near Richmond in the spring 1862, McClellan "consciously repeated aspects of the Anglo-French attack on Sebastopol."[193]

Although McClellan confidently wrote his wife that "I do believe that I am avoiding the faults of the Allies at Sebastopol," he aped their primary blunder.[194] The Union commander, who had been greatly affected by the "horribly bungled logistics of the Crimean War," emphasized organizational and support elements rather than exploiting favorable circumstances.[195] Thus, instead of rapidly advancing on weak Confederate positions at Yorktown, Virginia, McClellan remained in his Crimeanesque siege lines far from Richmond and attempted to crush the enemy with massive bombardment. Sears argues that McClellan's failure to appreciate two key aspects of the Crimean War greatly hampered his Civil War performance: (1) "he gave hardly a mention to the subject of high command," and (2) "because McClellan arrived too late to witness either battles or siege, the potential effect of the rifled musket on future tactics escaped him."[196] As has been discussed, both of these oft-cited failings are somewhat understandable. Regardless, McClellan exemplifies how a belief in understanding foreign combat can instill misplaced confidence on what to do on a battlefield with deleterious consequences.

For Lincoln and other Northerners, the Sebastopol analogy offered a political as well as military caution as US forces became mired on the peninsula.[197] The American system did not allow the type of no confidence vote that brought down Great Britain's Aberdeen government during the Crimean War's first winter, but looming November 1862 midterm elections marked an early referendum on the war effort. Severe Republican losses would complicate war management, potentially shift European attitudes about the Confederacy's prospects, and likely inspire the South to greater resistance. Thus, failure of the slow-moving, easily deterred McClellan to seize Richmond prompted Lincoln's increasing skepticism about an approach that seemed like the Sebastopol siege. After replacing McClellan as army commander in July 1862, Halleck added his pessimism about Union prospects to reach Richmond in part based on the British and French difficulty in overcoming field fortifications in the Crimea. Other knowledgeable Northerners had the same reaction, such as then–rear admiral Du Pont, who in early August 1862 wrote that "we are watching events at Richmond with painful anxiety. . . . I presume the rebels are making it their Sevastopol."[198] By then, however, Lincoln had come to regard the destruction of Lee's army as the key to victory.

For Southern leaders, such as Davis and Lee, Sebastopol offered a warning on the danger of allowing Union forces to besiege the Confederate capital.[199] In such a circumstance, they feared that, like the Russians, it would only be a matter of time before defeat resulted. Upon assuming command of the Army of Northern Virginia in early June 1862, the offensively inclined Lee wrote Davis that "it will require 100,000 men to resist the regular siege of Richmond, which perhaps would only prolong not save it."[200] The usually defense-favoring Joseph Johnston, who had directed the force before being wounded, agreed on the need to attack rather than attempt to survive a siege. Herman Hathaway and Archer Jones emphasize that "the Confederate leaders could hardly escape the analogy, because none other than McClellan had served as an official US observer at the siege of Sebastopol."[201] Belief in the "Sebastopol thesis" meant it was imperative to take the offensive to keep Union forces away from Richmond. The Army of Northern Virginia would be successful for over two years before wearing down. At this point a Sebastopol-style siege campaign commenced at Petersburg, Virginia, with the inevitable breakthrough nine months later heralding the war's end.

CONCLUSION

Even before the Civil War ended, participants and historians began penning works on the great struggle. Hundreds of volumes would soon emerge, many attacking

Jefferson Davis and George McClellan, both infamous in their own way. The vast shadow of the Civil War left no room for the Crimean War, which essentially disappeared from American discourse. Chief Engineer Delafield may have hoped his commission report was forgotten, as his Civil War postmortem focused on the vulnerability of masonry forts to modern artillery in direct opposition to his key finding from the Crimean War.[202] By contrast, he had reported from that earlier conflict the utility of mines. The consequences for not applying that lesson and others in the antebellum years were considerably mitigated by the United States essentially fighting itself in the Civil War instead of a European power.

As the first US Army commission to visit a war zone, there is no disputing its precedent-setting import, but how should we judge its effectiveness? Maureen O'Connor questions its potential, given that "the late date at which the United States decided to send observers combined with the red tape encountered by the Delafield Commission in both France and Russia caused the three American officers to miss altogether the opportunity to observe the important battles of the war."[203] She believes, however, that, as a result of the group's presence in Europe during the most significant war in forty years, their reports proved instructive in several ways: (1) ensuring awareness of current thinking about weapons' utility, (2) enhancing understanding on European general thinking about the dynamics of modern war, and (3) improving relations between the US Army and individual militaries.[204] Yet Bonura correctly notes that "the overall impression gained from these three works was that the Crimean War demonstrated nothing new in the military art, not in tactics or technology."[205] Moten, author of the most authoritative study on the Delafield Commission, finds significant lessons generated, but they proved of limited importance. Compared to the army, the navy's lack of a dedicated lesson-learning effort left it at a stark disadvantage in potentially benefiting from other people's mistakes.

As a first try, the Delafield Commission provided insights into the challenges of learning from foreign wars. Above all, this difficult task requires the assignment of high-quality personnel. Davis deserves praise for selecting three of the army's sharpest officers for this extended duty, despite many competing demands. Yet as a group they possessed limitations that would shape their observations in critical ways.[206] Davis, despite hoping to assist army operations in the West, selected officers only from the service's elite ranks, who tended to exude disdain for such "warfare." A veteran frontier infantryman instead of McClellan might have been a more appropriate choice, but the secretary attached great importance to obtaining information for the underdeveloped cavalry branch. Another valid appreciation was how the group's "lack of experience in high-level planning, coordination, and execution of operations, and a lack of focus on maneuver warfare" diminished appreciation of battlefield developments.[207] The inclusion of an officer familiar with high-level operations in the Mexican-American War would have better enabled such insights.

For example, Col. Ethan Hitchcock, inspector general for Scott's expeditionary force in the Mexican-American War, would have been a good candidate, if not for his poor health. Much more problematic was the War Department's formation of the Delafield Commission only a year after the fighting started and the failure to obtain prior permission for the American observers to be attached to frontline forces, which resulted in them reaching Sebastopol only after the fighting was essentially over. Finally, the decision to produce three separate reports, albeit for understandable reasons, meant, as Moten relates, that "working separately and writing on matters assigned individually—mentally 'paddling his own little canoe'—each commissioner focused on his own task and matters of import in his own branch."[208] This approach reduced the potential for identifying overarching dynamics as well as reconciling conflicting positions of subjects due to their different perspectives.

The Americans discovered a wealth of information from touring the recent battlefields and discussions with combatants, albeit with a narrow, technical focus. That is, the commissioners excelled at identifying innovative developments, which allowed for improved ways to perform existing tasks. The best example is Mordecai's appreciation of how beneficial the French 12-pound gun would be for the US field artillery. The group spent considerable time attempting to determine the most effective ordnance, from small arms to large guns. They even did a good job discovering advances in the less exciting support areas (e.g., medical transports, dehydrated food). This type of data not only fit the outlook of the commissioners but also responded to the secretary's tasking. The pursuit of such details, however, appears to have obscured generating broader insights about the evolving nature of warfare. Moten persuasively criticizes that by providing the commissioners with a long, nonprioritized list of requirements, Davis promoted "a tendency to concentrate on technical matters almost to the exclusion of higher-level thinking."[209] Yet, given the nature and experience of group members, it seems unlikely that the commissioners—even operating without any formal tasking—would have produced a significantly different response.

Beyond concentrating on technical details, the commissioners tended to embrace data that affirmed the status quo as exemplified by their extensive reporting on masonry fortifications' resistance to modern naval warships and rifled artillery. This lesson bolstered senior army engineers engaged in a heated dispute about the obsolescence of such works. Critics complain that they neglected contrary information, but even Dahlgren—the navy's leading ordnance expert—agreed with their basic assessment on the fortification–warship balance. Although Delafield and McClellan included data on Sebastopol's earthen works that proved so problematic for the British and French, these classically trained engineers disparaged their strength relative to masonry fortifications. Bureaucratic incentives and personal predispositions inclined experienced observers to adopt a conservative outlook, but such likelihood does not diminish its negative effect, especially at times of rapidly changing technology. Less than a decade later, during the Civil War, masonry fortifications proved extremely vulnerable to rifled artillery, while earthen works generally absorbed such firepower. Davis had explicitly inquired about the much-touted rifled Lancaster gun. Its poor showing indicated the time had not arrived for such weapons, but their day would not be long in coming. These examples highlight a critical danger for lessons-learning efforts—the accurate but counterproductive finding.

The navy's "approach" to discovery about Crimean combat clearly left much to be desired. Given the new technologies employed, Farragut was right to want a firsthand assessment. The void left by Secretary Dobbin ignoring his plea was only partially filled by the informal efforts of Dahlgren and Porter, given the former's focus on ordnance and the latter's brief time in the Crimea. As undoubtedly the department's leadership expected, forward-deployed officers absorbed some of the knowledge through conversations with their British and French naval colleagues. For example, Du Pont discovered the floating machine ship's utility during his service off China in the late 1850s.[210] Despite the efforts of the most inquisitive and thoughtful officers (e.g., Dahlgren, Du Pont, Porter), the lack of direct access and operating in isolation hindered appreciating the synergistic impact of new technologies suggested by events in the Crimean War.

Application of findings deemed germane for the US military varied depending on the nature of the lessons. Much of the information was ignored as irrelevant, given the War Department's preoccupation with operations in the West. Findings that reinforced the status quo (sustaining information) were used to bolster arguments for continued spending and activity such as a call for expanding the number and scale of masonry fortifications. Particularly embraced were insights that offered better ways to do tasks the army was already pursuing, especially in the field artillery. As a senior member of Ordnance Board, Mordecai could shepherd his findings, such as the French 12-pound gun, through the testing and approval process. The Napoleon gun would be the most common artillery piece for both sides in the Civil War, providing excellent service, especially with rapidly firing antipersonnel canister rounds. Plus, the wrought iron gun carriages were a marked success. Two British artillery experts sent to study the US Civil War for their own lessons-learning effort commended American use of such carriages, commenting that they "stood the test of actual service" and contributed significantly to the speed and reliability in firing large guns.[211]

Alternatively, a lack of appreciation about the tactical implications of infantry armed with rifled muskets and the benefits of effective operational staffs contributed to a series of excessively deadly battles and ineffectual fighting during the early years of the latter conflict. Observations like the commissioners' discussion of rifle pits suggested an evolving battlefield, but their conveyance was unlikely to precipitate recognition of the need for a more fundamental reassessment of strategy, operations, and tactics. It certainly did not occur in this case. As Bonura concludes, while the Delafield Commission reporting supplied technical data, "it did very little to in-form the army's intellectual framework of the battlefield or even the art of war in a greater sense."[212] The result reflects that the lessons had instructional and instrumen-tal influences but not inspirational, as they did not identify challenges of the modern battlefield that needed to be addressed, let alone take steps to respond. The minimal analytical capability of the pre–Civil War army made it unlikely the service would explore such dynamics without clear and persuasive cues from Crimean combat.

The navy, with less investment in discovering what happened and seeing even fewer relevancies for what occurred despite the introduction of key new weapons and technologies, deserves a lower evaluation. The navy took some easy and produc-tive actions such as assigning Dahlgren a gunnery practice ship to improve marks-manship and modifying the *Cumberland*. It undoubtedly gave a boost to Dahlgren's big guns and steam propulsion. These steps, however, amounted to little, especially given the prodigious postwar activity sparked in European navies. In large part, the war's focus on naval power projection and attacking coastal fortifications dimin-ished the US Navy's responsiveness. Given budget limitations, one might applaud the Navy Department leadership for not being distracted, yet the subsequent events of the Civil War show the narrowness of that perspective. A proper appreciation for the prior war's lessons would have forced a reconsideration of what qualified as appropriate US naval activities, something that its conservative leadership would not even ponder. In other words, the classification of some findings as "irrelevant" reflected a cultural predisposition rather than truly being irrelevant (e.g., floating batteries, mines).

Finally, the application of lessons and analogies from the Crimean War to the conduct of the US Civil War can be judged as mixed at best. Key decision-makers drew wisdom from that far-off conflict at times, such as Du Pont basing his suc-cessful attack plan against Port Royal on the Royal Navy's assaults on Odessa and Sebastopol and Lamb using the latter's defenses as a model for his stout Fort Fisher guarding Wilmington, North Carolina. Yet in other cases they did not, such as the navy's foolish rejection of joint land–sea operations against coastal fortifications at Charleston in 1863. Political, bureaucratic, and cultural factors largely prompted such neglect, which greater appreciation or study of lessons would have been un-likely to overcome. Perhaps most dangerous, as McClellan exemplified in the 1862 peninsula campaign, is when decision-makers operate with misplaced confidence that they are properly applying findings from the prior war. Although the Union commander believed he could avoid the mistakes the Anglo-French made in assault-ing Sebastopol, he repeated the core failing by not advancing quickly. By the time of the next case (the Russo-Japanese War), a half century had elapsed, and the US mili-tary services had undergone significant institutional development. Did such growth improve learning from foreign war?

NOTES

Epigraph: Richard Delafield, *Report on the Art of War in Europe in 1854, 1855, and 1856* (Washington, DC: George Bowman, 1860), 1.

1. David Farragut to Secretary of Navy James Dobbin, April 12, 1854, in Loyall Farragut, *Life of David Glasgow Farragut: First Admiral of the United States Navy, Embodying His Journal and Letters* (New York: D. Appleton & Company, 1879), 166.

2. Jefferson Davis, *Report of the Secretary of War*, December 4, 1854 (Washington, DC: A.O.P. Nicholson, 1854), 19–20; and Matthew Moten, *The Delafield Commission and the American Military Profession* (College Station: Texas A&M University Press, 2000), 88.

3. In mid-1815, Capt. Sylvanus Thayer and Maj. William McRee embarked for Europe to see Napoleonic warfare, as did Brig. Gen. Winfield Scott (technically on leave but attached to the French as a military observer), who traveled separately. Unfortunately, all arrived after the Battle of Waterloo.

4. Robert Edgerton, *Death or Glory: Legacy of Crimean War* (Boulder, CO: Westview Press, 1999), 29.

5. William Skelton, *American Profession of Arms: The Army Officer Corps, 1784–1861* (Lawrence: University Press of Kansas, 1992), 187; and Robert Utley, *Frontiersmen in Blue: The US Army and the Indian, 1848–1865* (Lincoln: University of Nebraska Press, 1981), 45.

6. Jay Luvaas, *The Military Legacy of Civil War: The European Inheritance* (Lawrence: University Press of Kansas, 1988), 7.

7. John Dahlgren, *Shells and Shell-Guns* (Philadelphia: King & Baird, 1856), 124.

8. Dunbar Rowland, ed., *Jefferson Davis, Constitutionalist* (hereafter, *JDC*), vol. 2: *His Letters, Papers, and Speeches* (Jackson: Mississippi Department of Archives and History, 1923), 373, 444; Lynda Crist and Mary Dix, eds., *Papers of Jefferson Davis* (hereafter, *PJD*), vol. 5: *1853–1855* (Baton Rouge: Louisiana State University Press, 1985), 103–4, 372; and Maureen O'Connor, "In the Eye of the Beholder: Western Military Observers from Buena Vista to Plevna" (PhD diss., Harvard University, 1996), 65–76.

9. Dahlgren, *Shells and Shell-Guns*, 334.

10. Wayne Hsieh, *West Pointers and the Civil War: The Old Army in War and Peace* (Chapel Hill: University of North Carolina Press, 2009), 19–23; Skelton, *American Profession of Arms*, 240–41; and Moten, *Delafield Commission*, 30–31, 83–87.

11. William J. Cooper Jr., *Jefferson Davis, American* (New York: Vintage Books, 2000), 146, 261–69, 272–73, 282; and *PJD* 5:v–viii.

12. *PJD* 5:v.

13. Moten, *Delafield Commission*, 83.

14. Arthur Frame, "US Military Commission to Crimean War and Influence on the US Army before the American Civil War" (PhD diss., University of Kansas, 1993), 116, 148–49; and Moten, *Delafield Commission*, 75, 88.

15. For paragraph, see Stanley Falk, "Soldier-Technologist: Major Alfred Mordecai and the Beginnings of Science in the US Army" (PhD diss., Georgetown University, 1959), 240, 274, 427–28; Moten, *Delafield Commission*, 85, 88–93, 98–100, 104–8; O'Connor, "Eye of the

Beholder," 121n215; and Stephen Sears, *George B. McClellan: The Young Napoleon* (New York: Da Capo Press, 1999), 42–44.

16. Moten, *Delafield Commission*, 93.

17. Moten, 100.

18. Davis to Delafield, Mordecai, and McClellan, April 2, 1855, letter in *JDC* 2:446; for the complete tasking list, see *JDC* 2:446–48; and Moten, *Delafield Commission*, 108–14.

19. Davis to Delafield, Mordecai, and McClellan, April 2, 1855, letter in *JDC* 2:447.

20. For paragraph, see Moten, *Delafield Commission*, 114–23; O'Connor, "Eye of the Beholder," 29, 32–33, 78, 82–87, 98–99; Falk, "Soldier-Technologist," 434–35; and Crimean Commission to Davis, April 4, 1856, in *PJD*, vol. 6, *1856–1860*, p. 394.

21. For paragraph, see Moten, *Delafield Commission*, 124, 128–32, 135–36; George McClellan, *Report of the Secretary of War: Communicating the Report of Captain George B. McClellan, One of the Officers Sent to the Seat of War in Europe in 1855 and 1856* (Washington, DC: A.O.P. Nicholson, 1857), 62; Frame, "US Military Commission," 171–82; and O'Connor, "Eye of the Beholder," 79, 87–88, 283.

22. Alfred Mordecai to Sara Mordecai, June 20–21, 1855, letter quoted in Moten, *Delafield Commission*, 132.

23. For paragraph, see Moten, *Delafield Commission*, 153–54, 158–59, 175, 177; Frame, "US Military Commission," 182, 195, 200; Falk, "Soldier-Technologist," 456, 459–60, 468–69; and O'Connor, "Eye of the Beholder," 80–82, 87–91, 94–95.

24. Moten, *Delafield Commission*, 147.

25. Moten, 145.

26. Delafield to Davis, November 5, 1855, quoted in O'Connor, "Eye of the Beholder," 80.

27. See *PJD* 5:427–29 for the dates and subjects of these letters.

28. Davis to Delafield, February 9, 1856, in *PJD* 6:393.

29. For paragraph, see *PJD* 6:394–96; Moten, *Delafield Commission*, 171–77, 202; Frame, "US Military Commission," 198, 204, 467; Falk, "Soldier-Technologist," 465–73; and O'Connor, "Eye of the Beholder," 92, 96.

30. Moten, *Delafield Commission*, 175.

31. Michael Bonura, *Under the Shadow of Napoleon: French Influence on the American Way of Warfare from the War of 1812 to the Outbreak of World War II* (New York: New York University Press, 2012), 99–100.

32. Jefferson Davis, *Report of the Secretary of War*, December 1, 1856 (Washington, DC: Cornelius Wendell, 1856), 16.

33. For paragraph see *PJD* 6:395; Richard Delafield, *Report on the Art of War in Europe in 1854, 1855, and 1856* (Washington, DC: George W. Bowman, 1860), 1–3; Frame, "US Military Commission," 204–6, 238–39; Moten, *Delafield Commission*, 175–76, 194, 202; and Falk, "Soldier-Technologist," 251, 483.

34. Moten, *Delafield Commission*, 175.

35. McClellan, *Report of the Secretary of War*, 21–22.

36. Delafield, *Report on the Art of War*, 176.

37. Brent Nosworthy, *The Bloody Crucible of Courage: Fighting Methods and Combat Experience of the Civil War* (New York: Carroll & Graf, 2003), 83–84.

38. Ian Hope, *A Scientific Way of War: Antebellum Military Science, West Point, and the Origins of American Military Thought* (Lincoln: University of Nebraska Press, 2015), 146–49, 184–88; and Thomas Greiss, "Dennis Hart Mahan: West Point Professor and Advocate of Military Professionalism, 1830–1871" (PhD diss., Duke University, 1968), 254–55, 263, 271.

39. Henry Halleck, *Elements of Military Art and Science*, 2nd ed. (New York: D. Appleton, 1859), 438.

40. Dobbin to Farragut, April 15, 1854, in Farragut, *Life of David Glasgow Farragut*, 167.

41. Kenneth Hagan, *This People's Navy: The Making of American Sea Power* (New York: Free Press, 1991), 140.

42. J. D. Hayes, ed., *Samuel Francis Du Pont: Selection from His Civil War Letters* (hereafter, *SDP letters*), 3 vols. (Ithaca, NY: Cornell University Press, 1969), 1:lxiv; and Hagan, *This People's Navy*, 151–53, 159.

43. Robert Schneller, *A Quest for Glory: Biography of Rear Admiral John A. Dahlgren* (Annapolis, MD: Naval Institute Press, 1996), 69–72.

44. For paragraph, see Schneller, 76–77, 157, 167–68; Falk, "Soldier-Technologist," 398, 404–6; Chester Hearn, *Admiral David Dixon Porter: The Civil War Years* (Annapolis, MD: Naval Institute Press, 1986), 33–34; and Paul Lewis, *Yankee Admiral: A Biography of David Dixon Porter* (New York: D. McKay, 1968), 88.

45. James Dobbin, *Report of the Secretary of Navy*, December 4, 1854 (Washington, DC: A.O.P. Nicholson, 1854), 393.

46. "USS Cumberland and CSS Florida," Department of Navy, Naval History and Heritage Command, http://www.history.navy.mil/.

47. James Dobbin, *Report of the Secretary of Navy*, December 3, 1855 (Washington, DC: Cornelius Wendell, 1855), 393; Davis, *Report of the Secretary of War*, December 1, 1856, p. 22–23; and *JDC* 2:461–66.

48. Dahlgren, *Shells and Shell-Guns*, 391.

49. Dahlgren, 295.

50. O'Connor, "Eye of the Beholder," 97; for paragraph, see O'Connor, 96, 100–102, Delafield, *Report on the Art of War*, 1–3, 24, 36, 39, 49–57, 63, 97, 136, 214–15; Alfred Mordecai, *The Military Commission to Europe in 1855 and 1856: The Report of Major Alfred Mordecai, 1856* (Washington, DC: George Bowman, 1860), 13, 61, 63; and McClellan, *Report of the Secretary of War*, 7, 22–23.

51. Davis, *Report of the Secretary of War*, December 1, 1856, p. 15.

52. For paragraph, see Delafield, *Report on the Art of War*, 3, 36, 53, 56–57, 97; Dahlgren, *Shells and Shell-Guns*, 121–22, 416; and McClellan, *Report of the Secretary of War*, 23.

53. Dahlgren, *Shells and Shell-Guns*, 416.

54. Delafield, *Report on the Art of War*, 53.

55. For paragraph, see Delafield, *Report on the Art of War*, 109–10; Norman Youngblood, *The Development of Mine Warfare: A Most Murderous and Barbarous Conduct* (Westport, CT: Praeger, 2006), 13–22, 28–33; Howard Levie, *Mine Warfare at Sea* (Dordrecht, Netherlands: Martinus Nijhoff, 1992), 11, 119; and Jack Greene and Alessandro Massignani, *Ironclads at War: The Origin and Development of the Armored Warship, 1854–1891* (New York: Da Capo Press, 1998), 21–22.

56. For paragraph, see Delafield, *Report on the Art of War*, 10, 12, 34, 168, 172–76; Dahlgren, *Shells and Shell-Guns*, 313–14, 387, 412–15, 430–31; Dobbin, *Report of the Secretary of Navy*, December 3, 1855, p. 13; James Dobbin, *Report of the Secretary of Navy*, December 1, 1856 (Washington, DC: Cornelius Wendell, 1856), 412, 414; Greene and Massignani, *Ironclads at War*, 24–33; Nosworthy, *Bloody Crucible*, 112–20; and Lewis, *Yankee Admiral*, 88.

57. Falk, "Soldier-Technologist," 435.

58. Quoted in Greene and Massignani, *Ironclads at War*, 30.

59. Delafield, *Report on the Art of War*, 172.

60. Dahlgren, *Shells and Shell-Guns*, 412.

61. For paragraph, see Mordecai, *Military Commission to Europe*, 134, 142–45; and Falk, "Soldier-Technologist," 488–89.

62. Delafield, *Report on the Art of War*, 5.

63. Mordecai, *Military Commission to Europe*, 143.

64. Delafield, *Report on the Art of War*, 12–17, 25–26; and Mordecai, *Military Commission to Europe*, 64, 121–22, 127, 135, 191.

65. For paragraph, see Delafield, *Report on the Art of War*, 58, 61, 68–72; *PJD* 5:248; and McClellan, *Report of the Secretary of War*, 42–44, 80, 255, 283.

66. Delafield, *Report on the Art of War*, 58, emphasis original.

67. Nosworthy, *Bloody Crucible*, 82.

68. Delafield, *Report on the Art of War*, 90–91.

69. For paragraph, see Delafield, *Report on the Art of War*, 18, 24, 49–50, 136; Brian McAllister Linn, *The Echo of Battle: The Army's Way of War* (Cambridge, MA: Harvard University Press, 2007), 13–16, 19, 25–26; and Samuel Watson, "Knowledge, Interest, and the Limits of Military Professionalism: The Discourse on American Coastal Defence, 1815–1860," *War in History* 5, no. 3 (July 1998): 280–307.

70. Delafield, *Report on the Art of War*, 39.

71. Joseph Totten, "The Effects of Firing with Heavy Ordnance from Casemate Embrasures," Papers on Practical Engineering, no. 6 (Washington, DC: Taylor and Maury, 1857), 137–39.

72. McClellan, *Report of the Secretary of War*, 23.

73. Davis, *Report of the Secretary of War*, December 1, 1856, p. 15.

74. Dobbin, *Report of the Secretary of Navy*, December 1, 1856, p. 412.

75. Dahlgren, *Shells and Shell-Guns*, 405–7.

76. Dahlgren, 411.

77. For paragraph, see *JDC* 2:446–47; Mordecai, *Military Commission to Europe*, 61, 63, 110, 118; Delafield, *Report on the Art of War*, 5, 9–10, 24, 42–43, 135–36; and Dahlgren, *Shells and Shell-Guns*, 124–28, 393–94, 397, 403–7, 413–14.

78. Dahlgren, *Shells and Shell-Guns*, 112.

79. Mordecai, *Military Commission to Europe*, 61.

80. Delafield, *Report on the Art of War*, 19.

81. Dahlgren, *Shells and Shell-Guns,* 405.

82. Delafield, *Report on the Art of War*, 110; and *PJD* 5:427.

83. Delafield, *Report on the Art of War*, 110.

84. J. D. Hittle, *The Military Staff: Its History and Development* (Westport, CT: Greenwood, 1975), 151.

85. Mordecai, *Military Commission to Europe*, 30, 58; and Falk, "Soldier-Technologist," 474.

86. For paragraph, see McClellan, *Report of the Secretary of War*, 124–26; Mordecai, *Military Commission to Europe*, 18, 162; Delafield, *Report on the Art of War*, 9; *PJD* 6:505; and Moten, *Delafield Commission*, 183–87, 191.

87. For paragraph, see Mordecai, *Military Commission to Europe*, 157–58, 162–65, 172–76, 209; McClellan, *Report of the Secretary of War*, 42, 44; Delafield, *Report on the Art of War*, 5–6, 8; Moten, *Delafield Commission*, 151, 180, 198; and Nosworthy, *Bloody Crucible*, 647.

88. Mordecai, *Military Commission to Europe*, 176.

89. Mordecai, 176.

90. McClellan, *Report of the Secretary of War*, 16.

91. Moten, *Delafield Commission*, 151; Delafield, *Report on the Art of War*, 50–51; Mordecai, *Military Commission to Europe*, 176; and McClellan, *Report of the Secretary of War*, 12.

92. Edward Hagerman, *The American Civil War and the Origins of Modern Warfare: Ideas, Organization, and Field Command* (Bloomington: Indiana University Press, 1988), 22–23; and Hsieh, *West Pointers*, 83; see also Moten, *Delafield Commission*, 83; and Earl Hess, *Field Armies and Fortifications in the Civil War: The Eastern Campaigns, 1861–1864* (Chapel Hill: University of North Carolina Press, 2005), 7.

93. Mordecai, *Military Commission to Europe*, 147.

94. For paragraph, see Mordecai, *Military Commission to Europe*, 64; McClellan, *Report of the Secretary of War*, 14–23; Delafield, *Report on the Art of War*, 20, 43, 53–54; and Linn, *Echo of Battle*, 27–29.

95. See three works by James St. Clair Morton, *Memoir on Fortification* (Washington, DC: William A. Harris, 1858); *Memoir on the Dangers and Defences of New York City: Addressed to the Hon. John B. Floyd, Secretary of War* (Washington, DC: William A. Harris, 1858); and *Memoir on American Fortification: Submitted to the Hon. John B. Floyd, Secretary of War* (Washington, DC: William A. Harris, 1859); and see Edward Hunt, *Modern Warfare: Its Science and Art* (New Haven, CT: T. J. Stafford, 1860).

96. McClellan, *Report of the Secretary of War*, 16.

97. For paragraph, see Mordecai, *Military Commission to Europe*, 13, 61–64; McClellan, *Report of the Secretary of War*, 22; Delafield, *Report on the Art of War*, 11, 53–55, 214–15; and Moten, *Delafield Commission*, 149–51.

98. Delafield, *Report on the Art of War*, 11.

99. Quoted in Moten, *Delafield Commission*, 196.

100. Moten, 196.

101. For paragraph, see *PJD* 5:vi–ix; *PJD* 6:110; Davis, *Report of the Secretary of War*, December 4, 1854, p. 11–14; Cooper, *Jefferson Davis*, 68, 199–200, 232, 236, 262–72, 302; Skelton, *American Profession of Arms*, 221, 232–35, 291; and J. P. Clark, *Preparing for War: The Emergence of the Modern US Army, 1815–1917* (Cambridge, MA: Harvard University Press, 2017), 58.

102. *PJD* 5:vi.

103. Nosworthy, *Bloody Crucible*, 95.

104. For paragraph, see Davis, *Report of the Secretary of War*, December 4, 1854, p. 6–7; Jefferson Davis, *Report of the Secretary of War*, December 3, 1855 (Washington, DC: Beverly Tucker, 1855), 3–6, 15–16, 22; John Floyd, *Report of the Secretary of War*, December 5, 1857 (Washington, DC: Cornelius Wendell, 1857), 3, 6, 12; John Floyd, *Report of the Secretary of War*, December 6, 1858 (Washington, DC: William A. Harris, 1858), 3–5; John Floyd, *Report of the Secretary of War*, December 1, 1859 (Washington, DC: George Bowman, 1859), 3–4, 7–9, 16; *PJD* 5:vii, 74–75; *PJD* 6:92; Utley, *Frontiersmen in Blue*, 13–17, 111, 128, 140–42, 209–10; and Boyd Dastrup, *King of Battle: A Branch History of the US Army's Field Artillery* (Fort Monroe, VA: Office of the Command Historian, TRADOC, 1992), 86–87.

105. *PJD* 5:64; and Jefferson Davis, *Report of the Secretary of War*, December 1, 1853 (Washington, DC: Beverly Tucker, 1853), 7.

106. *Historical Statistics of the United States Millennial Edition Online*, Table Ea636–643 ("Federal Government Expenditures by Major Function, 1789–1970"), http://www.hsus.cambridge.org.

107. For paragraph, see Moten, *Delafield Commission*, 24, 55, 107, 194; Hope, *Scientific Way*, 136, 148–52, 177–81, 195, 209–10; Skelton, *American Military*, 167–72, 238–39; Hsieh, *West Pointers*, 11–12, 19, 36, 46, 74; Clark, *Preparing for War*, 31–36, 42–43, 55–60; Greiss, "Dennis Hart Mahan," 250, 259, 265, 285–86; and Watson, "Knowledge, Interest, and the Limits of Military Professionalism," 298–301.

108. Skelton, *American Profession of Arms*, 139.

109. Skelton, 255.

110. Moten, *Delafield Commission*, 55.

111. Quoted in Hope, *Scientific Way*, 181.

112. Hsieh, *West Pointers*, 74.

113. Skelton, *American Profession of Arms*, 175.

114. For paragraph, see Bonura, *Under the Shadow*, 103–15; Hope, *Scientific Way*, 200–203, 209–10; Clark, *Preparing for War*, 59–60; and Moten, *Delafield Commission*, 24, 30–31, 83–87.

115. Delafield, *Report on the Art of War*, 277.

116. Cooper, *Jefferson Davis*, 273.

117. Bonura, *Under the Shadow*, 131.

118. Cooper, *Jefferson Davis*, 274.

119. For paragraph, see Janice McKenney, *The Organizational History of Field Artillery, 1775–2003* (Washington, DC: Center of Military History, 2007), 48–49; Dastrup, *King of Battle*, 74–75, 86–87; Skelton, *American Profession of Arms*, 248, 252; Falk, "Soldier-Technologist," 488–91, 496; Davis, *Report of the Secretary of War*, December 1, 1856, p. 12; and Mordecai, *Military Commission to Europe*, 145.

120. For paragraph, see Davis, *Report of the Secretary of War*, December 1, 1856, p. 12; Mordecai, *Military Commission to Europe*, 145, 147; Dastrup, *King of Battle*, 82–83, 118; Nosworthy, *Bloody Crucible*, 82–83, 88–92; Falk, "Soldier-Technologist," 477, 490–91, 524; and McKenney, *Organizational History of Field Artillery*, 49–50.

121. For paragraph, see Falk, "Soldier-Technologist," 484–85, 508–9, 523, 525, 535; Davis, *Report of the Secretary of War*, December 1, 1856, p. 11–12; Floyd, *Report of the Secretary of War*,

December 1, 1859, p. 10; Moten, *Delafield Commission*, 181–82; and Angus Konstam, *American Civil War Fortifications (1): Coastal Brick and Stone Forts* (New York: Osprey, 2003), 40–41.

122. Floyd, *Report of the Secretary of War*, December 1, 1859, p. 10.

123. Cooper, *Jefferson Davis*, 273.

124. For paragraph, see Konstam, *Civil War Fortifications*, 11–17, 21, 33–34, 39; Skelton, *American Profession of Arms*, 125, 132, 243–44, 225, 229, 244–45, 293; Linn, *Echo of Battle*, 13–16, 19, 25–26; Hope, *Scientific Way*, 54–59, 129–32, 138–39, 184–93; and Watson, "Knowledge, Interest, and the Limits of Military Professionalism," 289–92, 302–6.

125. For paragraph, see Davis, Report of the Secretary of War, December 1, 1856, p. 11–12; Skelton, *American Profession of Arms*, 245–46; Halleck, *Elements of Military Art*, 429–32; Linn, *Echo of Battle*, 37–38; and Greiss, "Dennis Hart Mahan," 279.

126. Davis, *Report of the Secretary of War*, December 1, 1856, p. 15.

127. Floyd, *Report of the Secretary of War*, December 5, 1857, p. 17.

128. John Barnard, *Dangers and Defence of New York* (New York: D. Van Nostrand, 1859).

129. For paragraph, see Morton, *Memoir on American Fortification*, 50, 66, 77; Youngblood, *Development of Mine Warfare*, 34–35; Aurora Hunt, *Major General James Henry Carleton, 1814–1873: Western Frontier Dragoon* (Glendale, CA: Arthur H. Clark, 1958), 910–13; Linn, *Echo of Battle*, 27–29; and Greiss, "Dennis Hart Mahan," 268–76.

130. Greiss, "Dennis Hart Mahan," 279.

131. For paragraph, see Davis, *Report of the Secretary of War*, December 3, 1855, p. 10; Konstam, *Civil War Fortifications*, 49, 63; and Greiss, "Dennis Hart Mahan," 269–70, 279, 282.

132. Edwin Bearss, *Fort on Ship Island (Fort Massachusetts), 1857–1935* (Denver: Denver Service Center, National Park Service, 1984), 16–17.

133. Davis, *Report of the Secretary of War*, December 3, 1855, p. 10.

134. For paragraph, see Falk, "Soldier-Technologist," 421–22, 486, 504–7; Nosworthy, *Bloody Crucible*, 82–83, 104–8; Floyd, *Report of the Secretary of War*, December 1, 1859, p. 11; Dastrup, *King of Battle*, 86–87; and McKenney, *Organizational History of Field Artillery*, 50–51.

135. Hsieh, *West Pointers*, 32; Floyd, *Report of the Secretary of War*, December 3, 1859, p. 5; Hittle, *Military Staff*, 187; and Falk, "Soldier-Technologist," 478.

136. *PJD* 6:106; Davis, *Report of the Secretary of War*, December 3, 1855, p. 15–16, 22; Floyd, *Report of the Secretary of War*, December 5, 1857, p. 17; and Floyd, *Report of the Secretary of War*, December 6, 1858, p. 11.

137. Delafield, *Report on the Art of War*, 90; and Frame, "US Military Commission," 243–44.

138. Hunt, *Major General James Henry Carleton*, 170.

139. For paragraph, see Hsieh, *West Pointers*, 43, 51–52; Utley, *Frontiersmen in Blue*, 21, 115; McClellan, *Report of the Secretary of War*, 125, 277–88; *PJD* 6:396; Frame, "US Military Commission," 211–16, 258–63, 270–72; Hunt, *Major General James Henry Carleton*, 166–70; Herman Hattaway and Archer Jones, *How the North Won: A Military History of the Civil War* (Champaign: University of Illinois Press, 1991), 50–51; and Moten, *Delafield Commission*, 183–89.

140. *PJD* 6:55.

141. *PJD* 6:55.

142. Quoted in Frame, "US Military Commission," 270.

143. For paragraph, see Falk, "Soldier-Technologist," 482–88, 537, 542–43; Davis, *Report of the Secretary of War*, December 1, 1856, p. 11–12; Moten, *Delafield Commission*, 196; and Nosworthy, *Bloody Crucible*, 104.

144. For paragraph, see Davis, *Report of the Secretary of War*, December 4, 1854, p. 17–21; Davis, *Report of the Secretary of War*, December 3, 1855, p. 11; Davis, *Report of the Secretary of War*, December 1, 1856, p. 8; Mordecai, *Military Commission to Europe*, 172, 176; Delafield, *Report on the Art of War*, 5–6; Falk, "Soldier-Technologist," 412–13, 422–24, 476; Nosworthy, *Bloody Crucible*, 78–81, 84–85; Skelton, *American Profession of Arms*, 254–55; Hsieh, *West Pointers*, 38–39, 76–79; and Bonura, *Under the Shadow*, 93–96.

145. Moten, *Delafield Commission*, 82.

146. Nosworthy, *Bloody Crucible*, 82.

147. Davis, *Report of the Secretary of War*, December 1, 1856, p. 13–14.

148. Hsieh, *West Pointers*, 79.

149. For paragraph, see Hsieh, *West Pointers*, 8, 79–81, 85–86, 216; Nosworthy, *Bloody Crucible*, 87–93, 96–99, 647; Falk, "Soldier-Technologist," 477–78; Bonura, *Under the Shadow*, 94–96; Hagerman, *American Civil War*, 18–19; Frame, "US Military Commission," 242, 255–56; Moten, *Delafield Commission*, 199; Clark, *Preparing for War*, 61–62; and Luvaas, *Military Legacy*, 3, 5, 25, 65.

150. Greiss, "Dennis Hart Mahan," 305.

151. Greiss, 305.

152. Nosworthy, *Bloody Crucible*, 647.

153. For paragraph, see Donald Canney, *The Old Steam Navy*, vol. 1: *Frigates, Sloops, and Gunboats, 1815–1885* (Annapolis, MD: Naval Institute Press, 1990), 45; Hagan, *This People's Navy*, 139–40; and Schneller, *Quest for Glory*, 98, 112, 116, 121.

154. For paragraph, see *SDP letters*, 1:lxii–lxiii; Dahlgren, *Shells and Shell-Guns*, 275–77; Hagan, *This People's Navy*, 124, 138–41; and Schneller, *Quest for Glory*, 97, 112.

155. Lewis, *Yankee Admiral*, 90.

156. Schneller, *Quest for Glory*, 172.

157. *Historical Statistics of the United States*, Table Ea636-643.

158. Dahlgren, *Shells and Shell-Guns*, 222; emphasis original.

159. For paragraph, see Schneller, *Quest for Glory*, 49, 54, 100, 112; Hagan, *This People's Navy*, 2, 15, 20, 140; Lewis, *Yankee Admiral*, 89; and Greene and Massignani, *Ironclads at War*, 56.

160. Quoted in Hagan, *This People's Navy*, 140.

161. For paragraph, see Schneller, *Quest for Glory*, 59–60, 84, 87, 107–16, 124, 156–57, 160, 163–72, 175; Canney, *Old Steam Navy*, 1:45, 48, 50, 71–72, 83; and Greene and Massignani, *Ironclads at War*, 75, 90.

162. Schneller, *Quest for Glory*, 166.

163. For paragraph, see Dahlgren, *Shells and Shell-Guns*, 397, 403–4; Dobbin, *Report of the Secretary of Navy*, December 1, 1856, p. 411; Isaac Toucey, *Report of the Secretary of Navy*, December 3, 1857 (Washington, DC: Cornelius Wendell, 1857), 579; and Schneller, *Quest for Glory*, 147, 150, 158–59.

164. Dobbin, *Report of the Secretary of Navy*, December 3, 1855, p. 19.

165. For paragraph, see Canney, *Old Steam Navy*, 1:61, 71; and Hagan, *This People's Navy*, 140.

166. "USS Cumberland and CSS Florida."

167. Dobbin, *Report of the Secretary of Navy*, December 3, 1855, p. 13.

168. For paragraph, see Greene and Massignani, *Ironclads at War*, 31–35, 56; Hagan, *This People's Navy*, 140, 160; Lewis, *Yankee Admiral*, 88–89; and Donald Canney, *The Old Steam Navy*, vol. 2: *The Ironclads, 1842–1885* (Annapolis, MD: Naval Institute Press, 1993), 5–6.

169. Lewis, *Yankee Admiral*, 88.

170. Greene and Massignani, *Ironclads at War*, 109–12.

171. For paragraph, see Levie, *Mine Warfare*, 12,119; Schneller, *Quest for Glory*, 313; and Youngblood, *Development of Mine Warfare*, 34–35, 37, 72.

172. Linn, *Echo of Battle*, 29.

173. David Detzer, *Allegiance: Fort Sumter, Charleston and the Beginning of the Civil War* (New York: Harcourt, 2001), 198–200, 226; Craig Symonds, *Lincoln and His Admirals: Abraham Lincoln, the US Navy, and the Civil War* (New York: Oxford University Press, 2008), 8–12; and Greene and Massignani, *Ironclads at War*, 48–49.

174. Nosworthy, *Bloody Crucible*, 83; and Bonura, *Under the Shadow*, 114, respectively; for paragraph, see Hsieh, *West Pointers*, 8, 72, 144–45, 255; Moten, *Delafield Commission*, 177, 202–3; Mark Moore, *The Wilmington Campaign and the Battles for Fort Fisher* (New York: Da Capo, 1999), 136; and Falk, "Soldier-Technologist," 472–73.

175. Moten, *Delafield Commission*, 202.

176. Nosworthy, *Bloody Crucible*, 83.

177. Quoted in Moten, *Delafield Commission*, 203.

178. For paragraph, see Donald Stoker, *The Grand Design: Strategy and the US Civil War* (New York: Oxford University Press, 2010), 103; Konstam, *Civil War Fortifications*, 21, 42, 55; Ron Field, *American Civil War Fortifications (3): The Mississippi and River Forts* (New York: Osprey, 2007), 4–5, 13–17, 27–28; *SDP letters*, 2:19, 69, 394; Canney, *Old Steam Navy*, 2:22–23; Moore, *Wilmington Campaign*, 137–38, 145, 151; Delafield, *Report on the Art of War*, 20, 43; McClellan, *Report of the Secretary of War*, 16, 19, 22–23; and John Keegan, *The American Civil War: A Military History* (New York: Alfred A. Knopf, 2009), 278–79.

179. Cooper, *Jefferson Davis*, 416.

180. Greene and Massignani, *Ironclads at War*, 42, 46–47, 80, 242–43; Canney, *Old Steam Navy*, 2:6–7, 57–58; Schneller, *Quest for Glory*, 190, 194, 200–203; and Hagan, *This People's Navy*, 165–70.

181. For rest of paragraph, see Youngblood, *Development of Mine Warfare*, 37–61, 72, 209n36; Schneller, *Quest for Glory*, 235, 314; *SDP letters*, 3:3–5, 12; and Hagan, *This People's Navy*, 170, 173.

182. Schneller, *Quest for Glory*, 263.

183. For paragraph, see Canney, *Old Steam Navy*, 1:91, 137–38; Canney, *Old Steam Navy*, 2:47, 55; *SDP letters*, 1:137–38, 235; *SDP letters*, 2:33, 446; and Stoker, *Grand Design*, 11–16, 134–37.

184. Andrew Lambert quoted in Moore, *Wilmington Campaign*, 136.

185. For paragraph, see Konstam, *Civil War Fortifications*, 22, 34, 40, 45–48, 53; Hagan, *This People's Navy*, 172–73; and Linn, *Echo of Battle*, 29.

186. Konstam, *Civil War Fortifications*, 48.

187. For paragraph, see Schneller, *Quest for Glory*, 155, 218–19, 234–42, 252, 263–64, 268–73, 290, 313; Hagan, *This People's Navy*, 170–73; *SDP letters*, 2:443–45, 547; and Canney, *Old Steam Navy*, 2:73, 79, 93.

188. Moore, *Wilmington Campaign*, 150; emphasis in original.

189. Hagan, *This People's Navy*, 172.

190. Hagan, 172.

191. For paragraph, see Keegan, *American Civil War*, 120–22; Hattaway and Jones, *How the North Won*, 51–52, 145, 265, 333–34; and Stoker, *Grand Design*, 64, 70–72, 88–89, 143.

192. Sears, *McClellan*, 45.

193. Lambert quoted in Moore, *Wilmington Campaign*, 136.

194. Quoted in Sears, *McClellan*, 180; for paragraph, see Sears, *McClellan*, 46–49; McClellan, *Report of the Secretary of War*, 5–24; Stoker, *Grand Design*, 168; and Hattaway and Jones, *How the North Won*, 145.

195. Falk, "Soldier-Technologist," 472.

196. Sears, *McClellan*, 48–49.

197. For paragraph, see Hattaway and Jones, *How the North Won*, 265, 333–34; Stoker, *Grand Design*, 141, 148, 150, 159, 410; and Bevin Alexander, *How the South Could Have Won the Civil War: The Fatal Errors That Led to Confederate Defeat* (New York: Crown, 2007), 67, 70, 87, 212–13.

198. *SDP letters*, 2:177.

199. For paragraph, see Hattaway and Jones, *How the North Won*, 188, 192, 200–201, 588, 593; Stoker, *Grand Design*, 148, 151–57, 161; and Alexander, *How the South*, 53–54.

200. June 5, 1862, letter from Lee to Davis in Cliff Dowdey and Louis Manarin, eds., *Wartime Papers of R. E. Lee* (New York: Bramhall House, 1961), 183–84.

201. Hattaway and Jones, *How the North Won*, 188.

202. Linn, *Echo of Battle*, 29.

203. O'Connor, "Eye of the Beholder," 92.

204. O'Connor, 93.

205. Bonura, *Under the Shadow*, 116.

206. For paragraph, see Moten, *Delafield Commission*, 75, 79, 105–67; Skelton, *American Profession of Arms*, 255; Linn, *Echo of Battle*, 20–21; and Clark, *Preparing for War*, 34–36.

207. Moten, *Delafield Commission*, 107; see also Clark, *Preparing for War*, 34–36.

208. Moten, *Delafield Commission*, 173–74.

209. Moten, 173.

210. *SDP letters*, 1:235.

211. Quoted in Luvaas, *Military Legacy*, 39.

212. Bonura, *Under the Shadow*, 114.

CHAPTER 2

THE RUSSO-JAPANESE WAR
Enthusiastic but Encumbered Exploration

He is no patriot who despises lessons that may be drawn from
the mistakes of other nations, and foolishly believes that in
its policies our country may follow courses that have
involved other great nations in ruin and disaster.
—*Capt. William Judson, Russo-Japanese War observer*

President Theodore Roosevelt reflected the views of many American civilian and
military leaders in writing that "I am greatly interested in the Russian and Japanese
War" two days after the Imperial Japanese Navy's surprise attack on Port Arthur
(February 8, 1904).[1] With the conflict's potential strategic significance, given the recent American acquisition of the Philippines as well as its expected military lessons,
correspondent Charles à Court Repington commented that the Americans, along
with the English, "were more deeply interested in this great quarrel than in any
other campaign that had been fought by foreign nations within the memory of living
man."[2] He was among fifty-plus reporters who reached Tokyo by March to satisfy
such curiosity.[3] US soldiers and sailors, however, desired more expert examination of
a conflict they expected to reveal valuable insights. With the last major ground combat more than twenty-five years earlier, technological developments had generated
sharp disagreements over proper organization, equipment, and doctrine. It had been
almost forty years since the last large-scale naval combat, and intense debates existed
over warship designs and combat tactics.

The growing complexity of battle since the Crimean War had prompted increasing efforts to obtain information about foreign militaries and third-party conflicts.
The perceived value gleaned from witnessing the Russo-Turkish War (1877–78) and
the War of the Pacific (1879–1884) contributed to the establishment of the Military
Information Division and the Office of Naval Intelligence as well as full-time attachés.[4] By 1904 the number of attachés had risen above twenty, including army and
navy postings in St. Petersburg and Tokyo. The two services, however, believed that
coverage of the first great-power fight in decades required dedicated observers. As
a result, twenty-three Americans would be sent for varying parts of the conflict,

trailing only the British among the more than a dozen nations that dispatched military personnel.

HOW DID THE AMERICANS ATTEMPT TO IDENTIFY LESSONS?

A flood of volunteers, including a young second lieutenant, Douglas MacArthur, contacted the War Department, but the General Staff's Second Division, which oversaw the effort, had already identified candidates and quickly dispatched eight observers.[5] Unlike the Delafield Commission's problematic attempt to investigate both sides, the service, in accord with now standard practice, attached officers to each force. The highly intelligent captain Peyton March possessed ideal attributes—successful command of a field artillery battery during the Spanish-American War, work with Maj. Gen. Arthur MacArthur in the Philippines, and service on the General Staff since its 1903 formation. March, along with his boss, Col. Enoch Crowder, went to the Japanese side, where both collected staff information while Crowder additionally addressed the cavalry and March the field artillery. Joining them were Maj. Joseph Kuhn (engineering) and Capt. John Morrison (infantry). Additionally, the president arranged a six-month leave and semiofficial observer status with the Japanese for Lt. Granville Fortescue, his uncle's illegitimate son and a former Rough Rider. On the Russian side, Lt. Col. Walter Schuyler, an unenthusiastic cavalry officer, was the senior American. Capt. Carl Reichmann, a German immigrant who had served as an observer during the Boer War, covered the infantry while Capt. William Judson followed engineering matters. Finally, Maj. Montgomery Meigs Macomb examined artillery and staff operations. Beside recent Ordnance Board service, Macomb valuably had experience with the machine gun, a weapon of considerable interest at the time.

Although instructed to note any seemingly valuable finding, the General Staff provided each observer with specific tasking, and improved communication facilitated a more iterative process than during the Crimean War.[6] In August 1904 March, who was with the Japanese First Army, watched from a great vantage point the war's first major battle (Liaoyang), while Morrison and Kuhn, present with the Second Army, struggled to eyeball events as its commander maintained a tighter leash on foreigners. A mid-September Imperial Edict, probably prompted by Japan's battlefield success, relaxed the restrictions on observers. Still, the Americans suffered from a lack of Japanese language proficiency and host interference. On the other side, although generally more accommodating to foreigners, the Russians regarded the United States as a potential Japanese ally and closely monitored the Americans. Beyond this hindrance, the observers suffered from high operating expenses, a lack of accurate maps, and, above all, an inability to speak Russian. A discouraged Schuyler urged the recall of two Americans and the assignment of a general, like the European delegations, to obtain better treatment. US observers augmented their direct efforts through contacts with representatives from other militaries. The mutual benefit from such exchanges resulted in essence an international clearinghouse in which, as Schuyler noted, "almost everything which came under the observation of one was soon known by all."[7] Still, no foreigner possessed the detailed data needed for some taskings, which prompted rarely successful solicitations of Russian and Japanese authorities.

The army leadership, under pressure from the White House, decided to modify the group's composition in October 1904.[8] That month, in a speech after returning from Japan, Dr. Louis Seaman extolled Japan's military medical and sanitation practices and complained that all American observers were from the "killing departments."[9] Given army struggles to keep soldiers healthy during the Spanish-American War, this critique had weight, prompting Roosevelt to "ask" if medical officers could be dispatched. Expectation of host opposition to an increase in the number of Americans meant they would have to be substitutes. Thus, the secretary of war on October 17 recalled Morrison and Kuhn from the Japanese side and Reichmann and Schuyler from the Russian side, although March, due to his wife's death, left instead of Kuhn. The army then detailed Col. Valery Havard, chief surgeon for the Department of the East, and Capt. Charles Lynch to study Russian and Japanese practice, respectively. In mid-December 1904 the eagerly awaited first returnees (March and Morrison) arrived in Washington and quickly met with senior officials including President Roosevelt, Secretary of War William Howard Taft, and Chief of Staff Lt. Gen. Adna Chaffee. Arriving a month later from Russia, Reichmann and Schuyler received similar audiences. Roosevelt, demonstrating his level of interest, lunched with March on March's third day back and read Morrison's final report the day he received it.

The war continued with two notable actions—the siege of Port Arthur (August–December 1904) and the battle at Mukden (February 1905).[10] No American army officer was inside the stubbornly defended key Russian port or initially with the besieging Japanese force, although the on-leave Fortescue was briefly present. Kuhn and Morrison spent a few days with the Japanese Third Army in early November, and the Japanese finally agreed in late December to allow the former's attachment. He witnessed the collapse of the worn-down defenders and subsequently investigated the captured Russian works until news of an approaching major fight prompted him to scurry north. With the Russian and Japanese armies converging at Mukden, every observer wanted to be present for the largest battle in modern history (over six hundred thousand combatants). Judson, Macomb, and Havard were with the Russians, while Kuhn, Crowder, and Lynch were with the Japanese. Major General MacArthur and new military attaché, Capt. John J. Pershing, reached Japanese forces only after the battle. Mukden turned into something of a debacle for the Americans when the

Map 2.1 The Russo-Japanese Theater of War

Japanese seized an ailing Judson and the caregiving Havard as they dallied during the Russian retreat.

This battle would be the war's last significant ground combat, but that was not evident at the time, so the army continued to dispatch observers.[11] The high-ranking MacArthur's receipt of better treatment from the Japanese prompted assignment of Brig. Gen. Thomas Barry to the Russian side. The army replaced the captured Havard with another surgeon, Col. John Van Rensselaer Hoff. In June the US cohort on the Japanese side peaked at six with the addition of Lt. Col. Edward McClernand, an experienced cavalry officer and senior staff aide. The lull in fighting afforded observers the opportunity to conduct inspections, interview veterans, and attend lectures by host staff officers, although such sessions revealed limited data. In response to complaints, Maj. Gen. Shigeta Fukii, First Army chief of staff, typified Japanese sentiment by declaring "we are paying for this information with our blood."[12]

Attachés continued to collect data after the September 1905 peace agreement, while the War Department moved expeditiously to make information available.[13] Even though some witnesses did not produce final reports because of high rank, other duties, or illness, the army published ten observer accounts. A few of the witnesses also penned articles for military journals, while the General Staff provided Macomb's report on machine guns in the Russian army to the *Journal of the US Infantry Association*. The General Staff produced an official history ("The Epitome of the Russo-Japanese War") and printed translations of well-regarded foreign accounts.[14] Moreover, the British published considerable material, including the widely read *A Staff Officer's Scrap Book during the Russo-Japanese War* by Sir Ian Hamilton, the senior British observer. Almost one hundred articles on various aspects of the Russo-Japanese War appeared in US military journals in the first five years after the conflict.

The US Navy's interest in the Russo-Japanese War probably even exceeded the army's interest, but information-gathering at sea represented a greater challenge.[15] Chief of the Office of Naval Intelligence (ONI), Capt. Seaton Schroeder, prioritized collection on the Far East and prepared for study of the anticipated conflict. The president, however, rejected the plan to forward deploy warships to monitor events, given his fear of neutrality violations. The fleet was kept south of Shanghai, although initially small warships protected threatened American concerns, especially in Korea. Instead the Americans, like the British and Germans, attempted to place officers on board combatant warships. The department dispatched Lt. Irving Gillis in late January 1904 to be assistant naval attaché in Tokyo and, if war occurred, a shipboard observer. It sent Lt. Lloyd Chandler, commanding a destroyer flotilla in the Philippines, north to witness events, possibly from Korea. Lt. Cdr. Newton McCully, proficient in Russian, had been designated for service on a Russian vessel and reached Manchuria in late April. Like the army, the navy would later assign two surgeons (William Braisted and Raymond Spear) to examine medical care.

Unfortunately, the belligerents rejected American requests for warship observer status.[16] The US Navy received no reciprocity for having allowed Lt. Akiyama Saneyuki, then a naval attaché and future planner for the Battle of Tsushima, to observe Spanish-American War operations with Rear Adm. William Sampson's staff off Cuba. The Japanese only permitted on board British officers, who would not share findings lest they upset their hosts and lose the treasured access. In response to American protests, officials periodically briefed navy attaché Lt. Cdr. Charles Marsh and Gillis, albeit withholding almost all meaningful details. McCully overcame Russian resistance and entered Port Arthur in early May 1904, but naval officials rejected his sailing with the fleet. Instead he attempted, with limited results, to obtain information from loose-lipped sailors and foreign naval attachés. After the Battle of the Yellow Sea (August 1904), McCully obtained permission for a cursory visit to the heavily damaged *Peresviet* and *Poltava* battleships and spoke with participants in what would be the war's second-largest sea action. Yet, with the Japanese siege of Port Arthur commencing, and after an unproductive visit to Vladivostok, he began the long trip home.

With warships held back and observers marooned on land, the Navy Department struggled to identify lessons about the fighting.[17] ONI tracked newspaper stories and scrutinized observer and attaché reporting. The navy employed unconventional methods such as using *Colliers'* correspondent James Archibald as an informant and having a marine pose as an English draftsman to gain access to the battle-damaged cruiser *Askold* undergoing repairs in Shanghai. When Asiatic Fleet commander Rear Adm. Charles Train interred three Russian cruisers escaping the climactic Battle of Tsushima, the Navy Department cabled that the president wanted officers interviewed for data on "the recent battle and effects of Japanese gun fire, torpedo boats and tactics and whether they believe mines and subs were used," asking, "What do they attribute the Japanese victory to?"[18] Gillis and McCully met with senior officials upon their return, but neither could provide the desired technical details, although the latter relayed some useful insights from his conversations with combat participants.

Naval leaders hoped more information would become available after the war's conclusion.[19] Cdr. Nathan Sargent, captain of the Asiatic Fleet's protected cruiser *Baltimore*, was a highly regarded former aide to Adm. George Dewey who wrote his ex-boss about the war's lessons. Dewey at that time headed the influential General Board, which had become "an effective mechanism for reflecting upon current experience and learning from it."[20] Naval War College faculty and students repeatedly reenacted Russo-Japanese naval battles to identify key findings and develop more knowledgeable sailors. The US Naval Institute's professional journal, *Proceedings*, functioned as a platform for prominent sailors to probe for lessons, especially from the Battle of Tsushima. ONI Chief Schroeder examined the struggle in the March 1906 issue, while the influential Naval War College professor Alfred Thayer Mahan provided his assessment of Tsushima three months later.[21] That same issue Lt. R. D. White conveyed a detailed description of the battle based on information from a Russian naval constructor present.[22] In the December issue, Lt. Cdr. William Sims, a talented and increasingly important officer, effectively rebutted Mahan's interpretation of the combat.[23] Yet, the following year, an anonymous British author ("Black Joke") replied with an essay challenging Sims's account. Problematically, neither Sims nor Mahan had actual figures on Japanese and Russian firing at Tsushima, leaving them to make critical assumptions about gunnery. Writing almost five years after the battle, Lt. Lyman Cotten lamented that "in attempting to make a study of this subject, one is immediately impressed with the paucity of reliable data."[24]

WHAT LESSONS DID THE ARMY IDENTIFY?

World War I erupted in the summer of 1914 with violence of unprecedented scale, scope, and lethality. Although military powers had been arduously preparing to fight for years, they were surprised by the rapid emergence of a defense-dominated battle-field. Attacking troops faced daunting challenges, including strong field fortifications and deadly machine-gun fire. In search of a way to break the stalemate, both sides amassed huge artillery forces. At sea, the naval powers, with their large battleship armadas, experienced an unexpected focus on the submarine and its threat to merchant shipping. Except for a single indecisive engagement at Jutland, the expensive surface fleets played no active role.

Soldiers in World War I, unlike sailors, should not have been surprised as the Russo-Japanese War featured many elements that came to define the later conflict, albeit in less developed form. There were highly lethal battles between forces of unprecedented size. Competing armies depended heavily on field artillery and machine guns for fire support. The superiority of and victory by the attacking Japanese obscured the emerging defense-dominant battlefield, but evidence was available for observant analysts. By contrast, the naval struggle with two major fleet engagements contrasted sharply to World War I as Russia and Japan did not employ submarines. Still, the earlier conflict yielded a number of relevant lessons in areas such as mine danger, utility of shipboard telegraph, and destroyer requirements. Even lessons regarding battleship characteristics had relevance as, without application, the British could have lost at Jutland with potentially critical consequences.

The Russo-Japanese War offered much of value, and the American observers relayed voluminous data, but a number of factors complicate identifying lessons. In contrast to the Delafield Commission, which traveled together, observers witnessed different types of actions at different times. For example, the combatants significantly increased usage of machine guns as the war progressed. Even when present at the same battle, descriptions by Japanese- and Russian-attached officers could be markedly different. This variance in part resulted from observers' divergent preexisting beliefs on how best to prepare for and conduct warfare.[25] Given distinct perspectives and experiences, as John Greenwood finds, the "conclusions they drew and the recommendations they made in the *Reports* were just as often contradictory as confirmatory."[26] Of course, the views of some soldiers by virtue of rank and position (Barry, MacArthur) or reputation and initiative (Macomb, March, Morrison, and Pershing) carried greater influence.

The observers did agree that the Russo-Japanese War signaled no fundamental departure in the nature of combat. Given the magnitude and duration of great powers fighting with modern arms, Kuhn thought it reasonable to expect "some startling and original methods." Yet he stressed "so far as I am able to judge, the recognized rules and principles for conducting warfare underwent no serious modification in their application."[27] Similarly, Judson observed "on the whole, there was little development of novelties in the recent war."[28] Morrison relayed that the victorious

Japanese "have shown us little that is not in the books, little that can be truly called original."[29] Although it had not undergone revolutionary development necessitating entirely new approaches, combat had evolved in notable and important ways. Some of these the Americans grasped; others they did not.

Enlightening Lessons: Broad Themes

Unprecedented scale. Enlightening findings—those foreshadowing future conflicts—consisted of broad themes and specific insights. With regard to the former, no point received more emphasis than that modern war required enormous resources.[30] The first large battle (Liaoyang) in August 1904 involved nearly three hundred thousand soldiers, six months later double that number fought at Mukden. Beyond sheer number of troops, the latter's eighty-mile front illustrated the modern battlefield's vast size. Judson explained the implications by noting that the "length of the line tends to prevent the spread of local disaster."[31] As a result, the duration of engagements kept increasing—Liaoyang (five days) to Shaho (eight days) to Mukden (almost twenty days)—which exhausted personnel and consumed huge amounts of materiel. Kuhn projected even greater demands in future battles, with large field guns requiring up to five or six tons of ammunition per piece. He appreciated that "these figures seem appalling, but they will have to be reckoned with if an adequate ammunition supply is to be maintained."[32]

Thus, the Americans highlighted the importance of transportation capability.[33] Reichmann observed that in this "competition between a long line of communication by railroad and a short line by steamer," Japan possessed an inherent advantage.[34] He pointed out that, with control of the seas, its ground commander "could make a landing and establish bases and starting points for campaigns wherever he pleased."[35] Kuhn added that Japanese "possession of a heavily subsidized merchant marine made a large fleet of transports immediately available upon the outbreak of the war."[36] Several Americans endorsed Japan's use of soldiers dedicated to transportation tasks, enabling frontline troops to focus on combat. On land, in areas like Manchuria with poor roads, Kuhn stressed that "the existing railway lines play a most important part, so important, in fact, that they may be said to have dominated to a large extent the strategy of the war" (battles primarily fell along the Mukden–Port Arthur line).[37] Critically, when conducting envelopments, armies could not be cut off from "supply depots for longer than seven to ten days."[38]

Prewar preparation critical. Given that a resource-intensive conflict should have favored the larger, wealthier Russian empire, the Americans explained Japan's surprising victory in large part by its superior prewar preparation.[39] Reichmann noted that

65

"an inquiry into the Russian forces and their organization leaves no doubt as to the absolute unpreparedness of Russia for a war in the Far East."[40] Observers highlighted three particularly harmful mistakes. First, St. Petersburg invested heavily in building the commercial port of Dalny prior to the completion of Port Arthur's fortifications. When war came, the Russians scrambled to improve defenses at the latter and lacked the ability to safeguard the former. Judson concluded that this experience "suggests the advisability of confining our plants to be developed across the sea for commercial and naval purposes to the same harbors."[41] Plus, Port Arthur's works focused on protecting against naval attack, but the key Russian position fell from land-side assault. This result, as Brian McAllister Linn points out, "showed some American coast artillerymen that 'without the co-operation of mobile forces our seacoast defenses cannot endure.'"[42] As will be discussed, this insight had significant repercussions for US defense of the Philippines.

Second, the Americans stressed that Russian prewar training badly lagged the German-influenced Japanese forces.[43] Morrison, Reichmann, and Pershing argued that the war demonstrated that peacetime tactical training was of the "utmost importance" for commanders as well as troops. Observers pointed out that such training in combination with the promotion of capable, energetic officers enabled the Imperial Japanese Army to employ a highly praised decentralized approach. McClernand bluntly averred that "in this matter their [the Japanese] system and ours furnish the two extreme examples. . . . That the former method is the correct one can not, it is thought, be seriously questioned."[44] The Americans noted that the peacetime existence of larger Japanese units eased the transition to war.

Finally, the Russians struggled to introduce reserves at a commensurate rate to the Japanese, who showed the value of a well-developed mobilization and replacement system.[45] McClernand differentiated the Japanese "clocklike precision and smoothness" from the chaotic US experience in the Spanish-American War.[46] The Americans also praised the Japanese for anticipating reserve needs, forwarding troops ahead of combat rather than waiting for losses to be reported. Reichmann and Judson fretted that the US traditional reliance on untrained volunteers would no longer suffice. Still, as Kuhn reported, even Japan's much lauded system had its limits in the causality-intensive crucible of twentieth-century conflict, with soldier skills, especially junior officers, declining after heavy losses.

Increased fire support essential. The question of whether the combat signaled warfare's shift toward defense dominance belongs in the later discussion of disputed findings, but the Americans almost universally emphasized that both attackers and defenders sought greater fire support.[47] No witness was more impressed by these efforts than Reichmann, a veteran infantryman, who declared, "If I were not too old to learn a new trade, I would like to go into the artillery business myself."[48] Although

Morrison—an inveterate infantryman present early in the war when Russian fire was least effective—disagreed, most observers believed the combat demonstrated that the US Army needed to increase the number of guns per unit. Expecting study of the Manchurian fighting to prompt militaries to bolster their gunnery capability, Reichmann declared that "a nation that enters to-day upon war with palpable inferiority in artillery incurs the gravest risks."[49] In contrast to conventional wisdom, McClernand pointed out the fighting revealed that "the guns of the assailants will frequently perform a more important part than those of the defense" by hampering and demoralizing entrenched forces.[50]

The Americans posited three explanations for the superiority of Japanese artillery. First, better training and experience enabled surpassing selection of gun positions, identification of targets, and recognition of proper fuses/ranges. Second, the Japanese artillery's regimental organization facilitated getting more guns into battle. McClernand averred that "the need for regimental organization for the field artillery is believed to be beyond question."[51] Finally, while Russian gunners possessed a better field piece (the Model 1900, quick-firing three-inch gun), they lacked the high-explosive shells used extensively by the Japanese. Kuhn argued that this edge "turned out to have been a most important one and went far toward maintaining a balance in the artillery equipment of the belligerents."[52]

Superiority of indirect fire. US witnesses highlighted the emergence of indirect fire (shooting at targets not visually identifiable) as field artillery's main form of battle support.[53] The Japanese employed this approach from the start, and Russians eventually adopted it. Reichmann emphasized that "the increasing use of indirect fire as the war progressed is worthy of careful study; the advantages of its effective use are obvious."[54] First, it facilitated massing fire. Initially the Russians relied on a high rate of fire, but as Capt. Tiemann Horn, USA, wrote in a postwar review, "The idea of *rapidity* taking the place of *concentration* was exploded."[55] Second, indirect fire enabled gun batteries to establish better protection on the increasingly dangerous battlefield. As Kuhn noted, the Japanese took advantage of increased distance afforded by indirect fire to maximize concealment. Even with the development of improved locating equipment (e.g., range finders) and techniques (e.g., crater analysis), indirect fire enhanced survivability as reduced gun movement permitted constructing stronger shelters. The observers described how the armies surmounted long-standing targeting and communication challenges with spotting teams attached to infantry units, "squared maps" (grids) and, above all, telephones connecting artillery commanders with widely dispersed gun positions.

Surprising frequency and utility of night attacks. With increased fire support adding to the modern battlefield's lethality, the Americans reported the combatants, especially the Japanese, sought to reduce vulnerability by employing night attacks.[56] Armies had previously been reluctant to engage in large-scale night action. March regarded the repeated use of such attacks as "the most important development of the war."[57] The inherent challenge of fighting in this environment caused casualties for both the Japanese and Russians, but the observers noted they learned how to operate in it. McClernand found that success required "painstaking reconnaissances," detailed instructions on the line of direction and objectives, and awaiting moonlit or starlit nights.[58] The bottom line, as Kuhn expressed, was "night attacks and maneuvers will receive a wide application in future wars, and troops should be carefully trained for this work in time of peace."[59]

Extensive construction of field fortifications. Whether attacking or defending, fighting day or night, the extensive use of field fortifications generated observer attention.[60] Kuhn noted that "the whole country was literally honeycombed with Russian trenches" as multiple defense lines protected important positions.[61] He added that Japanese trenches, even hasty arrangements, proved formidable in safeguarding advanced forces against counterattacks. Reichmann pointed out that "in order to be able to withstand this artillery fire and enable his infantry to repulse the attacker's infantry, the general on the defensive must provide effective shelter for his men."[62] Morrison averred that "once in the presence of an enemy the intrenching tool seemed next in importance to the rifle and ammunition."[63] The American engineers (Kuhn and Judson) discovered no "startling developments in the matter of field fortifications," but they noted the value of head cover over trenches and effective Japanese inclusion of a "small berm, about 10 inches below the crest, designed as an elbow rest and to give greater steadiness to the rifle."[64]

Increased casualty treatment requirements. Medical observers stressed that Manchuria illustrated the need to better prepare for the inevitable high number of casualties in modern war.[65] Havard argued that "we must have a large reserve corps of able physicians and surgeons willing, when the emergency comes, to be mustered into service."[66] Lynch concluded that Japan's unmatched wartime medical performance resulted from careful integration of medical and operational planning, proper resourcing, and conduct of frequent medical maneuvers. In contrast, Havard sharply criticized the lack of cooperation between Russian line officers and army doctors. The Americans observed that modern war complicated casualty identification, treatment, and evacuation with the spread of units, lengthier battles, and increased night engagements. Given the US Army's long-standing difficulty identifying wounded and dead soldiers, Lynch endorsed the circular brass tags containing name, rank, and unit worn around the necks of Japanese soldiers.[67]

Enlightening Lessons: Specific Weapons/Systems

These broad findings led to identification of a number of lessons relating to weapons or supporting materiel, although none of these findings involved a discovery of the magnitude of French 12-pound cannon, discussed in the previous chapter.

Surprising bayonet utility. For most American witnesses, the prevalence of night attacks unexpectedly restored the utility of the bayonet.[68] March declared that "one of the most striking lessons" was "that the bayonet is not an obsolete weapon by any means in modern warfare in spite of the increased effectiveness of the modern rapid-fire field gun and magazine rifle."[69] McClernand found "in night attacks the bayonet is essential" given the heightened risk of friendly fire.[70] The Japanese emphasized that using bayonets in such circumstances required thorough training. Enthusiasm for the bayonet was not universal, as evidenced by Pershing downplaying its value. Still, for most US officers, the bayonet, especially the shorter Japanese variant, had demonstrated its relevance in modern war.

Machine-gun emergence. Much less surprising, the machine gun became an increasingly significant provider of fire support.[71] At the siege of Port Arthur in late 1904, Kuhn found Russian machine-gun fire to be "murderously effective."[72] Macomb reported the two sides during the Battle of Mukden employed almost three hundred machine guns. Observers stressed not only their frequent use but also the importance attached to them by Russian and Japanese officers. Kuhn relayed the Japanese equipped cavalry brigades with six machine guns and infantry regiments with three, but they were considering further increases. Reflecting a predominant view, he wrote that "it seems certain that this weapon will play an important part in the future, and the equipment and tactics of machine guns should receive serious and prompt consideration for our army."[73] Still, Macomb, whose opinion carried particular weight on the subject, provided a measured assessment—it "played a useful but not a great part in the war."[74] By this statement he meant this weapon had not revolutionized warfare as some had anticipated or were claiming based on the Russo-Japanese experience.

Beyond its overall increased importance, machine-gun use in Manchuria offered some tactical cues.[75] While Pershing and Kuhn recorded its expected effectiveness defending against troops crossing open terrain, Macomb pointed out that the fighting revealed "it is equally valuable on the offensive or defensive to an active moving force which knows how to use it."[76] McClernand added that "their rapid fire frequently silenced the fire of the Russian infantry and caused the latter to crouch down in their trenches."[77] Macomb and McClernand relayed that machine gunners strenuously argued for using them in pairs, given the benefits of crossfire and the weapon's mechanical fragility. Macomb noted that machine guns should be kept in reserve as long as possible to minimize vulnerability. Finally, on the question of where to put machine guns organizationally (a subject of considerable debate in the US Army), the Americans indicated, as McClernand wrote, that "the propriety of attaching them to the infantry was never heard questioned."[78]

Although providing salient lessons regarding general machine-gun use, observers could not obtain the detailed data about operational requirements sought by the War Department. Given logistical concerns about this weapon, they regrettably supplied only anecdotal accounts on ammunition expenditure rates (e.g., the Japanese carried 4,200 rounds per gun at one point, or an eight-gun battery expended 6,000 rounds in ninety seconds in an engagement). Such information provided a sense of scale, but it did not allow serious consideration of what to expect in future battle or facilitate whether the benefit was worth the investment. David Armstrong argues that the inability to acquire better information exemplifies how the "failure to ask the right questions robbed the attaché reports of much of their usefulness in the area of machine guns."[79] Yet such criticism seems unfair as they could have only obtained this data from their hosts, who were not willing to provide such assistance.

Necessity for telephonic connectivity. The prior reference to the telephone's utility for artillery commanders represented only one way in which this device enhanced operations. Above all, observers stressed that the widespread use of the telephone, as well as the telegraph, enabled effective communication among increasingly dispersed units.[80] They noted that the Japanese maintained such links in the field between division and brigades and often down to battalion headquarters. Behind the front lines, telephones ensured rapid exchanges with various depot and administrative locations. The clear value of such communications prompted increased Russian use by late 1904. Judson described how "the Russians had four or five telephones to the mile, along the fortified belt, in addition to many behind it, and in addition to telephones for fire direction of artillery."[81] A prewar concern about telephone lines' vulnerability to sabotage proved unmerited, although Kuhn cautioned against the war being viewed as dispositive given "the passive attitude of the Chinese and the lack of enterprise of the Russian cavalry."[82]

Missed Lessons

Mounting cavalry difficulties. The cavalry seemingly faced an ominous future, given the war's negligible role for horse soldiers, but the Americans were mostly dismissive about the generalizability of this experience.[83] Observers usually ignored the limited cavalry actions that occurred, but some of these witnesses indicated that traditional roles, especially shock attack and exploitation of a beaten force, were becoming less feasible. These tasks had long been the focus on European, not American, cavalry, but Reichmann warned that even reconnaissance missions "are becoming more and more difficult, owing to the long range of firearms."[84] The most constructive cavalry operations occurred with the Japanese use of dismounted infantry, another long-standing role for US horsemen, albeit one conducted with trepidation if subordinated to the infantry. Horrifyingly to US cavalry officers, Judson wrote in his final report that, based on Manchuria and a fixed budget, it seemed worthy of inquiry whether "money could not be saved on our cavalry to increase the strength of our field artillery and the mobility of at least a portion of our infantry."[85] Fortunately for cavalry officers, some of the Americans in Manchuria provided reasons to question generalizing about the cavalry's diminished utility. Schuyler and Kuhn noted that the much-hyped Russian cavalry "simply accomplished nothing" due to ineptitude.[86] Reichmann contended that "the character of the country greatly detracted from the efficiency of the cavalry service."[87] Ultimately, observer and cavalry officer McClernand conveyed branch member sentiment that "it is believed we have nothing to learn from the Russo-Japanese war about the proper use of that arm."[88]

Disputed Lessons

Tactical defense stronger, but offensive still possible? The preceding list of findings tends to be overlooked as a result of criticism of Americans for not recognizing the extent of the battlefield shift toward the defensive or appreciating the demanding requirements for success in such a context.[89] Observers could not agree on the meaning of what they witnessed. Advocates of different approaches and representatives for particular army components seized on evidence to support their divergent preferences. Before addressing these differences, general agreement existed on two fundamental points—growing tactical strength of the defense and continuing viability of the offensive at the operational and strategic levels as demonstrated by the attacking Japanese winning every major battle. Observers pointed out that the extremely high cost of those victories compromised the Japanese army's ability to exploit success. The Japanese loss of ninety thousand soldiers in capturing Port Arthur despite the haphazard preparation and limited manning of Russian works displayed the severe consequences for an attacking force when maneuver was not possible. Yet the witnesses added that flanking proved challenging, as such maneuvers now required traveling far greater distances, resulting in exhausted forces less able to pursue the retreating enemy. The increased importance and difficulty of flanking operations prompted Reichmann to declare, "I was strongly impressed with the importance of mobility" and Judson to conclude, "With regard to infantry, the lesson, as I see it, is beyond all other things, to make it more mobile."[90]

Proper combined-arms approach? Even though commentators stressed that the increased lethality of the modern battlefield required greater combined-arms proficiency, they disagreed on what that meant in practice.[91] A postwar *Army-Navy Journal* editorial opined that, whereas the cavalry had been the primary arm in the Indian wars and the infantry dominant in the turn-of-century colonial wars, the future lay with the artillery.[92] As noted, in the field artillery discussion, Reichmann supported this perspective, which was of course popular with artillery officers. Yet many observers, led by Morrison, continued to place primacy on the infantry. Despite emphasizing the increased importance of artillery-based fire support, Judson found that "nothing in the Russo-Japanese War demonstrated that, in field battles, the infantry has lost its supreme importance."[93] Bottom line, as Greenwood stresses, "any number of tactical conclusions could have been reached on the subject of artillery and infantry and their influence upon one another on the battlefield."[94]

Viability of frontal attacks? Observers also disagreed sharply on what the fighting indicated about potential for frontal assaults.[95] Having witnessed the repeated repulse of Japanese troops, Americans attached to the Russians tended to be pessimistic about attacks against fortified lines. For example, Reichmann relayed that, despite 250 Japanese guns pummeling a one-thousand-yard section of the Russian front at Liaoyang, the defenders stood firm in their almost fortress-like positions.[96] Judson simply declared such positions "invulnerable."[97] Yet Americans with the Japanese regarded penetrations against such "zones of death" as possible, albeit requiring high casualty acceptance. In a September 1904 letter, Morrison wrote that Manchurian combat had reinforced his prior view, that "the right kind of infantry can carry anything if you have enough of it. It is cheaper to do it some other way than by frontal attack if possible but frontal attack can win."[98] He and Kuhn pointed out that tactical changes (e.g., skipping the expected preliminary bombardment, using engineer troops to clear paths, and placing forward reserve troops to participate in the initial battles) aided attacking forces.

Further split existed among Japanese-based observers over whether their host increased spacing in attacking ranks and, if so, did it contribute to success.[99] March noted early in the war that they began deviating from the so-called German method of attack by enlarging the spacing of soldiers and using cover as much as possible. Yet Morrison, present at the same time, found this modification limited, arguing "there is a decided reaction from the great extension advocated by some and used in South Africa [the Boer War]."[100] McClernand, a late-war witness, found that "the Japanese made a considerable change in their extended-order formations and attacked in much wider and looser ones than in the earlier battles fought."[101] Yet Kuhn, with the Japanese throughout the war, reiterated Morrison's earlier view that "for infantry attacks the Japanese adhered closely to the principles laid down in the drill regulations of all nations having modern armies."[102] Given that the need to disperse attacking infantry formations had been a major lesson from the Boer War, Greenwood argues, "A repetition of similar extensions in Manchuria would have proved quite significant."[103] Observers' contrasting reports, in part due to differing definitions of "dispersed," precluded such a determination.

What accounted for healthier soldiers? The decision to dispatch medical observers reflected a priority on learning how to better care for soldiers in what turned out to be the first major conflict in which combat deaths exceeded disease-related fatalities. The key question was what accounted for such health—the hardy peasant composition of the two armies, the salubrious Manchurian environment, or the forces' hygiene/sanitation practices. The aforementioned Dr. Seaman and Dr. Anita Newcomb McGee of the American Red Cross highly praised the Japanese army's sanitary methods, but March, Kuhn, and Lynch did not believe they did anything noteworthy except use boiling water and abdominal bandages.[104] Rather, they attributed Japanese soldiers' good health to their cleanliness, sobriety, and diet. Lynch applauded the Japanese army's placement of responsibility for soldier health on both regular and medical officers, enabling the early isolation of contagious soldiers and the elimination of tainted food and water. Havard, Hoff, and Reichmann, on the Russian side, emphasized proper nourishment, strongly endorsing the wheeled field kitchens that provided soldiers hot meals and boiling water.[105]

WHAT LESSONS DID THE NAVY IDENTIFY?

In his 1905 Annual Report, Navy Secretary Charles Bonaparte asserted that "very impressive lessons as to naval problems of the highest importance have been afforded by the bloody war in eastern Asia."[106] Yet, without American witnesses to the sea combat, formulation and articulation of those lessons fell to leading naval figures such as Mahan and Sims, who already possessed strong and somewhat contradictory views.[107] No one considers an event with a completely open mind, but the influence of prior sentiment seems particularly acute in this case, especially as pertains to the battleship. Still, this debate ultimately resulted in a dominant understanding of events' meaning. Almost all naval findings from the Russo-Japanese War could technically be classified as misleading if World War I combat is used as the evaluation criterion, but that standard seems too narrow. Thus, I have sorted lessons by not only their impact on preparation for that global struggle but also the pursuit of fleet effectiveness in the intervening decade.

Reaffirmed Lessons

Mahanian validation. The Russo-Japanese War revealed, according to Rear Adm. George Converse, the Bureau of Navigation chief, that "no new military principles have been evolved, but the important ones of all ages have been re-demonstrated."[108] By this statement he meant the conflict reaffirmed the core Mahanian concepts. The war actually served as a laboratory test for them, given that, as the august American naval theorist explained, "more of my works have been done into Japanese than into any other tongue" and that the country showed unmatched "attention to the general subject."[109] Above all, Americans stressed that the Far East fight demonstrated the importance of commanding the seas and that such command resulted from winning fleet engagements. Converse declared that "land battles in which nearly three-quarters of a million men have been engaged at once have not settled as much as two fleet engagements [Battle of the Yellow Sea and Battle of the Tsushima Strait]."[110] For Mahan, the defensive-oriented alternatives employed by the Russians—"Fortress Fleet" (protecting fixed positions in particular at Port Arthur) and "Fleet in Being" (preoccupying the enemy by avoiding battle)—proved "in my judgment fundamentally erroneous" and offered a cautionary tale for the Americans.[111] Lieutenant Cotten added that the fleet's presence at Port Arthur "made it a double objective, since the fall of the port would eliminate both army and fleet."[112]

The conflict reiterated that concentrating capital warships was the key to winning fleet engagements.[113] Mahan characterized as one of the war's most important and clearest lessons "the inexpediency, the terrible danger, of dividing the battle-fleet, even in times of peace, into fractions individually smaller than those of a possible enemy."[114] While the Japanese navy maintained all its battleships together under Adm. Heihachiro Togo, the Russian navy, which if combined would "have outweighed decisively" its enemy, had been separated into the Pacific Ocean, Black Sea, and Baltic Fleets.[115] Admiral Dewey expressed the same sentiment in July 1905.[116] Mahan concluded that "we Americans have luckily had an object lesson, not at our own expense, but at that of an old friend."[117]

Qualified personnel critical. American officers also stressed that the Japanese sailors' superior fleet handling and gunnery critically contributed to their success.[118] Converse's 1905 Annual Report stated that "the lesson of greatest moment taught by this war is the importance of the personnel."[119] ONI Chief Schroeder concurred that "after all is said and done, nothing remains so steadily confirmed as the supreme influence of the human factor."[120] Cdr. Bradley Fiske highlighted that, after displaying poor gunnery skills during the Battle of the Yellow Sea, the Japanese conducted intense training "under conditions of the most intense realism" to be prepared for the next major engagement.[121] In contrast, White and Schroeder condemned the Russian navy's minimal gun practice and fleet-wide maneuvers before the Battle of Tsushima. If Togo won because of superior training, Fiske asked, "does this not guide us to the conclusion that our own drills and maneuvers should be made as realistic as much like battle, as possible?"[122]

Enlightening Lessons

Armored cruiser ineffectiveness. The conflict revealed some clear data about cruisers and destroyers, classes previously untested in major war and subject of much speculation. Although Secretary Bonaparte's 1905 Annual Report politically cited "much difference of opinion as to the value of armored cruisers," of which the United States had just built or was building a total of ten, sentiment on their wartime performance was overwhelmingly negative.[123] Converse pointed out that although Russians and Japanese placed all their armored cruisers in the line at Tsushima "to pad out the orders of battle," they had little worth as the decisive combat phase occurred beyond their gun range.[124] If the battle had occurred at a closer distance, they would have lacked the protection to slug it out with battleships. Thus, Schroeder harshly but accurately summed up that, based on the war, "the armored cruiser has failed to justify its existence."[125] Instead, it was the nonarmored cruisers' multirole performance (e.g., scout, convoy escort, blockade sentinel) that garnered praise.

Upgraded destroyers needed. The war highlighted the worth of the relatively new torpedo boat destroyers, more commonly referred to as destroyers, albeit revealing needed design improvements.[126] Schroeder observed that it may "be emphatically stated that no naval force can be considered complete or in the plenitude of its powers without a large number of both destroyers and torpedo boats."[127] He added that the latter's propensity to sink damaged vessels "points to the necessity of destroyers for the defense of the big ships after the main battle."[128] Cdr. Cameron Winslow conveyed to the president that the Russo-Japanese War showed going forward that the battleship fleet "must be accompanied, particularly at night and in foggy weather," by destroyers.[129] For operating during rough weather as well as battle, Schroeder and McCully observed that the war indicated that destroyers had to be larger and better armed.

Wireless telegraphy essential. In the first war in which navies used wireless telegraphy (radio), American commentators related its considerable benefit for Japanese scouting missions, especially prior to the Battle of Tsushima.[130] A Japanese auxiliary cruiser spotted the Russian warships and quickly informed Admiral Togo of their position, course, speed, and formation. US commentators criticized the Russians for not even attempting to block that transmission, despite having present an auxiliary cruiser outfitted with a strong wireless set. Togo had correctly anticipated the enemy's path, but Schroeder dismissed suggestions that a less orthodox approach might have succeeded as scouts formed wireless chains that "would infallibly keep the Japanese admiral cognizant of such a move."[131] McCully reported the firmly held view of Russian sailors that "every ship employed for military purposes in time of war should have a wireless outfit."[132]

Mine danger. The conflict also offered opportunities to assess the threats of mines and torpedoes. Unsurprisingly, given that mines sank eighteen warships, Secretary Bonaparte declared their utility a prominent war lesson.[133] The Japanese laid mines outside Port Arthur to force the Russians either to conduct lengthy clearance operations or to accept grave risk in launching rapid sorties. In doing the latter, the battleship *Petropavlovsk* sank after hitting a mine, taking with it the fleet's irreplaceable commander, Vice Adm. Stepan Makarov. After this April 1904 incident, the Russians, according to McCully, "became rather mine-struck."[134] Their increased minelaying paid huge dividends a month later when two Japanese battleships (*Yashima* and *Hatsuse*) went down after contacting devices placed across their usual track. McCully noted the advantage of Russia's dedicated mine-layer *Amur* and the greater use of contact over electric-observation types.

Deficient but impactful torpedo. The Americans judged the torpedo's performance far less positively, although noting its potential and psychological influence.[135] Schroeder and McCully observed that the celebrated torpedo attack on Port Arthur at the war's outset caused little physical damage despite the aggressors benefiting from surprise, smooth water, and short-range shooting. Subsequent efforts scored even worse, revealing to US commentators deficiencies with both the torpedoes and the tactics employed in their delivery. Some commentators praised Japanese torpedo boats at Tsushima, but others noted that they only succeeded in sinking damaged warships unable to defend themselves.[136] Nonetheless, US sailors appreciated that the threat of torpedo attack hampered Russian naval operations. The Bureau of Navigation chief's 1905 Annual Report declared that the initial surprise attack critically "paralyzed the initiative of one sea power, giving the other the command of the sea."[137] Moreover, the Americans believed that Baltic Fleet commander, Adm. Zinovy Rozhestvensky, fearing a night torpedo attack, painted his warships black, which left them more visible in the daytime. Thus, Secretary Bonaparte concluded after the war that torpedo craft "have a real, although a somewhat restricted, field of usefulness in naval warfare."[138]

Disputed Lessons (at Least Initially)

Key aspects of battleship design and employment initially did not yield agreed-on findings among the Americans except that the battleship remained supreme. Writing shortly after the Battle of the Yellow Sea (August 1904), Navy Secretary Paul Morton declared in his annual report that "the day of the battle ship is not over" as "events of the past few months in Eastern seas confirm in a most striking manner."[139] The subsequent Battle of Tsushima (May 1905) only reinforced this judgment. Beyond this conclusion and changes to reduce warship vulnerability (e.g., need to bolster underwater protection, especially in vicinity of magazines and steering gear; benefit of reducing topside clutter), division existed on critical questions: How important was warship speed? What was the best range to engage the enemy? What was the appropriate armament for battleships? How were modern gunnery techniques evolving?[140]

Value of warship speed? The Japanese used their superior fleet-handling skills to maneuver into advantageous firing positions, but the contribution of an edge in speed became a contentious issue among Americans.[141] Needing to cover vast distances, the US Navy traditionally prioritized range over speed compared to other sea powers. Secretary Bonaparte's 1905 Annual Report, however, concluded that the war showed with practical certainty "that superior speed is of value in a fleet, not merely because it enables the commander to force or avoid battle, but because it is a source of strength in actual conflict."[142] Sims wrote the president that the Russians, even if they matched the Japanese in every other way and had 50 percent more guns, "would still have been easily defeated if we assume the Japanese fleet speed to have been appreciably greater."[143] Yet other prominent American analysts, led by Mahan, diminished the importance of speed, in part because they believed Japan's edge to be only a few knots, far less than Sims asserted. ONI Chief Schroeder contended that the "apparently prevalent argument that it was by their superior speed that the Japanese were able to press the heads of the Russian columns and cap them does not appear to be tenable."[144] Instead they asserted that the outcome resulted from the Japanese commander's interior lines and adroit maneuvering combined with Russian mistakes.

Decisive gunnery range? The salience of speed depended to a degree on the optimal range for engaging the enemy.[145] Sims, Fiske, and others believed that fleets possessing "scientific gunnery" could now produce victory through the physical destruction of warships at long range with heavy guns. Evidence of such potential occurred at Tsushima when the Russian battleship *Oslyabya* became the first all-steel battleship sunk exclusively by naval gunfire. For long-range gunnery advocates, a speed edge enabled maneuvering into lethal firing positions as well as reduced vulnerability to enemy warships. It allowed the Japanese at Tsushima to get more of their heavy guns into the fight despite the Russian fleet actually possessing a numerical superiority. Less concerned about speed were officers who continued to believe that victory required a high volume of fire from intermediate- or close-range guns to overwhelm the enemy and crew, prompting capitulation as warships rarely sank. Mahan argued that "the so-called secondary battery is really entitled to the name primary, because its effect is exerted mainly upon the personnel rather than the material of a vessel."[146] He and McCully cited the Russian withdrawal at the Battle of Yellow Sea after Adm. Wilgelm Vitgeft's death as evidence that this traditional view of naval combat held. At Tsushima, they stressed how the Russians reported being "blinded" by intermediate six- and eight-inch caliber guns. Schroeder added that "throughout the entire war the favorite practice of the Japanese appears to have been to use common shell to wreck the unarmored parts and demoralize and kill the personnel."[147] Yet Fiske and other long-range gunnery proponents rejected this interpretation, asserting that the extensive damage from intermediate-caliber guns at Tsushima only occurred *"after the Russians had been whipped"* and it was safe to close within their range.[148]

By the end of 1906 the Sims–Fiske position prevailed. From the beginning most senior line officers favored this perspective, as evidenced by Dewey in July 1905 attributing Japanese victory at Tsushima to "big guns on battleships."[149] Likewise, Bureau of Navigation chief Converse's 1905 Annual Report concluded that "the extent of the damages inflicted at long range by heavy guns confirms previously existing growing opinion in favor of armaments of heavier caliber for all armored ships."[150] Still, Roosevelt, the war's most important student, had remained uncertain. In a December 1905 letter to the navy secretary, he noted an article stressing the key role of the secondary battery at Tsushima and emphasized that before its elimination "we ought first to have the full facts before us."[151] Back-and-forth debate continued for most of 1906 until Sims so convincingly explained how the Japanese battleships' large guns dominated that Mahan declared his withdrawal from the warship design debate, given a limited understanding of modern technology.[152]

Imagined Lesson

Fire control advantage. At times uncertainty about what transpired in combat combines with wish fulfillment to produce inaccurate findings. An example of this phenomenon occurred in the Russo-Japanese War naval combat. Proponents of "scientific gunnery" possessed significant interest in obtaining data regarding the relatively new and untested system of fire control (centralized launching of all warship guns).[153] McCully errantly reported that "in battle of Japan Sea [the] Japanese first showed application of a system of fire control, while the Russians never used any."[154] Sims trumpeted the Japanese as benefiting from such an advantage. Yet, as the anonymous "Black Joke" correctly argued in 1907, the Japanese "are believed to have had little of what we would now understand by the term 'fire-control.'"[155] Norman Friedman points out that it was actually the Russians who had begun employing the type of system being developed by the Americans (and British). Lacking the evidence available to this naval historian, Sims associated fire control with the victorious Japanese, which aided his campaign for the American Navy to embrace it.

HOW DID THE US MILITARY APPLY ITS FINDINGS?

Abandonment of the Subig Bay Stronghold

It is appropriate to begin with an interservice matter—how best to defend the Philippine Islands—indisputably influenced by a lesson.[156] Appreciation of their growing codependency prompted the War and Navy Departments to establish the Joint Army and Navy Board, or Joint Board, in 1903 with identification of overseas base locations among its first tasks. The navy wanted to place its main Pacific outpost at Subig Bay, a deep, sheltered harbor approximately sixty miles from Manila and thirty-five miles from Corregidor Island at the entrance of Manila Bay.[157] The Joint Board approved the location with the secretary of war expressing the army's view that "the selection of the site for the naval base was a matter which concerned the Navy alone."[158] President Roosevelt provided full-throated support, but Congress limited funding before the Russo-Japanese War. The conflict, especially starting with a surprise naval attack, provided excellent lobbying material. Roosevelt exclaimed that the opposition of House Minority Leader John Sharp Williams to Subig Bay "is monstrous in view of what we have seen happen before our eyes to the Russians at Port Arthur because of their unpreparedness."[159] Legislators subsequently approved significant money for the planned works, and army leaders agreed to split their Philippines construction funds between Subig Bay and Manila.[160]

Local army resistance unsuccessfully challenged the project.[161] In June 1904 Maj. Gen. Leonard Wood, governor of the Moro Province and close friend of the president, implored Roosevelt to shift the main naval base to Manila Bay as the existing "plan if carried out will be a colossal mistake."[162] In response to Wood's letter, Dewey noted that the superiority of Subig Bay had been determined by the navy's General Board, Joint Board, two successive secretaries, and every commander-in-chief of the Asiatic Fleet since the Spanish-American War. The admiral concluded his lengthy rebuttal by rejecting Manila Bay given "the fallacy of concentrating the means of the mobile naval defense at the centre of attack—as if a boxer should try to defend himself by holding his fists against his own breast."[163] For naval leaders, this error was precisely what was then happening at Port Arthur. Viewing the issue as primarily a maritime matter and noting the Joint Board's endorsement, the president wrote Wood in early August that "I agree entirely with the decision to which they came."[164] As Richard Challener put it, "The sailors had won the Subig battle of 1904," but Congress appropriated only modest funds the following year, and construction progress was slow.[165] The military's perception of Subig Bay's importance initially increased in the aftermath of the Russo-Japanese War. A major 1906 army review of coastal fortifications (the Taft Board) identified it as vital, as did the newly crafted war plan against Japan (eventually to be known as War Plan Orange), which called for maintaining a toehold at Subig Bay until the US battleship fleet arrived from Norfolk.

Consideration of Russia's Port Arthur experience, however, hardened Philippines-based soldiers' opposition to the naval base and ultimately converted the rest of the army against it.[166] Whereas previously the primary threat appeared to be European navies, ground officers now regarded expeditionary forces as the main danger. They questioned the practicality of holding Olongapo (the Subig Bay port) for months, noting that its physical environs were remarkably similar to Port Arthur, which proved vulnerable after the Japanese Third Army's artillery reached the surrounding high hills. American observers' conclusion that Russian separation of its main commercial port (Dalny) and naval base (Port Arthur) on the Liaodong Peninsula eased their capture reinforced Philippines-based soldiers' angst about the distance between Manila and Subig Bay. An early indication of the siege's influence on army thinking appears in Capt. Edward Schulz's January 1905 article, "Land Defense of Seacoast Fortifications."[167] Whereas army critics of the naval base had previously not gained the attention of service leaders, Challener explains that "the more the Army studied the presumed 'lessons' of the Russo-Japanese war the less it liked Subig Bay."[168]

During 1907 the War Department shifted firmly against Subig Bay, with decisive consequences.[169] First, Chief of Staff Maj. Gen. J. Franklin Bell fought the navy's request for concentrating the islands' defense construction funds there. Then, in June, when the Joint Board and the president endorsed Subig Bay's prioritization over Manila in the war plan, the army objected. Three months later Wood convinced visiting Secretary of War Taft to abandon his support for the naval base, and a team of artillery experts judged Olongapo indefensible after exploring the hills surrounding it. In October the army leadership persuaded a reluctant Roosevelt to halt construction

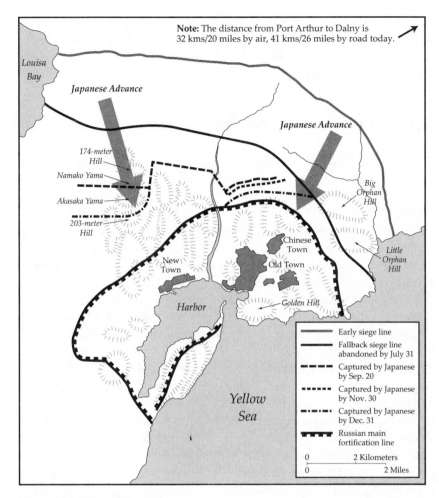

Map 2.2 *The Siege of Port Arthur*

until the Joint Board reconsidered the matter. At its subsequent late January 1908 session Bell declared Subig Bay indefensible against a strong land-side attack. Unable to rebut this assessment, the navy capitulated.

The reversal on Subig Bay soured relations between the army and navy, alienated the president, and bequeathed an impractical plan for defense of the Philippines, but it represented a clear and beneficial application of a finding from the Russo-Japanese War. Largely on the basis of the recent conflict, the critical decision criteria had shifted from being primarily a naval problem to primarily a land challenge.[170] When criticized about its new stance, the General Staff explained it was simply following

81

the war's insights.[171] News of the Joint Board's changed position outraged Roosevelt, who felt betrayed after years of steadfastly lobbying for Subig Bay's defenses, but he accepted the military's recommendation that Pearl Harbor now be the main naval base in the Pacific, and work commenced there in 1909.

HOW DID THE ARMY APPLY ITS FINDINGS?

The army's recent combat experience, reorganization, expanded mission, and increasingly professionalized officer corps encouraged the application of Russo-Japanese War lessons, but other contextual factors worked against their embrace.[172] The War Department's woefully inadequate support for soldiers during the Spanish-American War had prompted President William McKinley to establish the Dodge Commission, which urged institutional changes. More generally, the emergence of the Progressive Era created favorable political and cultural conditions for reforms to increase effectiveness. Plus, the need for improved management grew with the army having to defend the recently acquired overseas possessions. In response, Secretary of War Elihu Root shepherded a major reorganization, including the General Staff's 1903 establishment. Supporting this effort and overall service preparedness was an enthusiastic "Colonel Roosevelt."

Bolstering the army's educational system was a core component of the Root reforms as service leaders worried about its adequacy.[173] The War Department established a four-tier hierarchy to upgrade advanced study: (1) garrison schools, (2) special service schools (e.g., Artillery School, School of Submarine Defense), (3) the General Service and Staff College (GSSC), and (4) the Army War College (AWC). The Fort Leavenworth–based GSSC combined the former Infantry and Cavalry School (closed since the Spanish-American War) with instruction to prepare officers for high-level command and staff positions. After a problem-plagued first year, Bell took over as commandant and split the two-year program so that only distinguished graduates of the Infantry and Cavalry School advanced to the Staff College. While improving performance, this change problematically resulted in attendance by engineers and artillerists declining by nearly 50 percent, which impeded combined-arms instruction. The War Department created the AWC for exceptional officers. Attached to the General Staff with responsibility for developing war plans, the AWC emphasized realistic campaign study.

Army leaders ensured that these schools considered the recent conflict.[174] The secretary of war declared in his 1905 Annual Report that "a high technical efficiency is growing more and more necessary in order to keep abreast of modern progress in the art and science of war."[175] He added that "particularly instructive and interesting" were lectures on the Russo-Japanese War given at the AWC by returned observers, and he directed "the attention of the college authorities and students to lines of inquiry certain to prove of great value."[176] The War Department assigned some of the returning observers to key educational positions. Barry took over the AWC in December 1905, while a few months later Havard became head of the Army Medical School. Most influentially, as will be discussed, Bell appointed Morrison to the GSSC faculty. To improve AWC instruction, Maj. Eben Swift spent the 1907 summer in Manchuria exploring the battlefields.[177]

These institutional and educational developments contributed to the officer corps' increasing sophistication.[178] Edward Coffman points out that "with the advent of the twentieth century and the Root reforms, the level required of a military professional rose considerably."[179] Soldiers looked to general (e.g., *Journal of the Military Service Institution of the United States*) and branch (e.g., *Artillery Journal*) periodicals for information about martial developments and debates on their implications. Some army intellectuals, such as John Bigelow and Arthur Wagner, had attempted since the late nineteenth century to reduce European influence by arguing that the service's own military experience was more germane. German and French military thinking, however, remained important. Timothy Nenninger finds that the tension between so-called Americanists and Europeanists seemed to foster "a renaissance in the study of military art within the army."[180]

Unfortunately, as Coffman notes, "older officers who had spent most of their careers in the nineteenth century still dominated the Army."[181] A frustrated Roosevelt failed to overcome congressional and institutional opposition to replace an essentially seniority-based personnel system with a merit-based approach. The former, along with a high mandatory retirement age of sixty-four, meant promotions occurred slowly, blocking talented, energetic officers (e.g., second lieutenants averaged almost twenty-nine years to become majors). The president could elevate officers out of order to the brigadier general rank (e.g., a forty-six-year-old Captain Pershing passed over 862 soldiers in 1906). Such moves, however, generated accusations of favoritism within the service and resistance from the Senate Military Affairs Committee, which had to sign off, sharply limiting their employment. Age-based tension combined with strong branch and bureau parochialism to influence perspectives on the Manchurian combat. Linn points out that "the differing interpretations [of the Russo-Japanese War] were symptomatic of a growing division between Managers [organization-focused] and Heroes [battle-focused]," while Jonathan Bailey adds that "partisans of particular doctrinal approaches tended to find what they wanted to suit their own arguments."[182]

Although overcoming such schisms had been a key motivation for the General Staff's establishment, it initially possessed limited capability.[183] With fewer than fifty officers, the woefully undermanned body employed less than a third of the personnel of the British equivalent and less than a fifth of other European powers.

Moreover, the army lacked trained staff officers and restricted continuous service to four-year terms. In contrast to the German General Staff's focus on plans and operations, the American entity spent considerable time on administrative matters. Adding to its difficulties, War Department bureaus, despite being placed under the chief of staff, resisted their subordination. In particular, Steven Stebbins points out that "the early General Staff was ill-suited to direct major revisions of training and doctrine."[184]

Roosevelt hoped to energize the General Staff by tapping the dynamic Bell as chief of staff in April 1906.[185] He was the fourth man in four years to hold the army's top position, but the first to obtain it without seniority. This brilliant, progressive, and action-oriented officer with experience in all three line branches was, as Matthew Oyos notes, "Roosevelt's kind of soldier."[186] Believing the General Staff had concentrated excessively on administrative matters, the new chief "determined that strategic planning and intelligence gathering needed more attention."[187] He possessed a keen interest in the Manchurian conflict and its implications. Lacking bureaucratic experience, Bell sought to complement his own strengths by elevating the politically adroit and former Russo-Japanese War observer Barry to be assistant chief of staff. Although an enthusiastic reformer, Edgar Raines points out that Bell "favored a moderate rate of change" to avoid alienating the officer corps, especially given his limited authority.[188] Encouraging this view, a legislative effort to make the chief of staff the service's only lieutenant general had failed amid intense opposition.

A series of challenges in Latin America and Asia absorbed the understrength service in the immediate post-Russo-Japanese War period.[189] Beginning in late 1905 tension over China and Venezuela necessitated planning for possible operations. Then in 1906, with Cuban stability deteriorating, pressure grew on the president to dispatch an American force. Ultimately, the United States deployed over five thousand troops (nearly 10 percent of the total army) in October 1906. Problems with the first two designated commanders of this force necessitated that Bell assume direct charge and Barry replace him in early 1907. At the same time tension with Japan rapidly intensified and lingered for two years, prompting feverish planning activity and increased force deployments in the Philippines. In scrambling to meet these challenges, the army particularly suffered from having less than four thousand officers.

Finally, conservative and anti-imperial sentiment in Congress presented a hurdle to applying any lesson that required significant outlays or statutory reforms.[190] Although the army's budget had grown substantially from the pre-Spanish-American War period, a majority of legislators by mid-decade opposed further increases. Given that many of the war's findings related to large field engagements or siege operations that seemed inapplicable to US military needs, reformers faced a high bar to convince Congress of relevancy. Despite senior army officials repeatedly stressing the need for a sufficient training budget, they were repeatedly rebuffed. Besides limited funds, tight congressional control over military policy complicated reform efforts as soldiers strove for perfect, not workable, solutions, given the difficulty of modifying initial legislation.

In general, historians have concluded that, despite Secretary of War Taft asserting in his 1905 Annual Report that the army was applying lessons from the Russo-Japanese War, the effort produced limited effects.[191] Greenwood, author of the most in-depth examination of the US Army observer effort, judges that its influence was "virtually nil," given the lack of perceived relevance of some findings, while the more utile ones suffered from an inadequate threat impetus.[192] He adds that even though the army eventually introduced some ideas, "there was no direct link between the observers' recommendations and the Army's adoption of similar programs."[193] Similarly, Bailey finds that although many European and American officers "were eager to seize on new ideas and their consequences . . . unfortunately such lessons generally remained no more than the ideas of those junior officers with the time to write articles."[194] Analysts attribute exceptions primarily to personal agency by observers. Such judgments are not inaccurate in a narrow sense, but as the previously discussed Subig Bay example shows, the influence of foreign war lessons needs to be considered through a wider lens. That is, while the army clearly failed to take full advantage of their potential benefits, observations affected the service in meaningful—albeit not always positive—ways if one considers their impact on materiel, educational, organizational, doctrinal, and training decisions.

In assessing the army's application of lessons, some clearly positive and negative outcomes occurred, as I will articulate, but judging the War Department's response should largely be a product of how it addressed four key findings from the Russo-Japanese War: the criticality of more effective field artillery, the increasing importance of the machine gun, the challenge of the more lethal battlefield, and the vital need for prewar preparation. The army did not fully embrace any of these findings, but neither did it completely ignore them. Rather, the responses fell along a spectrum. What accounts for the divergent outcomes yields insight into the process of learning lessons and how to improve the results. Some impact had already occurred when, in July 1905, President Roosevelt, although an enthusiastic consumer of observer reporting, cautioned the chief of staff against a rapid embrace of lessons from the victorious Japanese, as "not all of the things they have done have been wise, and some of the wise things they have done are not wise for us."[195] Army leaders concurred with this perspective, prompting experimentation to validate discoveries. Relevance, however, was not something that can be demonstrated with a test, and perceptions of it tended to diverge depending on bureaucratic and cultural considerations.

Beneficial but Incomplete Application

Field artillery change quickly adopted. The response to the field artillery cues is particularly interesting given their perceived relevance, recognized branch deficiency, introduction of postwar reforms, and ultimate failure to obtain significantly improved effectiveness.[196] In his 1904 Annual Report, Secretary Taft endorsed allocating a greater share of the budget to the artillery as suggested by early reporting from the Russo-Japanese War.[197] Infantry and cavalry officers on the General Staff, however, swiftly mobilized against any reallocation. As a result, Taft, in his 1905 Annual Report, declared that any increase in funds for the artillery should not come at the expense of the other branches.[198] This perspective reflected the broader problem that tribalism continued to undermine combined arms despite the war reaffirming its importance. Change was much more likely within service components than in areas requiring cooperation between them. For the field artillery, as Capt. William Snow averred in an important 1908 paper, observer reports from the Russo-Japanese War should be regarded as the "final arbiter of all differences of military opinion."[199]

The long-neglected US field artillery had improved since its poor performance in the Spanish-American War, but bureaucratic, cultural, and resource constraints limited progress.[200] Working with a rejuvenated Ordnance Bureau, the branch in 1904 finally obtained a modern weapon—the high-volume, low-recoil 3-inch M1902. Their primary gun now qualitatively matched European models, but the Americans severely trailed quantitively with a planned wartime ratio of 2.5 guns per thousand infantrymen. Additionally, the field artillery remained organizationally linked with the politically dominant coastal artillery and lacked authority to establish units larger than a battery. Direct fire continued to be the main support method, despite it proving increasingly hazardous. Some artillerists argued that the new gun's characteristics warranted a shift to indirect fire, but the War Department, infantry, and even some gunners regarded it as an auxiliary technique that did not produce the physical and especially psychological benefits of direct fire. This debate, as artillery historian Vardell Nesmith notes, "was all theory."[201]

The obsolescence of direct fire as well as the inadequacy of US Artillery's organization quickly became evident when observer dispatches began arriving.[202] Based on Japanese gunnery effectiveness, Chief of Artillery Brig. Gen. John Story, in late 1904, lobbied the War Department for greater resources and adoption of the indirect fire method. As discussed, this push to grow at the expense of infantry and cavalry failed, prompting a frustrated Story to write that "there is no first-class power which has so systematically neglected its field artillery as the United States."[203] Then the president, after meeting with the returned observers, inquired about the state of the field artillery. Taft, when supplying General Story's response on February 8, 1905, added that it "clearly shows the fact that the present status of the field artillery is most unsatisfactory."[204] The following month Roosevelt directed Story to submit recommendations. Story's response indicated that the United States needed to follow lessons from the Russo-Japanese War showing that effective field artillery required well-trained gunners in echeloned organizations directed via telephonic communication and under almost all circumstances using indirect fire.

Absorption of these findings began prompting significant changes by mid-1905.[205] In May the General Staff reversed itself, supporting an increase in the number of field guns from thirty-six to forty-eight per wartime division. Story, March, and others used the Russo-Japanese War to convince the War Department of indirect fire's superiority. The Board on the Preparation of Drill Regulations for Field Artillery began laying out an indirect-fire control system, which the army soon adopted as the standard method of support. Nesmith, who closely examines this transition, characterizes the conflict in the Far East as *"the right war at the right time."*[206] In June the army established two provisional field artillery regiments. To validate lessons, the Fort Riley–based regiment in late summer 1906 tested a range of artillery pieces with varying types of ammunition, including the high-explosive shells used so effectively by the Japanese. The War Department appointed Macomb and Judson as two-thirds of the board directing this effort, with the former reporting that "the experiments tended to confirm in every particular the lessons learned in the Russo-Japanese war on the Manchurian battlefields."[207] Above all, they highlighted that attacking forces needed to coordinate closely infantry assaults with field artillery and machine gun fire. Artillery historian Boyd Dastrup points out that within a year of the Manchurian conflict's conclusion, the army had "introduced technology and tactics that rivaled their European counterparts and revolutionized its field artillery."[208]

The two provisional regiments facilitated experimentation, but Japanese success prompted the War Department to seek a more fundamental reorganization.[209] The growing specialization of the coastal and field artillery missions had driven their partial separation in 1901, but both remained in the Corps of Artillery. Observer comments exacerbated the perceived risk from this arrangement, especially given the field artillery's second-class treatment. Branch members published a series of articles stressing that effective mass fire required grouping guns into regiments and brigades. The War Department established an investigatory Committee on the Reorganization of Artillery, with March as a key member. For the sub-regimental structure, the service adopted March's recommendation of two battalions of three batteries, about which the chief of artillery wrote, "follows more closely the teachings of the Russo-Japanese War" than the three-battalion, two-battery structure preferred by many artillery officers.[210] The first session of the 59th Congress did not act on the proposed legislation, but the following year the Roosevelt administration won passage of a bill that split the Artillery Corps into the Coastal Artillery and Field Artillery, authorized field artillery units larger than batteries, and raised the pay for specially trained personnel. In mid-1907 the War Department followed up by establishing six field artillery regiments and expanding the wartime infantry division's field artillery component from a regiment to a two-regiment artillery brigade.

Failure to lead to fire-support proficiency. Although the above changes seem to represent a textbook case of lessons learned, the result proved disappointing and instructive to the challenges faced when attempting to benefit from externally prompted cues. That is, despite positive doctrinal and organizational change, human and fiscal resource constraints along with cultural predilections ultimately prevented the army from developing a proficiency with indirect fire and combined arms in the decade between the Russo-Japanese War and World War I.[211] As Stebbins notes, the army leadership "tended to perceive field artillery reform vaguely and over-optimistically, often equating the establishment of institutions with successful reform."[212] Exacerbating this deficiency, legislators refused to establish a chief of field artillery as the prior artillery branch chief became responsible only for the coastal artillery. After the split, Bell complained that "the Coast Artillery gets all the money, all the promotion, all of everything worthwhile that Congress has to give."[213] In his 1907 Annual Report, Bell relayed Ordnance chief Brig. Gen. William Crozier's concern that although the reserve supply of gun ammunition "is in a more backward state than that of any other element of the fighting equipment for an army," the field artillery's goal of tripling stockpiles to at least one thousand rounds per gun went unfunded.[214] So did an adequate supply of training rounds, which restricted live fire to once a year. Moreover, despite the peacetime establishment of six field artillery regiments to facilitate preparation for mass fire, training above battery level rarely occurred as the army dispersed these smaller units across the United States and overseas.

The field artillery's difficulties extended beyond inadequate resources as it struggled not only to cooperate with the infantry but to understand how to cooperate.[215] In 1907 Bell appropriately changed the name of the Fort Riley–based School of Application for Cavalry and Field Artillery to the Mounted Service School since it neglected gunnery. That same year, the School of Artillery became the School of Coastal Artillery and the *Journal of US Artillery* subsequently published almost exclusively on coastal gunnery matters. Yet the logical and necessary step of establishing a field artillery school did not occur, essentially leaving inadequate garrison schools to instruct new lieutenants in conducting artillery fire. Plus, the paucity of field artillerists attending the army's top-tier schools (Snow in 1908 became the first one to graduate from the AWC) hampered obtaining knowledge about complex tactical operations and prevented infantry officers from understanding how to work with gunners. As a result, Stebbins emphasizes, "nowhere in the Army schools did anyone attempt to practically work out the synchronization of modern field artillery fires with maneuver."[216] Without clear guidance on coordination, artillerists' understanding and proficiency with the more complex indirect-fire approach lagged.

Chief of Staff Wood warned in 1910 that the "existing deficiency in the field artillery constitutes one of the greatest menaces to our country in case of war," but ameliorative measures were not a sufficient corrective.[217] With the belated establishment of the School of Fire in September 1911, six years after the Russo-Japanese War's conclusion, "field artillery reform finally seemed to be well-underway."[218] Yet the school's first commandant "quickly found that reversing decades of neglected gunnery training demanded all of the School's energy," impeding his aim of training with the infantry.[219] Likewise, in its first two years (1911–12), the *Field Artillery Journal* published more than five articles on branch-specific techniques and training for every one on combined arms. Bailey notes that, as late as 1916, when the prospect of joining World War I loomed, "there was concern that officers graduating from the US Army's School of Fire could not conduct indirect fire missions effectively."[220] This concern proved warranted as the initial field artillery units sent to Europe in 1917 struggled to synchronize fire with infantry movement.

How should the army be judged in its application of field artillery lessons from the Russo-Japanese War? Its vivid demonstration of modern gunnery contributed significantly to positive changes: adoption of indirect fire, establishment of an autonomous field artillery branch, introduction of field artillery battalions and regiments, and increased divisional firepower. Yet these actions were not sufficient to produce the requisite capability as the army proved unable to educate and train personnel to obtain proficiency with the new approach. It had a dozen years to become competent in modern field artillery, but gains were almost exclusively technical, leaving the service completely unprepared tactically for what would be needed in France. The lack of a strong, effective branch leadership undoubtedly hampered developing indirect fire and combined-arms capability, as did senior army officers' beliefs that they had addressed the problem by simply creating institutions and organizations. Only in February 1918, eleven years after the branch's creation and almost a year after entering World War I, would a chief of field artillery (William Snow, by then a major general) be appointed. Hard-gained experience with the American Expeditionary Force (AEF) spurred necessary changes, but the objective of learning from foreign wars is to avoid such a costly education.

Failed Inspiration

Insufficient response to the machine gun's emergence. While the army's response to the field artillery lessons was inadequate, its reaction to information on the machine gun's increasing role proved worse. The disparate outcomes resulted largely from two differences—one informational and one bureaucratic. For the field artillery, the war provided clear guidance on necessary doctrinal and organizational reforms, whereas the conflict only indicated the machine gun would be significant for future conflict but didn't indicate how best to organize and use it. Moreover, in contrast to a dedicated branch that absorbed and acted on the field artillery data, no such entity existed for machine gunners.

The army had hoped for instructional guidance similar to that available for field artillery. The General Staff delayed addressing organizational and tactical issues with the machine gun, as Armstrong relates, "until a thorough evaluation could be made of the information contained in the reports of the observers of the Russo-Japanese War."[221] Yet, although the American witnesses described their extensive use, the reports did not clarify how to proceed. Arthur MacArthur, in October 1905, typified observers in calling for "a careful and exhaustive investigation by the General Staff, as to the best type of gun, the organization of tactical units, and their distribution to commands."[222] Critics, including then interim chief of staff Lt. Gen. John Bates, found their long-standing concerns reinforced as machine guns in Manchuria frequently suffered mechanical failure and expended enormous amounts of ammunition. Many officers, however, agreed with Bell, who, after replacing Bates in April 1906, wrote that "the automatic machine gun is an implement of war of great importance."[223] Yet he added "just how great cannot be known from the experience at hand."[224]

Thus, the chief of staff increased experimentation with recently acquired Maxim machine guns.[225] The aforementioned late summer 1906 Fort Riley trials reinforced the need for closely coordinating machine-gun fire with advancing infantry. With the aim of increasing experience, the army established provisional two-gun machine-gun platoons in every infantry and cavalry regiment. This approach adhered to the one specific wartime lesson, as March wrote in a supporting paper, that "all observers agree that machine guns should never work singly, but should be handled in pairs."[226] Another influence of reports from the Far East was in the potential for machine guns to provide direct fire support as the field artillery shifted to providing indirect fire from behind the front lines. For example, Fort Leavenworth instructor Capt. J. A. Woodruff described how machine guns enabled viable defenses with fewer troops in smaller works with shorter flanks.[227]

Yet, despite influential supporters, including the chief of staff and president, the army's machine-gun program achieved fleeting and grossly insufficient progress.[228] The distribution of two Maxims to each regiment actually impeded experimentation by limiting larger-scale operational tests and placing the development onus on junior officers who wrote enthusiastic articles but mostly stoked debate. Furthermore, an ammunition budget that allowed less than five minutes of rapid fire for the entire year hindered learning. In his 1908 Annual Report, Bell declared machine-gun platoons "not satisfactory," and interest shifted to creating an experimental six machine-gun company.[229] He unwisely assigned direction of this effort to Capt. John Parker, who counterproductively focused on generating support for an independent machine-gun branch. An August 1908 General Staff report stressed that evidence from the Russo-Japanese War strongly supported the weapon's integration into the infantry and cavalry. By the end of the decade, its prospects as a separate branch were over, but so were the terms of Roosevelt and Bell and much of the impetus for machine-gun development. Peacetime six-gun machine-gun companies would not be established until 1916, and the army entered World War I without a standard weapon. Pershing, in his memoirs, understandably laments that, despite observers stressing its increased importance, the machine gun "was much to our disadvantage."[230]

Harmful Embrace

Infantry dismissive of need for more assistance. A central factor in the army's failure to respond adequately to field artillery and machine-gun cues from the Russo-Japanese War was the infantry branch's embrace of a culturally preferred interpretation of the Manchurian fighting that facilitated dismissiveness of growing fire-support requirements.[231] While the Far East combat was under way, the General Staff introduced a new capstone guidance document—the *Field Service Regulations* (*FSR*). Senior officers had identified the need for more direction on force structure and combat principles at the brigade and division level than provided in the administrative-focused General Regulations. The resulting 250-page *FSR*, accepted in February 1905, was, as J. P. Clark points out, "the first American manual to bind the drill regulations of the various branches together with a holistic set of principles for combined arms tactics."[232] The section on combat stressed that the "decisive results can usually be obtained only by the offensive," and the defense should be conducted "with a view to eventual assumption of the offensive."[233] This promising initiative, however, did not prompt the desired improvement in combined-arms capability. Parochial factors helped shape the infantry's perspective, particularly its belief that the army had a disproportionate number of artillery and cavalry units.

Information from Manchuria reinforced rather than modified the infantry's core beliefs.[234] Japan's success as the aggressor in all major battles affirmed to most American infantrymen the faith that élan and closing speed would be sufficient for frontal assaults to overcome acknowledged stronger defensive positions. The challenge was matching the spirit, endurance, and skill of Japanese soldiers, as a belief existed that technological developments had softened men. Chief of Staff Bell conveyed to the president in January 1907 that "frontal attacks and assaults with the bayonet are still *possible* but only with *well trained* troops."[235] Engineers added that field fortifications in the recent combat had demonstrated value in facilitating offensive operations as well as defense. The Russo-Japanese War simply did not provide clear evidence of defense dominance, and without such "proof" the infantry and army as a whole maintained its preferred approach. Although data from the Far Eastern fighting should have at least generated caution about the durability of this status quo orientation, the infantry's interpretation of Manchuria actually bolstered their confidence that reforms were unnecessary.

Contributing significantly to this result was the empowerment of Morrison as arbiter on the nature of the Russo-Japanese combat. Wanting to leverage the observer experience, then GSSC commandant Bell decided to add one of the witnesses from the infantry branch to the faculty.[236] Bell initially requested Reichmann, but the War Department said no because of the latter's extended absence from his regiment. Despite discovering that this opposition was not strong, Bell switched to Morrison, who possessed a sharply contrasting professional outlook and understanding of events in Manchuria. Although Bell's views about modern combat generally aligned with Reichmann's, Clark explains that "conceptual matters were of secondary importance for Bell. He wanted 'practical' officers like Morrison who had served under Bell in the Philippines."[237] In praising the performance of Morrison, who arrived at Fort Leavenworth in September 1906, new commandant Brig. Gen. Charles Hall wrote that "his observations and deductions there [Manchuria] have been of great help to him as an instructor in military art and also of much value and interest to the students."[238] Within a year, as planned, Morrison began what became a five-year stretch as head of the school's influential Military Art Department. As Linn notes, officers at the time regarded Morrison as "one of the most respected tactical minds in the army."[239] Typifying student sentiment, George C. Marshall credited him with having "taught me all I have ever known of tactics."[240] Yet historians such as Clark, Nenninger, and Stebbins criticize the instructor for promoting a retrograde, infantry-centric view of battle.[241]

His influence extended beyond instruction, as evidenced in the contrary influences of Russo-Japanese War lessons on the revised *FSR* and *Infantry Drill Regulations* (*IDR*).[242] Walter Kretchik points out that a number of positive changes in the 1910 *FSR* "were inspired by the reports of" the observers.[243] It codified the increased fire support adopted in 1907 with a two-regiment field artillery brigade (forty-eight guns and sixteen howitzers) as a part of a wartime infantry division, introduced a separate section on entrenchments including discussions of their relationship to offensive and defensive operations, and conceptually integrated artillery with infantry and cavalry. Yet, while the *FSR* emphasized the importance of combined arms, the army failed to provide practical guidance on how to achieve it. As Stebbins notes, although the *FSR* "urged combined arms cooperation," the individual branch drill regulations simply "did not explain how to coordinate."[244] Leaving command-and-control issues unresolved was particularly problematic given how the infantry's embrace of Morrison's interpretation of the Russo-Japanese War fostered the "illusion of needing no assistance."[245] For example, in the first new *IDR* since 1904, Morrison, in drafting the 1911 guidance, conveyed his certainty, as Clark relates, "that machine guns were nothing more than mere 'weapons of emergency' and artillery would have only a negligible effect upon defending infantry."[246] If Reichmann had composed this document, it would undoubtedly have contained very different language based on his contrasting insights from witnessing Manchurian combat. Of course, such a scenario is hard to imagine given that the infantry officers' sentiment cohered with Morrison's view.

Insufficient Instrumental Influence

Peacetime preparedness continues to lag. The overarching lesson of peacetime preparedness being key to wartime success warranted application in a number of areas, including unit structure, force mobilization, training, and coastal defenses, but insufficient progress occurred largely because the army leadership could not leverage this information to obtain adequate support both within the service and especially in Congress. For example, the Russo-Japanese War highlighted the advantages of standing brigades and divisions, but a lack of legislative concurrence constrained the War Department's response.[247] In his December 1905 State of the Union, Roosevelt declared that "the number of posts in which the Army is kept in time of peace should be materially diminished and the posts that are left made correspondingly larger."[248] In testimony before the Senate Military Affairs Committee the following March, Taft forcefully argued that establishing brigade and division posts would aid training.[249] When legislators, preferring the political benefits of dispersed bases, continued to prevent peacetime units bigger than a regiment, Taft used his discretionary power in the Philippines to establish experimental brigades and expanded some stateside bases to comparable size without acknowledging them as "brigade posts." In July 1907 the army issued General Order #146, which "authorized the organization of tactical brigades and divisions for the purpose of instruction."[250] These were notable steps, but most army garrisons remained regimental size or smaller.

Besides buttressing the perceived need for bigger standings units, the huge size of the Russian and Japanese armies, combined with the increased US role in world affairs, reinvigorated efforts to address mobilization requirements.[251] Difficulty in the Spanish-American War led to the Militia Act of 1903, or the Dick Act, which changed the traditional state militias into better-funded and theoretically more prepared National Guard units. The bill for the Dick Act initially included a one-hundred-thousand-man federal reserve force, but Secretary Root dropped it when opposition threatened the entire legislation. Observer reports on the importance of skilled soldiers led to a renewed attempt to obtain a federal reserve of up to fifty thousand veterans to fill out cadre units and reduce dependence on the lowly regarded National Guard. In his 1907 Annual Report, the chief of staff argued that "a suitable mobilization reserve" would do more to improve the efficiency of the line army than any single action.[252] The Interstate National Guard association, however, countered that expanding and upgrading its member units offered the best manpower solution. Ultimately, Bell appreciated that, given that the forces at Mukden totaled over 600,000 combatants, the service needed mobilization plans and programs that bolstered the potential contributions from reservists, the National Guard, and volunteers.

Yet enacting such measures proved challenging as doubts, especially among legislators, existed about the relevance of this lesson for the United States.[253] The War Department negotiated an amendment to the Dick Act, gaining more control over National Guard units in exchange for an increased federal subsidy and commitment to mobilize them before volunteers. National Guard forces, however, remained disproportionally infantry units, lacking the specialized troops and weapons, which proved so critical in Manchuria. Congress continued to reject a reserve force although a small breakthrough occurred in 1908 for doctors. Beyond a potential need for a million bodies, data from the Russo-Japanese War highlighted the military need for stockpiled weapons and munitions. Shortly after the conflict, the Army and Navy Joint Board investigated wartime ammunition requirements, but political resistance blocked the Ordnance chief's follow-up efforts. Since the army had muddled through previous conflicts, it was difficult for civilians, including veterans, to appreciate that the scale and complexity of modern war necessitated a more structured process. Repeated references to Manchuria by army preparedness advocates such as Bell and Pershing failed to correct that misperception.

Even more than obtaining larger peacetime units and better mobilization measures, the army sought to leverage the Russo-Japanese War lessons to enable more frequent and realistic training.[254] Difficulties during the Spanish-American War and a recognized requirement to practice modern warfare prompted the War Department to initiate large-scale, "more realistic" maneuvers in 1902. Reflective of the importance attached to this activity, the army over the next few years dispatched senior officers, including Chief of Staff Chaffee, GSSC Commandant Bell, and Major General Wood to observe French and German field exercises. The significantly expanded 1904 army maneuvers, however, generated congressional backlash over the cost and forced cancellation of the next year's underfunded activity. In his 1905 Annual Report, Secretary Taft declared that, based on recent combat, the lack of realistic large-scale, combined-arms maneuvers "is perhaps the most radical defect in our present system of military training."[255] He instructed the General Staff "to prepare a solution to this 'radical defect.'"[256] In January 1906 Roosevelt strongly endorsed the General Staff's plan, including summer field maneuvers, directing that "every effort be made to secure the appropriations from Congress, and if Congress will not take action that we do all we can with the appropriations that we have."[257]

Two months later the army initiated an unprecedented service-wide training program involving garrison (Phase 1) and field (Phase 2) activity.[258] In June Congress finally provided the necessary money for twenty thousand regular soldiers and fifty thousand militia to conduct summer maneuvers at seven locations. Lessons from the Russo-Japanese War not only contributed to gaining this money but also shaped the activity. Coffman notes that an emphasis on physical conditioning and realistic tactical problems, including night combat, almost certainly reflected the influence of information from the Far East. In particular, the Fort Riley effort, with the participation of the provisional field artillery regiment "to employ 'modern tactical methods,'" had been shaped by the Manchurian combat.[259] Above all, as Bell conveyed to Roosevelt in early 1907, "there is one thing the recent war taught us and it should never be forgotten, namely: that it takes time, a long time in fact, to make really *good* Infantry."[260]

Nonetheless, the army failed to employ the necessary rigor and realism to maximize the summer maneuvers' educational value.[261] Stebbins cautions that "although Chief of Staff Bell had begun extensive improvements of Army training in 1906, his efforts did not change entrenched attitudes overnight."[262] Beyond the old army's "parade ground mentality," sparse funds for training ammunition limited a soldier to sixty rounds a year, making it, as Charles McKenna points out, "'next to impossible' consistently to simulate conditions of war during maneuvers."[263] Moreover, overseas needs exacerbated the Corps of Engineers and Signal Corps' inability to properly support the field camps, frustrating the army leadership's desire to mimic the Far Eastern combat environment with field fortifications and modern communications. For the next round of biennial summer maneuvers (1908), the army sought more central control and evaluation, which March characterized as a "distinct improvement."[264] Designer and chief umpire of the Fort Riley effort, March, as Coffman points out, "called upon his Russo-Japanese War experience to emphasize night attacks and the increased effectiveness of modern weapons, particularly the machine gun."[265] Still, core deficiencies continued with the other efforts, and the objective of training realism was not met.

Most problematically, the maneuvers lacked sufficient combined-arms activity.[266] Progressive officers pushed for such instruction in accordance with their understanding of the Russo-Japanese War, but the increased presence of Leavenworth faculty, recent graduates, and students as umpires and instructors imbued the training with the infantry-centric bias articulated above. Moreover, addressing another war lesson (the need to develop reserve soldier skills) compromised combined-arms training as the War Department regarded National Guard participation as essential. Militia troops' limited ability handicapped designing activity that would enhance their improvement as well as facilitate instruction on large-scale advanced operations. The greater ease of obtaining money for National Guard training ensured their involvement, even if senior army officers shared the president's view that "it is ten times as important to maneuver the regulars."[267] In the Philippines, Pershing demonstrated what could have been achieved after taking command of one of the recently created experimental brigades.[268] The new brigadier general, who valuably exercised his unit in tactics employed in Manchuria, lamented in his memoirs that US officers and soldiers "rarely had the opportunity for practical field training especially the higher units."[269]

Finally, the Russo-Japanese War, which began with a surprise assault on Port Arthur, highlighted the continuing significance of coastal defenses and US deficiencies with fire control, searchlights, and submarine defenses (mines).[270] The effectiveness of mines prompted greater attention to this traditionally neglected weapon. As the artillery chief related at the end of 1904, concern about the inadequacy of US submarine defenses grew as "the most valuable lesson learned thus far from the Russo-Japanese war is their paramount importance for harbor protection."[271] The president echoed this view in his 1904 State of the Union and in February 1905 asked Taft "what action has been taken by the Chief of Artillery in this matter."[272] The secretary of war, chief of staff, and chief of artillery all enthusiastically endorsed a plan to complete submarine defenses at key US harbors and sought funds to double the number of students at the Submarine Defense School. Additionally, study of the war's long-range naval engagements prompted department approval of installing a coastal defense system with position-finding and fire control elements.[273] Finally, the War Department intensified pursuit of funds to equip harbor defenses with searchlights, given the increased likelihood of night combat as evidenced by the Far Eastern fight.

Russo-Japanese War lessons, however, proved insufficient to obtain the necessary resources.[274] Secretary of War Luke Wright declared at the end of 1908 that deficiencies remained in the critical areas of fire control, sea mines, searchlights, and electric power plants, despite aggressive lobbying.[275] When members of the coastal artillery sought budget prioritization given critical needs, legislators were not the only obstacles; as Linn points out, "their peers emphatically repudiated this claim," hampering even relatively cost-effective measures such as mines and searchlights.[276] Further creating headwinds, prominent military correspondent James Archibald informed the president that, based on his observations and careful study of key positions on the West Coast and Hawaiian Islands, submarines were vastly superior to mines in defending such places.[277] The president, however, remained supportive of army efforts after the chief of artillery replied that both the Russo-Japanese War and US exercises show the proposal to substitute submarines for completed harbor defenses "is preposterous."[278] Nonetheless, Chief of Staff Wood lamented in his 1910 Annual

Report that "the great reduction in appropriations has delayed the completion of important seacoast defenses and the installation of very necessary equipment."[279] The difficulty in judging the efforts to learn lessons is evident from this area. Practitioners of coastal defense identified foreign war findings, designed responses, and won support of senior officials such as the secretary of war and the president, but they failed to convince their army colleagues and legislators of the relative importance. Is this a failure or a proper result based on appropriate threat perception and prioritization?

Beneficial Application

Bolstered signal corps. Beyond these four primary issues, some clearly beneficial applications of lessons occurred as well as harmful rejections of information. Importantly, the illustrated value of new communication technology helped fuel army efforts to bolster the Signal Corps.[280] In his 1905 Annual Report, the chief signal officer noted the fighting showed "the indispensability of a fire-control and fire-direction system which, if properly devised and operated, must greatly increase the efficiency of field artillery."[281] The General Staff quickly approved such a system, and the Signal Corps equipped gunnery units with the necessary telephonic gear. In 1905 the army doubled the number of Signal Corps personnel and opened a dedicated Signal School. The following year the first wireless field platoon deployed to Cuba, and the service installed wireless stations at key bases in the United States and overseas territories. Bell emphasized in his 1907 Annual Report that as a "result of the last great war military men all over the world have come to recognize as an absolute essential to success in warfare the ability to keep the commander in chief in reliable communication with every fraction of his command."[282] The resultant expanded Signal Corps, however, struggled to meet the heavy operational and training demands for its services.

Renewed value of the bayonet. Whereas reports from the Russo-Japanese War energized pursuit of better communication, they prompted a sharp reversal in attitude about the bayonet.[283] The army in 1903 had replaced the knife bayonet with a rod bayonet as a part of the new Springfield rifle. The change reflected a belief that the modern gun's range and rate of fire would sharply diminish hand-to-hand fighting. The 1904 *IDR* dropped bayonet fighting exercises. Then observers began reporting extensive bayonet use. Roosevelt, in early January 1905, inquired about the bayonet's utility after meeting with the first returnees. In response, Ordnance chief Crozier modified his prior dismissal of the weapon, writing that the prevalence of night attack "heretofore considered almost impracticable . . . constitutes a new consideration" and "the question of its [the bayonet] use would therefore seem to be one which should properly be reopened."[284] Chief of Staff Chaffee, in late January, convened a special committee with Schuyler as president and March as recorder, which concluded that "the use of the bayonet in the Russo-Japanese war by both combatants shows conclusively that the bayonet is not a weapon of the past."[285] The chief of staff endorsed the committee's recommendation "that we should no longer attempt a combination tool, viz, bayonet and intrenching tool."[286] Beyond adopting a knife bayonet of the same length that the Japanese used, the army increased bayonet training. While the president questioned the bayonet's appropriateness given the nature of the American soldier, Bell in January 1907 emphasized to Roosevelt that "the experience of the Manchurian war demonstrated the necessity of such a weapon and we have no thought of giving it up."[287]

Better digging tools obtained. Similarly, the frequent use of entrenchments prompted an effort to provide soldiers the requisite digging tools.[288] In May 1905 Chaffee explained to an inquiring Taft that two years earlier the army, aiming to lighten the soldiers' load, had adopted the aforementioned combination bayonet-entrenchment tool.[289] Yet, by the time of this letter, war reports had resulted in the formation of the Entrenching Tools Board to review the subject. The ever-present March also served on this body, relaying how the Japanese used such implements, while Reichmann testified about the Russian experience. According to the committee's final report, information that the laying-down trench in Manchuria was "of little or no value in modern fighting . . . has been of first importance in determining the type of intrenching tool to be recommended."[290] The War Department quickly approved the board's conclusions that infantry kneeling or standing trenches could only practically be dug with a pick and spade, and companies should carry a two-foot rule, four hand axes, three wire cutters, fourteen pick mattocks, and forty-two shovels. Crozier reported that entrenching tools for sixty thousand men had been acquired by mid-1906.[291] After the Russo-Japanese War, American officers generally believed, as Capt. Sherwood Cheney uttered in a June 1908 AWC lecture, that "in future wars, there will be more digging and less marching."[292]

Enhanced medical capability. The unprecedented attention to the conflict's medical/health aspects reflected the importance attached to the subject, with findings leading to positive educational and doctrinal responses but limited organizational development.[293] After the war the GSSC Department of Military Art placed instruction on the "Care of Troops" into its core "Troops in Campaign" course, while West Point established a Department of Hygiene. The army successfully tested the placement of sanitary squads under unit medical officers during the 1906 and 1908 summer camps and instituted a correspondence school for medical officers on sanitation management. The War Department adopted the Japanese model of joint responsibility for medical and line officers in the *FSR* 1910 and revised the *Manual for the Medical Depart-ment*. The army also embraced an evacuation system from battalion aid stations to rear hospitals similar to the Japanese method. Although these steps were not matched with the necessary organizational reforms, the service successfully recruited about one hundred physicians and surgeons for its newly established medical reserve and added four ambulance companies to the wartime division in the *FSR* 1910.

One small but important finding that appears to have gained traction was the utility of dog tags.[294] Various identification means initiated by soldiers had been common since the Civil War, but the army had never adopted an official approach to facilitate recognition of wounded and deceased troops. Dr. Lynch endorsed the use of the circular ID discs that Japanese soldiers wore around their necks. On December 20, 1906, the War Department issued General Order 204, which stated that an aluminum identification tag "will be worn by each Officer and Enlisted Man of the Army whenever the field kit is worn."[295] The quartermaster general quickly procured seventy-five thousand such discs to be issued to soldiers. Although I have not been able to identify a direct link between information on the Japanese benefit from using such discs and the introduction of the "dog tag," the timing is highly suggestive.

Data Denial

Reactionary cavalry response. Offsetting these benefits, the army missed opportunities because the decision-makers deemed collected information as irrelevant or believed its application entailed culturally unappealing consequences. Best exemplifying the latter was the cavalry.[296] For some time the battlefield's increasing lethality had threatened the cavalry, which performed poorly during the Spanish-American War. Before retiring in 1903, Lt. Gen. Nelson Miles, commanding general of the US Army, recommended replacing horses in five cavalry regiments with automobiles, motorcycles, and bicycles. This initiative gained no traction, but concerned horse officers had initially hoped the Far East conflict would provide evidence boosting their importance. As discussed, observers quickly dashed such anticipation. Rather than try to apply lessons from an objective study of Manchuria, cavalry officers concentrated on undercutting any perceived relevance from the experience and somewhat inexplicably put more emphasis on traditional, European-style horse operations. They penned numerous articles highlighting the inferiority of Russian and Japanese horsemen and Manchuria's unsuitability for cavalry operations. In direct opposition to evidence, the 1906 Cavalry Board declared that "the charge is the decisive and most important and characteristic cavalry movement."[297] It added that future wars would involve "great cavalry combats, taking place far in advance of the main body," and battles "must be decided largely by shock action."[298] Given that US cavalry had never focused on that role, making such a declaration after the Russo-Japanese War seems bizarre. Essentially, American horse soldiers, fighting to preserve their position and believing their own rhetoric, performed "the most intricate mental gymnastics" to support all traditional missions.[299]

Although US cavalry had performed as dismounted infantry with notable success in prior wars, the branch fought emulation of the Japanese use of horse soldiers in this manner.[300] This bureaucratically based perspective reflected concern about being placed under command of infantry officers, even though—as the pro-cavalry Roosevelt acknowledged in early 1905—"the modern cavalryman is nine times out of ten on foot."[301] In his 1907 and 1908 Annual Reports, Bell suggested that such dismounted infantry could provide needed rapid reinforcement, given that the Russo-Japanese War showed foot soldiers struggled to possess sufficient mobility on the large, modern battlefields.[302] Yet, the 1912 Cavalry Service Regulations declared, "habitual reliance on dismounted action will weaken and eventually destroy initiative."[303] Rather than embrace the opportunity to satisfy an identified army requirement, the cavalry moved in a reactionary direction.

Engineering company deficiency unaddressed. In contrast to the aforementioned positive changes regarding the bayonet and digging tools, a lack of resources prevented a similar benefit for engineering companies.[304] Elaborate field fortifications evidenced in the Russo-Japanese War could not be constructed by infantrymen using basic tools. They required more knowledgeable and better-equipped engineering companies. Yet, despite Judson and Kuhn providing many examples of such units' value, insufficient funding and competing needs prevented establishing a sufficient number of such units. In his 1907 Annual Report a frustrated Bell noted the army had lacked an adequate number of engineers to meet field needs on at least ten occasions since the Russo-Japanese War.[305] Their inability to support summer maneuvers was problematic, as Kuhn explained in his *Notes on Field Fortifications*, given the difficulty in instructing line officers how to understand field fortifications' tactical employment. The army did take low-cost steps (e.g., increasing the study of such defenses at Fort Leavenworth; establishing a dedicated Field Engineering School; directing greater attention to such works in the revised *FSR*).

Sustained resistance to the increased force management and support capability. Regarding managing and supporting large field forces, the war's lessons failed to motivate a sufficient response as many legislators and some officers questioned not only the utility but the wisdom of such military capability.[306] March and other observers could not precipitate augmentation of the General Staff based on Japanese effectiveness. Similarly, findings about fielding and sustaining huge armies proved insufficient to overcome bureaucratic and political opposition. Prior to reports from

Manchuria, initiatives to assign a permanent body of trained enlisted personnel to the logistics departments as well as to establish a single Department of Supply (combining the Quartermaster, Subsistence, and Pay departments) had been blocked on Capitol Hill. Witnesses to the Far East fighting gave these efforts renewed impetus. Roosevelt wholeheartedly agreed, writing the chief of staff, in early July 1905, where "we really ought to perfect ourselves after the Japanese model is their commissary and quartermaster arrangements."[307] Urging legislative action, Chaffee, in his 1905 Annual Report, declared that "it is doubtful if any measure to improve the efficiency of the Army would be more far-reaching."[308] Yet the subsequent bill for a General Service Corps failed, as would follow-on attempts.

Neglect of food preparation cue. The area of food preparation represented another missed opportunity as progress after some initial steps stalled amid higher peacetime priorities.[309] In 1905 the army's food preparation "took a giant leap forward" with the long-advocated establishment of a school for bakers and cooks.[310] The commissary general, in late 1906, related to the General Staff that Lynch's report on food in the Russo-Japanese War had been "considered so valuable that (a) copy was sent to all Commissaries, for their information."[311] After observers' lavish praise of the Russian wheeled field kitchen's contribution to soldier health, the commissary general highlighted in his 1905 and 1906 Annual Reports the advantages of fireless cooking in the field. In a February 1906 report to Taft, the chief of staff wrote that "we are at a period now when rapid advance may be expected in our methods of preparing food for men in the field."[312] Yet "rapid advance" did not occur, as the army continued low-priority experimentation for the next decade. Thus, the AEF would largely be without such a benefit until the large-scale procurement of the Liberty rolling kitchen commenced in July 1918.

HOW DID THE NAVY APPLY ITS FINDINGS?

The first decade of the twentieth century was both a great and trying time for the US Navy, which had rapidly grown into one of the world's sea powers.[313] Six men served as secretary of navy under Theodore Roosevelt, but, as Oyos notes, "none of this rapid turnover mattered because Roosevelt intended to run the navy himself."[314] The large sums of money needed for the ambitious naval-building program ensured legislators considerable involvement. Closely allied with key members of Congress were the engineer-dominated technical bureaus (Construction and Repair, Steam Engineering, and Ordnance), which primarily designed warships. Yet line officers, in addition to their control over ship deployments and personnel assignments through the Bureau of Navigation, had gained greater input into warship plans in the prior half decade. An informal group of younger reformers, including Sims and Fiske, possessed the energy, intellectual prowess, and connections with a few progressive senior officers and Roosevelt to exert considerable pressure for improvement in warship design and sea operations.

The maritime threat perceptions of US officials shifted during the Russo-Japanese War.[315] The Japanese navy's wartime success combined with the European navies' diminished presence in the Pacific sharply elevated concern about the former. Roosevelt wrote Senator Henry Cabot Lodge shortly after the Battle of Tsushima that "most certainly the Japanese soldiers and sailors have shown themselves to be terrible foes. There can be none more dangerous in all the world."[316] Although the US Navy possessed a superior number of battleships, their presence primarily on the East Coast meant that the main fleet was essentially three times as far from San Francisco as the Japanese fleet at Yokohama. Still, the German naval buildup was also a growing source of anxiety, given its threat to American interests in the Caribbean. The Royal Navy's early 1905 decision to build the revolutionary fast, all-big-gun battleship *Dreadnought* alarmingly exploded the Anglo-German naval competition.

For some American naval officers, the *Dreadnought* produced excitement, but for others it inspired dread given the tightening budget environment.[317] In April 1904 Congress appropriated an almost 20 percent increase in the navy's budget. Seven months later, the service submitted its largest funding request ever, including construction of three battleships, five cruisers, six destroyers, six torpedo boats, and two colliers. Secretary Bonaparte argued that the amount, significantly reduced from bureau demands, "can hardly be deemed unreasonable," especially with the need to reach forty-eight battleships to base strong fleets in both the Atlantic and Pacific Oceans.[318] Now, however, after providing outlays that allowed the US Navy's expansion over fifteen years from thirteenth to second in number of capital ships (third in overall tonnage), congressional sentiment shifted against further fleet growth. In a March 1905 letter to Wood, even Roosevelt accepted the adequacy of the forty capital ships (twenty-eight battleships, twelve armored cruisers) in service, under construction, or authorized. He added in a September letter to Republican congressman Richard Bartholdt that "we ought to replace worn-out units, or obsolete units, by thoroughly efficient ones, but I do not think we now need any increase."[319] The navy obtained funding for two battleships in 1905 by promising that it would subsequently ask for one replacement battleship annually unless faced with unforeseen events. Unfortunately, construction of the *Dreadnought* threatened to make all preceding battleships obsolete. Such concern sparked Roosevelt to explore restricting *Dreadnought*-type vessels, but he determined that "after sounding France, Germany, England and Italy in the matter, I see no hope of accomplishing this result."[320] Regardless, naval expenditures declined by almost 20 percent over the next two years and remained below the 1905 level for five years.[321]

Although the navy wanted to maintain its recent battleship construction pace, the service struggled to operate its rapidly growing fleet.[322] In part, the president's willingness to slow fleet expansion reflected a necessity "while we bring up the personnel."[323] An extreme shortage of junior officers prompted the navy to graduate the senior class at Annapolis early in 1905. As a result, passed midshipman Chester Nimitz, serving on the battleship *Ohio*, found himself at a party in Tokyo where he met Admiral Togo shortly after Japan's victory.[324] Inadequate personnel combined with insufficient funds, especially for coal, constrained the navy's ability to act on the Japanese demonstrated value of training. In early 1906 the service actually had to request additional appropriations just to operate its ships. Ultimately, after much complaining, Congress provided the funds but "the fall-out placed extra scrutiny on all naval expenditures."[325] Personnel quality as well as quantity was an issue, with the navy continuing to employ a largely seniority-based system.[326] Merit-based promotions remained a decade away, but recognition that the average age of a Japanese battleship captain in the recent war was more than ten years younger than his American counterpart led to a policy essentially reducing the eligibility age for US Navy battleship skippers.

Beneficial Application

Although the aforementioned difference of opinion existed regarding some Russo-Japanese War lessons, the Navy Department ultimately embraced three main insights from the conflict—one strategic (superiority of concentration), one tactical (future engagements would take place at greater range), and one design (long-range combat required all-big-gun, fast battleships). These findings shaped policy for many years as students at Annapolis and the Naval War College studied and refought the Battle of Tsushima. If the measurement of lessons learned is whether they better prepared the US Navy for World War I, the answer of course is an overwhelming no, given the nature of maritime activity. Yet such a standard seems excessively narrow given the active role the service played in protecting US national security in the intervening dozen years. The navy eagerly and usefully implemented some of the most salient lessons for warship design of battleships and smaller surface warfare vessels as well as tactics and strategy in their use. The findings exerted influence instrumentally, instructionally, and inspirationally.

Embrace of the all-big-gun battleship. Although the navy benefited from data about the previously untested armored cruiser and destroyer classes, senior civilian officials and sailors eagerly focused on the war's reaffirmation of battleship primacy.[327] Thus, whether the Americans responded appropriately to the findings about battleships would largely be determinative of the service's overall success at applying lessons from the Russo-Japanese War. This question is complicated by the initially sharp schism over the appropriate takeaways, but, as noted, one interpretation gained ascendance within a year, enabling action. At the beginning of the twentieth century, improved technology and shooting tactics prompted calls for a radical new design—the all-big-gun battleship. Dewey, in October 1903, requested that the Bureau of Construction and Repair conduct a feasibility study. It did not respond to this request or subsequent ones, but proponents used a basic plan generated by Lt. Cdr. Homer Poundstone to pique Roosevelt's interest. In early October 1904 the president conveyed to the secretary of navy his regret that the newest battleship, the *New Hampshire*, would have intermediate 7-inch and 8-inch guns, as it "should be composed simply of 12″ and 11″ guns, and of a secondary battery of 3″ guns [for use against torpedo boats]."[328] While Congress, in March 1905, authorized the relatively slow *South Carolina* and *Michigan* as the first battleships without an intermediate battery, Mahan and most navy engineers regarded eliminating these guns as a significant error, which left the issue in flux as the Russo-Japanese War continued.

In pressing for the all-big-gun battleship, Dewey and the General Board had been influenced by Sargent's letters from the Far East on the increased range of naval battles, but navy leaders had to overcome considerable resistance.[329] As Oyos points out, "from 1904 to 1906 T. R. would be uncharacteristically indecisive on the all-big-gun ship question."[330] In a late December 1905 letter, the president wrote to Navy Secretary Charles Bonaparte that, given the Russians' claim "that the Japanese superiority in secondary battery fire was one of the main causes of their defeat," the service should not pursue the all-big-gun battleship until it had a proper understanding of what occurred.[331] By June 1906 proponents of this new type of warship had gained sufficient support of Roosevelt and key members of Congress to win authorization of the first true American dreadnought, the *Delaware*, with ten 12-inch guns and a twenty-one-knot speed. Even then, the matter remained in some doubt as the legislation did not specify design parameters, and Mahan's Battle of Tsushima assessment in that month's issue of *Proceedings* again raised doubt about the all-big-gun battleship. In early September 1906 the president wrote Converse that, based on the recent war, "I am not at all sure that the destructive effect to the personnel of the five and six-inch guns is something that we can safely disregard in eliminating these guns from our batteries."[332]

Support for the intermediate battery, however, soon collapsed for good. In response to Roosevelt soliciting his view, Sims provided the previously discussed, technically devastating rebuttal to Mahan's interpretation of the Russo-Japanese combat.[333] In late September the president replied that "I regard your article as convincing and have modeled the recommendation [for an all-big-gun battleship] in my message accordingly."[334] The following month Dewey emphasized the need for two, not one, dreadnought-types per year, as they were "now deemed necessary for maintaining sea power by the principal nations."[335] Reinforcing Sims's argument was Roosevelt's conversation with the recent Civilian Lord of the Admiralty, from which he relayed to the lieutenant commander that the "knowledge acquired by the British representatives with the Japanese fleet, [was] exactly the ground you took in your paper."[336] A few weeks later, in discussing the 1907 building program, the president wrote dreadnought skeptic Senator Eugene Hale, chairman of the Senate Naval Affairs Committee, that after careful study of the Russo-Japanese War, he was convinced of "advantages of having battleships carrying say eight twelve-inch guns, are very, very great."[337] Congress, in early 1907, appropriated funds for the already authorized *Delaware* as well as a second dreadnought, the *North Dakota*. The follow-ing year, the administration obtained funding for two more such battleships as well as congressional acceptance that two such vessels per annum represented the fleet requirement. Information from the Russo-Japanese War precipitated some other changes, including the replacement of the inadequate 3-inch small guns with 5-inch weapons to counter the increased torpedo range and addition of better underwater protection to guard against mines.[338]

Introduction of fire control. The all-big-gun battleship's viability depended on accurate long-range gunnery, which the war indicated was possible, but required improvements, especially "fire control" (an information-management system that coordinated at a central point simultaneous salvos from all guns on a warship).[339] Since his October 1902 appointment as inspector of target practice, Sims had achieved significant progress in fleet gunnery through the introduction of continuous aim fir-ing and rigorous practice. He and other progressive officers, however, believed that further gains required "fire control." The navy had not aggressively pursued this capability when "reports" of use in the Russo-Japanese battle inspired the Ameri-cans to take action. That is, armed with inaccurate information that fire control had provided the Japanese an advantage in combat, along with positive results from ex-perimentation by the battleship *Alabama*, Sims lobbied successfully for the late 1905 establishment of a special fire control board. Based on the board's recommendation, the navy placed spotters with telescopic sights aloft above the gun smoke, marking the service's first major step toward fire control. The Americans, responding to the vulnerability of warship superstructures demonstrated in the recent war, introduced "cage" masts fore and aft to protect these personnel and their equipment and to pro-vide redundancy. By 1908 US battleships deployed to sea with rudimentary versions of the initial system, although effective fire controlled, long-range gunnery would prove more difficult than anticipated and would require another decade of concep-tual and technological improvements. This example represents a productive applica-tion of a false finding, but such positive outcomes are likely to be rare.

Armored cruiser obsolescence. The US Navy deemphasized the armored cruiser after its limited utility in the Russo-Japanese War.[340] It had invested heavily in this vessel with the view, as Capt. Royal Bradford declared, that they "should be ready to fight almost anything, even a battleship."[341] Attitudes rapidly changed toward the previously much-touted "Big Ten" armored cruisers, of which six still remained to be commissioned when the Russo-Japanese War concluded. After that conflict, the navy abandoned consideration of it as a capital ship. Dewey explained that improved battleship gunnery had compromised the armored cruiser's effectiveness.[342] Writing the chairman of the House Naval Affairs Committee in June 1907, the president lamented that it would "have been infinitely better to have spent the money which actually was spent on them in the construction of first-class battleships."[343] In his Annual Report that year, Navy Secretary Victor Metcalf pointed out that the US and other leading navies planned no more armored cruisers.[344] European naval powers shifted to building battlecruisers, which combined big guns and fast speed by sacrificing armor, but the US preferred to concentrate on battleship construction.

Oceangoing destroyers. Even though the checkered wartime performance of destroyers and torpedo boats had reinforced some American sailors' disdain for small boat combat, the conflict enhanced the navy's understanding of their requirements, which led to more and better variants.[345] No new destroyers had been procured during the first four years of the Roosevelt administration, as much debate existed over proper ship characteristics and tactics. Information from the Russo-Japanese War prompted Roosevelt in mid-September 1904 to order formation of a torpedo boat board to review the destroyer's roles and requirements. Consideration of the fighting contributed heavily to its January 1905 assessment that this vessel should be optimized for fleet protection, with sufficient reliability and seaworthiness to stay with battleships. The navy leadership endorsed these findings, and Congress authorized the first three truly ocean-capable destroyers in June 1906. Of particular note, this and subsequent classes possessed five 3-inch guns, given, as the General Board stated, "the great value of a powerful battery had been emphasized in the Russo-Japanese War."[346] Whereas navy planning in 1903 required one destroyer per battleship, by 1907 it was four destroyers per battleship, causing the president in that year's State of the Union to declare that the US needed "plenty."[347] Congress concurred, approving twenty in Roosevelt's second term.

Selective Embrace between Conflicting Lessons

Fleet concentration over Pacific presence. While senior officers and civilian decision-makers stressed the war's important strategic lessons, two conflicting signals complicated application.[348] It is notable that the president and even Mahan accepted Bureau of Navigation Chief Rear Adm. Henry Taylor's caution against removing all battleships from the Pacific Ocean when the navy, in 1902, established the North Atlantic and Asiatic Fleets. The Far Eastern conflict prompted a reconsideration of that position by demonstrating the severe consequences for Russia not concentrating its capital ships. As Mahan emphasized, Americans considering the conflict needed to "SUBSTITUTE THEREIN, IN THEIR APPREHENSION, ATLANTIC FOR BALTIC, AND PACIFIC FOR PORT ARTHUR."[349] Contrasting the impetus to relocate the Pacific-based battleships to create a unified fleet, the enhanced threat perception of the Japanese encouraged maintaining a strong regional presence. In response, the General Board's committee on ship distribution proposed, during the 1904–5 winter, splitting the force between the Atlantic and Pacific Oceans. Acknowledging that such a basing scheme might weaken the navy on specific occasions, the committee argued it would deter foreign governments more than a far larger force an ocean away. The full General Board tabled this proposal as the perceived twenty-battleship level necessary to allow such a split would not be reached until 1907.

Ultimately, the navy prioritized the fleet concentration lesson even as increasing tension with Japan generated congressional and popular pressure from Western states for an enhanced presence in the Pacific.[350] In 1906 the navy replaced the Asiatic Fleet's battleship squadron with newly commissioned armored cruisers. Service leaders hoped the armored cruisers could at least function symbolically as "a kind of subsidiary capital ship."[351] With all battleships concentrated in the Norfolk-based Atlantic Fleet, the ONI stressed that the US possessed a decisive 3:1 advantage over the Japanese. When growing US–Japanese tension and a larger number of American battleships prompted the General Board's ship deployment subcommittee to call for relocating some of these vessels to the Pacific in early 1907, the full General Board rejected this proposal. It argued, as Ronald Spector notes, that "it would be better to station the *entire* fleet in the Pacific," although such relocation was not seriously considered.[352] After a concerned Mahan wrote the president about rumors of battleship transfers to the Pacific, the latter replied, "I have no more thought of sending four battleships to the Pacific while there is the least possible friction with Japan than I have of going thither in a rowboat myself."[353] Rather, sentiment existed for a temporary show of force, which evolved into the much-hyped Great White Fleet's unprecedented, fourteen-month circumnavigation (December 1907–February 1909). As Roosevelt prepared to vacate the White House, he advised Taft to never divide the fleet, citing such a mistake as the most critical factor in Russia's defeat.[354] The navy's commitment to concentration necessitated in a war with Japan that the Atlantic Fleet steam approximately twenty thousand miles to face a rested, ready enemy force in a decisive engagement. As Ian Toll observes, this approach "seemed to recap the dismal career of the Russian fleet under Admiral Rozhestvensky in 1905, and who could say with confidence that the result would not be the same?"[355]

Neglected Lessons

Mine warfare remained undeveloped. For other types of vessels, weapons, and systems, the navy either failed to respond to Russo-Japanese War cues (in part because of disagreement over their meaning) or proved unable to leverage the information to obtain necessary civilian support. The US Navy, like other sea powers, noted how the conflict vividly illustrated the danger of sea mines, but this recognition did not lead to the service developing capability in this area.[356] The prewar view of the mine as a coastal defense weapon in the army's domain had contributed to its prior neglect. In his 1905 Annual Report, Navy Ordnance Bureau chief Capt. Newton Mason claimed with regard to mines that "much progress was made as a result of a widely increased service interest in this branch, for which the events of the Russo-Japanese war are perhaps largely responsible."[357] The department procured several European mine types, including the Elia that McCully praised for its effectiveness off Port Arthur. Yet the Americans conducted only modest experimentation with them and achieved no meaningful increase in preparedness. Rather, reflective of the service focus on battleships, the primary reaction to this lesson was designing these vessels to better withstand detonations. Such a step fit within the basic service culture, whereas developing better mines, minelaying, and minesweeping capability did not. Almost inexplicably, Gregory Hartmann and Scott Truver point out that the US Navy before World War I remained "in much the same position with respect to mine warfare that it had been in at the conclusion of the Civil War; it had no usefully functioning mines."[358] The department's request for a minelaying vessel led to the slow, low-priority conversion of an old protected cruiser beginning in 1908, but it failed to lay down its first minesweeper until 1917.

Regular cruisers not impacted. While the navy responded to the lesson on the armored cruiser's limited utility by ending their acquisition, it largely ignored findings related to regular cruisers amid dislike for and disagreement over collected data. Effusive praise of Japanese cruisers' use of wireless by McCully and Schroeder did not prompt enthusiastic embrace of wireless telegraphy, which had been first introduced on US warships in 1903.[359] Considerable culturally based resistance to this important technology remained among line officers fearing a loss of independence. Although protected and unprotected cruisers had, as Converse in his 1905 Annual Report noted, "rendered invaluable aid" during the conflict, these classes did not see a boost analogous that occurred with destroyers.[360] Prewar concern that protected cruisers lacked the speed to keep up with the increasingly fast battleships led to the April 1904 authorization of three experimental, lightly protected scout cruisers. The technical bureaus argued that the war showed the utility of this *Chester*-class, but the General Board contended that it demonstrated cruisers needed to be larger and faster. The division contributed to congressional refusal to fund additional cruisers in the post-Russo-Japanese War years.

Support ships did not generate much interest. Reports on the nature of battle highlighted the importance of noncombat ships, but they remained a lower priority for the navy and frustratingly of even less concern to legislators. For example, the General Board, after learning about the recent combat's intensity, sought an ammunition supply vessel, which, as Dewey explained in 1906, was "considered necessary on account of the present great rapidity of fire, and the probable early exhaustion of ships' ammunition supply in battle."[361] Yet the navy obtained neither the requested money for such a ship nor the nearly $5 million ($139.5 million constant dollars) worth of reserve ammunition sought.[362] The Baltic Fleet's challenging efforts to obtain coal during the long transit to Tsushima reiterated the already appreciated need for oceangoing colliers.[363] The first two such fleet colliers had been authorized in 1904, but not much progress had occurred when Dewey in late 1906 urged the construction of two more as soon as the initial vessels were complete.[364] The admiral described them as "an indispensable adjunct to a fighting fleet," and colliers of sufficient speed and capacity could not be improvised from existing merchant marine ships.[365] It took the experience of the Great White Fleet, however, for the navy to obtain funding for five fleet colliers at the end of the decade. Despite Japan's benefit from purpose-built hospital ships prompting the navy to reiterate with urgency its post-Spanish-American War desire for two such vessels, Congress would not allocate the necessary funds.[366] The first dedicated hospital ship would only be laid down after US entry into World War I.

CONCLUSION

When 1st Lt. George Marshall toured the Manchurian battlefields in 1913, the Russo-Japanese War remained a reference point of modern war for US soldiers and sailors, but it would soon be eclipsed by a much greater conflagration.[367] One would expect World War I to consume the American army, especially given European combatants' claims of astonishment about the nature of the fighting even though, as Bailey points out, "any officer with his extensive knowledge of the Russo-Japanese War should have believed his views confirmed rather than voiced surprise."[368] The War Department dispatched officers, including now lieutenant colonel Kuhn, to support the work of military attachés, but belligerents with the exception of Great Britain restricted observers' access far more than in past practice.[369] More problematic, as Clark criticizes, "in contrast to the curiosity evidenced during the Russo-Japanese War, the prevailing mood in the U.S. Army from 1914 was smug certainty."[370] He adds that American officers dismissively concluded that "the European armies simply failed to apply what were still assumed to be correct tactical principles."[371] Unsurprisingly, when the United States finally entered the war in April 1917, its forces were woefully unprepared. It would be over a year before the AEF contributed meaningfully on the battlefield, and even then its soldiers mostly employed British and French weapons. US Army officers struggled to grasp the essentiality of infantry-artillery coordination as the key to modern combat despite this being a lesson available from the Russo-Japanese War and stressed by many American observers of that conflict. While "Leavenworth men" (graduates of the GSSC) gained great praise based on their ability to keep the large AEF functioning, their faith in the rifleman to overcome all proved badly misguided.[372] Dastrup notes that "modern field artillery weapons and equipment existed, but the Army lacked qualified personnel to exploit the new technology."[373]

In contrast to their army brethren, American naval officers had good reason to be surprised about World War I's naval component, which entailed fundamental differences from the Russo-Japanese War.[374] Yet, for US sailors, the submarine-centered action appeared largely irrelevant, and they maintained focus on major fleet engagement. When now rear admiral Sims, after being dispatched to London as senior naval representative in March 1917, sent back word of a desperate need for destroyers and antisubmarine craft, the navy's prior neglect in developing such capabilities complicated responding to the requirements for convoy escort. The same was true for mine warfare, as the service possessed only two minelayers and a small, obsolete mine inventory, delaying for months its ambitious plan to establish a 240-mile-wide minefield ("the North Sea Mine Barrage") between Scotland and Norway.

Although today the Russo-Japanese War barely registers among even the historically aware, at the time American military and civilian leaders eagerly anticipated its potential to provide insights into the dynamics of modern war. It had been decades since great-power armies met on the battlefield and even longer since their navies had a full-scale engagement. The expectation of valuable information prompted the US government to underwrite a vast collection effort that would include sending twenty-three officers to the Far East at varying points of the war. In comparison to the Crimean case, the US military engaged a more committed and intelligent discovery approach. Most importantly, the army and navy moved with dispatch to place generally excellent officers in the war zone once the fighting commenced. Still, constraints affected the collection of information, including a lack of local language skills, insufficiently senior officers, and especially sporadic and limited combatant cooperation.

Despite host restrictions, army observers identified and reported notable developments in the ground war. As Greenwood points out, their reports "provided a great wealth of invaluable and irreplaceable impressions and facts, interpretations and experiences, of the war in Manchuria."[375] The Americans appropriately stressed a shocking increase in the scale of war and the value of peacetime preparation and planning. They highlighted the shift in artillery from direct fire to indirect fire, the widespread use of the telephone, and the sharply increased role for machine guns. US observers also identified the expanded use of field fortifications and greater lethality of combat as well as belligerent responses to this environment such as night fighting and the associated surprising utility of the bayonet.

Historians criticize this effort for its failure to produce recognition of the modern battlefield's fundamental shift toward the defensive and the deficiency of an infantry-centric approach, but is this judgment warranted? As discussed, some observers, particularly those attached to the Russian side, did stress the implications of the defenders' tactical strength against frontal assaults. The problem occurred when Americans on the other side pointed out that the attacking Japanese won every battle and the war. What accounted for their success prompted a myriad of explanations—soldiers' superior spirit and determination, greater combat skill, prodigious fire support, and operational/tactical adjustments. These divergent reasons complicated identifying the extent to which the tactical offense/defense balance was tilting toward the latter and the resultant operational and strategic implications. The battles revealed that successful attacks required greater resources, produced higher casualties, and left worn-down victors less able to exploit their success, but stalemated trench warfare had not been observed and thus was not reported.

One could argue that greater imagination should have precipitated a more insightful appreciation by witnesses of the increasingly defense-dominant battlefield, but such assessments represent a much harder challenge than identifying specific weapons or tactics, especially when a preexisting preference exists for the status quo. As Yigal Sheffy explains, even though all appreciated modern weapons increased destructiveness, "the more abstract meanings of the subject remained vague to contemporaries . . . they therefore received contradictory interpretations, while observers from the same army reached completely different conclusions on the same specific subject."[376] Given this context, commentators on lessons learned from the Russo-Japanese War have found that many officers focused on finding ammunition to bolster the existing and preferred notion of offensive supremacy.[377] Historians such as Bailey and Sheffy stress this dynamic in the European armies, but American officers reacted similarly, despite being less "bound by any nationalistic school of

military thought."³⁷⁸ As discussed, the outsize influence of Morrison on army educational and doctrinal development ensured that his conservative, infantry-centric
understanding of the conflict carried enormous weight. Deserving the most criticism was the infantry's dismissiveness about the vital need for effective fire support
to compete on the modern battlefield and the army's resultant failure to develop
combined-arms proficiency.

The War Department's decision to forgo an officially sanctioned analysis of
the fighting that attempted to reconcile the range of observer interpretations on
the offense/defense balance diminished the potential to appreciate the degree of
change and battlefield requirements. Rather than establish a body or clearinghouse
to analyze and deconflict reports, the army published hundreds of pages from individual witnesses containing many contrasting observations and insights. Given the
prevailing view in favor of an offensive-orientation and infantry-centric approach,
quite likely any effort to form an institutional judgment would have reinforced this
perspective with the bonus of official sanction. Still, the absence of any attempt to
resolve differences ensured that the status quo understanding remained operative. A
well-structured, balanced effort, minimizing cultural and bureaucratic influences—
undoubtedly difficult to establish and execute—has the best potential to distill accurate lessons, especially those disruptive of current practice. Such efforts require
strong service leadership, a quality not present at the time even though Chief of Staff
Bell himself was open-minded about the changes in modern battle.

The navy similarly did not pursue an officially sanctioned assessment, but sailors faced an even greater hurdle to discovery as they had to debate lessons without any Americans present at the engagements. Conveyance of findings took place
piecemeal on the pages of *Proceedings*, in correspondence between US officers in the
Asiatic Fleet and Washington, in informal conversations with British naval officials,
and at educational forums. For broad, strategic issues, this was not problematic as
the value of fleet concentration and central role of the battleship were abundantly
evident. Yet, regarding battleship design and tactics, it proved a hindrance. Given
two contrasting preexisting perspectives, naval officers grasped at different metrics to
explain what happened (e.g., volume of fire [Mahan] versus accuracy of fire [Sims]).
Moreover, analysts of sea battles tended to identify the data in a way that reflected
favorably on their preferred interpretation (e.g., Mahan and Sims contrasting understanding of Togo's speed advantage at Tsushima). Still, the *Proceedings*-centered debate allowed Sims and his allies to gain the upper hand by weight of argument. The
British observer presence with the Japanese fleet assisted this process as information
filtered to the Americans. Given that Admiral Togo's naval victories reinforced prior
sentiment, the war's core lessons did not involve any painful adjustment in American sailors' worldview, unlike for soldiers. They almost gleefully took note of the

torpedo's poor performance and the nonuse of submarines ("pigboats"), although the danger from mines could not be denied.

The application of lessons, or the failure thereof, has been the most criticized stage of the learning process regarding the Russo-Japanese War for the army. Typically, Greenwood points out that "many of the conclusions reached and recommendations made by the Army officers upon their return to the United States were simply rejected."[379] The War Department leadership, to its credit, attempted to transfer findings to key audiences through assigning returned observers as (1) organizers and judges of exercises/tests, (2) members of investigating committees, and (3) leadership positions at educational institutions. Plus, some of the most talented observers were placed in charge of new, experimental units (e.g., Pershing at Fort McKinley, with its composite brigade; Macomb, with the Fort Riley field artillery regiment). As the chapter shows, several findings, deemed relevant and actionable, influenced choices, but judging responses as either a success or a failure depends significantly on the evaluation standard. Application of informational cues follows a progression of stages: (1) validating findings through testing/exercises; (2) adjusting educational curriculum, modifying doctrine, developing weapons, and reforming organizations; and (3) acquiring the necessary materiel and conducting frequent and widespread training with new doctrine/equipment/organizations to develop proficiency. Completion of this progression requires buy-in by necessary decision-makers operating at distinct levels—practitioners, senior service leadership, and executive officials and legislators. No major finding traversed all these stages and levels, but the army benefited to some degree from the partial application of notable lessons in the preparation for war (e.g., peacetime operational plans, training), conduct of war (e.g., indirect fire, night attacks) and support of war (e.g., telephones, medical corps).

These accomplishments, however, did not significantly upgrade combat capability, as branch components failed to take advantage of the Russo-Japanese War, albeit in distinct ways. The cavalry, not surprisingly, completely rejected information from a war that signaled its declining influence. This branch foresaw danger from acknowledgment of not only this overarching finding but the war's indication of a potentially valuable adjustment—use as highly mobile, dismounted infantry—given that it entailed subordination to foot soldiers. The attitude highlights the difficulty of applying "disruptive" lessons. While the infantry responded to clear cues such as the bayonet's surprising utility and the need for more entrenching tools, such reactions did not directly challenge its understanding of war. Observers' divergent reporting on frontal assault viability, the need for field artillery and machine-gun support, and offensive and defensive balance left in question what action to take, if any. The infantry ultimately resolved the problem by selectively embracing information that fit with its preexisting preferences. In particular, Morrison, with the Japanese army early in the conflict, prioritized his view that the Russo-Japanese War validated a retrograde infantry-centric approach to battle. This interpretation contrasted with other observers, such as March and Reichmann, but Morrison exercised an outsize influence on the army in the years after the conflict through his position at Fort Leavenworth and his role as the main drafter of infantry guidance.

Frustratingly, the army proved unable to develop a strong machine-gun capability. Although some skepticism persisted about this weapon, many American soldiers as well as Chief of Staff Bell and President Roosevelt regarded its growing use throughout the Russo-Japanese War as illustrative of the future. Yet, lacking an institutional base, the machine-gun program suffered from a time-consuming, distracting debate about its proper organizational place even after Manchuria clearly demonstrated it belonged in the infantry. Within that branch, key officers such as Morrison were somewhat dismissive of its value in part because of limited expectation to engage in the mass, static-type battles that would reflect much of World War I fighting. Thus, no bureaucratic entity exerted a concentrated effort to foster reform and obtain resources as occurred with the field artillery's application of relevant lessons. Moreover, the machine-gun findings were of more inspirational than informational value, as the war—with some minor exceptions (e.g., using guns in pairs)—did not provide clear direction on how to employ the weapon, again unlike for the field artillery. It did spark testing after the war, with provisional platoons and an experimental company, but these efforts did not lead to the development of requisite capabilities.

While the lack of machine-gun development was frustrating, most disappointing was the army's inability to obtain proficiency with indirect-fire support, undermining or at least greatly circumscribing the value of changes to the field artillery prompted by findings from the Russo-Japanese War. Evaluating the application of lessons regarding the field artillery is difficult. The army, within two years, responded to cues from the conflict by adopting indirect fire as primarily a fire-support method, separating the field artillery from the coastal artillery, and establishing larger peacetime units (e.g., battalions and regiments). Advocacy for these changes predated the Russo-Japanese War, but it provided the critical impetus for their implementation. Alas, educational, training, and resource deficiencies over the ensuing decade, exacerbated by the infantry's discounting the importance of cooperation, meant when US gunners in 1917 marched into twentieth-century warfare, they were unable to provide the required type of modern fire support. The failure to obtain proficiency with indirect-fire method does not vitiate the benefit derived from study of the Russo-Japanese War, but it highlights the challenge of fully applying lessons without shared agreement on a subject deemed of high priority.

Division on the proper lessons regarding fleet engagements and warship design also affected the navy, but advocates of change generally won the interpretive struggle, especially in support of the all-big-gun battleship. Whether such lessons would have exerted sufficient influence to win approval for the *Delaware*—America's first dreadnought—without the prior British decision to build the *Dreadnought* is unknowable. Yet, especially given Sargent's letters to Dewey and the latter's role in the decision, American findings about the war can be said to have been applied at a minimum as strong reinforcement. Insights regarding armament, armor, shooting, and superstructure improved the design of these mammoth vessels. Sailors took note of specific design and tactical lessons for other warship types and supporting vessels. Still, with the exception of the destroyer, their application proved limited and sporadic, given lower prioritization relative to the battleship in the smaller budgets of the postconflict years. Although senior naval officers would have welcomed congressional funding of such ships, they could comfortably tolerate their neglect and an increasingly top-heavy fleet because they regarded themselves as embracing the war's overarching lesson—concentrating all battleships in a single fleet remained the key to sea dominance. Such learning may not rank with the discovery of a new wonder weapon or revolutionary tactical innovation, but it has importance for improving military preparedness and should not be dismissed.

This case provides multiple examples of how accepting one lesson undermines addressing another significant finding (e.g., army inclusion of reservists in summer maneuvers hampered combined-arms training for active-duty soldiers, navy fleet concentration weakened presence in the Pacific). Perhaps no lesson had a more direct influence on US military policy than the difficulty of safeguarding naval bases from land-side attack as Japan exhibited at Port Arthur. This finding prompted a previously deferential army to vigorously oppose establishing the main Pacific naval base at Subig Bay in the Philippines and ultimately prevent its construction. Without the analogous Port Arthur example, it is difficult to see prewar army critics of this base gaining the War Department's support, let alone prevailing over the navy. The army's position was correct, but the warranted victory came at the cost of poisoning interservice relations. This effect compromised another key lesson learned from the Far East, as observers noted cooperation between Japan's army and navy contributed significantly to their military effectiveness. In a lecture on the Russo-Japanese War, even the tireless naval booster Mahan criticized soldiers and sailors for "cooperation" efforts that consisted of attempts at supremacy when "coordination of the two, which I conceive to be the proper solution, can scarcely be said to exist."[380] How to deconflict and address such conflicting lessons is an interesting and important question.

This chapter exemplifies well both the potential of and danger from studying foreign wars. As the first major conflict of the twentieth century, the Russo-Japanese War occurred at a transitional time for warfare as well as US military institutions. Regarding ground combat, it signaled a new era that, with a better understanding of what happened and more imagination of what it signaled, could have profited

army preparedness for the future battlefield. For naval combat, it marked the climax
of centuries of the seas being dominated by battleships (or their earlier equivalents).
Alas, soldiers generally failed to appreciate the changes that required unappealing
departures from their cultural and bureaucratic preferences, while sailors embraced
the lessons that reinforced their cherished way of doing things even though they
would soon be under assault from below and above the water.

NOTES

Epigraph: Quoted in John Greenwood, "The American Military Observers of the Russo-
Japanese War (1904–1905)" (PhD diss., Kansas State University, 1971), 491–92.

1. Theodore Roosevelt to Theodore Roosevelt Jr., February 10, 1904, in *The Letters of Theodore Roosevelt*, vol. 4: *The Square Deal, 1903–1905*, ed. Elting Morison (Cambridge, MA: Harvard
University Press, 1951), 274.

2. Quoted in Greenwood, "American Military Observers," 121.

3. Rotem Kowner, *The A to Z of the Russo-Japanese War* (Lanham, MD: Scarecrow, 2009), 413.

4. Greenwood, "American Military Observers," 101, 110–13, 116, 130, 132; Maureen
O'Connor, "In the Eye of the Beholder: Western Military Observers from Buena Vista to
Plevna" (PhD diss., Harvard University, May 1996), 271–72, 410–50; and Jeffrey Dorwart, *The
Office of Naval Intelligence: Birth of America's First Intelligence Agency, 1865–1918* (Annapolis, MD:
Naval Institute Press, 1979), 9–12, 28.

5. For paragraph, see "Report of Capt. Peyton C. March, General Staff, Observer with the
Japanese Army," and "Report of Lieut. Col. Walter S. Schuyler, General Staff, Observer with
the Russian Army," in *Reports of Military Observers Attached to the Armies in Manchuria during
the Russo-Japanese War*, Part 1 (Washington, DC: Government Printing Office, 1906), 25–26,
105–6, respectively; Greenwood, "American Military Observers," 113, 121–30, 135–36, 149–51,
155–58, 173, 183, 191, 230–32, 249, 283–84, 330–32; Edward Coffman, *The Hilt of the Sword: The
Career of Peyton March* (Madison: University of Wisconsin Press, 1966), 22–23, 26–27; Roosevelt
to Theodore Roosevelt Jr., February 19, 1904, in Morison, *Letters*, 4:732; and Roosevelt to
Lloyd Griscom, February 22, 1904, and Roosevelt to Robert Roosevelt, February 27, 1904, in
Theodore Roosevelt Center Digital Library (hereafter, TRCDL), Dickinson State University.

6. For paragraph, see "Report of Capt. Peyton C. March," 5, 24–25, 55; "Report of Capt.
John F. Morrison, 20th Infantry, Observer with the Japanese Army," and "Report of Capt. Carl
Reichmann, 17th Infantry, Observer with the Russian Forces," in *Reports of Military Observers
Attached to the Armies in Manchuria during the Russo-Japanese War*, Part 1 (Washington, DC:
Government Printing Office, 1906), 57 and 86, and 173–75, respectively; Maj. Joseph Kuhn,
Corps of Engineers, "Report on Russo-Japanese War," in *Reports of Military Observers Attached
to the Armies in Manchuria during the Russo-Japanese War*, Part III (Washington, DC: Govern-
ment Printing Office, 1906), 5; Greenwood, "American Military Observers," 136, 158, 172–73,
182–83, 217, 256, 259–74, 280–82, 306; "Report of Lieut. Col. Walter S. Schuyler," 101–2, and
"Report of Capt. William V. Judson, Corps of Engineers, Observer with the Russian Forces in

Manchuria," in *Reports of Military Observers Attached to the Armies in Manchuria during the Russo-Japanese War*, Part V (Washington, DC: Government Printing Office, 1907), 147.

7. Quoted in Greenwood, "American Military Observers," 185.

8. For paragraph, see "Report of Capt. Peyton C. March," 5; "Report of Capt. John F. Morrison," 57; "Report of Capt. Carl Reichmann," 173; Greenwood, "American Military Observers," 198, 200–201, 210, 216–17, 305, 357–59, 366–72; Coffman, *Hilt of the Sword*, 31; and Adna Chaffee to William Loeb, January 14, 1905, in TRCDL.

9. Quoted in Greenwood, "American Military Observers," 200.

10. For paragraph, see "Report of Capt. John F. Morrison," 57; Kuhn, "Report on Russo-Japanese War," 5; Chaffee to Loeb, January 12 and 17, 1905, in TRCDL; "Report of Col. Valery Havard, Assistant Surgeon-General, USA, Observer with the Russian Forces in Manchuria," in *Reports of Military Observers Attached to the Armies in Manchuria during the Russo-Japanese War*, Part II (Washington, DC: Government Printing Office, 1906), 5; "Report of Maj. Charles Lynch, Medical Department, General Staff, USA, Observer with the Japanese Forces in Manchuria," in *Reports of Military Observers Attached to the Armies in Manchuria during the Russo-Japanese War*, Part IV (Washington, DC: Government Printing Office, 1907), 11; "Report of Capt. William V. Judson," 147; Greenwood, "American Military Observers," 305–8, 311, 322–25, 328, 331; and Gene Smith, *Until the Last Trumpet Sounds: The Life of General of the Armies John J. Pershing* (New York: Wiley, 1998), 80, 83–88.

11. For paragraph, see "Report of Col. John Van R. Hoff, Assistant Surgeon-General, USA, Observer with the Russian Forces in Manchuria," in *Reports of Military Observers Attached to the Armies in Manchuria during the Russo-Japanese War*, Part II (Washington, DC: Government Printing Office, 1906), 113; "Report of Lieut. Col. Edward J. McClernand, 1st Cavalry, Observer with the Japanese Forces in Manchuria," in *Reports of Military Observers Attached to the Armies in Manchuria during the Russo-Japanese War*, Part V (Washington, DC: Government Printing Office, 1907), 8; John J. Pershing, *My Life before the World War, 1860–1917* (Lexington: University of Press Kentucky, 2013), 222–27; Smith, *Until the Last*, 84, 87–90; and Greenwood, "American Military Observers," 225–26, 232–35, 331–35, 374.

12. Quoted in Smith, *Until the Last*, 87.

13. For paragraph, see Greenwood, "American Military Observers," 2, 6, 150, 375–82, 393–420, 427, 432, 446.

14. For example, see L. Z. Soloviev, *Actual Experiences in War: Battle Action of the Infantry: Impressions of a Company Commander* (Washington, DC: Government Printing Office, July 1906).

15. For paragraph, see Greenwood, "American Military Observers," 104, 113, 144, 147–48; Bruce Swanson, *A Plain Sailorman in China: Life and Times of Commander I. V. Gillis* (Annapolis, MD: Naval Institute Press, 2012), 51–56, 61–62, 67; William Braisted, *The US Navy in the Pacific, 1897–1909* (Annapolis, MD: Naval Institute Press, 2008), 57, 154, 159–61, 168; Dorwart, *Office of Naval Intelligence*, 28, 31, 45, 51–52, 55–56, 68, 70, 78–80; Newton McCully, *The McCully Report: The Russo-Japanese War, 1904–05* (Annapolis, MD: Naval Institute Press, 1977), viii, 5, 26; and Charles Darling to Roosevelt, February 6, 1904, William Moody to Robley Evans, February 9, 1904, General Order #154, March 11, 1904, and H. C. Taylor to Roosevelt, August 23, 1904, all in TRCDL.

16. For paragraph, see Swanson, *Plain Sailorman*, 59, 61–68, 72; Dorwart, *Office of Naval Intelligence*, 80–81; Greenwood, "American Military Observers," 145–48; Kowner, *A to Z*, 30,

168, 280–81, 388; and McCully, *McCully Report*, v, viii–ix, 27, 41, 47–48, 89, 108, 137, 149, 166–70, 194–95, 212–16, 255–56.

17. For paragraph, see Swanson, *Plain Sailorman*, 66, 73–75; and Dorwart, *Office of Naval Intelligence*, 81–82.

18. Quoted in Richard Challener, *Admirals, Generals, and American Foreign Policy, 1898–1914* (Princeton, NJ: Princeton University Press, 1973), 223.

19. For paragraph, see George Converse, Report of the Chief of the Bureau of Navigation (hereafter, *ARND/BON* 1905), September 30, 1905, in *Annual Reports of the Navy Department for the Year 1905* (Washington, DC: Government Printing Office, 1906), 368; Swanson, *Plain Sailorman*, 77, 93–99; Ronald Spector, *Admiral of the New Empire: The Life and Career of George Dewey* (Columbia: University of South Carolina Press, 1988), 173–75; William McBride, *Technological Change and the United States Navy, 1865–1945* (Baltimore: Johns Hopkins University Press, 2000), 71–73; and William Vacca, "Learning about Military Effectiveness: Examining Theories of Learning during the Russo-Japanese War" (PhD diss., Rutgers University, 2009), 194, 364–65.

20. Trent Hone, *Learning War: The Evolution of Fighting Doctrine in the US Navy, 1898–1945* (Annapolis, MD: Naval Institute Press, 2018), 30.

21. Seaton Schroeder, "Gleanings from the Sea of Japan," US Naval Institute *Proceedings* 32, no. 1 (March 1906): 47–93; and Alfred Mahan, "Reflections, Historic and Other, Suggested by the Battle of the Sea of Japan," US Naval Institute *Proceedings* 32, no. 2 (June 1906): 447–71.

22. R. D. White, "With the Baltic Fleet at Tsushima," US Naval Institute *Proceedings* 32, no. 2 (June 1906): 597–620.

23. William Sims, "The Inherent Tactical Qualities of the All-Big-Gun, One-Caliber Battleships of High Speed, Large Displacement, and Gun-Power," US Naval Institute *Proceedings* 32, no. 4 (December 1906): 1337–66.

24. Lyman Cotten, "The Naval Strategy of the Russo-Japanese War," US Naval Institute *Proceedings* 36, no. 1 (March 1910): 42.

25. J. P. Clark, *Preparing for War: The Emergence of the Modern US Army, 1815–1917* (Cambridge, MA: Harvard University Press, 2017), ix–xi; and Brian McAllister Linn, *The Echo of Battle: The Army's Way of War* (Cambridge, MA: Harvard University Press, 2007), 104–5.

26. Greenwood, "American Military Observers," 426.

27. Kuhn, "Report on Russo-Japanese War," 227.

28. "Report of Capt. William V. Judson," 216.

29. "Report of Capt. John F. Morrison," 98.

30. For paragraph, see Kuhn, "Report on Russo-Japanese War," 214, 229–30; "Report of Capt. William V. Judson," 173; "Report of Capt. Peyton C. March," 31–37; "Report of Capt. John F. Morrison," 79, 83; "Report of Lieut. Col. Walter S. Schuyler," 114, 137; "Report of Capt. Carl Reichmann," 261–64; and Carl Reichmann, "Chances in War," *Journal of the US Infantry Association* 3, no. 1 (July 1906): 26–27.

31. "Report of Capt. William V. Judson," 173.

32. Kuhn, "Report on Russo-Japanese War," 230.

33. For paragraph, see "Report of Capt. John F. Morrison," 67–68; Kuhn, "Report on Russo-Japanese War," 56–57, 87, 228; "Report of Maj. Charles Lynch," 17; "Report of Lieut. Col. Edward J. McClernand," 39, 46, 140; and "Report of Capt. William V. Judson," 191–92.

34. "Report of Capt. Carl Reichmann," 185.

35. Reichmann, "Chances in War," 18.

36. Kuhn, "Report on Russo-Japanese War," 67.

37. Kuhn, 74.

38. Greenwood, "American Military Observers," 467.

39. For paragraph, see "Report of Capt. William V. Judson," 149, 217; McCully, *McCully Report*, 65; J. Franklin Bell to Roosevelt, January 10, 1907, in TRCDL; Vacca, "Learning about Military Effectiveness," 234, 333; and James Sisemore, "Russo-Japanese War, Lessons Not Learned" (Master's thesis, USA Command and General Staff College, 2003), 25, 29–30, 49.

40. "Report of Capt. Carl Reichmann," 180.

41. "Report of Capt. William V. Judson," 208.

42. Linn, *Echo of Battle*, 103.

43. For paragraph, see "Report of Capt. John F. Morrison," 98–99; "Report of Lieut. Col. Walter S. Schuyler," 137; "Report of Capt. Carl Reichmann," 270; "Report of Lieut. Col. Edward J. McClernand," 20–22, 84–85, 124–25; Bell to Roosevelt, January 10, 1907, p. 1, in TRCDL; and Greenwood, "American Military Observers," 415, 469, 486–87.

44. "Report of Lieut. Col. Edward J. McClernand," 85.

45. For paragraph, see "Report of Capt. John F. Morrison," 67; Kuhn, "Report on Russo-Japanese War," 83, 90; "Report of Lieut. Col. Edward J. McClernand," 120–21, 143, 205–6; "Report of Capt. William V. Judson," 205–6; and "Report of Capt. Carl Reichmann," 279.

46. "Report of Lieut. Col. Edward J. McClernand," 120–21.

47. For paragraph, see "Report of Capt. John F. Morrison," 83–84; "Report of Capt. Peyton C. March," 20, 25, 42; "Report of Capt. Carl Reichmann," 184–85, 266, 269–71, 276–80; Kuhn, "Report on Russo-Japanese War," 31–35, 221; "Report of Lieut. Col. Edward J. McClernand," 103, 119, 143; "Report of Capt. William V. Judson," 211–14; and Vardell Nesmith, "Quiet Paradigm Change: Evolution of the Field Artillery Doctrine of US Army, 1861–1905" (PhD diss., Duke University, 1977), 324–25.

48. Carl Reichmann, "Chances in War—Concluded," *Journal of the US Infantry Association* 3, no. 2 (October 1906): 21.

49. "Report of Capt. Carl Reichmann," 270.

50. "Report of Lieut. Col. Edward J. McClernand," 103.

51. "Report of Lieut. Col. Edward J. McClernand," 143.

52. Kuhn, "Report on Russo-Japanese War," 31.

53. For paragraph, see Kuhn, "Report on Russo-Japanese War," 32–34, 181; "Report of Lieut. Col. Edward J. McClernand," 36, 117, 119–20; "Report of Lieut. Col. Walter S. Schuyler," 111–12, 115; "Report of Capt. Carl Reichmann," 201, 267, 269, 280; "Report of Capt. William V. Judson," 211; and Nesmith, "Quiet Paradigm Change," 309–10, 314, 317, 319.

54. "Report of Capt. Carl Reichmann," 280.

55. Tiemann N. Horn, "Present Method and Lessons in Regard to Field Artillery Taught by the Russo-Japanese War," *Journal of the US Artillery* 30, no. 3 (November–December 1908): 259; emphasis original.

56. For paragraph, see "Report of Capt. Peyton C. March," 12, 43, 51–53; "Report of Capt. Carl Reichmann," 269, 278–79; Kuhn, "Report on Russo-Japanese War," 229; "Report

of Lieut. Col. Edward J. McClernand," 98–99; and "Report of Capt. William V. Judson," 200–201, 213.

57. Quotation from his 1905 Army War College lecture on lessons learned from the Russo-Japanese War, Coffman, *Hilt of the Sword*, 31.

58. "Report of Lieut. Col. Edward J. McClernand," 98.

59. Kuhn, "Report on Russo-Japanese War," 229.

60. For paragraph, see "Report of Capt. John F. Morrison," 80–84, 90, 95; "Report of Lieut. Col. Walter S. Schuyler," 134–35; "Report of Capt. Carl Reichmann," 262–64, 269, 271, 280; Kuhn, "Report on Russo-Japanese War," 108–15, 138, 189; and "Report of Capt. William V. Judson," 200–202.

61. Kuhn, "Report on Russo-Japanese War," 108.

62. "Report of Capt. Carl Reichmann," 264.

63. "Report of Capt. John F. Morrison," 81.

64. Kuhn, "Report on Russo-Japanese War," 112, 114.

65. For paragraph, see "Report of Col. Valery Havard," 5–8; "Report of Maj. Charles Lynch," 36–37, 190–91, 199, 204–5; and Richard Milloy, "The Influence of the Russo-Japanese War on Medical and Engineer Operations in the US Army" (Monograph, School of Advanced Military Studies, May 2014), 13–14.

66. "Report of Col. Valery Havard," 7.

67. "Report of Maj. Charles Lynch," 143–44; and Greenwood, "American Military Observers," 476–77.

68. For paragraph, see "Report of Capt. Peyton C. March," 52–54; "Report of Lieut. Col. Walter S. Schuyler," 127; "Report of Capt. Carl Reichmann," 278; "Report of Col. Valery Havard," 33; "Report of Lieut. Col. Edward J. McClernand," 97–99; and Greenwood, "American Military Observers," 443, 449–50.

69. "Report of Capt. Peyton C. March," 53–54.

70. "Report of Lieut. Col. Edward J. McClernand," 98.

71. For paragraph, see "Report of Capt. Peyton C. March," 51; Kuhn, "Report on Russo-Japanese War," 106–8, 230; "Report of Lieut. Col. Edward J. McClernand," 94; Montgomery Macomb, "Machine Guns in the Russian Army," *Journal of the US Infantry Association* 3, no. 3 (January 1907): 16; "Report of Capt. William V. Judson," 194–97; and David Armstrong, *Bullets and Bureaucrats: Machine Gun and the US Army, 1861–1916* (Westport, CT: Greenwood Press, 1982), 138–39.

72. Kuhn, "Report on Russo-Japanese War," 128.

73. Kuhn, 230.

74. Macomb, "Machine Guns," 18.

75. For paragraph, see Macomb, "Machine Guns," 12–20; Kuhn, "Report on Russo-Japanese War," 107–8; "Report of Lieut. Col. Edward J. McClernand," 94–97, 103; Greenwood, "American Military Observers," 420–21, 446–48; and Armstrong, *Bullets and Bureaucrats*, 138–42.

76. Macomb, "Machine Guns," 19.

77. "Report of Lieut. Col. Edward J. McClernand," 95.

78. "Report of Lieut. Col. Edward J. McClernand," 94.

79. Armstrong, *Bullets and Bureaucrats*, 140.

80. For paragraph, see Kuhn, "Report on Russo-Japanese War," 34, 63, 191; "Report of Capt. Carl Reichmann," 196, 267; "Report of Lieut. Col. Walter S. Schuyler," 153; and "Report of Lieut. Col. Edward J. McClernand," 140.

81. "Report of Capt. William V. Judson," 202.

82. Kuhn, "Report on Russo-Japanese War," 64.

83. For paragraph, see "Report of Lieut. Col. Edward J. McClernand," 112–14; "Report of Capt. Carl Reichmann," 200, 279; "Report of Lieut. Col. Walter S. Schuyler," 119, 123; Kuhn, "Report on Russo-Japanese War," 22–23, 27–28, 228; and "Report of Capt. William V. Judson," 160, 210.

84. "Report of Capt. Carl Reichmann," 279.

85. "Report of Capt. William V. Judson," 210.

86. Kuhn, "Report on Russo-Japanese War," 228; and "Report of Lieut. Col. Walter S. Schuyler," 119.

87. "Report of Capt. Carl Reichmann," 185.

88. "Report of Lieut. Col. Edward J. McClernand," 114.

89. For paragraph, see Reichmann, "Chances in War," 26–27; "Report of Capt. John F. Morrison," 59, 84, 97; "Report of Capt. William V. Judson," 211; "Report of Capt. Peyton C. March," 30; Kuhn, "Report on Russo-Japanese War," 205, 214–15, 228; "Report of Lieut. Col. Walter S. Schuyler," 125; "Report of Capt. Carl Reichmann," 265; Nesmith, "Quiet Paradigm Change," 367; Greenwood, "American Military Observers," 439, 444; and Vacca, "Learning about Military Effectiveness," 156, 160–61.

90. Reichmann, "Chances in War—Concluded," 19; and "Report of Capt. William V. Judson," 214.

91. For paragraph, see Kuhn, "Report on Russo-Japanese War," 122–23, 126–27; "Report of Lieut. Col. Edward J. McClernand," 102–3; "Report of Capt. Carl Reichmann," 271; Reichmann, "Chances in War—Concluded," 4; "Report of Capt. William V. Judson," 213; Oliver Wood, *From the Yalu to Port Arthur: Epitome of the First Period of the Russo-Japanese War* (Kansas City, MO: Franklin Hudson, 1905), 32–33, 37–38; Walter Kretchik, *US Army Doctrine: From the American Revolution to the War on Terror* (Lawrence: University of Kansas Press, 2011), 115; and Vacca, "Learning about Military Effectiveness," 254–56.

92. *Army-Navy Journal* 64 (January 26, 1907), 594.

93. "Report of Capt. William V. Judson," 213.

94. Greenwood, "American Military Observers," 429.

95. For paragraph, see "Report of Capt. Carl Reichmann," 269; "Report of Capt. John F. Morrison," 82, 98; Kuhn, "Report on Russo-Japanese War," 83, 142, 229; Clark, *Preparing for War*, ix–x, 221; Greenwood, "American Military Observers," 437–39; Timothy Nenninger, *The Leavenworth Schools and the Old Army: Education, Professionalism, and the Officer Corps of the United States Army, 1881–1918* (Westport, CT: Greenwood Press, 1978), 88; and Vacca, "Learning about Military Effectiveness," 155.

96. Reichmann, "Chances in War—Concluded," 20.

97. "Report of Capt. William V. Judson," 202.

98. Quoted in Nenninger, *Leavenworth Schools*, 88.

99. For paragraph, see "Report of Capt. Peyton C. March," 43; "Report of Capt. John F. Morrison," 95–98; Kuhn, "Report on Russo-Japanese War," 229; "Report of Lieut. Col. Edward

J. McClernand," 101–2; Montgomery Macomb, "Notes on the Russian Infantry Soldier," *Journal of the US Infantry Association* 2, no. 4 (April 1906): 31–32; Nenninger, *Leavenworth Schools*, 88; Greenwood, "American Military Observers," 439–40; and Pershing, *My Life*, 254–55.

100. "Report of Capt. John F. Morrison," 95.

101. "Report of Lieut. Col. Edward J. McClernand," 101–2.

102. Kuhn, "Report on Russo-Japanese War," 229.

103. Greenwood, "American Military Observers," 439.

104. "Report of Capt. Peyton C. March," 41; Kuhn, "Report on Russo-Japanese War," 47–48; "Report of Maj. Charles Lynch," 45, 57–58, 61, 145, 151–52, 167, 170–71, 174, 178, 208–9; Greenwood, "American Military Observers," 475–78, 484; and Milloy, "Influence of the Russo-Japanese War," 10–12.

105. "Report of Capt. Carl Reichmann," 256–57; "Report of Lieut. Col. Walter S. Schuyler," 126, 139; "Report of Col. Valery Havard," 7–10, 27–28, 77, 109–11; "Report of Col. John Van R. Hoff," 121, 160, 164–66, 184; and Milloy, "Influence of the Russo-Japanese War," 12.

106. Charles Bonaparte, Report of the Secretary of the Navy (hereafter, *ARND/SON 1905*), December 4, 1905, in *Annual Reports of the Navy Department for the Year 1905* (Washington, DC: Government Printing Office, 1906), 19.

107. Vacca, "Learning about Military Effectiveness," 377.

108. *ARND/BON 1905*, p. 368; for paragraph, see Paul Morton, Report of the Secretary of the Navy (hereafter, *ARND/SON 1904*), November 23, 1904, in *Annual Reports of the Navy Department for the Year 1904* (Washington, DC: Government Printing Office, 1904), 7; Cotten, "Naval Strategy," 42, 45–46, 52; Alfred Thayer Mahan, *Naval Strategy, Compared and Contrasted with the Principles and Practice of Military Operations on Land* (Boston: Little, Brown, 1911), 383–401; and George Baer, *One Hundred Years of Sea Power: The U.S. Navy, 1890–1990* (Stanford, CA: Stanford University Press, 1993), 11–17, 20.

109. Mahan, quoted in Ian Toll, *Pacific Crucible: War at Sea in the Pacific, 1941–1942* (New York: Norton, 2012), xix.

110. *ARND/BON 1905*, p. 391.

111. Mahan, *Naval Strategy*, 385.

112. Cotten, "Naval Strategy," 53.

113. For paragraph, see Mahan, *Naval Strategy*, 391–92, 398–400; Alfred Thayer Mahan, "Retrospect upon the War between Japan and Russia" (May 1906) in *Naval Administration and Warfare: Some General Principles* (Boston: Little, Brown, 1918), 167–73; Cotten, "Naval Strategy," 49; McCully, *McCully Report*, 244; and Braisted, *US Navy in the Pacific*, 175, 199, 212.

114. Mahan, "Retrospect," 167.

115. Mahan, 167.

116. Dewey to Secretary of Navy, July 26, 1905, cited in Robert O'Connell, *Sacred Vessels: Cult of the Battleship and the Rise of the US Navy* (New York: Oxford University Press, 1993), 109.

117. Mahan, "Retrospect," 169.

118. For paragraph, see *ARND/BON 1905*, p. 368, 392–93; Schroeder, "Gleanings from Sea of Japan," 48, 55, 69–70, 92; and White, "With the Baltic Fleet," 613–15.

119. *ARND/BON 1905*, p. 368.

120. Schroeder, "Gleanings from Sea of Japan," 92.

121. Bradley Fiske, "Why Togo Won," US Naval Institute *Proceedings* 31, no. 4 (December 1905): 808.

122. Fiske, 809.

123. *ARND*/SON 1905, p. 20.

124. *ARND*/BON 1905, p. 392.

125. Schroeder, "Gleanings from Sea of Japan," 92.

126. For paragraph, see Schroeder, 75, 83; McCully, *McCully Report*, 161–62, 247; and Roosevelt to William Moody, September 15, 1904; and Roosevelt to Paul Morton, September 26, 1904, both in TRCDL.

127. Schroeder, "Gleanings from Sea of Japan," 75.

128. Schroeder, 75.

129. Quoted in Norman Friedman, *US Destroyers: An Illustrated Design History*, rev. ed. (Annapolis, MD: Naval Institute Press, 2004), 22.

130. For paragraph, see White, "With the Baltic Fleet," 598; Schroeder, "Gleanings from Sea of Japan," 58–61, 82–83; and Mario de Arcangelis, *Electronic Warfare: From the Battle of Tsushima to the Falklands and Lebanon Conflicts* (Poole, UK: Blandford Press, 1985), 11–16.

131. Schroeder, "Gleanings from Sea of Japan," 58.

132. McCully, *McCully Report*, 251.

133. For paragraph, see McCully, *McCully Report*, 79–83, 90, 98–101, 156–59, 195, 199, 248; Vacca, "Learning about Military Effectiveness," 379–80; Norman Youngblood, *The Development of Mine Warfare: A Most Murderous and Barbarous Conduct* (Westport, CT: Praeger, 2006), 76–79; and Gregory K. Hartmann with Scott Truver, *Weapons That Wait: Mine Warfare in the US Navy* (Annapolis, MD: Naval Institute Press, 1991), 38, 40.

134. McCully, *McCully Report*, 83.

135. For paragraph, see M. C. Ferrand, "Torpedo and Mine Effects in the Russo-Japanese War," trans. Philip Alger, US Naval Institute *Proceedings* 33, no. 4 (December 1907): 1479, 1481; Schroeder, "Gleanings from Sea of Japan," 48–49, 70–72; Vacca, "Learning about Military Effectiveness," 95–96; White, "With the Baltic Fleet," 606–7, 610–11; and McCully, *McCully Report*, 96, 246.

136. Ferrand, "Torpedo and Mine Effects," 1481; and White, "With the Baltic Fleet," 610.

137. *ARND*/BON 1905, p. 392.

138. *ARND*/SON 1905, p. 20.

139. *ARND*/SON 1904, p. 4–5.

140. Schroeder, "Gleanings from Sea of Japan," 81; McCully, *McCully Report*, 249–50; and Norman Friedman, *US Battleships: An Illustrated Design History* (Annapolis, MD: Naval Institute Press, 1985), 78.

141. For paragraph, see Sims, "Inherent Tactical Qualities," 1338, 1342, 1344; Mahan, "Reflections," 450, 456–57, 470; "Black Joke," "A.B.G.B.S.," US Naval Institute *Proceedings* 33, no. 2 (June 1907): 674–75; White, "With the Baltic Fleet," 614–15; Vacca, "Learning about Military Effectiveness," 208, 366, 371; and Hone, *Learning War*, 102.

142. *ARND*/SON 1905, p. 20.

143. Sims to Roosevelt, September 27, 1906, p. 6, in TRCDL.

144. Schroeder, "Gleanings from Sea of Japan," 77.

145. For paragraph, see Sims, "Inherent Tactical Qualities," 1341–42, 1349–53; Mahan, "Reflections," 460, 466; Vacca, "Learning about Military Effectiveness," 194, 207, 210, 217–18, 363–70, 377; McCully, *McCully Report*, 80–82, 249–50; McBride, *Technological Change*, 72, 75; Norman Friedman, *Naval Firepower: Battleship Guns and Gunnery in the Dreadnought Era* (Annapolis, MD: Naval Institute Press, 2008), 68; and Sims to Roosevelt, September 27, 1906, in TRCDL.

146. Mahan, "Reflections," 460.

147. Schroeder, "Gleanings from Sea of Japan," 89.

148. Bradley Fiske, "Compromiseless Ships," US Naval Institute *Proceedings* 31, no. 3 (September 1905): 552; emphasis original.

149. Quoted in O'Connell, *Sacred Vessels*, 109.

150. *ARND/BON* 1905, p. 393.

151. Roosevelt to Bonaparte, December 20, 1905, in *The Letters of Theodore Roosevelt*, vol. 5: *The Big Stick, 1905–1907*, ed. Elting Morison (Cambridge, MA: Harvard University Press, 1952), 121.

152. Sims, "Inherent Tactical Qualities," 1338–39, 1348–52; McBride, *Technological Change*, 72, 75; and Wayne Hughes, "Mahan, Tactics, and Principles of Strategy," in *The Influence of History on Mahan*, ed. John Hattendorf (Newport, RI: Naval War College Press, 1991), 25–26.

153. For paragraph, see McCully, *McCully Report*, 249, 251; Sims to Roosevelt, September 27, 1906, p. 10, in TRCDL; Elting Morison, *Admiral Sims and the Modern American Navy* (New York: Russell and Russell, 1942), 145–46, 170; and Friedman, *Naval Firepower*, 37–39, 272–73.

154. McCully, *McCully Report*, 249.

155. "Black Joke," "A.B.G.B.S.," 678.

156. For paragraph, see Spector, *Admiral of the New Empire*, 3, 122–23, 127, 137, 146, 163–65; Challener, *Admirals, Generals*, 38–39, 47–48, 193, 233–35; Braisted, *US Navy in the Pacific*, 116, 119–20, 175–76, 316–19; and Matthew Oyos, *In Command: Theodore Roosevelt and the American Military* (Lincoln: Potomac, 2018), 319–23.

157. Subig Bay was the more commonly used spelling at that time for what today is better known as Subic Bay.

158. Quoted in Brian McAllister Linn, *Guardians of Empire: The US Army and the Pacific, 1902–1940* (Chapel Hill: University of North Carolina Press, 1997), 83.

159. Roosevelt to Theodore Elijah Burton, February 23, 1904, in Morison, *Letters*, 4:737.

160. William Taft, Report of the Secretary of War (hereafter, *ARWD/SOW* 1904), November 28, 1904, in *Annual Reports of the War Department for the Year Ended June 30, 1904*, vol. 1 (Washington, DC: Government Printing Office, 1904), 17; and William Taft, Report of the Secretary of War (hereafter, *ARWD/SOW* 1905), December 9, 1905, in *Annual Reports of the War Department for the Fiscal Year Ended June 30, 1905*, vol. 1 (Washington, DC: Government Printing Office, 1905), 26–27.

161. For paragraph, see Braisted, *US Navy in the Pacific*, 171, 176–80, 216–18; Challener, *Admirals, Generals*, 225, 232, 235–39, 246; Spector, *Admiral of the New Empire*, 165–68; Edward Miller, *War Plan Orange: The US Strategy to Defeat Japan, 1897–1945* (Annapolis, MD: Naval Institute Press, 2007), 53, 65–67, 86–87; Linn, *Guardians of Empire*, 81, 84; and Oyos, *In Command*, 59, 193–94, 210–11.

162. Leonard Wood to Roosevelt, June 1, 1904, p. 2, in TRCDL.

163. Dewey to Roosevelt, August 4, 1904, p. 9, in TRCDL.

164. Roosevelt to Leonard Wood, August 5, 1904, in Morison, *Letters*, 4:881.

165. Challener, *Admirals, Generals*, 240.

166. For paragraph, see Spector, *Admiral of the New Empire*, 148, 168–69; Linn, *Guardians of Empire*, 84; Cotten, "Naval Strategy," 45–46; Challener, *Admirals, Generals*, 24–25, 215, 228, 231, 237–38; Baer, *One Hundred Years*, 34–37; and William Taft, Report of the Secretary of War (hereafter, *ARWD/SOW* 1906), December 12, 1906, in *Annual Reports of the War Department for the Year Ended June 30, 1906*, vol. 1 (Washington, DC: Government Printing Office, 1906), 45–46.

167. Edward Schulz, "Land Defense of Seacoast Fortifications," *Journal of the Military Services Institution of the United States* 36, no. 133 (January–February 1905): 101.

168. Challener, *Admirals, Generals*, 237.

169. For paragraph, see Roosevelt to Victor Metcalf, February 11, 1908, in *The Letters of Theodore Roosevelt*, vol. 6: *The Big Stick, 1907–1909*, ed. Elting Morison (Cambridge, MA: Harvard University Press, 1952), 937–39; Braisted, *US Navy in the Pacific*, 216–17, 220–21, 243; Linn, *Guardians of Empire*, 86–87; Edgar Raines, "Major General J. Franklin Bell and Military Reform: The Chief of Staff Years, 1906–1910" (PhD diss., University of Wisconsin–Madison, 1976), 594–95; Challener, *Admirals, Generals*, 240–41, 247; and Spector, *Admiral of the New Empire*, 162, 168–69.

170. For paragraph, see Braisted, *US Navy in the Pacific*, 219–22; Challener, *Admirals, Generals*, 41, 48–49, 241–42; Miller, *War Plan Orange*, 44–46; Linn, *Guardians of Empire*, 89–90, 112–13; and Roosevelt to Victor Metcalf, February 11, 1908; Roosevelt to Key, March 26, 1908; and Roosevelt to Richmond Hobson, April 16, 1908, in Morison, *Letters*, 6:937–39, 982–83, 1008.

171. Challener, *Admirals, Generals*, 241.

172. For paragraph, see Daniel Beaver, *Modernizing the American War Department: Change and Continuity in a Turbulent Era, 1885–1920* (Kent, OH: Kent State University Press, 2006), 21–22, 26–30; Clark, *Preparing for War*, 120–21, 168–73, 182–83, 189–91, 210–13, 232; Linn, *Echo of Battle*, 94–95; and Oyos, *In Command*, 66, 81, 85, 99, 115–18, 197.

173. For paragraph, see Clark, *Preparing for War*, 121, 130–31, 160–62, 199–203, 207–15; Edward Coffman, *The Regulars: The US Army, 1898–1941* (Cambridge, MA: Harvard University Press, 2007), 50, 143, 176–78, 182–83; Raines, "Bell and Military Reform," 13, 36, 357, 359; and Nenninger, *Leavenworth Schools*, 55–58, 70–75, 85–86, 112, 119–20.

174. For paragraph, see Nenninger, *Leavenworth Schools*, 77–79, 83–85, 88, 104; Raines, "Bell and Military Reform," 354, 356, 366; John Pershing, *My Experiences in the World War*, vol. 1 (New York: Frederick Stokes, 1931), 41; and Clark, *Preparing for War*, 227–28.

175. *ARWD/SOW* 1905, p. 17.

176. *ARWD/SOW* 1905, p. 19.

177. Among the lectures generated by Swift were "The Influence of Peace Training as Shown in the Battle of Liaoyang" (1910) and "The Influence of Peace Training as Shown in the Battle of Mukden" (1910), available at the US Army Heritage and Education Center at Carlisle Barracks, Pennsylvania.

178. For paragraph, see Carol Reardon, *Soldiers and Scholars: The US Army and the Uses of Military History* (Lawrence: University Press of Kansas, 1990), 3, 5, 87–89, 92, 94–95, 106–7, 147–48; Linn, *Echo of Battle*, 53–54, 82, 86–87; Kretchik, *US Army Doctrine*, 87–88, 91–95, 104–6; Nenninger, *Leavenworth Schools*, 82–83, 86, 121; and Clark, *Preparing for War*, 156–58.

179. Coffman, *Regulars*, 190.

180. Nenninger, *Leavenworth Schools*, 82.

181. Coffman, *Regulars*, 184; for paragraph, see 53, 87–88, 298; Clark, *Preparing for War*, 106, 109, 134–35, 138–39, 148–50, 185–86; Raines, "Bell and Military Reform," 293–96, 331, 333, 336, 347; Oyos, *In Command*, 146–72, 304–11; Pershing, *My Life*, 242, 244–45; Roosevelt to Wood, June 4, 1904, and Roosevelt to Wood, June 8, 1904, both in Morison, *Letters*, 4:820, 826–28; and Roosevelt to John Hull, May 28, 1908, in Morison, *Letters*, 6:1039.

182. Linn, *Echo of Battle*, 104–5; and Jonathan Bailey, "Military History and the Pathology of Lessons Learned: The Russo-Japanese War, a Case Study," in *The Past Is Prologue: The Importance of History to the Military Profession*, ed. Williamson Murray and Richard Hart Sinnreich (New York: Cambridge University Press, 2006), 185.

183. For paragraph, see Beaver, *Modernizing the American War Department*, 21–22, 32–34; Raines, "Bell and Military Reform," 26, 38, 42–44, 57, 137, 149–50, 170, 179, 187; Linn, *Guardians of Empire*, 54–55, 126; Clark, *Preparing for War*, 194–96, 241; and Oyos, *In Command*, 152–54, 196–205, 215–16.

184. Steven Stebbins, "Indirect Fire: The Challenge and Response in the US Army, 1907–1917" (Master's thesis, University of North Carolina-Chapel Hill, 1993), 44.

185. For paragraph, see Raines, "Bell and Military Reform," 7, 13–14, 63, 137, 152, 177–78, 199, 203, 396, 398, 503; Beaver, *Modernizing the American War Department*, 22, 33–36; Oyos, *In Command*, 152–54, 164–71, 200–205, 211; and Roosevelt to Hull, February 16, 1906, in Morison, *Letters*, 5:155.

186. Oyos, *In Command*, 201–2.

187. Oyos, 211.

188. Raines, "Bell and Military Reform," 24.

189. For paragraph, see *Historical Statistics of the United States Millennial Edition Online*, Table Ed26-47 ("Military Personnel on Active Duty by Branch of Service and Sex, 1789–1995"), http://www.hsus.cambridge.org; *ARWD/SOW* 1906, p. 7, 9–10, 24; Thomas Barry, Report of the Chief of Staff (hereafter, *ARWD/COS* 1906), November 20, 1906, in *Annual Reports of the War Department for the Fiscal Year Ended June 30, 1906*, vol. 1 (Washington, DC: Government Printing Office, 1906), 549; J. Franklin Bell, Report of Chief of Staff (hereafter, *ARWD/COS* 1907), August 31, 1907, in *War Department, USA Annual Reports, 1907*, vol. 1 (Washington, DC: Government Printing Office, 1907), 171; Raines, *Bell and Military Reform*, 64, 318, 357, 599; Oyos, *In Command*, 211–16; Roosevelt to Taft, January 11, 1906, Roosevelt to General Staff War Department, January 22, 1906, Roosevelt to Bell, September 1, 1906, and Roosevelt to William Howard Taft, September 17, 1906, all in Morison, *Letters*, 5:132–35, 391, 414–15, 420; and Roosevelt to J. Franklin Bell, January 13, 1908, in Morison, *Letters*, 6:905–6.

190. For paragraph, see *Historical Statistics of the United States Millennial Edition Online*, Table Ea636-643 ("Federal government expenditures by major function, 1789–1970"), http://www.hsus.cambridge.org; *ARWD/SOW* 1904, p. 40–41; *ARWD/SOW* 1905, p. 62–63; Samuel Mills, Report of the Chief of Artillery (hereafter, *ARWD/COA* 1905), October 30, 1905, in *Annual Reports of the War Department for the Year Ended June 30, 1905*, vol. 2 (Washington, DC: Government Printing Office, 1905), 249; John Bates, Report of the Board of Ordnance and Fortification (hereafter, *ARWD/BOF* 1905), October 24, 1905, in *Annual Reports of the War*

Department for the Year Ended June 30, 1905, vol. 2 (Washington, DC: Government Printing Office, 1905), 282; *ARWD/SOW 1906*, p. 73–74; and Luke Wright, Report of the Secretary of War (hereafter, *ARWD/SOW* 1908), December 10, 1908, in *War Department Annual Reports*, vol. 1 (Washington, DC: Government Printing Office, 1908), 62–63.

191. *ARWD/SOW* 1905, p. 30.

192. Greenwood, "American Military Observers," 500; also see 2–3, 501–4.

193. Greenwood, 3.

194. Bailey, "Military History," 185.

195. Roosevelt to Chaffee, July 3, 1905, in Morison, *Letters*, 4:1261.

196. For paragraph, see "Report of Capt. Carl Reichmann," 269–70; "Report of Capt. William V. Judson," 214; Vacca, "Learning about Military Effectiveness," 252, 263–66; and Boyd Dastrup, *King of Battle: A Branch History of the US Army's Field Artillery* (Fort Monroe, VA: TRADOC, 1992), 149.

197. *ARWD/SOW* 1904, p. 16.

198. *ARWD/SOW* 1905, p. 25–26.

199. William J. Snow, "The Functions of Field Artillery," quoted in Clark, *Preparing for War*, 219.

200. For paragraph, see Janice McKenney, *The Organizational History of Field Artillery, 1775–2003* (Washington, DC: Center of Military History, 2007), 90, 95–96, 99; Nesmith, "Quiet Paradigm Change," 261, 267–77, 287–88, 294, 299, 301–8, 323, 340; Raines, "Bell and Military Reform," 149, 390, 394, 455, 477; and Dastrup, *King of Battle*, 127, 137, 140–42, 147–50, 157.

201. Nesmith, "Quiet Paradigm Change," 304.

202. For paragraph, see "Report of Capt. Carl Reichmann," 269, 280; Nesmith, "Quiet Paradigm Change," 59, 321–25, 329, 332, 340; *ARWD/COA* 1905, p. 255–56; Robert Shaw Oliver to Roosevelt, December 2, 1904, in TRCDL; and Roosevelt to Taft, March 13, 1905, in Morison, *Letters*, 4:1138.

203. John Story, Report of the Chief of Artillery (hereafter, *ARWD/COA* 1904), November 3, 1904, in *Annual Reports of the War Department for the Fiscal Year Ended June 30, 1904*, vol. 2 (Washington, DC: Government Printing Office, 1904), 420.

204. Taft to Roosevelt, February 8, 1905, in TRCDL.

205. For paragraph, see *ARWD/COA* 1905, p. 260–61; J. Franklin Bell, Report of the Board of Ordnance and Fortification, October 25, 1907, in *War Department, U.S.A. Annual Reports, 1907*, vol. 2 (Washington, DC: Government Printing Office, 1907), 228; William Crozier, Report of the Board of Ordnance and Fortification, November 1, 1906, in *Annual Reports of the War Department for the Year Ended June 30, 1906*, vol. 2 (Washington, DC: Government Printing Office, 1906), 239; Raines, *Bell and Military Reform*, 467–69, 477; Nesmith, "Quiet Paradigm Change," 2–4, 309, 322–27, 331–34, 340; Dastrup, *King of Battle*, 148–49; and McKenney, *Field Artillery*, 99–101.

206. Nesmith, "Quiet Paradigm Change," 340; emphasis original.

207. Montgomery Macomb, "Attack and Defense of an Experimental Redoubt," *Journal of the US Infantry Association* 5, no. 3 (November 1908): 368.

208. Dastrup, *King of Battle*, 150.

209. For paragraph, see *ARWD/COA* 1905, p. 259–61; *ARWD/SOW* 1906, p. 50–51; *ARWD/COS* 1906, p. 557; Arthur Murray, Report of the Chief of Artillery (hereafter, *ARWD/COA*

1906), November 23, 1906, in *Annual Reports of the War Department for the Year Ended June 30, 1906*, vol. 2 (Washington, DC: Government Printing Office, 1906), 211–12; Arthur Murray, Report of the Chief of Artillery (hereafter, *ARWD/COA* 1907), July 29, 1907, in *War Department, U.S.A. Annual Reports, 1907*, vol. 2 (Washington, DC: Government Printing Office, 1907), 217; Raines, *Bell and Military Reform*, 455–56, 465–66; Frederick Grant, Report for the Department of the East, August 16, 1906, in *Annual Reports of the War Department for the Year Ended June 30, 1906*, vol. 3 (Washington, DC: Government Printing Office, 1906), 36; McKenney, *Field Artillery*, 91–92, 100–101; Dastrup, *King of Battle*, 157–59; and Nesmith, "Quiet Paradigm Change," 323–25, 329–30.

210. *ARWD/COA* 1907, p. 217.

211. For paragraph, see *ARWD/COA* 1905, p. 260; Dastrup, *King of Battle*, 153–54; Nesmith, "Quiet Paradigm Change," 323–25; McKenney, *Field Artillery*, 103–6; Stebbins, "Indirect Fire," 25–33, 40–43; and Roosevelt to Bell, April 28, 1906, in TRCDL.

212. Stebbins, "Indirect Fire," 28.

213. Quoted in Stebbins, 26–27.

214. *ARWD/COS* 1907, p. 186.

215. For paragraph, see Stebbins, "Indirect Fire," 29–32, 37–42, 47–50, 69–72; *ARWD/COS* 1906, p. 559; J. Franklin Bell, Report of the Chief of Staff (hereafter, *ARWD/COS* 1908), December 9, 1908, in *War Department Annual Reports, 1908*, vol. 1 (Washington, DC: Government Printing Office, 1908), 354; Dastrup, *King of Battle*, 153; and Raines, "Bell and Military Reform," 360–62, 482.

216. Stebbins, "Indirect Fire," 37.

217. Leonard Wood, Report of Chief of Staff (hereafter, *ARWD/COS* 1910), October 1, 1910, in *Annual Report of the War Department, 1910*, vol. 1 (Washington, DC: Government Printing Office, 1910), 130; for paragraph, see Stebbins, "Indirect Fire," 44–45, 51–54, 66, 78–79; Clark, *Preparing for War*, 142, 236; and Dastrup, *King of Battle*, 176.

218. Stebbins, "Indirect Fire," 54.

219. Stebbins, 58.

220. Bailey, "Military History," 178.

221. Armstrong, *Bullets and Bureaucrats*, 138; for paragraph, see Armstrong, 136–42, 161; Macomb, "Machine Guns in the Russian Army," 3–4, 18–21; "Report of Lieut. Col. Edward J. McClernand," 96; Greenwood, "American Military Observers," 395, 446–48; Daniel Kenda, "Lessons Learned from the Use of the Machine Gun during the Russo-Japanese War and the Application of Those Lessons by the Protagonists of World War I" (Master's thesis, USA Command and General Staff College, 2005), 4–5, 72–78, 84, 92; and Raines, "Bell and Military Reform," 413–16.

222. Quoted in Kenda, "Lessons Learned," 76.

223. Quoted in Raines, "Bell and Military Reform," 416.

224. Raines, 416.

225. For paragraph, see Raines, "Bell and Military Reform," 414–16, 469; Armstrong, *Bullets and Bureaucrats*, 140–42; Kenda, "Lessons Learned," 77; Greenwood, "American Military Observers," 446; and Charles McKenna, "The Forgotten Reform: Field Maneuvers in the Development of the United States Army, 1902–1920" (PhD diss., Duke University, 1981), 118–19.

226. Quoted in Armstrong, *Bullets and Bureaucrats*, 141.

227. Milloy, "Influence of the Russo-Japanese War," 30.

228. For paragraph, see Armstrong, *Bullets and Bureaucrats*, 105–6, 112, 142–44, 151–52, 159–64, 177–78, 183–84; Kenda, "Lessons Learned," 13, 77–78; Raines, "Bell and Military Reform," 408, 412–16, 423, 426, 429, 432–37; Roosevelt to Luke Wright, October 26, 1908, in Morison, *Letters*, 6:1319–20; Beaver, *Modernizing the American War Department*, 64–67; and John Wilson, *Maneuver and Firepower: Evolution of Divisions and Separate Brigades* (Honolulu: University Press of the Pacific, 2001), 28.

229. *ARWD/COS* 1908, p. 365–66.

230. Pershing, *My Life*, 255.

231. For paragraph, see Clark, *Preparing for War*, 216–18, 228–29; Wilson, *Maneuver and Firepower*, 23–25; Kretchik, *US Army Doctrine*, 105, 109–11; and Michael Bonura, *Under the Shadow of Napoleon: French Influence on the American Way of Warfare from the War of 1812 to the Outbreak of WWII* (New York: New York University Press, 2012), 193–200.

232. Clark, *Preparing for War*, 217.

233. *Field Service Regulations, US Army, 1905* (Washington, DC: Government Printing Office, 1906), 101.

234. For paragraph, see Reichmann, "Chances in War," 26–27; "Report of Capt. John F. Morrison," 84, 97–98; "Report of Capt. William V. Judson," 211; Kretchik, *US Army Doctrine*, 115–16; and Clark, *Preparing for War*, 232–33.

235. Bell to Roosevelt, January 10, 1907, p. 2, in TRCDL (emphasis original).

236. Clark, *Preparing for War*, 227–28.

237. Clark, 227.

238. Charles Hall, Report of the Infantry and Cavalry School, Staff School, and Signal School, August 31, 1907, in *War Department, U.S.A. Annual Reports, 1907*, vol. 4 (Washington, DC: Government Printing Office, 1907), 242.

239. Linn, *Guardians of Empire*, 100.

240. Quoted in Forrest Pogue, *George Marshall: Education of a General, 1880–1939* (New York: Viking, 1963), 99.

241. Clark, *Preparing for War*, 228; Stebbins, "Indirect Fire," 37; and Nenninger, *Leavenworth Schools*, 87–89, 104.

242. For paragraph, see Kretchik, *US Army Doctrine*, 111–21; Raines, "Bell and Military Reform," 478–82; Wilson, *Maneuver and Firepower*, 27–28; Clark, *Preparing for War*, 222–25, 236; Nenninger, *Leavenworth Schools*, 88, 92–94, 127; and Bonura, *Under the Shadow*, 196–202.

243. Kretchik, *US Army Doctrine*, 114.

244. Stebbins, "Indirect Fire," 69.

245. Clark, *Preparing for War*, 224.

246. Clark, 225.

247. For paragraph, see Adna Chaffee, Report of the Chief of Staff (hereafter, *ARWD/COS* 1905), November 8, 1905, in *Annual Reports of the War Department for the Year Ended June 30, 1905*, vol. 1 (Washington, DC: Government Printing Office, 1905), 378–79; *ARWD/SOW* 1906, p. 48–50; *ARWD/COS* 1906, p. 552–53; Raines, "Bell and Military Reform," 521, 527–33, 577–78; and Wilson, *Maneuver and Firepower*, 25.

248. Theodore Roosevelt, "Annual Message of the President Transmitted to the Congress," December 5, 1905 (Washington, DC: Government Printing Office, 1906), 38.

249. *Army Appropriation Bill for the Fiscal Year 1906–7: Hearing before the Senate Committee on Military Affairs*, 59th Congress (Washington, DC: Government Printing Office, 1906), March 26, p. 68–69.

250. McKenna, "Forgotten Reform," 111.

251. For paragraph, see *ARWD/COS* 1907, p. 189–90; Raines, "Bell and Military Reform," 518–25, 539–40, 552–53, 585; Linn, *Guardians of Empire*, 53, 85; Greenwood, "American Military Observers," 123–24, 487; and Oyos, *In Command*, 173–77.

252. *ARWD/COS* 1907, p. 191.

253. For paragraph, see *ARWD/SOW* 1905, p. 31–32, 35–36; William Taft, Report of the Secretary of War (hereafter, *ARWD/SOW* 1907), January 4, 1908, in *War Department, U.S.A. Annual Reports, 1907*, vol. 1 (Washington, DC: Government Printing Office, 1907), 27; *ARWD/SOW* 1908, p. 34–37; *ARWD/COS* 1908, p. 360; Wilson, *Maneuver and Firepower*, 25; Raines, "Bell and Military Reform," 446, 451, 540, 542–47, 585; and Bonaparte to Roosevelt, February 8, 1906; Dan Moore to William Loeb, February 9, 1906; Newberry to Roosevelt, February 12, 1908; and Bonaparte to Roosevelt, February 14, 1908, all in TRCDL.

254. For paragraph, see Clark, *Preparing for War*, 146–48, 204–6; Oyos, *In Command*, 178–87; McKenna, "Forgotten Reform," 92–100, 111; and Stebbins, "Indirect Fire," 33–34.

255. *ARWD/SOW* 1905, p. 31.

256. McKenna, "Forgotten Reform," 99.

257. Roosevelt to Taft, January 11, 1906, in Morison, *Letters*, 5:133.

258. For paragraph, see *ARWD/SOW* 1905, p. 39–40; *ARWD/SOW* 1906, p. 47; *ARWD/COS* 1906, p. 552; Coffman, *Regulars*, 91, 107; Raines, "Bell and Military Reform," 469, 485–88; and McKenna, "Forgotten Reform," 101–6.

259. McKenna, "Forgotten Reform," 105.

260. Bell to Roosevelt, January 10, 1907, p. 2, in TRCDL; emphasis original.

261. For paragraph, see Raines, "Bell and Military Reform," 486; *ARWD/COA* 1905, p. 249; *ARWD/BOF* 1905, p. 282; *ARWD/SOW* 1907, p. 31; *ARWD/COS* 1907, p. 175–76; *ARWD/SOW* 1908, p. 24, 37; *ARWD/COS* 1908, p. 351; Stebbins, "Indirect Fire," 64–65; and McKenna, "Forgotten Reform," 106–20.

262. Stebbins, "Indirect Fire," 34.

263. McKenna, "Forgotten Reform," 107.

264. Quoted in McKenna, 116.

265. Coffman, *Hilt of the Sword*, 34.

266. For paragraph, see McKenna, "Forgotten Reform," 104, 107–10; Stebbins, "Indirect Fire," 35–36; and Oyos, *In Command*, 183.

267. Roosevelt to Hull, February 16, 1906, in Morison, *Letters*, 5:154.

268. Pershing, *My Life*, 246–50, 256; and Smith, *Until the Last*, 92, 96.

269. Pershing, *My Life*, 248.

270. For paragraph, see *ARWD/COA* 1904, p. 386–87, 410–13; *ARWD/SOW* 1904, p. 11–14; Alexander Mackenzie, Report of Chief of Engineers, Military Affairs, September 28, 1904, in *Annual Reports of the War Department for the Fiscal Year Ended June 30, 1904*, vol. 2 (Washington,

DC: Government Printing Office, 1904), 284–86; *ARWD/SOW* 1905, p. 22–24; *ARWD/COA* 1905, p. 250, 257–58; Arthur Murray, Report of the School of Submarine Defense, August 15, 1905, in *Annual Reports of the War Department for the Year Ended June 30, 1905*, vol. 4 (Washington, DC: Government Printing Office, 1905), 112–16; Charles Humphrey, Report of the Quartermaster-General (hereafter, *ARWD/QG* 1906), September 30, 1906, in *Annual Reports of the War Department for the Year Ended June 30, 1906*, vol. 2 (Washington, DC: Government Printing Office, 1906), 32–35; *ARWD/COA* 1906, p. 204–6, 222–23; James Allen, Report of the Chief Signal Officer (hereafter, *ARWD/CSO* 1906), July 1, 1906, in *Annual Reports of the War Department for the Year Ended June 30, 1906*, vol. 2 (Washington, DC: Government Printing Office, 1906), 197–98; *ARWD/COA* 1907, p. 201; *ARWD/SOW* 1908, p. 26–27; Arthur Murray, Report of Chief of Coastal Artillery, October 3, 1908, in *War Department Annual Reports, 1908*, vol. 2 (Washington, DC: Government Printing Office, 1908), 234; and Terrance McGovern and Bolling Smith, *American Coastal Defenses, 1885–1950* (Oxford: Osprey, 2006), 13, 48–52, 57.

271. *ARWD/COA* 1904, p. 410.

272. Roosevelt to Taft, February 7, 1905, in Morison, *Letters*, 4:1117.

273. *ARWD/COA* 1906, p. 205.

274. For paragraph, see *ARWD/SOW* 1906, p. 43; *ARWD/COS* 1906, p. 557; *ARWD/SOW* 1907, p. 8, 26–27; *ARWD/COS* 1907, p. 177; *ARWD/COA* 1907, p. 201; *ARWD/SOW* 1908, p. 32–33; and William Howard Taft to Roosevelt, June 24, 1907, in TRCDL.

275. *ARWD/SOW* 1908, p. 26–27.

276. Linn, *Echo of Battle*, 99.

277. James Archibald to Roosevelt, January 2, 1907, in TRCDL.

278. Arthur Murray to James Franklin Bell, January 12, 1907, p. 2, in TRCDL.

279. *ARWD/COS* 1910, p. 131.

280. For paragraph, see "Wireless Telegraphy," Report of the Inter-Departmental Board submitted to the President by Navy Secretary Paul Morton, July 29, 1904 (Washington, DC: Government Printing Office, 1905), 119–23, 126, 136–42, http://www.earlyradiohistory.us/; Adolphus Greely, Report of the Chief Signal Officer (hereafter, *ARWD/CSO* 1905), September 30, 1905, in *Annual Report of the War Department for the Year Ended June 30, 1905*, vol. 2 (Washington, DC: Government Printing Office, 1905), 207, 240, 242; *ARWD/CSO* 1906, p. 197–98; *ARWD/COS* 1907, p. 183, 196; and Raines, "Bell and Military Reform," 476–77.

281. *ARWD/CSO* 1905, p. 242.

282. *ARWD/COS* 1907, p. 196.

283. For paragraph, see William Crozier, Report of Chief of Ordnance, Appendix I, Exhibits A & B (hereafter, *ARWD/COO* 1905), in *Annual Reports of the War Department for the Year Ended June 30, 1905*, vol. 9 (Washington, DC: Government Printing Office, 1905), 75–95; Kretchik, *US Army Doctrine*, 105; Raines, "Bell and Military Reform," 482–83, 486; Bonura, *Under the Shadow*, 196–97; Roosevelt to Taft, June 4, 1905, in Morison, *Letters*, 4:1090–91; and Greenwood, "American Military Observers," 364, 372, 450.

284. *ARWD/COO* 1905, p. 85.

285. *ARWD/COO* 1905, p. 90.

286. *ARWD/COO* 1905, p. 86.

287. Roosevelt to Chaffee, July 3, 1905, in Morison, *Letters*, 4:1261; and Bell to Roosevelt, January 10, 1907, p. 2, in TRCDL.

288. For paragraph, see "Report of Lieut. Col. Edward J. McClernand," 102; *ARWD/COS* 1905, p. 374; *ARWD/COO* 1905, Correspondence Relating to the Adoption of Intrenching Tools for Infantry, May 6, 1905, p. 143–44, May 23, 1905, p. 150–53, and May 26, 1905, p. 154; and Oyos, *In Command*, 236–37.

289. *ARWD/COO* 1905, Correspondence from Chief of Staff to Secretary of War, May 23, 1905, p. 152–53.

290. *ARWD/COO* 1905, Correspondence from Chief of Staff to Secretary of War, May 23, 1905, p. 152.

291. William Crozier, Report of Chief of Ordnance, October 13, 1906, in *Annual Reports of the War Department for the Year Ended June 30, 1906*, vol. 6 (Washington, DC: Government Printing Office, 1906), 24–25.

292. Quoted in Charles Payne, "The Russo-Japanese War: Impact on Western Military Thought Prior to 1914" (Master's thesis, University of Georgia, 1990), 38.

293. For paragraph, see *ARWD/SOW* 1905, p. 28–30; *ARWD/SOW* 1906, p. 37–38, 40, 121; *ARWD/COS* 1906, p. 557; *ARWD/COS* 1907, p. 181; *ARWD/SOW* 1907, p. 27–29; *ARWD/COS* 1908, p. 360; Robert O'Reilly, Report of the Surgeon-General, August 24, 1906, in *Annual Report of the War Department for the Year Ended June 30, 1906*, vol. 2 (Washington, DC: Government Printing Office, 1906), 121, 139; Milloy, "Influence of the Russo-Japanese War," 7, 15–20, 23, 41; Raines, "Bell and Military Reform," 476–77; and Wilson, *Maneuver and Firepower*, 28.

294. "Report of Maj. Charles Lynch," 143–44; James Aleshire, Report of Quartermaster-General, July 1, 1907, in *War Department, U.S.A. Annual Reports, 1907*, vol. 2 (Washington, DC: Government Printing Office, 1907), 46; and Steven Casey, *When Soldiers Fall: How Americans Have Confronted Combat Losses from World War I to Afghanistan* (New York: Oxford University Press, 2014), 19.

295. General Order 204, quoted in "USA World War II Dog Tags," World War II US Medical Research Center, http://www.med-dept.com.

296. For paragraph, see Coffman, *Regulars*, 155–56; Linn, *Echo of Battle*, 66; Greenwood, *American Military Observers*, 433–35; Reardon, *Soldiers and Scholars*, 141–42; Payne, "Russo-Japanese War," 90–91, 97, 108, 113–14; and Vacca, "Learning about Military Effectiveness," 106, 130, 258, 282, 314.

297. Quoted in Linn, *Echo of Battle*, 99.

298. Quoted in Linn, 99.

299. Vacca, "Learning about Military Effectiveness," 282.

300. For paragraph, see Coffman, *Regulars*, 155–56; Reardon, *Soldiers and Scholars*, 141–42; Payne, "Russo-Japanese War," 90–91, 97, 108, 113–14; and Vacca, "Learning about Military Effectiveness," 106, 130, 258, 282, 314.

301. Roosevelt to Taft, January 4, 1905, in Morison, *Letters*, 4:1091.

302. *ARWD/COS* 1907, p. 192–94; and *ARWD/COS* 1908, p. 357.

303. Quoted in Reardon, *Soldiers and Scholars*, 142.

304. For paragraph, see "Report of Capt. William V. Judson," 200–202; Kuhn, "Report on Russo-Japanese War," 114–15; *ARWD/COS* 1907, p. 195–96; Nenninger, *Leavenworth Schools*,

102–3; Raines, "Bell and Military Reform," 478; and Milloy, "Influence of the Russo-Japanese War," 29–39.

305. *ARWD/COS* 1907, p. 195–96.

306. For paragraph, see Charles Humphrey, Report of the Quartermaster-General, November 10, 1904, in *Annual Reports of the War Department for the Year Ended June 30, 1904*, vol. 2 (Washington, DC: Government Printing Office, 1904), 80; *ARWD/COS* 1905, p. 376; *ARWD/QG* 1906, p. 55; Henry Sharpe, Report of the Commissary-General (hereafter, *ARWD/CG* 1906), October 1, 1906, in *Annual Report of the War Department for the Year Ended June 30, 1906*, vol. 2 (Washington, DC: Government Printing Office, 1906), 79; *ARWD/SOW* 1907, p. 17; *ARWD/COS* 1907, p. 191, 196; Greenwood, "American Military Observers," 364–65, 469, 500–501; Beaver, *Modernizing the American War Department*, 32, 37–38, 40–42; Raines, "Bell and Military Reform," 192–93; and Nenninger, *Leavenworth Schools*, 124–26.

307. Roosevelt to Chaffee, July 3, 1905, in Morison, *Letters*, 4:1261.

308. *ARWD/COS* 1905, p. 376.

309. For paragraph, see John Fisher and Carol Fisher, *Food in the American Military: A History* (Jefferson, NC: McFarland, 2011), 118, 123–24; John Weston, Report of the Commissary-General, 1905, September 30, 1905, in *Annual Report of the War Department for the Year Ended June 30, 1905*, vol. 2 (Washington, DC: Government Printing Office, 1905), 80; *ARWD/CG* 1906, p. 73; and Harry Rogers, Report of the Quartermaster, September 30, 1920, in *1920 Secretary of War Annual Report* (Washington, DC: Government Printing Office, 1921), 90–91.

310. Fisher and Fisher, *Food in the American Military*, 118.

311. Quoted in Greenwood, "American Military Observers," 381.

312. Quoted in *ARWD/CG* 1906, p. 74.

313. For paragraph, see Morison, *Admiral Sims*, 71, 73, 78, 90, 114–15, 178–81, 219, 475–76; Oyos, *In Command*, 32–36, 118–19, 216–30, 281–94; Paul Pedisich, *Congress Buys a Navy: Politics, Economics, and the Rise of American Naval Power, 1881–1921* (Annapolis, MD: Naval Institute Press, 2016), 3–6, 17, 28, 41, 60–61, 74, 129–30, 142, 151, 156–57, 161–62, 171, 177; McBride, *Technological Change*, 20, 39–40, 47–48, 51–57; and Hone, *Learning War*, 23–38, 88–89.

314. Oyos, *In Command*, 118–19.

315. For paragraph, see Dorwart, *Office of Naval Intelligence*, 81–82; Baer, *One Hundred Years*, 33–34; Hone, *Learning War*, 96–98; and Oyos, *In Command*, 122–23, 129, 251–52, 257–58.

316. Roosevelt to Henry Cabot Lodge, June 5, 1905, in Morison, *Letters*, 4:1205.

317. For paragraph, see *ARND/SON* 1904, p. 3; *ARND/SON* 1905, p. 17; Pedisich, *Congress Buys a Navy*, 76, 149–52, 159–69, 173; Spector, *Admiral of the New Empire*, 150–53; Baer, *One Hundred Years*, 9–11, 18, 33–34; Braisted, *US Navy in the Pacific*, 173, 185; and Oyos, *In Command*, 222–25, 258–60.

318. *ARND/SON* 1905, p. 17.

319. Roosevelt to Richard Bartholdt, September 25, 1905, in Morison, *Letters*, 5:35.

320. Roosevelt to Eugene Hale, October 27, 1906, in Morison, *Letters*, 5:475.

321. *Historical Statistics of the United States*, Table Ea636-643.

322. *ARND/SON* 1905, p. 4; *Historical Statistics of the United States*, Table Ed26-47; John Alden, *The American Steel Navy* (Annapolis, MD: Naval Institute Press, 1989), 251–52, 266; and Pedisich, *Congress Buys a Navy*, 66, 96, 132–33, 139–40, 167.

323. Roosevelt to Wood, March 9, 1905, in Morison, *Letters*, 4:1136.

324. E. B. Potter, *Nimitz* (Annapolis, MD: Naval Institute Press, 1976), 56–57.

325. Pedisich, *Congress Buys a Navy*, 163.

326. O'Connell, *Sacred Vessels*, 20–24, 126; Hone, *Learning War*, 22–23, 43–45; Victor Metcalf, Report of the Secretary of the Navy (hereafter, *ARND/SON 1907*), November 18, 1907, in *Annual Reports of the Navy Department for the Fiscal Year 1907* (Washington, DC: Government Printing Office, 1908), 6; and Roosevelt to Key, April 10, 1908, and Roosevelt to Newberry, May 12, 1908, both in Morison, *Letters*, 6:999–1001, 1029.

327. For paragraph, see O'Connell, *Sacred Vessels*, 48–49, 76, 79–80, 106–12, 134; McBride, *Technological Change*, 63, 66–69, 71–72; Friedman, *US Battleships*, 51–55; and Baer, *One Hundred Years*, 18–19, 23, 30–31.

328. Roosevelt to Morton, October 6, 1904, in TRCDL.

329. For paragraph, see *ARND/SON 1907*, p. 7; Mahan, "Reflections," 460, 466; McBride, *Technological Change*, 69, 72, 75, 87; Sims, "Inherent Tactical Qualities," 1362–63; Spector, *Admiral of the New Empire*, 175–77; Oyos, *In Command*, 248–60, 278–80, 286; Roosevelt to Sims, October 5, 1904, Roosevelt to George Albert Converse, October 31, 1904, Roosevelt to Morton, February 20, 1905, Roosevelt to William Rockhill, August 29, 1905, all in Morison, *Letters*, 4:973, 1006, 1123, 1326; Roosevelt to Metcalf, January 27, 1907, in Morison, *Letters*, 5:572; and William Cowles to Roosevelt, August 27, 1906, in TRCDL.

330. Oyos, *In Command*, 255.

331. Roosevelt to Bonaparte, December 20, 1905, in Morison, *Letters*, 5:121.

332. Roosevelt to Converse, September 10, 1906, in Morison, *Letters*, 5:403.

333. Sims to Roosevelt, September 27, 1906, in TRCDL.

334. Roosevelt to William Sims, September 27, 1906, in Morison, *Letters*, 5:427.

335. Dewey to Bonaparte, October 2, 1906, p. 2, in TRCDL.

336. Roosevelt to Sims, October 13, 1906, in Morison, *Letters*, 5:455.

337. Roosevelt to Hale, October 27, 1906, in Morison, *Letters*, 5:475.

338. McCully, *McCully Report*, 62; Friedman, *US Battleships*, 62–63, 66, 78–79; and Converse to Roosevelt, October 16, 1906, in TRCDL.

339. For paragraph, see Hone, *Learning War*, 55–91; Oyos, *In Command*, 130–43; Friedman, *Naval Firepower*, 20, 60, 79, 176–87; Morison, *Admiral Sims*, 83, 89, 135, 145, 147, 170, 236–37, 241; O'Connell, *Sacred Vessels*, 98, 102, 106, 109, 118–19; McCully, *McCully Report*, 251; and Sims to Roosevelt, October 1, 1905, Sims to Roosevelt, July 5, 1906, Sims to Roosevelt, September 27, 1906, p. 10–12, 23, and Converse to Roosevelt, October 16, 1906, all in TRCDL.

340. For paragraph, see *ARND/BON 1905*, p. 392; *ARND/SON 1905*, p. 20; Norman Friedman, *US Cruisers: An Illustrated Design History* (Annapolis, MD: Naval Institute Press, 1984), 61–65; Alden, *American Steel Navy*, 368–76, 381; and McBride, *Technological Change*, 75, 87, 113–14.

341. Friedman, *US Cruisers*, 45.

342. Dewey to Roosevelt, January 15, 1907, p. 1–2, in TRCDL.

343. Roosevelt to Foss, January 11, 1907, in Morison, *Letters*, 5:545.

344. *ARND/SON 1907*, p. 7.

345. For paragraph, see *ARND/SON 1907*, p. 7; Alden, *American Steel Navy*, 149–50, 157, 368–69, 375–76; Friedman, *US Destroyers*, 16–24; McCully, *McCully Report*, 161–62, 247; Roosevelt to

Cannon, February 29, 1908, in Morison, *Letters*, 6:956, 1516; and Dewey to Bonaparte, October 2, 1906, p. 5, 8, in TRCDL.

346. Quoted in Friedman, *US Destroyers*, 21.

347. Theodore Roosevelt, "Annual Message of the President to the Congress," December 3, 1907 (Washington, DC: Government Printing Office, 1910), 56.

348. For paragraph, see Mahan, "Retrospect," 167–73; Braisted, *US Navy in the Pacific*, 173, 181, 199; O'Connell, *Sacred Vessels*, 129; and Oyos, *In Command*, 123–29.

349. Mahan, "Retrospect," 173; emphasis original.

350. For paragraph, see Baer, *One Hundred Years*, 24–26, 34–35, 40–47; Hone, *Learning War*, 96–104; Challener, *Admirals, Generals*, 34, 248, 251–52; Spector, *Admiral of the New Empire*, 148–49, 161–62; Braisted, *US Navy in the Pacific*, 188, 193–200, 206, 212; Richard Turk, *The Ambiguous Relationship: Theodore Roosevelt and Alfred Thayer Mahan* (Westport, CT: Greenwood Press, 1987), 50–61, 90; Oyos, *In Command*, 124–25, 325–28; Roosevelt to Bonaparte, August 10, 1906, Roosevelt to Lodge, May 22, 1907, and Roosevelt to Newberry, August 6, 1907, all in Morison, *Letters*, 5:353, 670, 743; and Roosevelt to Charlemagne Tower Jr., February 12, 1908, in Morison, *Letters*, 6:941.

351. Friedman, *US Cruisers*, 57.

352. Spector, *Admiral of the New Empire*, 162; emphasis original.

353. Roosevelt to Mahan, January 12, 1907, in Morison, *Letters*, 5:551.

354. Roosevelt to Taft, March 3, 1909, in Morison, *Letters*, 6:1543.

355. Toll, *Pacific Courage*, xxxiv.

356. For paragraph, see O'Connell, *Sacred Vessels*, 141, 145; Hartmann and Truver, *Weapons That Wait*, 36–37; McCully, *McCully Report*, 248; and "USA Mines" in http://www.navweaps.com.

357. Newton Mason, Report of the Chief of Bureau of Ordnance, October 1, 1905, in *Annual Reports of the Navy Department for the Year 1905* (Washington, DC: Government Printing Office, 1906), 501.

358. Hartmann and Truver, *Weapons That Wait*, 37.

359. Schroeder, "Gleanings from Sea of Japan," 58–61; McCully, *McCully Report*, 251; Alden, *American Steel Navy*, 234; and Susan Douglas, "The Navy Adopts the Radio, 1899–1919," in *Military Enterprise and Technological Change*, ed. Merritt Roe Smith (Cambridge, MA: MIT Press, 1985), 119, 126–28, 132–39, 146–49, 152–53.

360. *ARND/BON* 1905, p. 392–93; for rest of paragraph, see Charles Bonaparte, Report of the Secretary of the Navy (hereafter, *ARND/SON* 1906), November 28, 1906, in *Annual Reports of the Navy Department for the Year 1906* (Washington, DC: Government Printing Office, 1907), 20, 26; Friedman, *US Cruisers*, 45, 55, 57, 67–71; Dewey to Bonaparte, October 2, 1906, in TRCDL; Roosevelt to Foss, January 10, 1905, in Morison, *Letters*, 4:1097; and Roosevelt to George Turner, February 10, 1909, in Morison, *Letters*, 6:1516.

361. Dewey to Bonaparte, October 2, 1906, p. 6, in TRCDL.

362. Bonaparte to Roosevelt, February 8, 1906, Newberry to Roosevelt, February 12, 1906, Bonaparte to Roosevelt, February 14, 1906, and Roosevelt to Eugene Hale, February 21, 1906, all in TRCDL.

363. *ARND/SON* 1906, p. 26; Schroeder, "Gleanings from Sea of Japan," 79–80; Miller, *War Plan Orange*, 75, 91, 94; Alden, *American Steel Navy*, 123–24, 224; and Friedman, *US Cruisers*, 55–56.

364. Dewey to Bonaparte, October 2, 1906, p. 6, in TRCDL.

365. Dewey to Bonaparte, October 2, 1906, p. 6 in TRCDL.

366. Presley Rixey, Report of the Surgeon General, US Navy, October 1, 1905, in *Annual Reports of the Navy Department for the Year 1905* (Washington, DC: Government Printing Office, 1906), 1211–14.

367. Coffman, *Regulars*, 95.

368. Bailey, "Military History," 190.

369. Alfred Vagts, *Military Attaché* (Princeton, NJ: Princeton University Press, 1967), 266, 270–71.

370. Clark, *Preparing for War*, 259.

371. Clark, 259.

372. Clark, 265.

373. Dastrup, *King of Battle*, 160.

374. For paragraph, see O'Connell, *Sacred Vessels*, 211, 222–23; Baer, *One Hundred Years*, 74, 78–79; Morison, *Admiral Sims*, 360, 413–15; and Hartmann and Truver, *Weapons That Wait*, 36–37, 48–49, 52–55.

375. Greenwood, "American Military Observers," 506.

376. Yigal Sheffy, "A Model Not to Follow: European Armies and the Lessons of War," in *The Impact of the Russo-Japanese War*, ed. Rotem Kowner (New York: Routledge, 2007), 266.

377. McBride, *Technological Change*, 237; Vacca, "Learning about Military Effectiveness," 348–51; Kenda, "Lessons Learned," 95; Sheffy, "A Model Not to Follow," 255, 265; Payne, "Russo-Japanese War," 124; and Bailey, "Military History," 176.

378. Greenwood, "American Military Observers," 2.

379. Greenwood, 2.

380. Quoted in Vacca, "Learning about Military Effectiveness," 248.

CHAPTER 3

THE SPANISH CIVIL WAR
Desired but Disputed Data

It is generally accepted that the civil war in Spain had not only been a
laboratory for testing equipment—particularly of German and
Russian designs, but a "dress rehearsal" for the next war.
—*US military attaché Col. Stephen Fuqua*

In contrast to the eagerly anticipated Russo-Japanese War, news of the Spanish Civil
War's outbreak in July 1936 generated scant interest among American officers. Understandably, they did not expect a struggle between elements of this lowly regarded,
poorly equipped military to yield valuable insights on modern warfare. Foreign
power intervention, however, rapidly intensified the combat's scale and significance.
The initial success of the German- and Italian-backed Nationalist rebels prompted a
reluctant Joseph Stalin in late September to provide the leftist government with sufficient assistance to reverse battlefield fortunes. Adolf Hitler and Benito Mussolini
responded by increasing their contribution, resulting in stabilized front lines by year's
end. Besides wanting to bolster their respective allies, these outside powers, most notably the Germans, tested new tactics and weapons.[1] For example, the German Condor
Legion established an "Experimental Flight" section to evaluate prototypes as they
became available (e.g., Heinkel He-111, Junkers Ju-87, and Messerschmitt Bf-109).

The transformed Spanish Civil War prompted the US Army to reassess its informational value shortly after the November 1936 battle for Madrid, with the General Staff's Military Intelligence Directorate (MID) initiating an enhanced collection
effort. Extensive coverage of the war in American and international military periodicals complemented the official investigation. Reflecting the sentiment of many
American officers, Col. Conrad Lanza observed in mid-1938 that "the fact that this
war is occurring just at the time when there has been a change of tactics, organization, and weapons among nations, makes it important, and desirable of close
study."[2] By contrast, most members of the US Army Air Corps dismissively grouped
it with the "small" conflicts in Ethiopia and China as not germane to understanding
airpower. Given that "air power as an instrument of war remained largely in the
realm of theory and conjecture," this neglect, motivated by strategic preferences and

bureaucratic considerations, is a key element of this chapter.[3] The need to adopt a bifurcated examination of the US Army lessons-learning dynamics combined with American sailors' lack of interest prompted exclusion of the US Navy in this chapter.[4]

HOW DID THE ARMY ATTEMPT TO IDENTIFY LESSONS?

This conflict required a markedly different information collection approach. The pre–World War I norm of providing access to third-party observers had significantly eroded, diminishing the utility from dispatching designated officers.[5] Reflective of the War Department's initial disinterest in the fighting, MID rejected the army attaché in Spain's request for attachment to Republican forces, believing, as the assistant chief of staff for intelligence wrote, that "little could be gained, judging by the lack of any reports of importance from Colonel Stephen Fuqua to date" and fearing that "embarrassing incidents" from the placement of official observers on one side.[6] The lack of diplomatic relations with the Nationalists precluded assigning personnel to their forces. With the combat's most interesting features involving foreigners, the Americans recognized that better sources of information might exist outside of Spain. An anonymous American war correspondent argued in late 1937 that "the lessons learned will be seen in what the interested powers do by way of modification or change in materiel and organization within the next few years" after their battlefield experiences.[7]

Thus, both necessity and virtue prompted the War Department to adopt an attaché-centric investigatory approach.[8] On December 11, 1936, MID executive officer Lt. Col. Oliver Wood cabled army representatives in London, Paris, Berlin, Rome, and Moscow that "the conflict [in Spain] has now reached a stage of acute interest," as important "aircraft, weapons and armored vehicles are undergoing the practical test of war."[9] Wood tasked them to "utilize every appropriate opportunity to obtain data on the types, performances, and tactical use of these materiels."[10] The attachés with primary responsibility for Spanish Civil War coverage were a relatively educated, experienced group, but largely lacking in technical expertise. Of the ten officers who filed the most reports about the conflict, nine had graduated from the Command and General Staff School (CGSS); eight, the Army War College (AWC); and most had World War I combat experience. Unfortunately, given that the tank and aircraft would be key subjects of inquiry, they possessed infantry or artillery backgrounds, with the exception of pilot Capt. Townsend Griffiss and ordnance officer Lt. Col. Philip Faymonville.

These key attachés occupied three distinct vantage points. First, Fuqua and Griffiss operated inside Spain. Colonel Fuqua possessed significant attributes and even stronger negatives.[11] A much more experienced officer (nearly forty years of service, including three wars) than a typical attaché, he had requested assignment to Madrid in 1933 at reduced rank in lieu of retirement after completing a four-year stint as the chief of infantry. Fuqua maintained good relationships with Spanish officials and other attachés, took at least twenty-five trips to observe combat, and produced voluminous reports (some two thousand pages). These documents, however, focused on the preparations for and general conduct of battles resulting in complaints from MID over his failure to provide more technical information. With Fuqua ill equipped to understand aviation matters, MID wisely transferred Assistant Air Attaché Griffiss from Paris to Spain in December 1936. This experienced fighter pilot possessed strong acumen, attention to detail, and enthusiasm for the task. In a study of US Army reporting on the Spanish Civil War, Kim Juntunen found that Griffiss, more than any other attaché, "relied on personal observation for information, and he often analyzed the information he received, and tried to draw conclusions from what he was learning."[12] During his first eight months in country, Griffiss benefited from contact with American mercenary pilots fighting for the Republicans but, like Fuqua, lacked access to the Nationalist side.

Attachés based in Germany, Italy, and Russia represented a potentially important group of collectors, but they struggled to obtain information as these belligerents carefully shielded their insights. Maj. Truman Smith in Berlin, perhaps the best American military attaché at the time, frustratingly relayed to Washington in August 1937 that "all information on Spanish combat experience is guarded as a state secret."[13] Even his successful gambit to employ Charles Lindbergh, whom German aviators revered, to gain greater access to the Luftwaffe in a series of visits failed to produce much data on the Condor Legion. Likewise, the Americans in Italy supplied little of value on Spain.[14] The attachés in Moscow and Riga, who were the "principal windows" into the remote Red Army, passed along war information primarily from conversations with other foreign representatives and translated articles from Russian military journals.[15] Although historian David Glantz lauds Faymonville for providing "particularly accurate and perceptive" reports, as the first US military attaché to Moscow, he endured much criticism for being excessively sympathetic to the Soviets, and MID dismissively treated his cables as tainted.[16]

By contrast, attachés in London and Paris dispatched voluminous and valuable data.[17] Given their concern about the Germans, the French paid close attention to the Spanish combat, albeit tending to draw conclusions that reinforced their prevailing views. Beyond French military sources, Lt. Col. Horace Fuller and his assistant, Lt. Col. Sumner Waite, learned about the fighting from a well-informed attaché community including the German Karl-Erich Kühlenthal. Juntunen characterizes their reporting as "especially impressive" given its depth, variety, and attempts "to analyze the information they gathered and point out trends and possible lessons."[18] Although the British, particularly the Royal Air Force, devoted less attention to the Spanish Civil War, Lt. Col. Raymond Lee and his assistant, Lt. Col. Hayes Kroner, also collected meaningful data, especially from the Nationalist side.

A lack of resources hampered MID's ability to analyze events.[19] The office periodically produced memorandums for the chief of staff and other senior leaders on the war, but it usually passed along reports without assessment. Thus, as Bruce Bidwell highlights, findings "seldom received any suitable evaluation to the point where they could be effectively translated into improvements in our own tactics, techniques, or weapons."[20] William Odom adds that this deficiency was particularly problematic given that other army organizations lacked intelligence sections. Moreover, although MID provided a weekly list of received reports and would loan copies upon request if available, it only produced a small number and prohibited duplication, resulting in the most desired information often being unattainable. In a study of the Ordnance Department, Constance McLaughlin Green, Harry Thomson, and Peter Roots note the failure to provide lower-level and technical personnel access to valuable documents.[21] Still, Thomas Mahnken argues that US military intelligence "did a surprisingly good job" of monitoring foreign military activity given its deficient budget and limited number of personnel.[22] Supplementing army-collected information were numerous articles on the war, some authored by combat participants or extended battlefield visitors, in professional publications (e.g., *Infantry Journal*, *Army Ordnance*).[23]

With MID focused on information collection, analyses of the combat and its implications largely fell to the army's leading educational institutions, especially the Army War College.[24] With the service "more at peace than ever before in its history" and lacking the funds to sustain large forces or engage in much field training, officers gravitated toward army schools as students and instructors.[25] As Edward Coffman points out, the school system was "the most vital element in the Army."[26] The AWC class that began with the start of year two of the Spanish Civil War directed particular attention to the conflict as data accumulated. In October 1937 a group of students in the G-3 (operations) course analyzed the war's combat, especially for tanks. The following January a committee in the G-2 (intelligence) course considered lessons from the fighting, including "weapons development, tactical changes, and innovative techniques."[27] The army encouraged students to criticize standing policy and recommend changes, with their work reviewed by the school commandant, MID chief, and even army chief of staff. The CGSS, which served as a critical institution both for career development and understanding combined-arms warfare, exhibited less interest in the conflict, while the influential Air Corps Tactical School (ACTS) actively attempted to undermine its relevance, as will be discussed.

WHAT LESSONS DID THE ARMY IDENTIFY?

Before addressing army insights, it is helpful to briefly lay out key elements of the rapidly approaching World War II, for which the Americans were trying to prepare. The global struggle's intense combat consisted of unprecedented scale, technical sophistication, and destruction. On the ground, mechanized forces came of age, contributing significantly to the restoration of an advantage for attacking forces. Gradually, improved weapons and tactics emerged to restore some balance to the defense, especially in countering tanks, but military success remained heavily dependent on adequate mechanization and motorization as well as sustained logistical support. Above all, airpower was indispensable for offensive and defensive ground operations. Strategic bombing represented a major component of the combat, inflicting enormous devastation but not achieving the decisive victory predicted by prewar advocates. Moreover, the high attrition rate for bombers lacking proper fighter escort raised doubts about this approach. Finally, orchestrating all these land and air assets in a synergistic fashion required major improvements in command, control, communications, and intelligence.

The key question for our purposes is how well the US military learned lessons from the Spanish Civil War that prepared it for the above combat. A crucial prior query is what it would have been reasonable for the US—or anyone else—to discover from the conflict. Ending only six months before the start of World War II, the Spanish Civil War contained many elements present in the subsequent fight but also some stark differences. Students of the earlier fighting could have learned about the increasing role for the tank and aircraft in combination with traditional infantry and artillery forces as well as the command, control, communications, and intelligence challenge to integrating such arms productively. In particular, Spain illustrated the vital role aviation would perform in ground operations. It also revealed that all air-to-ground missions—close air support (CAS), light bombardment, and strategic bombing—benefited greatly from fighter protection, while preventing such strikes required air superiority. The conflict highlighted the potential for antitank and antiaircraft artillery (AAA) assets to counter tanks and aircraft. Contributing to their effectiveness were deficiencies in the still immature technologies that underlay armor and aviation as well as ignorance about how to employ them. Experience in Spain, however, contributed considerably to changes in weapons and tactics, especially by the Germans, that precipitated the offense-favoring blitzkrieg approach that dominated in the early years of World War II. Thus, while providing much useful data, the Spanish Civil War was less of a mirror than a pathway to future war. A pathway that a military neglected at its own peril.

Drawing lessons from any military experience appropriately warrants prudence about the danger of extrapolating given the unique context, but investigators of the Spanish Civil War particularly emphasized this risk given its unusual dynamics. Typifying this sentiment, the London-based attaché Lee endorsed British major C. A. de Linde's caution about forming conclusions, given that "it will be possible to prove almost any theory by the exercise of a little adroitness in selection or interpretation."[28] Manipulative potential existed in part because, as retired British major general Arthur Temperley warned in October 1937, "accurate information as to the performance of the various weapons is exceedingly hard to obtain; the secrets are jealously guarded."[29] The following year Griffiss added that, "primarily due to its limited strength and composition, the role of aviation in the Spanish civil war has not reached the importance and development that it would have in a European conflict."[30] Yet they and many others, after inoculating themselves with such qualifications, proceeded to describe a wide range of findings. Commentators generally concurred with Brig. Gen. Henry Reilly, USA (Ret.), a journalist who, after spending several months in country, wrote that the conflict "has been on a sufficiently large scale with respect to numbers engaged, training of troops, and leadership of officers, to be worth serious study. The weapons used have been sufficiently modern and numerous both on land and in the air to make the lessons learned worthy of acceptance."[31]

Above all, the US Army sought insights on four basic questions. Had the overall nature of warfare undergone fundamental change, with modern weapons restoring maneuver to the battlefield? How would the new and improved tanks and aircraft be employed? What were the practical design lessons regarding these weapons and counters to them? Finally, did strategic bombing, as American aviators asserted, obviate the need for ground combat? In discussing responses to these questions, one must be aware of the potential for shifting lessons in a conflict that lasted 989 days. Such changes, however, rarely occurred. Rather, as James Cortada found, attaché cables from the second half of the war generally "add little to the story, often reconfirming information learned earlier, either from the same writer or another observer."[32] Exceptions such as combatants' growing preference for larger-caliber antitank weapons are noted.

A more problematic issue was the significant schisms within the service over the findings' generalizability. Proponents of armored warfare argued that Spain was not a suitable environment for evaluating the tank, with its hilly terrain, large vineyards and groves, small villages, and ample trees.[33] Plus, both sides lacked a sufficient number of tanks to facilitate concentrated use. Finally, the Spanish crews that mostly operated these vehicles lacked adequate training and skill. In a January 1938 memorandum, MID executive officer Lt. Col. Charles Busbee acknowledged these factors contributed to tanks' lack of success.[34] Still, while acknowledging contextual limitations, MID and army leadership attached great weight to the collected information, as will be seen in the subsequent discussion. An even sharper division existed between the regular army and army air corps over the utility of lessons for aviation.[35] Air corps leaders viewed the conflict through the lens of absolute faith in strategic bombing, blinding them to data that challenged that approach. Encouraging their comfort with neglecting aerial combat in Spain was a lack of awareness of what actually transpired in the skies above Spain. Historian James Corum discovered that a "surprising level of ignorance and naivete regarding the war in Spain seems to have permeated the Air Corps to the highest levels."[36] In his memoirs, former chief of the air corps Gen. Hap Arnold complained that "where our Army observers watched the actual air fighting, reports were not only weak but unimaginative."[37] In reality, as Mahnken notes, "Hap Arnold received regular reports on the war but dismissed them as irrelevant."[38] As will be discussed, these same documents left a striking impression on non–air corps officers.

Enlightening Lessons

For certain subjects these schisms further clouded confusing signals, but in other areas the Americans identified clear lessons. Some of the findings represented valuable insights about the dynamics of future battle, while others proved misleading with dangerous implications if aggressively applied. I begin with the former, which tend to get overshadowed by the latter among historians criticizing the US Army's preparatory efforts in the late 1930s.

More complicated combined-arms challenge. Above all, reporting emphasized the critical need for effectively integrating different battlefield elements. The value of combined arms had been a central theme of the Russo-Japanese War and fully demonstrated in World War I, but it had then been about infantry–artillery cooperation. Information from Spain highlighted that militaries now had to ensure that tanks and aircraft acted in conjunction with those traditional ground components.[39] Typifying senior US ground officers reaction, field artillery chief Maj. Gen. Robert Melville Danford, in a September 1938 AWC lecture, emphasized that the fighting demonstrated a requirement for close cooperation between infantry, armor, field artillery, and air power.[40] Reilly stressed that accompanying fire, rather than being provided by artillery, was often "furnished by the tanks and by the assault aviation."[41] While strategic bombing zealots in the air corps rejected this perspective, Griffiss, the American aviator most exposed to the combat, emphatically declared that the conflict "shows the absolute dependency of Ground Forces upon Air Action and also that Air Operations in order to be successful on the field of battle must have ground support."[42] Appropriately, many commentators added that the war had illustrated not only the necessity of combining arms but the difficulty in doing so. For example, Lanza observed that "in the past we have found that coordination of artillery and infantry was far from simple. To add thereto two other arms, tanks and aviation, certainly complicates the question."[43]

Deficiency of light tanks. Armor, which had been integral to all major attacks, performed poorly in part because of the uniformly reported inadequacy of light tanks.[44] Before the war relatively fast, minimally armored tanks (known as tankettes in extreme variants) had been popular. Vehicles armed exclusively with machine guns such as the German Mark I and Italian CV-33 tankette suffered in engagements. Instead, the Americans praised the effectiveness of the Russian T-26's 45 mm cannon. Of the much-discussed March 1937 Battle of Guadalajara, the first combat of tanks versus tanks, Lanza explained that "the one with the heavier armament and armor won."[45] In May 1937 Waite added that, "for the combat tank, speed and radius of action are less important than armament which should include a gun and sufficient protection."[46] This same conclusion subsequently appears in the report of the January 1938 AWC Committee identifying war lessons and a July 1938 memorandum from MID director Col. E.R.W. McCabe to the chief of cavalry.[47]

Value of antitank guns. While the unexpected tank-on-tank combat contributed to appreciating the need for better protection, the flat-trajectory antitank gun's effectiveness garnered the most attention for stopping armor forces.[48] The Americans relayed battle reports and passed along commentary from European sources that tank attacks collapsed against 37 mm and 45 mm variants of this weapon in its baptism of fire. In particular, they highlighted the performance of the German Pak 36, a 37 mm antitank gun that Waite characterized in May 1937 as "very successful."[49] In articles written in the first half of 1938, British analyst J.F.C. Fuller and Italian reserve lieutenant colonel Emilio Canevari noted its advantageous mobility and rate of fire. Yet reports from later in the war indicated combatants' growing preference for larger, more powerful variants. Most notably, Reilly, after extensive conversations with Nationalist officers, wrote MID in October 1938 that "no one has any use for the 37 mm or similar small caliber weapon for antitank" guns.[50] He explained how the Germans employed their 88 mm Flak 18/36/37 gun with devastating effectiveness against enemy armor and other ground targets.

Continuing need for heavy field artillery. Limitations of the tank contributed to the continuing requirement for traditional field artillery.[51] Although the Americans noted, as will be discussed, that combatants' lack of guns resulted in both sides substituting CAS, planes could only deliver relatively small munitions. As a result, attaché reporting from Barcelona and London identified a need for heavier artillery.

Lanza explained in mid-1938 that, "if Spain has shown anything, it has been that even slenderly held positions can not be broken except through thorough artillery preparation. The rule has been—no artillery; no progress."[52] Despite not being a major lesson or an exciting new discovery, the continuing need for heavy field guns represents the type of useful revelation available from studying foreign wars as it ran counter to prevailing sentiment for sacrificing larger artillery to enhance force mobility.

The increased potential for and benefit from motorized transport. In general, the Spanish Civil War highlighted the criticality of rapid movement around the war zone, prompting commentators to identify a requirement for motorized forces.[53] Canevari, characterizing the conflict as a war "on wheels," argued that Spain "confirmed the absolute necessity of a strong effort to motorize the artillery and the services."[54] Lanza exclaimed that "the days of infantry operating on foot, except for defense, are disappearing."[55] He added that "the high rate of movement of motorized and mechanized troops enables forces 100 miles away to be in line over night."[56] Vincent Usera, a former US Marine who fought in the conflict for eighteen months, wrote that "no example in military history . . . affords a more extensive use of motor transport than the recent civil war in Spain."[57] The early 1938 AWC G-2 study on lessons recognized motorization's importance for moving men, weapons, and supplies. Yet, as a result of vehicles' vulnerability to air attack, small-arms fire, and physical obstacles, a CGSS lecturer asserted that Spain confirmed "troops in motors cannot fight," and Canevari cautioned that "employing motorized detachments in the fighting zone must be rejected."[58]

The potential for movement by air as well as ground represented one of the few Spanish Civil War lessons shared by air corps and regular army officers. The conflict would have been significantly different, if occurring at all, without German Ju-52 bombers flying Franco and more than twenty thousand soldiers from Spanish Morocco to the mainland ("the first successful major military airlift").[59] Appreciating this development, Arnold wrote in May 1938 that "troop transport by air can be expected to play a tremendous part in any future war."[60] Likewise, Maj. George Kenney, a leading ACTS instructor, began his discussion of findings from Spain with "air transportation of troops and supplies on a large scale to supplement and even to replace other means of transportation is definitely a part of modern warfare."[61] Maj. Thomas Phillips, a CGSS lecturer, elaborated on this subject in a mid-1938 article entitled "Air Power and Troop Movement."[62]

Increasing threat from and requirement for AAA. Among the lessons neglected by aviators, but not the regular army, was the increasing AAA threat to planes.[63] Lee reported in early 1937 that "one of the most interesting features of the struggle is the effectiveness of the German anti-aircraft guns."[64] When the chief of staff queried

MID after the air corps forwarded an article alleging AAA ineffectiveness, McCabe responded in July 1937 that the claim "is not borne out by the information at hand from reliable British, French, and German sources and from Spain itself."[65] Maj. Robert Mackin of the Coast Artillery Corps asserted in a September 1937 article that "all experts now agree that, in the great war laboratory in Spain, antiaircraft artillery has proved its value beyond all question and has firmly established its status as the foundation of sound antiaircraft defense."[66] In August 1938 Griffiss added that the French regarded antiaircraft (AA) defense as a key lesson and had given this position weight in their rearmament program.[67] Late in the war Reilly reported that "the height and speed of the heavy bombers necessitate antiaircraft guns light enough to be taken into the field but heavier than the usual 3-inch [76 mm] field gun."[68] Given the need for large numbers of such weapons, Reilly touted the German dual-purpose 88 mm flak gun, which could switch from firing at airplanes to ground targets in "only a few minutes."[69]

When aviators, such as Kenney, highlighted AAA's low rate for shooting down aircraft, others responded that Spain showed the value of AAA was in rendering air strikes ineffective, not downing planes.[70] As Basil Liddell Hart pointed out, AA guns "contributed much to the nullification of the effect by disturbing the bomber's aim."[71] Given the perceived danger, strike planes adopted a variety of attack approaches (e.g., higher altitude, greater speed, nighttime flight), which complicated hitting targets. By March 1938 heavier bombers on both sides operated above fifteen thousand feet. Horace Fuller added that Nationalist bombers raiding Barcelona and other coastal towns would even at times cut their engines on approach at twenty thousand feet and glide over the target.[72] The finding of AAA effectiveness was important for attacking not only air forces but defenders on the ground. The Americans highlighted the particularly vivid example of Italian frontline units suffering at the Battle of Guadalajara from inadequate AA protection. Bottom line, Griffiss concluded that the Spanish Civil War showed that AAA had become "an indispensable complement" to pursuit aviation in air defense.[73]

Misleading Lessons

Defense is dominant. The effort made by all major militaries to learn from the Spanish Civil War and to correct identified deficiencies meant that information could quickly become obsolete. This proved true for the conflict's most overarching takeaway for the Americans—defense remained the dominant form of warfare.[74] When discussing lessons, Lanza began by saying, "The outstanding one has been the power of the defense."[75] Usera elaborated that when equally strong forces meet, "all motion quickly congeals to a form of position warfare. The defense invariably is

Map 3.1 Major Spanish Civil War Battles

superior to the offense."[76] A December 1937 lecturer at CGSS added that surprisingly "mechanization, motorization and air power have benefited the defensive more than the offensive."[77] Observers pointed out that Nationalist breakthroughs only occurred when they possessed an overwhelming firepower advantage, such as during the Basque and Teruel campaigns. The chief of staff, chief of infantry, and other senior officers repeatedly noted this finding when projecting future battlefield dynamics.

Infantry-centric combined arms still proper orientation. Having already discussed the appreciation of combined arms' growing importance and increasing complexity as constructive lessons, the army leadership unfortunately interpreted the fighting as reaffirming the validity of an infantry-centric approach.[78] Witnesses repeatedly observed that armor advanced effectively at the outset of battles, but problems emerged after they lost contact with the infantry and artillery. US commentators, like others, paid particularly close attention to reports on the March 1937

Battle of Guadalajara, where Italian mechanized/motorized units became isolated and collapsed after Republican counterattacks.[79] Following the large-scale July 1937 Battle of Brunete, Fuqua passed along captured Nationalist documents indicating that "tanks operating alone are doomed to disaster."[80] Upon conclusion of the last major battle (Ebro River in late 1938), Reilly relayed that both sides regarded independent tank forces as "a delusion."[81] Armor historian Steven Zaloga complains that the vehicles' limited and improper use in forward advances rather than wide turning movements resulted in an "information gap" that "allowed military analysts of the period to give free rein to their own prejudices on the subject of army mechanization."[82] The army received similar information on the ineffectiveness of air strikes not conducted in direct support of ground troops, as will be discussed. Embrace of this lesson is evident from Chief of Staff Gen. Malin Craig's 1938 Annual Report, which declared that "we find current operations confirming anew the testimony of history that the Infantry is the core and the essential substance of an army."[83]

Superiority of antitank gun over the tank. The necessity of antitank guns provided the Americans a valuable finding, but it also misleadingly led them to believe that its advantage over the tank would not soon be reversed. Zaloga points out that the extensive coverage of the major July 1937 Battle of Brunete, where armor suffered severely against antitank guns, led it to have disproportionate influence on thinking.[84] After consulting reported data, the G-3 AWC committee on mechanized warfare concluded in October 1937 that "the gun-armor race favored antitank weapons."[85] Similarly, the January 1938 G-2 AWC committee identified the relative effectiveness of antitank guns as one of the conflict's clearest findings.[86] In a mid-1938 *Infantry Journal* article, Capt. Joseph Greene exuberantly declared the Spanish Civil War showed not only that the "antitank has the edge over the tank," but if further developed "we will have neutralized the greatest ground threat of modern warfare."[87] Ultimately, armor historian George Hofmann sums up that two years into the conflict "virtually all military writers and attachés had reported on the eclipse of the tank because of the emergence and dominance of the flat trajectory antitank gun."[88] This perspective endured among Americans, despite reports that the combatants indicated the telling need for larger, more powerful antitank guns as the war progressed.

Missed Lessons

The air corps unsuccessfully attempted to prevent the army from drawing aviation insights from the Spanish Civil War, an effort that contributed to its own neglect of available lessons.[89] In December 1936 the MID leadership ordered attachés to report all information on air operations as soon as gathered. This perspective was understandable, given that, as R. Dan Richardson highlights, aviation in Spain "became the first to put to the test the technological advances and the tactical and strategic theories that had been developed during the 1920s and 1930s."[90] With non–air corps officers touting aviation data, Kenney responded with a July 1938 essay rebutting the war's heuristic value. Although acknowledging that "we may still study the Spanish situation and find food for thought by analyzing certain air operations," he characterized collected data as "very meager" and contended the lack of real air forces precluded lessons.[91] Yet, as Juntunen notes, "thanks largely to Captain Griffiss, MID received more information about the air war than any other aspect of the war."[92] Even though the air attaché cautioned not to assume that the next air battle would emulate Spain, Griffiss stated that successes and failures "have shown us the power and limitation of an air arm from which we can better judge its future employment as well as the best means of defense against it."[93] Tami Davis Biddle adds that, ultimately, despite air corps officers' efforts to downplay the conflict, the extent of "incoming information prevented them from doing so."[94]

CAS critical for ground operations. Nonetheless, the US Army Air Corps largely ignored the critical role of close air support as well as data on how to do it properly because leading American aviators regarded this mission as unimportant.[95] In a fall 1937 speech, Arnold, then the assistant chief of the air corps, praised the Imperial Japanese Army because "she has not assigned her air force to operate against front-line trenches, as have the Spaniards."[96] He added that the latter suffered heavy losses because they used aircraft "promiscuously and indiscriminately to supplement artillery actions on a large number of petty, heterogeneous missions."[97] Arnold and Lt. Col. Ira Eaker observed, in a 1938 update to *This Flying Game*, that since planes in Spain had primarily attacked ground troops and equipment ("air cooperation missions") and only rarely engaged in bombing strategic targets ("air force missions"), the war had little relevance for the United States.[98] A focus on strategic bombardment and belief in the superiority of US technology prompted an insularity at the influential ACTS that diminished attention to Spain. Future key World War II tactical air commanders Elwood "Pete" Quesada and Otto Weyland recalled that, during their time as students in the 1930s, there was a dismissive, even hostile attitude toward "ground pounders" and neglect of CAS. Thus, unsurprisingly, Biddle finds the school "strangely indifferent" to the Spanish Civil War, offering only a single lecture on it during the 1937–38 academic year.[99]

Yet non-aviators repeatedly noted that the war showed how important CAS had become for ground operations.[100] Horace Fuller pointed out that in the July 1937 Battle of Brunete, "as at Guadalajara in March, the main offensive role fell to the air force."[101] Canevari highlighted that strike aircraft were "the only new factor tactically favoring the attack (or the counterattack) as against the other modern factors, all of which favor rather the defensive."[102] He added that the side with better attack aviation "secures for itself predominance in the offensive."[103] Attachés also passed along British, French, and Soviet assessments that sustained aerial attacks had a more damaging impact on troop morale than artillery fire. In his August 1938 review, Griffiss summed up this core finding that "there is no battle on Spanish soil that is not now prepared and supported by all available aviation. One cannot doubt that in a European war the armies would ask for the same support."[104]

Spain provided practical lessons in the execution of attack aviation, but unsurprisingly, given the air corps' orientation, it paid little attention.[105] Waite cabled that the best strike results came from low-altitude (200–600 meter) passes, which combined proximity to target, surprise, and less favorable conditions for both enemy fighters and AA guns. Griffiss, however, explained that, as the war progressed, combatants "found that the most successful method of executing ground attacks was by the 'dive and run' tactics."[106] Above all, the Americans stressed that the viability of air strikes depended on coordination. Griffiss underscored this lesson, writing that the key improvement for the Republican Air Force was "the tactical cooperation that now exists between the pursuit, bombardment and ground-attack aviation."[107] Although the inclusion of radios in attack planes represented a major technological improvement during the Spanish Civil War, the lack of portable field radios problematically prevented direct communication between aircraft and frontline troops. This deficiency increased, as Griffiss noted, the critical importance of training for "efficient liaison and cooperation between the Air and Ground Troops."[108]

Fighter escort required for strike missions. While the air corps missed CAS insights because of its disregard for that mission's importance, it neglected this lesson because acceptance "cast doubt on the invincibility of bombers."[109] That is, attaché reporting on the vital importance of air superiority for both offensive and defensive operations was not controversial, but the follow-on finding that pursuit (fighter) planes were the key to achieving air superiority prompted pushback as it jeopardized American aviators' preferred way of war. Griffiss cautioned that "the wars in both Spain and China have demonstrated the futility of relying upon one's own bombardment to find, to bomb and to destroy the enemy Air Force on the ground," threatening the air corps' "offense is the best defense" approach.[110] Instead, he emphasized that recent experience demonstrated that "the best available means of accomplishing the necessary task is by attacking the enemy aircraft in the air by one's own Air Force."[111] When the army chief of staff inquired about the veracity of a British article (sent him by air corps chief Maj. Gen. Oscar Westover in June 1937) that claimed Spain showed no need for escorts, MID head McCabe answered that a consensus of recent reporting existed "to the effect that pursuit protection of bombardment formations on daytime missions is still considered imperative by both the Rebel and Government Air Forces."[112] He did allow that "pursuit planes are having more and more difficulty getting in position to hit the new bombers [e.g., Soviet Katiuska SB-2; German He-111] as the latter become faster and install more machine guns."[113] Aviators seized on this comment, but US attachés subsequently reinforced McCabe's bottom line in describing how the key July 1937 Battle of Brunete shifted when the Germans introduced the much quicker and more lethal Messerschmitt Bf-109 fighter.[114] Griffiss summed up that after the war's first year "the peacetime theory" of bomber invulnerability no longer holds as "the increased speeds and modern armament of both the bombardment and pursuit plane have worked in favor of the pursuit."[115] Air corps' dismissiveness about the escort requirement and general importance of fighters resulted in insufficient attention to details about such planes: (1) superiority of single-seat variants, (2) sharply increased speed, and (3) significantly upgraded armament.

Unknown German innovative fighter tactics. The air corps missed the preceding lessons due to its myopic perspective, but pilots lost out on a third notable finding because the Americans lacked information about innovative German fighter tactics introduced in the skies above Spain.[116] Whereas Republican pilots continued to fly the traditional three-ship Vee formation, with a fourth plane usually trailing at higher altitude as a lookout, the Germans used dogfights from mid-1937 to develop and validate superior tactics. Given that faster monoplanes (e.g., Soviet I-16, German Bf-109) could not perform the tight turns of the older biplanes, combat revealed the need for change. The Germans had already obtained air superiority when they introduced the revolutionary "finger-four" formation during air battles over the Ebro in the summer of 1938. Neither Griffiss, who left Spain shortly thereafter, or other Americans reported this development, instead supplying a series of tactical observations (e.g., I-16s protecting bombers operated in pairs with a "scissor method of attack"; approaching from the rear worked best when facing faster Ju-86 and He-111 German bombers). They also relayed that combatants emphasized a need to improve peacetime flying and gunnery training.

Unavailable Information

Strategic bombing ineffectiveness? Whereas the air corps missed strongly supported findings on fighter escort and CAS requirements, it had more legitimate ground for disputing claims that strategic bombing had been shown to be ineffective.[117] After Nationalist air raids commenced on Madrid in late 1936, Fuqua reported that Madrileños' morale actually seemed to be strengthening and resistance hardening.[118] A few weeks later Lee relayed that, for the British, "one of the remarkable features of the war so far has been the amount of punishment the inhabitants of Madrid have taken from bombardment."[119] Later in the year Mackin asserted that Spain showed reason particularly to question the American variant of strategic bombing, given that "the bombardiers in the planes have had little difficulty in hitting those targets which cover large areas but small targets which require precision in bombing have seldom been hit."[120] Corum stresses that "this completely accurate analysis struck right at the heart of the Air Corps' doctrine which emphasized the destruction of small, specific, industrial targets."[121] Thus, by September 1937 an AWC course text ("Air Forces and War") characterized strategic bombing as ineffectual and boldly asserted that the Flying Fortress (B-17) concept had "died in Spain."[122]

Air corps officers such as Kenney, however, noted that attaché reporting showed that attacks had not occurred on a scale and intensity expected in a major conflict.[123] In contrast to the large, four-engine B-17-type bomber embraced by the army air corps, strike aircraft in Spain primarily consisted of two-engine medium bombers. Aviators identified a number of contextual factors that made Spain unsuitable for strategic bombing: an agrarian society lacking meaningful targets, civil war combatants' reluctance to strike nonmilitary targets, and an absence of armaments to carry out such missions, including chemical weapons. Arnold stressed it was particularly problematic for judging the viability of the American approach (versus Douhet-type terror strikes) given that "there has been no major effort to interrupt the commercial and industrial life in Spain by the use of large forces of heavy bombardment aviation."[124] Air corps officers believed that with better aircraft and the superior Norden bombsight, they would achieve far greater accuracy than air crews in Spain. Moreover, in his August 1938 review of the air war, Griffiss provided some support for the air corps by observing that although initial bombardments have produced anger, "in the few cases when the raids have been prolonged that first prompted 'will to resist' has been turned to 'terror' and then to 'panic.'"[125] Ultimately, as air force historian Michael Sherry observes, Spain and the other wars of the late 1930s exacerbated the preexisting schism as bomber "prophets found the evidence necessary to sustain their arguments or merely ruled the record before 1939 too inconclusive to merit much attention, while skeptics usually had their doubts reinforced."[126]

HOW DID THE ARMY APPLY ITS FINDINGS?

Lessons from the Spanish combat reached the army at a seemingly highly favorable time for application. The absence of fighting experience since World War I combined with a lack of exercise funds forced US officers largely to theorize about modern war during a period filled with the introduction of new and improved systems.[127] As a result, Chief of Infantry Maj. Gen. George Lynch wrote in early 1938, "There has seldom been a period in our peacetime history which has been so marked as the present era by diversity of view on all aspects of warfare—organization, tactics, equipment."[128] He continued that, fortunately, "the battlefields of Spain and China are offering proving grounds for testing various theories and contentions."[129] In particular, as the chief of staff noted, they provided "factual evidence of the roles in which the two relatively new arms, viz, tanks and aviation, can be employed effectively."[130] Of course, cynics would respond that Spain's provision of "answers" supporting Lynch and Craig's preexisting preferences accounted for their enthusiasm about this particular test. Regardless, identifying proper approaches had gained importance amid rising threat perceptions that left the army extremely concerned about its lack of preparedness.

The conflicting views of civilian and military US decision-makers, however, complicated reactions to Spanish Civil War findings, especially pertaining to aviation.[131] President Franklin Roosevelt favored building up the navy at the expense of the army until the September 1938 Munich crisis prompted his embrace of airpower as the key to national security. This perspective contrasted with the view of Secretary of War Harry Woodring, essentially an isolationist who opposed long-range bombers. Assistant Secretary of War Louis Johnson agreed with the air corps on the need for such aircraft and attempted to maneuver around Woodring. Caught between his civilian bosses, Craig stressed the need to procure modern arms and prepare a combat-ready force. Still, the chief of staff possessed a conservative, infantry-centric outlook, while his deputy (Maj. Gen. Stanley Embick) maintained an even more retrograde perspective that conflicted sharply with air corps leaders. George Marshall, who exerted growing influence as War Plans division chief (July 1938), deputy chief of staff (October 1938), and finally chief of staff (September 1939), demonstrated a more balanced appreciation of the need for building up air and ground forces.

Bureaucratic as well as ideational schisms hampered action in the decentralized army.[132] The 1920 National Defense Act established chiefs of infantry, cavalry, and field artillery, who, along with their preexisting counterparts in aviation and coastal artillery, possessed authority over branch equipment, doctrine, and training. At a time when evolving technology and tactics warranted greater integration, these powerful entities hindered efforts to develop common approaches, especially when their leaders perceived such initiatives as threatening branch status and funding. Moreover, their view of weapons' requirements precipitated frequent and sustained disagreements with the Ordnance Department. As Robert Cameron observes, the system "maximized the potential for criticism and obstruction of a recommended measure."[133]

The increasing availability of funds after a long period of deprivation actually exacerbated competition among army components.[134] The War Department's inadequate intrawar budgets bottomed out in the Roosevelt administration's first years (1932–35) as it grappled with the Great Depression. Economic improvement and rising threat perception resulted in the availability of more money beginning in FY36. Yet access to additional cash coincided with widely expanding military requirements. In particular, the high cost of modern aircraft stressed the army and heightened tension between aviators and ground officers. Craig stated in his 1938 Annual Report that, given the army had previously prioritized procuring aircraft, it needed to address areas shown to have been dangerously neglected from the Spanish Civil War.[135]

Attempting to address its woeful unpreparedness for war prompted a late-1930s shift in orientation from officer education and materiel development to force expansion and weapons procurement.[136] After many years of essentially experimentation, the army now moved toward "acquiring large quantities of the best available equipment."[137] Thus, while Ordnance Department appropriations rose sharply in the late 1930s, funds for research and development were essentially flat. Odom elaborates that "the army chose not to wait for new types of equipment to crawl through the procurement process. Instead, it opted for available standardized models, many of which had already grown obsolete."[138] While understandable, given preparedness concerns, as David Johnson adds, it "impeded American weapons research and development programs at a time when military technologies were rapidly changing."[139] Chief of Ordnance Maj. Gen. Charles Wesson complained to the General Staff in 1938 of his department's inability "to keep abreast of recent developments abroad."[140]

Inadequate weapons, insufficient training budgets, and an overburdened General Staff contributed to the army's continued use of two dated, conflicting doctrines.[141] Based on World War I lessons, the 1923 *Field Service Regulations* (*FSR*) specified that "the special mission of other arms are derived from their powers to contribute to the execution of the infantry mission," which was "the essential arm of close combat."[142] David Johnson criticizes that this doctrine "obscured the emerging need for a whole new structure to evaluate, assimilate, and utilize new technologies" in a true combined-arms approach.[143] In 1930, believing that the 1923 *FSR* provided "insufficient guidance," the army adopted a "complementary" document, *A Manual for Commanders of Large Units*. Essentially a copy of the French *Provisional Instruction on the Tactical Employment of Large Units* (1921), it laid out the "methodical battle" approach for divisions, corps, and army-level operations. As Walter Kretchik explains, problematically "the 1923 FSR stressed open warfare—the offense, maneuver, and the dominance of infantry—while the French-based *large units* favored attrition, firepower, and the defense."[144] Their difference "clearly warranted a choice between them," but the army maintained the discordant approaches throughout the 1930s despite increasing calls for doctrinal reassessment.[145]

Beyond consideration of war data from Spain and, to a lesser extent, China, the Americans sought to understand developments in leading European forces, particularly the Wehrmacht.[146] Although its participation in the Iberian struggle accounted for much of the US Army's interest in the war, information from Germany did not necessarily align with combat data. For example, Attaché Smith relayed that some German officers such as the highly regarded Heinz Guderian held a view of mechanized warfare that contrasted reports from Spain that the tank should be used in an infantry-support role. Guderian's view gained a wider audience in the United States when the *Infantry Journal*, in late 1937, published his two-part article on armored forces. Then, in mid-1937 Lt. Col. Adolf von Schell, chief of staff for the Inspector of the Panzer Corps and Army Motorization, visited a dozen American bases. A former student and lecturer at the US Army's Infantry School, this German pointed out numerous shortcomings with the American mechanized warfare program. In August 1938 Capt. Albert Wedemeyer, USA, a student at the Kriegsakademie (War College), provided information on German plans to conduct deep operations with a mobile, combined-arms force.

Despite their esteem for the Germans, American officers did not take their outlook as gospel to be aped, given the divergent perspectives of other military powers.[147] The sharply contrasting French approach reinforced the lessons that American attachés reported about the Spanish Civil War as "mechanized cavalry performed traditional cavalry missions, while tank units provided infantry support."[148] The Soviets, with their extensive participation in Spain and significant interest in mechanized warfare, potentially could have served as a fulcrum when weighing German and French approaches. Scholars disagree on whether Soviet participation in Spain contributed to the Russian army moving away from its Deep Battle mechanization concept.[149] Regardless, MID did not identify any change at the time, and American skepticism about reporting on the Red Army undermined its potential influence. Information on other armies (e.g., British, Italian, and Japanese) had little impact. Ultimately, Cameron stresses that Americans recognized that "no international consensus existed regarding the proper organization and use of mechanized combat forces."[150] Similarly, antitank weapons and tactics abroad "followed no discernible pattern."[151] Conservative US Army leaders generally hesitated to initiate reforms until the emergence of a consensus on what to do.

Given this context, especially the rapidly increasing threat perception, the US Army reacted more favorably to lessons that facilitated near-term preparedness. That is, findings tended to gain traction when they indicated what needed to be done as well as helped win support for what was already desired. By contrast, "inspirational" information indicating problems that needed to be solved or required major changes tended to be ignored or given lower priority. Ultimately, this lessons-learning case produces a disappointing outcome, but such a result was probably unavoidable given the misleading nature of some core findings and the air corps' dismissal of aviation data.

Beneficial but Incomplete Applications

AAA upgrade. The army had severely neglected antiaircraft artillery as air defense units faced considerable bureaucratic headwinds and funding shortages.[152] The War Department's decision to place the mission in the coastal artillery had a logic, but it meant that this critical component of modern warfare was relatively isolated. The AAA had to battle status quo forces in their home branch as well as other combat arms. As a result, the army employed insufficient .50 caliber machine guns as its main antiair weapon and rarely included air defense units when conducting maneuvers. Some recognition of the problem existed as the Modernization Board's late July 1936 guidance for testing the proposed triangular infantry division listed antiair as a critical requirement and urged close examination of such units in field testing. Still, the ground branches prioritized other elements amid tight budgets, while the air corps opposed AAA spending, given its belief that air strikes on enemy airbases offered a better "defense" against enemy bombers.

Reports from Spain (and China) on the import of airpower and the increasing effectiveness of AAA, however, heightened concern about prior neglect and prompted action.[153] In his 1937 Annual Report, the chief of staff listed AAA first in areas needing attention, identifying "major shortages include 3-inch AA guns, fire control directors, height finders, and .50 caliber machine guns" for both active and National Guard antiair units.[154] A few months later Craig instructed the chief of ordnance to "concentrate intensively" on obtaining an intermediate AA weapon, an unmet requirement since World War I.[155] With even stronger language in 1938, the chief of staff exclaimed that the army had mistakenly devoted "substantial little" appropriation to new defensive weapons such as AAA (and antitank guns).[156] He added that, with a larger budget, the deficiency "fortunately" could now be addressed.[157] Although the air corps remained reluctant to acknowledge AAA's threat to bombers, continuing information from Spain undermined such denial at a time when the entire US government had embraced airpower's significance. A concerned army leadership initiated a sharp increase in the procurement of AAA assets, as spending in this area trailed aviation only in the last years of the decade. In 1939 the army adopted the M-1 37 mm AA gun as its long-desired intermediate-range weapon, but poor performance prompted a swift switch to the Swedish Bofors 40 mm AA gun, which had performed well in Spain. Effusive reports on the German 88 mm flak gun's effectiveness in Spain contributed to the service's commencing development of a similar high-altitude AA gun (the 90 mm M-1) to replace its antiquated 3-inch weapon. Findings from Spain also influenced a 1938 revision of AA doctrine and considerable attention to the subject in the new *FSR* as well as a decision to pool AAA assets in the general headquarters units to maximize efficient use.

Still, while marked improvement occurred, the US Army did not fully respond to the lessons in this area.[158] The army ended the decade mostly employing inadequate 3-inch and .50 caliber machine guns as equipment deficiencies could not be quickly alleviated. The service deserves particular criticism for disproportionately neglecting protection of forward ground units, despite their need for safety being the most significant antiair insight from Spain. Given that the war illustrated the need for improved AAA in rear as well as forward areas, strategic bombing-oriented aviators focused attention on the former, as Bryon Greenwald explains, with "procurement of high altitude antiaircraft guns to defend against such an air attack and away from consideration of antiaircraft defense of the forward area."[159] Moreover, some ground officers foolishly resisted attaching significant antiair assets to frontline units, fearing a loss of mobility. As a result, the army entered World War II with a lack of organic division AA assets. Plus, although the 1938 and 1939 doctrinal changes reflected an increased appreciation of the antiair mission and somewhat better understanding of how to conduct it, they did not provide the guidance necessary for effective antiair operations against low-level attacks on field forces.

More mobile force. The clearest examples of the army productively implementing findings occurred in areas where the data eased addressing requirements previously recognized but neglected, given fiscal limitations. For example, information from Spain provided momentum for the army's pursuit of increased mobility.[160] Upon becoming chief of staff in late 1935, Craig had pushed for acquisition of motorized vehicles and adoption of a more mobile division structure. Senior officers had been reluctant to abandon the ponderous but battle-tested square (four regiment) division employed in World War I without definitive evidence of a need for change. In July 1936 the Modernization Board recommended a triangular three-regiment structure that would reduce the division's size by almost ten thousand soldiers. This effort advanced slowly, as did motorization, with Odom pointing out that the infantry in 1937 "still moved by foot, animal-drawn transport, or two-wheel drive motor vehicle."[161] Then, increased resources combined with the reports from Spain exalting the value of motorized transportation enabled progress. Lynch argued in early 1938 that "we are . . . from many points of view, more vitally affected by developments in motorization than by impending changes in the matériel of mechanization."[162] By his 1939 Annual Report, Craig reported significant improvement with the motorization program, even though the service's ongoing expansion resulted in deficiencies in notable areas (e.g., field artillery batteries).[163] Dan Fullerton accurately argues that the army's emphasis on motorization reflects better learning from the Spanish Civil War than historians usually credit the service, given their focus on the flawed tank policy.[164]

Validation of centralized control of air assets. Although air corps' lack of interest in the Spanish Civil War produced a desultory record of not learning, the conflict did prompt agreement between aviators and non-aviators on the correctness of a recently introduced key reform.[165] In 1936 the War Department established the General Headquarters Air Force with operational control of all army aircraft (except observation planes). Achievement of this long-sought air corps goal in part reflected, as Biddle notes, that "high-ranking officers in other branches of the army had also been growing gradually more aware of the combat potential of aircraft."[166] Arnold, in his memoir, wrote that by this time "in the Army, there was no responsible quarters . . . who still doubted that the airplane had become an indispensable military weapon."[167] Still, concern existed among ground force commanders about receiving adequate air support. The Spanish Civil War, however, reinforced the underlying belief of aviation's essential role in combat as well as the soundness of establishing centralized control. Craig simply declared in his 1937 Annual Report that the General Headquarters Air Force "is confirmed by the lessons of air operations in the current warfare abroad."[168]

Conflicting Signals Complicate Application

Debate over heavy field artillery retention. The Spanish fighting demonstrated the continuing value of heavier field artillery amid momentum for eliminating such weighty materiel.[169] The initial design for the new division's motorized field artillery regiment called for a mobility-emphasizing combination of 75 mm guns and 105 mm howitzers, eliminating the much heavier 155 mm howitzers. In his February 1938 final report on the provisional infantry division's field test, however, its chief of staff (Brig. Gen. Leslie McNair) indicated a preference for retaining the 155 mm howitzers (which had substituted for the not-yet-available 105 mm M2A1s). The extent to which the Spanish Civil War influenced McNair is unclear, but Field Artillery Chief Danford in June 1938 reacted to findings from Spain and concern about the lightened division artillery in directing a Field Artillery School investigation. Its report noted that the fighting reaffirmed the need for more firepower and adamantly rejected the 155 mm howitzer's replacement, contributing to the field artillery's recommendation for a more powerful 105–155 mm combination in the new division. Yet the mobility-emphasizing War Department was not persuaded and adopted a division artillery regiment of three 75 mm gun battalions and a 105 mm howitzer battalion. It would take further evidence supplied by the Germans early in World War II to convince army leaders that it was the 75 mm gun, not the 155 mm howitzer, that should be scrapped. More positively, the Spanish Civil War prompted a serious reexamination of fire-direction techniques and efforts to refine the branch's contribution to combined-arms operations.

Adjusted new division's table of organization and equipment. The War Department's decision to override the field artillery's preference for heavier field guns exemplified the army's struggle to implement conflicting lessons in the new infantry division.[170] On the one hand, battlefield information reiterated the importance of mobility, which was the overarching goal for designing a new organization. Motorization was the subject army officers most wanted explored in its late 1937 field test. At the same time, combat in Spain revealed a number of force requirements such as heavier field artillery and AAA that reduced mobility. In May 1937 Craig ordered antimechanized (antitank) and AAA battalions added to the Provisional Infantry Division to ensure a more realistic test and enable examination of these critical units, which resided at the corps level. The extent to which reports from early in the Spanish Civil War influenced this action is unclear, but their indicated high value suggests some impact. The field tests validated war lessons on the utility of antimechanized, antiair, and heavier field artillery, yet despite this result the Modernization Board introduced some changes to the new organizational structure that deviated from Spanish cues due to mobility concerns and lack of assets. For example, the revised division included no dedicated antitank unit in the infantry battalions, relying instead on .50 caliber machine guns in heavy weapon companies and 37 mm guns in regimental HQ companies. Recognizing that these changes would be controversial, Craig ordered a second field test to commence in February 1939 and closely scrutinize assets (e.g., antitank, antiair) pooled at higher levels. The outbreak of major war in Europe, however, prompted its early termination and the triangular infantry division's adoption. Although the new unit did not reflect all the cues from Spain (it could not, given the conflicting signals), the army used the collected data to conduct better experimentation and testing before ultimately taking a course of action based on a range of considerations.

Counterproductive Effects

Adopting an obsolescent antitank gun. Unfortunately, offsetting the above benefits was the regular army's harmful applications of information regarding antitank and tank operations, which contributed to the service's unpreparedness for World War II. The success of flat-trajectory antitank guns in defeating armor in Spain prompted enthusiastic pursuit of such a capability.[171] Although both the infantry and field artillery branches had responsibility for this mission, neither had displayed much interest until the German company Rheinmetall in December 1935 offered its Pak 36 37 mm gun for testing and sale. Yet no rapid action ensued as the Ordnance Department, infantry, and field artillery debated requirements. By mid-1937 accumulating reports on the utility of flat-trajectory antitank guns in Spain increased concern that the service lacked such an armament. As Lynch pointed out, although a .50 caliber machine gun was better than nothing, its ineffectiveness against vehicles with one inch or more of armor highlighted the need for a 37 mm or 47 mm antitank gun.[172] In September 1937 Craig told Ordnance chief Maj. Gen. William Tschappat that he regarded it of "urgent importance" that his department rapidly develops an efficient weapon.[173] This directive precipitated forward momentum. In testing, an experimental American 37 mm weapon actually outperformed the Pak 36, but the army adopted a design for what would become its M-3 37 mm antitank gun that "closely resembled the German Rheinmetall weapon."[174] Historians note that embracing the reliable foreign gun represented the fastest path to addressing what Craig lamented in his 1938 Annual Report was a "wholly lacking" capability.[175]

Yet, rather than being a triumphant example of a lesson learned, the 37 mm antitank gun's adoption illustrates the potential peril of well-intentioned efforts as it left the army with a weapon that "was obsolete before it was standardized."[176] Green, Thomson, and Roots note that Capt. Rene Studler, the London-based ordnance liaison officer, had cautioned as early as April 1937 that the Germans considered the 37 mm antitank gun inadequate and said its replacement by a 47 mm or 50 mm variant should be expected.[177] Studler's information, subsequent attaché reports on the shift to larger antitank weapons in Spain, and the Ordnance Department's preference for heavier antitank guns did not alter senior American officers' focus on the Pak 36. Rather, the War Department in August 1938 designated the infantry branch "as the most interested using arm" with authority over the gun choice to expedite progress.[178] Mobility concerns contributed to branch leaders' preference for the compact 37 mm weapon that could be wheeled by four men.

Although the critical need for an antitank weapon provides a reasonable rationale for the M-3's initial adoption, the army exacerbated the consequences of selecting an obsolete weapon by preventing development of a larger-caliber replacement.[179] As Odom observes, "had the Army waited to develop an entirely new gun, it may have been without any antitank weapon before 1941," instead of acquiring 2,500 before US entry into World War II.[180] Still, the same order that gave the infantry branch primacy dubiously barred the Ordnance Department from spending development funds in FY39 and FY40 on antitank weapons larger than 37 mm.[181] The army leadership apparently intended to block alternatives that might interfere with the M-3's acquisition. Over the next six months, the War Department received further reports documenting Spanish use of bigger calibers as well as news that the primary European militaries had commenced development of larger antitank guns. Citing such information, Danford, the field artillery chief, in December 1938 lobbied unsuccessfully for production of a more powerful antitank weapon. The infantry branch remained firmly against antitank guns larger than 37 mm, and the War Department continued to support that position. The army's new 90 mm high-altitude AA gun could not depress its barrel to fire at tanks as the German 88s had demonstrated in Spain.[182] German operations in the first year of World War II finally convinced the army of the need for a larger-caliber antitank gun, but by then it was unavoidable that American forces enter North Africa in late 1942 equipped with the inadequate M-3.

Moreover, in contrast to the materiel lesson about the antitank gun, Spain did not provide clear tactical guidance.[183] The Spanish Civil War, along with German practice, showed how defenders could channel armor attacks into lethal kill zones, but the Americans harbored some doubt about applicability of that finding to more open US terrain. In contrast to infantry primacy on gun selection, the War Department "left the question of overall proponency for antitank matters unresolved," which resulted in each branch developing its own approach.[184] Drawing on information from Spain and elsewhere, the CGSS's 1939 *Antimechanized Defense* contained "some sound fundamental principles" that would be embraced in the forthcoming 1939 *FSR*.[185] Yet Odom argues that even though "great concern for protection against a mechanized attack was evident throughout the manual . . . vague and sometimes conflicting guidance underlined the lack of well-formed doctrine."[186] After Brig. Gen. Adna Chaffee Jr.'s mechanized cavalry brigade dominated the August 1939 maneuvers, he acknowledged that the opposition force's lack of tactical awareness in using their antitank weapons artificially aided his unit's performance. Despite the signals from Spain on the importance of antitank guns, or perhaps because their success precipitated complacency about the tank threat, "the army had made even less progress by 1940 in this area than it had in tank development."[187]

Adoption of a conservative tank policy. The army leadership eagerly sought lessons about the tank, given that the War Department had previously been confined to evaluating between sharply contrasting theoretical arguments about what to do with this key weapon.[188] After abolishing the Tank Corps in 1920, the service placed armor in the infantry while allowing the interested cavalry to pursue an independent capability as long as it did not call its vehicles tanks. Although a more holistic approach briefly emerged in 1928 with the Experimental Mechanized Force, branch complaints led by then Chief of Infantry Fuqua resulted in its elimination a few years later. Historians lament this decision because, as Odom explains, "further experimentation with mechanization would focus on branch-specific requirements rather than on the operations of an independent, combined arms force."[189] For the infantry, as Cameron sums up, "tanks had a singular purpose—direct support of the foot soldier."[190] Whereas the infantry maintained tight control of its tankers, the cavalry established its mechanization center at Fort Knox, away from the branch leadership at Fort Riley. This decision assisted efforts by Chaffee and Brig. Gen. Daniel Van Voorhis to push for more autonomous use of "combat cars" (tanks). Despite their different requirements, the army's lack of funds necessitated the Ordnance Department develop a common base vehicle.

The debate over how best to use modern tanks intensified in late 1937, by which time attaché reports on the Spanish Civil War had circulated throughout the army leadership, branches, and school system.[191] In an October speech at the AWC, Van Voorhis, commander of the 7th Mechanized Cavalry brigade, highlighted contrasting opinions and asked, as Hofmann notes, "should tanks support the infantry or the infantry support tanks?"[192] Van Voorhis stressed that until the army answered this question, progress with mechanization would be stunted. Col. Bruce Palmer, another mechanized cavalry leader, contended that recent exercises indicated the need for a tank-centered combined-arms approach. With the army in possession of information from Spanish combat as well as Smith's reports on Wehrmacht armor developments, Chief of Staff Craig initiated a review of mechanization policy.

Advocates for differing approaches, including an independent mechanized arm, lobbied the General Staff G-3-led effort, but for it to recommend shifting tank policy away from the infantry-support role required a strong impetus from foreign military experience given leadership's preference for the status quo.[193] The German panzer divisions recommended such a reform, but the Iberian combat countered it. As Infantry Chief Lynch argued, "reports from the Spanish war theatre indicate that mechanized weapons have attained success only when used in close cooperation with infantry and artillery."[194] The overlapping AWC student committee investigations emphasized the same point. Recognizing Spain's potent influence, armor advocates, like strategic bombing proponents, argued that these findings were invalid, given "unsound organization and improper tactical doctrines."[195] Tank advocates acknowledged that they would fail without infantry and artillery support, but the solution was to motorize the other arms. Yet, as Mildred Gillie observes, accounts from Spain prompted infantrymen to feel that "it might well turn out that cavalry tankmen at Knox had been indulging in impossible daydreams all these years."[196] The bureaucratically stronger side had tangible combat-based evidence that trumped the behavior of a single military, even one as respected as the Germans. Armor historians such as Cameron and Hofmann, critical of the failure to embrace a tank-centric combined-arms approach, explain, as the latter writes, that the army's "reactive policy was primarily based on key information provided by attachés on military operations in Spain."[197]

Chief of Staff Craig conveyed the service's position during March 1938 congressional testimony, asserting that future military operations will "be carried out by the traditional arms. . . . Air and mechanized troops are valuable auxiliaries."[198] That same month, Craig selected Col. John Herr, an ardent traditionalist, to succeed the retiring chief of cavalry instead of Palmer, which would have propelled the cavalry branch toward a mechanized force capable of larger, independent operations. The following month, with the issuance of "Policies Governing Mechanization and the Tactical Employment of Mechanized Units," the War Department, as Gillie relates, "sought to end the destroying rivalry between infantry and cavalry tankmen, and to draw a clean-cut line between the two arms."[199] It stated that the "infantry was to develop tanks solely as an additional weapon for infantry, without reconnaissance, security, or support elements, while the mechanized cavalry was to continue its operations along cavalry lines by substituting the machine for the horse."[200] Yet harmony did not result. Based on armor's use in Spain, the infantry called for a "leading wave" of medium tanks to overwhelm enemy antitank guns and a second wave of light tanks advancing with the foot soldiers. While the War Department approved this concept in August 1938, mechanized cavalry officers labored to overturn the April policy. A critical Zaloga sums up that the American army employed "the Spanish experience to validate their own preconceptions about tank warfare, but this was a misuse of the lessons."[201] Validation is not always a "misuse," but in this case it proved counterproductive.

Neglected Findings

Failure to respond sufficiently to light-tank deficiency. The army leadership believed it was applying a core lesson by employing the tank in an infantry-support role, but it failed to respond adequately to the clearest armor lesson—the inadequacy of light tanks.[202] The Ordnance Department, after scrutinizing reports about Spain, found that "speed ceased to be the first requirement" of design as "heavier protective armor and, particularly, more powerful guns were of even greater importance than high speed."[203] It warned during the late 1930s, as Russell Weigley notes, that "American tanks were falling behind their European counterparts in both guns and armor."[204] Even after US experiments and maneuvers reinforced this lesson, army leaders retained their faith in light tanks. What accounts for the army leadership not seriously questioning the viability of this class and only belatedly bolstering capabilities?

Practical considerations certainly influenced senior officers, but their support also reflected a philosophical preference.[205] Deemphasizing the light tank would have prevented the priority equipping of armor units with a meaningful number of vehicles in the near term. The M2 infantry light tank (M1 combat car) only entered service in 1937. Knowledge that this tank had been based on the British Vickers 6-ton tank like the Russian T-26, then proving superior in Spain, helped army leaders downplay hypercritical reports on Nationalist armor. For example, Lynch wrote in early 1938 that "it is unfortunate, perhaps, that the failure of the light tank in Spain has given a bad name to the light tank in general."[206] Operators, as opposed to the Ordnance Department, continued to want vehicles as light and maneuverable as possible. With the infantry tanks required to fight alongside with foot soldiers, they had to be light enough to cross bridges and other obstacles. The mechanized cavalry was even less inclined than the infantry to abandon the light tank as its officers loathed any change reducing vehicle speed or handling. In contrast to the Germans' growing mechanized-centric perspective, the American mechanized cavalry officers at Fort Knox retained the outlook of cavalrymen. Bottom line, as Zaloga observes, for the US Army, the Spanish Civil War "did not provoke any serious questions about the viability of light tanks on the modern battlefield."[207] Even the usually laudatory Fullerton characterizes the continuing faith in the light tank as "the only real failure of the army's reading of the lessons from Spain."[208]

Ultimately, mounting combat evidence compelled army leaders to upgrade the M2 and devote greater resources to medium tanks, but these efforts did not yield satisfactory vehicles.[209] The M2A4 received a high-velocity 37 mm cannon as well as thicker armor. Adopted in December 1938 (although technical problems delayed production), this vehicle represented a "substantial improvement" and "marked a turning point in light tank design."[210] Nevertheless, the tank's gun compared unfavorably to the Russian T-26's 45 mm weapon and larger armament being developed in Europe, while its armor would not protect against even 37 mm antitank guns. The infantry continued to believe that armor thick enough to stop such shells represented a poor tradeoff for lost mobility. When US armor began operations in North Africa, as David Johnson remarks, "one of the first illusions to evaporate in the heat of battle was the effectiveness of the light tank."[211] The unprecedented and unexpected tank-on-tank battles in Spain prompted recognition of the army's problematic lack of any operational medium tanks. Even though a mechanized cavalry leader, Chaffee supported prioritizing medium infantry tanks, writing that they "are our most serious deficiency in mechanization at the present time."[212] The army intensified development of the T5 prototype during the second half of 1937, but the M2 production vehicle suffered from severe inadequacies with its small 37 mm gun (same as the light tank) and insufficient armor. Moreover, slow progress meant only eighteen had been obtained by the start of the war in Europe. The fighting in Spain had served as a catalyst for development of more capable medium tanks, but it would take evidence from early World War II battles to garner sufficient support for the much more powerful 75 mm armed M3.

Beneficial neglect of defense dominance lesson in new doctrine. Although neglecting lessons has a negative connotation, a military can benefit from not responding, as occurred when the army did not fundamentally reshape its doctrine to reflect the leadership-embraced findings of defense dominance.[213] Reports about the fighting in Spain, increased threat perceptions, and the army's growing budget intensified pressure for a long-delayed update to the 1923 *FSR*. The May 1937 appointment of Lynch as infantry chief added impetus, given his strong advocacy for such an effort, which began during the second half of 1937. Bureaucratic battling between the General Staff, CGSS, and the infantry delayed approval of the new guidance until early September 1939. The 1939 (tentative) *FSR* reflected positive and negative influences of findings as identified throughout this section, but critically it did not abandon the 1923 *FSR*'s offensive orientation. The new doctrine has long been criticized for almost doubling the length of its predecessor but failing in its stated goal of providing clear direction. While Michael Bonura complains that it "was a strange institutionalization of the diverging conceptualizations of the battlefield of the 1923 *FSR* and the [*Manual for Commanders of Large Units*]," Odom adds it confusingly "straddled the past and future battlefields."[214] Still, despite the *FSR* 1939 being an infantry-dominated doctrine, Kretchik points out that it "acknowledged that all arms and services contributed to success in war" and "redefined the concept of offense" with a greater appreciation for maneuver as well as firepower.[215] Thus, while confusing and contradictory, the guidance "contained most of the ingredients for blitzkrieg-style combined arms warfare."[216] This result has led revisionist historians to be far more positive, stressing that retention of a belief in the superiority of open or offensive warfare despite the defense's dominance in the Spanish Civil War enabled the Americans to react much more readily than the British and French after the Wehrmacht demonstrated modern warfare requirements early in World War II.[217]

Missed Opportunities

Given that the army air corps missed most of the salient lessons from the Spanish Civil War, a lack of response was almost certain despite non-aviators lobbying for indicated changes. Corum notes that so much of "the thoughtful and informed writing about operational air power was contributed by officers from the ground forces of the Army."[218] As he observes, "the fact that important doctrinal comment was being made by ground officers probably guaranteed that it would be ignored by the Air Corps officers."[219] The regular army leadership attempted to use Spain to precipitate necessary reforms to service aviation policy, but it proved very difficult given air corps resistance. Instead, aviators continued to pursue with vigor greater strategic bombing capability and bureaucratic independence. Bottom line, the service missed opportunities provided by collected combat data to be better prepared for World War II.

Less, not more attention to CAS. War Department pressure ensured that the air corps placed some attention on "aviation in support of ground forces," but its conceptualization of this mission had disturbingly, for ground soldiers, moved away from CAS and would continue to do so until faced with the realities of World War II.[220] In 1921 the US Army had been the first military to establish a dedicated attack aviation unit, but fifteen years later it still lacked an effective, heavily armored strike plane and adequate tactics for employing attack aircraft. Arnold claimed in his memoir that because the air corps, unlike the Royal Air Force, remained a part of the army, "the 'strategic bombardment' lectures of Hal George and the others at the Air Corps Tactical School were not allowed to obscure the need for 'tactical' ground-support operations."[221] Yet ACTS taught that "except in unusual situations airpower was not to be employed against targets within range of friendly artillery."[222] General Headquarters Air Force commander Maj. Gen. Frank Andrews, the third-ranking air corps officer, even objected to use of the term *air-ground military team* except for observation aviation.[223] As aviation historian Robert Futrell explains, Andrews "argued that pursuit, attack, and bombardment received no assistance from the ground forces in their combat operations."[224]

Information from the Spanish Civil War challenged the air corps' perspective and intensified tension between aviators and ground soldiers over the nature of the attack mission.[225] Reports from Europe prompted the War Department in mid-1937 to order an examination of strike aircraft, associated equipment, and CAS techniques. The air corps could not prevent the September 1937 introduction of an AWC course text (*Air Force and War*), which instructed that the best use of aviation was directly aiding ground operations (essentially, long-range artillery) as combat in Spain had illustrated. Futrell adds that "what made the text seem more authoritative" was that its author, AWC instructor Col. Byron Jones, had been a long-serving member of the air corps.[226] After outraged aviators charged Jones with contradicting army guidance, Deputy Chief of Staff Embick quickly responded that, given the newness of aviation, "our present War Department doctrine has had to be based necessarily on theory and assumption rather than on factual evidence. Now we are getting evidence of that character."[227]

Nonetheless, the air corps exerted decisive influence on air matters, and, despite accumulating evidence from Spain, the role of attack aviation "was gradually altered to that of more indirect support of ground forces."[228] Pilots maintained that the best way to achieve air superiority and weaken forward enemy units was through striking rear targets (e.g., transportation nodes, air bases, supply depots), not CAS, which required rigorous coordination with ground forces and resulted in greater attrition. They worried that based on the impact of CAS in Spain, as Maj. Omer Niergarth correctly predicted, "in all future wars, ground troops are going to demand much more of this close-in cooperation from air forces."[229] After receiving the mid-1937 tasker to investigate strike aircraft and CAS techniques, an uninterested air corps passed it to the Air Board and no action resulted. In 1938 an increasingly frustrated War Department directed the aviation branch to develop dedicated CAS aircraft, but air leaders, as Thomas Greer points out, were "wary lest changes in equipment provide an entering wedge for increased emphasis upon ground support functions."[230] The War Department and General Staff complained when they identified clear air corps transgressions, but, as Biddle adds, the ground army "was preoccupied with its own affairs and did little to force a change."[231] Reflective of the air corps emphasis on indirect support, it increasingly used the term *light bombardment* instead of *attack aviation*.

As a result, US CAS capabilities languished.[232] Lee Kennett, in an essay exploring this area, criticizes that "the lessons in tactical air power in the conflicts in China and Spain were often ignored or little noted."[233] He particularly complains that air corps' lack of interest meant "little effort was expended on joint exercises and maneuvers or on the formulation of doctrine," despite the fighting clearly illustrating the difficulty in providing effective CAS.[234] By 1939, to the frustration of senior ground commanders such as Marshall and McNair, the US Army "was among the least advanced" militaries in air attack techniques.[235] Revealingly, in the 1939 *FSR*, as Odom observes, "of the seven pages dedicated to the Air Corps, only two paragraphs specifically addressed close air support."[236] Moreover, whereas the Spanish experience spurred Soviet design of the excellent Il-2 Sturmovik ground-attack aircraft, the Americans ignored attaché-reported cues such as the value of armored seating protection for pilots. It took the 1940 Battle of France to galvanize the development of attack aircraft with 37 mm cannon, armor protection, and self-sealing fuel tanks. This belated acknowledgment versus a timely reaction to signals from Spain resulted in the US Army lacking not only optimized weapons but "an effective air/ground close air support doctrine until 1944."[237]

Spain fosters existential battle for the B-17. Intensifying the air corps' dismissiveness of Spain's lessons for attack aviation was a legitimate fear that information from that conflict jeopardized its top priority, the B-17 program.[238] Development of a prototype in 1935 finally provided American aviators with a machine to implement their preferred approach to war—unescorted, daylight, precision strategic bombing. Arnold, in his memoir, wrote that the plane "was the focus of our air planning, or rather of the Air Corps' fight to get *an* air plan—some kind of genuine air program— accepted by the Army."[239] The General Staff had actually selected the less capable but more affordable twin-engine B-18 in the mid-1930s competition for a new bomber. Still, with the air corps maintaining that the B-17 offered greater value despite its unprecedented unit cost, the army ordered thirteen YB-17s for testing in February 1936. Only three months later, the air corps sought fifty B-17s. The War Department, however, "instructed Westover to order no more B-17s until the thirteen on order had been delivered and tested."[240] Their successful summer 1937 testing did not transform the views of most ground officers, whose opposition emanated from a perceived lack of need for long-range, four-engine bombers rather than doubt about performance.

Reports about aerial combat in Spain reinforced this sentiment and prompted a concerted effort to kill the B-17 program.[241] Initially in early 1938, amid rising threat perceptions, expected funding increases, and political pressure, the General Staff and air corps agreed on the Balanced Air Force Program (144 four-engine bombers, 266 twin-engine bombers, 259 attack aircraft, and 425 pursuit planes) beginning in the FY40 budget. Nevertheless, as Richard Overy notes, "the army, impressed by the results of frontline support operations in Spain, thought medium bombers [B-18] promised 'greater efficiency, lessened complexity and decreased cost.'"[242] Critics of the B-17, led by Embick, sprang into action after Westover provided an opening in May 1938 by declaring essential the development of an even more advanced high-altitude, intercontinental bomber (the future B-29). First, they outmaneuvered aviators in getting the June 1938 Joint Army and Navy Board to assert that no foreseeable wartime mission existed for advanced bombers. Then, later that summer, the War Department instructed the air corps that development funds for FY39 and FY40 would be "restricted to that class of aviation designed for the close support of ground troops and the protection of that type of aircraft."[243] Most disturbing for aviators, Craig, in August 1938, told Westover that the army's aircraft requests for FY40 and FY41 "will include no four-engine bomber types."[244] When senior aviators aggressively challenged this decision, Embick responded that, in Spain and China, "the air forces have been unable to gain, by themselves, a victory which has been lasting or decisive."[245] Thus, he continued, "the bulk of the Air Corps strength in airplanes should be of the type suitable for the close support of the ground forces in the accomplishment of their missions."[246] A future with B-17s filling the skies seemed unlikely at the time.

Strategic bombing's prospects, however, soon reversed completely as new events outweighed the influence of Spain.[247] First, Westover's fatal plane crash in September 1938 resulted in the politically more astute Arnold becoming air chief. More importantly, American political leaders, including the president, attributed British and French capitulation at the Munich Conference at the end of that month to the Luftwaffe's "aerial threat." Roosevelt abandoned his prior dislike of strategic bombing and concluded that airplanes were the key to defeating Germany. In a mid-November 1938 meeting of senior officials, the president, as Futrell stresses, "issued instructions that General Arnold later described as the Magna Carta of the Air Force."[248] The army leadership fought back with some success against the White House's desire for an overwhelming emphasis on airpower, but subsequent budgets would clearly include the purchase of large numbers of B-17s. Marshall's October 1938 replacement of Embick as deputy chief of staff greatly improved aviator–soldier relations, given his appreciation of the need for balance between air and ground forces. Thus, as Overy avers, "the development of the B-17 was squeezed to the slenderest of margins. It was saved only by a sudden revolution in political support for the Air Corps."[249]

Costly neglect of fighter escort cue. If the aviation branch's dismissal of Spain as informative about the merit of strategic bombing was understandable, its neglect of strong signals regarding their need for fighter escort represented an egregious and costly mistake.[250] What accounted for this failing? British prime minister Stanley Baldwin uttered in 1932 the oft-repeated phrase that "the bomber will always get through" to assert the futility of robust defensive efforts, but subsequent technological progress bolstered this belief in the US Army Air Corps. When designed, the B-17's 250 mph speed exceeded the primary US pursuit planes and prevented accurate AA fire (at least according to the air corps). Strategic bombing acolytes viewed massed fighter responses to missions as impracticable given ignorance about radar's potential outside of senior officers and signal corps experts. With the B-17's high cost necessitating concentration of resources on this war-winning weapon, "every nickel spent on fighters seemed sheer waste" to bomber proponents.[251] By contrast, Lt. Col. A. H. Gilkeson, head of the 8th Pursuit Group, typified fighter pilots in complaining that this attitude at ACTS "has led to the teaching of doctrines which have not been established as being true and might even be fatally dangerous to our aims in the event of armed conflict."[252]

Although Spain provided evidence of the growing threat Gilkeson and Maj. Claire Chennault, former head of ACTS pursuit training, warned about, it did not lead to a long-range fighter escort.[253] Even when attaché reporting indicated that the Messerschmitt Bf-109 flew in excess of 300 mph, American aviators believed that pursuit planes would be "ineffective" against tight formations of the heavily armed Flying Fortress. Discussions about developing a long-range escort predated the Spanish Civil War, but it had received low priority, given not only a reluctance to acknowledge the requirement but also doubt about its technical feasibility. An early 1939 study of the subject concluded it was "desirable, but impractical" to develop escorts with the range and performance in battle (e.g., rate of climb, maneuverability) to defeat short-range interceptors.[254] Robert Finney, however, persuasively posits that "possibly had they insisted that the strategic air war would be dependent on fighter escort for the bombers, the engineering difficulties in producing such a plane would have been overcome sooner."[255] He adds that the air corps' "lack of emphasis on fighter escort was due in large measure to the fact that they did not know exactly how the air phase of the next war was going to be fought."[256] While they could not know exactly how the next air war would go, they had meaningful evidence from combat in Spain how it was likely to go. A highly critical Corum emphasizes that the air corps "ignored the clear and oft-repeated lesson from Spain that unescorted bombers were extremely vulnerable to modern high-performance fighters."[257] Instead, the air corps reacted by introducing a number of refinements into the B-17B, including increased armament. Continuing faith in unescorted strategic bombing despite combat evidence, as Biddle points out, even "helped to obscure avenues—such as the droppable auxiliary fuel tank—that might otherwise have been more readily recognized and explored."[258]

It would ultimately take painful direct experience to generate the needed response.[259] In November 1939, after the first few months of war in Europe, a belatedly worried Arnold complained about the neglect of fighter tactics and technology. Almost a year later the air corps placed a 1,500-mile range escort fighter at the top of its development priorities. Still, bomber advocates maintained confidence in their approach until a disastrous ten days in early October 1943, when the Germans downed 164 US bombers over Central Europe. David Johnson accurately characterizes that the long-range escort requirement "was a hard-learned lesson."[260] Sustained faith in unescorted, daylight, strategic bombing, despite the Spanish Civil War, as Col. Dennis Drew, USAF, observed nearly a half century later, explains why the United States entered the conflict "with the two best heavy bombers in the world (the B-17 and the B-24) but could not field a first-class fighter aircraft until 1943" (the P-51).[261] In his memoir Arnold blamed the air corps' lack of response to the escort requirement to insufficient awareness of reporting from Spain. He cited ignorance about a cable that relayed the following:

"We detected in one of the heavy bombardment squadrons a note of anxiety about the increased number of German fighters." (Apparently there were far more of the Me-109's in Spain than we knew of.) Item which might have affected our own ideas about bombers in regard to fighter escort: "The escort of bomber formations proceeding to and from their objectives, by double, or more than double, their number of fighters, has been found on both sides to be a necessity, notwithstanding the ability of the bomber to shoot down fighters." *Yet we in the US were still debating the need for fighter escorts for bombers.*[262]

As this chapter shows, this blatant attempt to deflect blame to MID does not reflect what happened.

CONCLUSION

The Spanish Civil War had been over less than six months when German troops, along with US Army attaché Maj. Percy Black, crossed the Polish border and commenced the long-feared major European war.[263] The resultant fighting generated high-level attention among American officials, with even the president inquiring about the dispatch of military observers.[264] Germany's battlefield success only intensified interest as the War Department ordered Black home in November 1939 for debriefing. Subsequently, the United States did not have direct access to the German forces, but American officers were attentive witnesses on the Allied side during the 1940 Battles of France and Britain. Of particular note, in contrast to the Spanish Civil War, the air corps exhibited a strong desire to learn about Royal Air Force engagements with the Luftwaffe. The scale and intensity of the combat produced considerable data, with Chief of Staff Marshall ordering the production and distribution of *Technical Lessons Bulletins* (first issued on May 22, 1940). The findings proved highly influential in changing army perspectives and practices. Unfortunately, the army obtained this information less than eighteen months before US entry into the war, leaving the service inadequate time to respond.

The basic lessons of the Spanish Civil War, which revealed themselves in its first year, predated US combat by nearly five years, providing a much better opportunity for application. The German military benefited enormously from scrutinizing the Iberian fighting, but it had the considerable advantages of being a direct participant and exceptionally good at experiential learning. Despite prompting some notable changes and reprioritizations, this case stands as the least effective of the American lessons-learning efforts examined in this book. Although the necessary attaché-centric approach had its limitations, especially in obtaining data from the Nationalist side, Juntunen finds "that the United States Army could not or would not make use of the 'lessons' of the war in Spain was not the fault of a lack of information."[265] Corum concurs that "failings were not due to any lack of solid factual information."[266] The US Army received plentiful reports on the inadequacy of light tanks, the value of flat-trajectory antitank guns, the necessity of motorization, the requirement for long-range fighter escorts, and the importance of CAS. Even though some complaints existed about accessing the collected information, MID did a credible job in circulating the data to relevant parties throughout the service.[267] Yet Green, Thomson, and Roots, in their history of the Ordnance Department, describe the limited influence of this information on weapon research and development as well as arms procurement.[268] Even less impact occurred in the organizational, doctrinal, and training dimensions of preparedness.

What accounts for this result? Juntunen charitably offers that "there was no time to ponder the data gathered and the conclusions reached by the attachés, war followed war too quickly."[269] That was true of the conflict's ending date (six months before the start of World War II in Europe), but much less so two years earlier, by which time the Americans had identified the basic elements of the fighting. Certainly, the sense of urgency about army unpreparedness in the late 1930s prompted a focus on acquiring the best available arms, not developing better weapons in response to cues from combat. In contrast to attention to early World War II lessons from combat between European military powers, Odom attributes Spanish Civil War findings' limited influence to Americans' low regard for combatants on the losing side of that conflict.[270] Exacerbating such attitudes was the learning process itself. Whereas personal agency had played an important role in the first two cases, not only was the army now much bigger and more complex but the group of reporting attachés also did not match the highly regarded and influential officers temporarily tasked to observe the Crimean and Russo-Japanese Wars (e.g., Richard Delafield, Alfred Mordecai, Peyton March, John Morrison, John J. Pershing).

The above factors mattered, but the major difficulty resulted from a combination of the core lessons and the nature of the army at the time. The American findings of defense dominance and infantry-centric combined arms correctly captured combat in the Spanish Civil War but ran counter to the trends that would emerge with German blitzkrieg operations early in World War II. This "evidence" from Spain reached the United States amid intense debates about modern battlefield dynamics, meaning it represented not only potential enlightenment but also powerful ammunition in the army's internal struggle over the proper approach required for future conflict. Given that the conflict appeared to validate the traditional views espoused by the army leadership (e.g., Craig, Embick, and Lynch) of tanks and aircraft as supporting not supported systems, the most innovative force components—the mechanized cavalry and air corps—worked aggressively to minimize the conflict's revelatory significance. For example, while the Germans used their experience to identify problems that needed to be solved and seek clues for doing so, especially with regard to tank operations and combined arms, the mechanized cavalry simply argued that "the Spanish civil war provided ample evidence of what not to do" to undermine traditionalists' use of the data.[271]

A similar but distinct dynamic undermined taking advantage of the fight's aviation lessons as the air corps dismissed the entire event as irrelevant. Although the Spanish Civil War did not represent a full-scale great-power air war, it offered considerable potential for learning valuable lessons with the involvement of advanced aircraft in a wide array of missions and the presence of an able chronicler (Griffiss). Senior army leaders, both appreciative of aviation's growing role in war and uncertain about the proper dimensions of that role, intensely examined the incoming information. That very eagerness, however, contributed to the air corps' reluctance to consider the Spanish Civil War as aviators regarded the "teaching" as a dangerous threat both to strategic bombing and obtaining an independent air force. Most frustratingly, the air corps neglected specific lessons that potentially would have enhanced, not undermined, the effectiveness of its own approach such as the need for a long-range escort.

The "battle" over the generalizability of the Spanish Civil War's instructional cues undermined its inspirational influence. The indication of the increased complexity to and importance of combined arms with the addition of the tank and aircraft did not produce the warranted exploration of modern fighting. Reilly, who spent as much time as any active or retired American soldier with the Nationalists, argued for such inspirational influence rather than using the Spanish Civil War lessons "to provide merely for improvements in existing types of weapons and weapon carriers."[272] As with the prior case in the Russo-Japanese War, appreciating the value of a weapon (machine gun) or tactical approach (indirect fire for field artillery) did not easily translate into skillful application at the more abstract level. The key to modern war was maximizing weapons' synergistic value. An army as bureaucratically decentralized and conceptually divided as the American service in the 1930s, however, was unlikely to apply lessons in this holistic fashion or be prompted to conduct the necessary experimentation to develop viable responses. Of course, the inability of most European militaries—both participants and observers in the Spanish Civil War—to benefit greatly from the conflict suggests that the Germans were exceptionally good rather than the Americans were exceptionally bad.

As a result, the most beneficial applications of findings from Spain involved elevating the priority of important but neglected elements of modern war, especially defensive weapons and force motorization. An awareness of the need for quantitatively and qualitatively better antimechanization and antiair weapons predated the conflict. It, however, provided the impetus (along with the availability of much greater funding) for measures to begin rectifying their deficiency. The information also aided efforts to obtain motorized transport for the artillery and other elements to begin enabling the type of mobility needed to reach the battlefield in a timely fashion. The army leadership embraced these lessons, both through obtaining needed equipment and encouraging doctrinal and organizational reforms to maximize their utility. Still, by the end of the decade, it had achieved insufficient progress from the severely deficient starting point to be ready for modern war.

Even the generally positive benefit from addressing neglected defensive capabilities yielded a cautionary tale involving the army's belated acquisition of a flat-trajectory gun. Widespread and emphatic reporting of its value against armor early in the conflict prompted Chief of Staff Craig and other senior officers to push for rapid procurement of this type of weapon. The fastest way to accomplish this goal was through essentially adopting (i.e., copying) the gun most responsible for that lesson, the 37 mm German Pak 36. Doubts about the adequacy of this caliber weapon existed especially in the Ordnance Department, a position increasingly supported by reporting during the later stages of the Spanish Civil War. Yet, rather than give weight to those concerns, the army leadership exacerbated the danger by preventing the Ordnance Department from developing a more powerful antitank weapon. This reaction was not driven by some nefarious intention but was apparently a belief that if the Ordnance Department generated an alternative to the M3 (the American version of the Pak 36), support for acquiring the existing weapon and learning how to use it would be undermined. The problem, however, quickly became evident in the early battles of World War II as the ground truth had rapidly changed. Armor advocates in Europe reacted to the poor performance of light tanks in Spain by replacing them with more heavily armed and armored variants. Such tanks rendered 37 mm antitank guns obsolete, and the American failure to develop a more powerful replacement left the army struggling to catch up with ever improving tanks throughout World War II. This example illustrates the potential peril from aggressively attempting to apply a lesson instructionally.

The bottom line is that this process must be a dynamic enterprise—one cannot be complacent because of a weapon's success in war. Other militaries are also learning lessons, including fixing, if possible, problems identified from the combat. This result is particularly true for relatively immature technologies and weapons, as has been shown with the tank and aircraft (Spanish Civil War), the machine gun and torpedo (Russo-Japanese War), and rifled artillery and rifled muskets (Crimean War). Such dynamism, of course, complicates using findings from foreign wars instructionally, but this difficulty does not diminish the value of the effort. It actually elevates using foreign war data inspirationally as other good militaries are going to attempt to use combat data to spark solutions to revealed problems. Future preparedness is not possible without learning from the learners, even when the collected information from the war under investigation creates a sense of urgency that encourages prioritization on fixing current deficiencies.

NOTES

Epigraph: Col. Stephen Fuqua to Military Intelligence Directorate (MID), April 26, 1937, quoted in Kim Juntunen, "US Army Attachés and the Spanish Civil War, 1936–1939: Gathering of Technical and Tactical Intelligence" (Master's thesis, Temple University, May 1990), 3.

1. James Corum, "The Spanish Civil War: Lessons Learned and Not Learned by the Great Powers," *Journal of Military History* 62, no. 2 (April 1998): 325–31; James Corum, "The Luftwaffe and Lessons Learned in the Spanish Civil War," in *Air Power History: Turning Points from Kitty Hawk to Kosovo*, ed. Sebastian Cox and Peter Gray (New York: Frank Cass, 2005), 175–78; James Sterret, "'Learning Is Winning' Soviet Air Power Doctrine, 1935–1941," in *Air Power History: Turning Points from Kitty Hawk to Kosovo*, ed. Sebastian Cox and Peter Gray (New York: Frank Cass, 2005), 68, 77, 83–85; William Astore and Eugenia Kiesling, "Tactics and Technology: Was the Spanish Civil War a Laboratory for Military Tactics and Technology?," in *History in Dispute*, vol. 18: *The Spanish Civil War*, ed. Kenneth Estes and Daniel Kowalsky (Detroit: St. James Press, 2005), 236–39; and Steven Zaloga and Kenneth Estes, "Armor: Was the Spanish

Civil War a Testing Ground for the Military Use of Tanks?," in *History in Dispute*, vol. 18: *The Spanish Civil War*, ed. Kenneth Estes and Daniel Kowalsky (Detroit: St. James Press, 2005), 259–62.

2. Conrad Lanza, "Lessons from Spain," *Field Artillery Journal* 28, no. 3 (May–June 1938): 183.

3. R. Dan Richardson, "The Development of Airpower Concepts and Air Combat Techniques in the Spanish Civil War," *Air Power History* 40, no. 1 (Spring 1993): 13.

4. Adam Siegel, "At the Tip of the Spear: The US Navy and the Spanish Civil War," *American Neptune* 61, no. 2 (Spring 2001): 185–204.

5. Alfred Vagts, *The Military Attaché* (Princeton, NJ: Princeton University Press, 1967), 270–72.

6. Quoted in Juntunen, "US Army Attachés," 15.

7. An American war correspondent, "Guns in Spain," *Coast Artillery Journal* 80, no. 6 (November–December 1937): 457.

8. For paragraph, see Bruce Bidwell, *History of the Military Intelligence Division, Department of the Army, General Staff, 1775–1941* (Frederick, MD: University Publications of America, 1986), 263, 381, 385; Juntunen, "US Army Attachés," 4–5, 9, 11, 17–18, 26; Thomas Mahnken, *Uncovering Ways of War: US Intelligence and Foreign Military Innovation, 1918–1941* (Ithaca, NY: Cornell University Press, 2009), 26–40, 165; William Odom, *After the Trenches: The Transformation of the U.S. Army, 1918–1939* (College Station: Texas A&M Press, 1999), 213–17; and James Cortada, ed., *Modern Warfare in Spain: American Military Observations on the Spanish Civil War, 1936–1939* (Washington, DC: Potomac Books, 2012), xi–xvi.

9. Quoted in Richardson, "Development of Airpower," 14.

10. Quoted in Richardson, 14.

11. For paragraph, see Cortada, *Modern Warfare*, xv, xx–xxv, 37, 45; Charles Burdick, "The American Military Attachés in the Spanish Civil War, 1936–1939," *Militärgeschichtliche Mitteilungen* 46, no. 2 (February 1989): 63, 66, 71, 75; Juntunen, "US Army Attachés," 12–19, 35–36, 87; George Hofmann, "The Tactical and Strategic Use of Attaché Intelligence: The Spanish Civil War and the US Army's Misguided Quest for a Modern Tank Doctrine," *Journal Military History* 62, no. 1 (January 1998): 104; Richardson, "Development of Airpower," 14, 16; and Richard Smith and R. Cargill Hall, *Five Down No Glory: Frank Tinker, Mercenary Ace in the Spanish Civil War* (Annapolis, MD: Naval Institute Press, 2011), 211, 314.

12. Juntunen, "US Army Attachés," 13.

13. Smith [Berlin] to MID, August 1937, quoted in Juntunen, "US Army Attachés," 13; also see Henry Gole, *Exposing the Third Reich: Colonel Truman Smith in Hitler's Germany* (Lexington: University Press of Kentucky, 2013), 99, 147–48, 167, 176, 180, 183–84, 193–200, 220; and Mahnken, *Uncovering Ways of War*, 89–90, 100–101, 118–19, 122, 127.

14. Juntunen, "US Army Attachés," 19–20, 26; and Astore and Kiesling, "Tactics and Technology," 240.

15. David Glantz, "Observing the Soviets: US Army Attachés in Eastern Europe during the 1930s," *Journal of Military History* 55, no. 2 (April 1991): 157–67, 181–82; and Juntunen, "US Army Attachés," 19–20.

16. Glantz, "Observing the Soviets," 182; also see Odom, *After the Trenches*, 189–90; and Mary Glantz, "An Officer and a Diplomat? The Ambiguous Position of Philip R. Faymonville

and United States—Soviet Relations, 1941–1943," *Journal of Military History* 72, no. 1 (January 2008): 141–77.

17. For paragraph, see Juntunen, "US Army Attachés," 13, 18–21, 36, 50; Cortada, *Modern Warfare*, xx, 37, 71, 273–76; and Astore and Kiesling, "Tactics and Technology," 237, 241.

18. Juntunen, "US Army Attachés," 12.

19. Bidwell, *History of MID*, 271; Cortada, *Modern Warfare*, xviii, 267–68, 277–79; Juntunen, "US Army Attachés," 8, 22–24, 31; Odom, *After the Trenches*, 213, 216; Mahnken, *Uncovering Ways of War*, 28; and Robert Cameron, *Mobility, Shock, and Firepower: The Emergence of US Army's Armor Branch, 1917–1945* (Washington, DC: US Army Center of Military History, 2008), 144–46.

20. Bidwell, *History of MID*, 267.

21. Constance McLaughlin Green, Harry Thomson, and Peter Roots, *The Ordnance Department: Planning Munitions for War* (Washington, DC: US Army Center of Military History, 1990), 214.

22. Mahnken, *Uncovering Ways of War*, 19.

23. For examples, Vincent Usera, "Some Lessons from the Spanish War," *Field Artillery Journal* 29, no. 5 (September–October 1939): 406–16; Emilio Canevari, "Forecasts from the War in Spain: Lessons Based on Technical and Tactical Experience," *Army Ordnance* 18, no. 107 (March–April 1938): 273–80; Henry Reilly, "Proving Ground in Spain," *Army Ordnance* 19, no. 114 (May–June 1939): 333–36; and Wendell Johnson, "Spanish War: A Review of the Best Foreign Opinion," *Infantry Journal* 45, no. 4 (July–August 1938): 351–56.

24. For paragraph, see Edward Coffman, *The Regulars: The American Army, 1898–1941* (Cambridge, MA: Harvard University Press, 2007), 281–85; Odom, *After the Trenches*, 86, 168–71, 196, 227–28; Mark Calhoun, *General Lesley J. McNair: Unsung Architect of the US Army* (Lawrence: University Press of Kansas, 2015), 19–20, 102–6, 109–10; 117–18; Michael Matheny, *Carrying the War to the Enemy: American Operational Art to 1945* (Norman: University of Oklahoma Press, 2012), 73–82; Cameron, *Mobility, Shock, and Firepower*, 145; Thomas Hughes, *Overlord: General Pete Quesada and the Triumph of Tactical Air Power in World War II* (New York: Free Press, 1995), 60–61; and Robert Finney, *History of the Air Corps Tactical School* (Maxwell AFB, AL: Research Studies Institute, USAF Historical Division, 1955), 56.

25. Coffman, *Regulars*, 233.

26. Coffman, 289.

27. Burdick, "American Military Attachés," 72.

28. Lee [London] to MID, May 17, 1938, in Cortada, *Modern Warfare*, 275.

29. Arthur Temperley, "Military Lessons of the Spanish Civil War," *Foreign Affairs* 16, no. 1 (October 1937): 34.

30. Griffiss to MID, August 1938, Subject: The Air Warfare in Spain and Its Effect upon the Air Rearmament of France," in *Volume II: Spanish War, August 17, 1937 to September 1, 1938: Reports and Articles*, collected by Col. Byron Q. Jones (Carlisle Barracks, PA: Army War College, 1938), 1.

31. Reilly, "Proving Ground," 333.

32. Cortada, *Modern Warfare*, xvii.

33. Hofmann, "Tactical and Strategic Use of Attaché Information," 17, 105, 113–14, 121, 128–29; Fuller [Paris] to MID, August 28, 1937, and Unnamed CGSS lecture, December 1,

1937, in Cortada, *Modern Warfare*, 178, 219; J.F.C. Fuller, "The Tank in Spain," *Army Ordnance* 19, no. 109 (July–August 1938): 26–27; John Weeks, *Men against Tanks: A History of Anti-Tank Warfare* (New York: Mason/Charter, 1975), 30; Cameron, *Mobility, Shock, and Firepower*, 185–86; and Steven Zaloga, *Spanish Civil War Tanks: The Proving Ground for Blitzkrieg* (Oxford: Osprey, 2010), 28.

34. Juntunen, "US Army Attachés," 111–12.

35. Corum, "Spanish Civil War," 318–20; Tami Davis Biddle, *Rhetoric and Reality in Air Warfare: Evolution of British and American Ideas about Strategic Bombing, 1914–1945* (Princeton, NJ: Princeton University Press, 2004), 166, 171–75; Hughes, *Overlord*, 52–59; Jeffrey Underwood, *Wings of Democracy: Influence of Air Power on the Roosevelt Administration, 1933–1941* (College Station: Texas A&M University, 1991), 9, 24, 41–42, 80, 94–96; Timothy Moy, *War Machines: Transforming Technologies in the US Military, 1920–1940* (College Station: Texas A&M University Press, 2001), 8–9, 29–31, 60–62, 67; and Gole, *Exposing the Third Reich*, 184–85, 211.

36. Corum, "Spanish Civil War," 318.

37. H. H. Arnold, *Global Mission* (Blue Ridge Summit, PA: TAB Books, 1989), 169.

38. Mahnken, *Uncovering Ways of War*, 127.

39. For paragraph, see Canevari, "Forecasts from the War in Spain," 274, 276; Usera, "Some Lessons," 406–10; Lanza, "Lessons from Spain," 191, 196; Griffiss to MID, August 1938, p. 1–2; Unnamed CGSS lecture, December 1, 1937, in Cortada, *Modern Warfare*, 215–18; and Robert Mackin, "Airplanes Can Be Stopped," *Coast Artillery Journal* 80, no. 5 (September–October 1937): 398.

40. Boyd Dastrup, *King of Battle: A Branch History of the US Army's Field Artillery* (Fort Monroe, VA: US Army Training and Doctrine Command, 1992), 200–201.

41. Reilly, "Proving Ground," 336.

42. Griffiss to MID, August 1938, p. 3.

43. Lanza, "Lessons from Spain," 191.

44. For paragraph, see Fuqua to MID, April 2, 1937, Waite [Paris] to MID, May 25, 1937, and unnamed CGSS lecture, December 1, 1937, all in Cortada, *Modern Warfare*, 108, 127–30, 220; Hofmann, "Tactical and Strategic Use of Attaché Information," 116, 127; Reilly, *Proving Ground*, 333–36; Juntunen, "US Army Attachés," 97–98, 101, 106–11; Cameron, *Mobility, Shock, and Firepower*, 125, 137–38; and Zaloga, *Spanish Civil War Tanks*, 6–7, 3, 44.

45. Lanza, "Lessons from Spain," 188.

46. Waite [Paris] to MID, May 25, 1937, in Cortada, *Modern Warfare*, 129.

47. Cameron, *Mobility, Shock, and Firepower*, 137–38, 185; and Reilly, "Proving Ground," 335–36.

48. For paragraph, see Lee [London] to MID, January 25, 1937, Waite [Paris] to MID, May 25, 1937, and Fuqua to MID, November 1, 1937, in Cortada, *Modern Warfare*, 60–61, 129, 188–89, 194–95; Canevari, "Forecasts from the War in Spain," 273–80; George Hofmann, *Through Mobility We Conquer: The Mechanization of U.S. Cavalry* (Lexington: University Press of Kentucky, 2006), 217–18; Cameron, *Mobility, Shock, and Firepower*, 37–38, 309–10; Juntunen, "US Army Attachés," 106–7, 113–19; and Reilly, "Proving Ground," 334–36.

49. Waite [Paris] to MID, May 25, 1937, in Cortada, *Modern Warfare*, 129.

50. Reilly to MID, October 13, 1938, quoted in Juntunen, "US Army Attachés," 116–17.

51. For paragraph, see Lanza, "Lessons from Spain," 189–90; unnamed CGSS lecture, December 1, 1937, and Fuqua to MID, February 12, 1938, in Cortada, *Modern Warfare*, 208, 219, 254–56; Hofmann, "Tactical and Strategic Use of Attaché Information," 127; and Dastrup, *King of Battle*, 194–95.

52. Lanza, "Lessons from Spain," 189.

53. For paragraph, see Canevari, "Forecasts from the War in Spain," 275–76, 280; unnamed, undated report (probably March 1937), and unnamed CGSS lecture, December 1, 1937, in Cortada, *Modern Warfare*, 84, 214–15; Lanza, "Lessons from Spain," 192–93; and Cameron, *Mobility, Shock, and Firepower*, 113.

54. Canevari, "Forecasts from the War in Spain," 276.

55. Lanza, "Lessons from Spain," 192.

56. Lanza, 193.

57. Usera, "Some Lessons," 415.

58. Unnamed CGSS lecture, December 1, 1937, in Cortada, *Modern Warfare*, 208; and Canevari, "Forecasts from the War in Spain," 275–76.

59. Corum, "Spanish Civil War," 316.

60. H. H. Arnold, "Air Lessons from Current Wars," *US Air Services* (May 1938): 17.

61. George Kenney, "The Airplane in Modern Warfare," *US Air Services* (July 1938): 22.

62. Thomas Phillips, "Air Power and Troop Movement," *Infantry Journal* 81, no. 3 (May–June 1938): 195–97.

63. For paragraph, see Fuller to MID, January 26, 1937, Fuller to MID, January 28, 1937, Fuller to MID, February 11, 1937, Kroner [London] to MID, March 9, 1937, Fuller to MID, March 25, 1937, MID Memorandum, McCabe to Chief of Staff, July 6, 1937, unnamed CGSS lecture, December 1, 1937, in Cortada, *Modern Warfare*, 59–60, 62, 64, 69, 76, 90–92, 164, 218–19; Mackin, "Airplanes Can Be Stopped," 397–99; Basil Liddell Hart, "Lessons of the Spanish War," *Army Ordnance* 18, no. 106 (January–February 1938): 203; Griffiss to MID, August 1938, p. 16, 19; Juntunen, "US Army Attachés," 119–23; Bryon Greenwald, *The Problems of Peacetime Innovation: The Development of US Army AAA during the Interwar Period—A Case Study in Preparing the Army for the Future* (Fort Leavenworth, KS: School of Advanced Military Studies, May 1995), 12; and Reilly, "Proving Ground," 333–34.

64. Lee to MID, January 25, 1937, in Cortada, *Modern Warfare*, 59.

65. MID Memorandum, McCabe to COS, July 6, 1937, in Cortada, *Modern Warfare*, 164.

66. Mackin, "Airplanes Can Be Stopped," 399.

67. Griffiss to MID, August 1938, p. 19.

68. Reilly, "Proving Ground," 333.

69. Reilly, 334.

70. For paragraph, see Kenney, "Airplane in Modern Warfare," 19; Waite to MID, February 8, 1937, Fuller to MID, March 10, 1937, Fuller to MID, March 25, 1937, Fuqua to MID, June 1, 1937, and unnamed CGSS lecture, December 1, 1937, all in Cortada, *Modern Warfare*, 66, 84, 92, 119, 207, 217; Juntunen, "US Army Attachés," 67, 76–77; Jack Rudolph, "Guadalajara: An Aerial Counter-Attack," *Infantry Journal* 45, no. 2 (March–April 1938): 113; Charles Noble, "Defense against Air Attack," *Cavalry Journal* 47, no. 4 (July–August 1938): 332–34; and Griffiss to MID, August 1938, p. 8.

71. Liddell Hart, "Lessons of the Spanish War," 203.

72. Fuller to MID, March 22, 1938, quoted in Juntunen, "US Army Attachés," 76–77.

73. Griffiss to MID, August 1938, p. 16.

74. Fuqua to MID, April 26, 1937, Fuqua to MID, July 17, 1937, Fuqua to MID, January 26, 1938, Fuqua to MID, July 20, 1938, and Fuqua to MID, October 12, 1938, all in Cortada, Modern Warfare, 123–26, 153–56, 245–46, 282, 293–94; Johnson, "Spanish War," 355–56; Lanza, "Lessons from Spain," 185–89; Canevari, "Forecasts from the War in Spain," 278, 280; and Basil Liddell Hart, "Lessons from Spain," section inserted in a revised edition of Europe in Arms (New York: Random House, 1937), 6–7.

75. Lanza, "Lessons from Spain," 185.

76. Usera, "Some Lessons," 414.

77. Unnamed CGSS lecture, December 1, 1937, in Cortada, Modern Warfare, 223.

78. For paragraph, see Waite [Paris] to MID, January 18, 1937, Lee to MID, January 25, 1937, Fuqua to MID, April 2, 1937, Kroner [London] to MID, April 20, 1937, Waite to MID, May 25, 1937, and Fuqua to MID, June 1, 1937, all in Cortada, Modern Warfare, 59, 61, 105–8, 111–19, 128–30; Lanza, "Lessons from Spain," 183–91; Canevari, "Forecasts from the War in Spain," 273–80; Cameron, Mobility, Shock, and Firepower, 125, 138, 185–86; and Hofmann, "Tactical and Strategic Use of Attachés Information," 107–10, 116, 127–28.

79. Some historians have strongly criticized this oft-cited example as a mischaracterization of what happened, but at the time the shared understanding impressed army officers. James Corum and Kenneth Estes, "Air Power: Did the Great Powers Gain Useful Information from the Use of Air Power during the Spanish Civil War?," in History in Dispute, vol. 18: The Spanish Civil War, ed. Kenneth Estes and Daniel Kowalsky (Detroit: St. James Press, 2005), 15; and Zaloga and Estes, "Armor," 37–39.

80. Fuqua to MID, February 26, 1938, quoted in Juntunen, "US Army Attachés," 110.

81. Reilly, "Proving Ground," 335.

82. Zaloga, Spanish Civil War Tanks, 40.

83. Malin Craig, Report of the Chief of Staff (hereafter, ARWD/COS 1938), in Annual Reports of the War Department, FY Ended June 30, 1938 (Washington, DC: Government Printing Office, 1938), 29–30.

84. Zaloga, Spanish Civil War Tanks, 28.

85. Hofmann, "Tactical and Strategic Use of Attaché Information," 121.

86. Cameron, Mobility, Shock, and Firepower, 137–38.

87. Joseph Greene, "The Case for Antitank," Infantry Journal 45, no. 3 (May–June 1938): 222.

88. Hofmann, "Tactical and Strategic Use of Attaché Information," 128.

89. For the paragraph, see Robert Futrell, Ideas, Concepts, Doctrine: Basic Thinking in the USAF, 1907–1960, vol. 1 (Washington, DC: Ross & Perry, 2002), 85; Odom, After the Trenches, 217–18; Juntunen, "US Army Attachés," 3, 21–22, 35, 66–67; and Richardson, "Development of Airpower," 13–14.

90. Richardson, "Development of Airpower," 13.

91. Kenney, "Airplane in Modern Warfare," 17, 19.

92. Juntunen, "US Army Attachés," 91.

93. Griffiss to MID, August 1938, p. 1.

94. Biddle, *Rhetoric and Reality*, 172.

95. For paragraph, see Underwood, *Wings of Democracy*, 24; Lee Kennett, "Developments to 1939," in *Case Studies in the Development of Close Air Support*, ed. Benjamin Cooling (Washington, DC: Office of Air Force History, 1990), 59; Hughes, *Overlord*, 52–58; Christopher Rein, *The North African Air Campaign: US Army Air Forces from El Alamein to Salerno* (Lawrence: University Press of Kansas, 2012), 13–14, 32; and Gregory Kreuder, "Lieutenant General 'Pete' Quesada and GeneralFeldmarschall Wolfram von Richtofen: What Made Them Great" (Master's thesis, School of Advanced Air and Space Studies, Air University, June 2009), 17.

96. Quoted in Kennett, "Developments to 1939," 48.

97. Quoted in Kennett, 48.

98. Biddle, *Rhetoric and Reality*, 171, 353n186.

99. Biddle, 171.

100. For paragraph, see Fuqua to MID, June 1, 1937, Griffiss and Fuqua to MID, June 14, 1937, and unnamed CGSS lecture, December 1, 1937, all in Cortada, *Modern Warfare*, 116–17, 144–45, 208, 212; Juntunen, "US Army Attachés," 66, 80–81; Kennett, "Developments to 1939," 39; and Richardson, "Development of Airpower," 20.

101. Fuller [Paris] to MID, August 28, 1937, in Cortada, *Modern Warfare*, 178.

102. Canevari, "Forecasts from the War in Spain," 279.

103. Canevari, 279.

104. Griffiss to MID, August 1938, p. 8.

105. For paragraph, see Griffiss to MID, August 1938, p. 10; Waite [Paris] to MID, February 8, 1937, Fuller [Paris] to MID, March 10, 1937, in Cortada, *Modern Warfare*, 66, 84; Juntunen, "US Army Attachés," 67–68, 76–77, 81–85; Biddle, *Rhetoric and Reality*, 173; Kreuder, "Quesada and Richtofen," 87–88; and Kennett, "Developments to 1939," 36.

106. Griffiss to MID, August 1938, p. 10.

107. Quoted in Juntunen, "US Army Attachés," 67.

108. Quoted in Juntunen, 89.

109. Biddle, *Rhetoric and Reality*, 173; for paragraph, see Griffiss to MID, August 1938, p. 3, 8–11, 16, 19; Lee [London] to MID, January 25, 1937, Fuller [Paris] to MID, January 28, 1937, Fuller (Paris) to MID, June 2, 1937, and unnamed CGSS lecture, December 1, 1937, all in Cortada, *Modern Warfare*, 60, 62–63, 132, 144–45, 163–64, 217; Juntunen, "US Army Attachés," 37–46, 52–58, 71, 84, 88–89, 176; Richardson, "Development of Airpower," 16, 20; and Smith and Hall, *Five Down*, 8, 11, 136, 256, 260–61, 264.

110. Griffiss to MID, August 1938, p. 15.

111. Griffiss to MID, August 1938, p. 16.

112. MID Memorandum, McCabe to Chief of Staff, July 6, 1937, in Cortada, *Modern Warfare*, 163.

113. MID Memorandum, 164.

114. Juntunen, "US Army Attachés," 41–42.

115. Griffiss to MID, August 1937 in *Volume I: Spanish War, September 1, 1936 to August 17, 1937: Reports and Articles*, collected by Col. Byron Q. Jones (Carlisle Barracks, PA: Army War College, 1938), 15–16.

THE SPANISH CIVIL WAR

116. For paragraph, see Juntunen, "US Army Attachés," 38–39, 57–58, 68, 74; Fuller [Paris] to MID, June 2, 1937, in Cortada, *Modern Warfare*, 131; Corum, "Luftwaffe and Lessons Learned," 70–71; Corum, "Spanish Civil War," 324–31; Astore and Kiesling, "Tactics and Technology," 236; and Smith and Hall, *Five Down*, 95, 99, 264–65.

117. For paragraph, see Fuqua to MID, September 1, 1936, Fuqua to MID, in Juntunen, "US Army Attachés," 78; Corum, "Spanish Civil War," 319–21, 329; Biddle, *Rhetoric and Reality*, 152–53; and Kenney, "Airplane in Modern Warfare," 17.

118. Fuqua to MID, January 8, 1937, in Cortada, *Modern Warfare*, 35.

119. Lee to MID, January 25, 1937, in Cortada, *Modern Warfare*, 60.

120. Mackin, "Airplanes Can Be Stopped," 399.

121. Corum, "Spanish Civil War," 321–22.

122. Quoted in Futrell, *Ideas, Concepts, Doctrine*, 85.

123. For paragraph, see Griffiss to MID, August 1938, p. 12–13; Juntunen, "US Army Attachés," 66, 78–79; Kenney, "Airplane in Modern Warfare," 19; Corum, "Spanish Civil War," 319; Biddle, *Rhetoric and Reality*, 152–53; Richardson, "Development of Airpower," 19; and Underwood, *Wings of Democracy*, 95–96.

124. Quoted in Biddle, *Rhetoric and Reality*, 353n187.

125. Griffiss to MID, August 1938, p. 14.

126. Michael Sherry, *Rise of American Air Power: The Creation of Armageddon* (New Haven, CT: Yale University Press, 1989), 69.

127. For paragraph, see Malin Craig, Report of the Chief of Staff (hereafter, *ARWD/COS* 1937), in *Annual Reports of the War Department, FY Ended June 30, 1937* (Washington, DC: Government Printing Office, 1937), 29; Louis Johnson, Report of the Assistant Secretary of War (hereafter, *ARWD/ASOW* 1938), in *Annual Reports of the War Department, FY Ended June 30, 1938* (Washington, DC: Government Printing Office, 1938), 25; Harry Woodring, Report of the Secretary of War, in *Annual Reports War Department, FY Ended June 30, 1939* (Washington, DC: Government Printing Office, 1939), 2; and Odom, *After the Trenches*, 168, 197–98.

128. George Lynch, "Current Infantry Developments," *Infantry Journal* 45, no. 1 (January–February 1938): 3.

129. Lynch, 3.

130. *ARWD/COS* 1937, p. 29.

131. For paragraph, see David Johnson, *Fast Tanks and Heavy Bombers: Innovations in the US Army, 1917–1945* (Ithaca, NY: Cornell University Press, 2003), 167–68; Underwood, *Wings of Democracy*, 68–69, 82, 101, 105, 110; Moy, *War Machines*, 94–97; Futrell, *Ideas, Concepts, Doctrine*, 84, 90–92; Forrest Pogue, *George Marshall: Education of a General, 1880–1939* (New York: Viking, 1963), 313, 318, 320, 323–25; and Russell Weigley, *History of the United States Army* (Bloomington: Indiana University Press, 1984), 416–17.

132. For paragraph, see Johnson, *Fast Tanks*, 53, 58–59; Hofmann, *Through Mobility*, 87, 188, 208, 236, 255, 259–60; Cameron, *Mobility, Shock, and Firepower*, 89–90, 97, 236; Green, Thomson, and Roots, *Ordnance Department*, 172, 204–5; and Odom, *After the Trenches*, 137, 146, 206–8, 213, 221.

133. Cameron, *Mobility, Shock, and Firepower*, 90.

134. For paragraph, see *Budget of the US Government for the Years FY36–40; ARWD/COS 1937*, p. 34–35; *ARWD/COS 1938*, p. 33–34; Malin Craig, Report of the Chief of Staff (hereafter, *ARWD/COS 1939*), in *Annual Reports War Department, FY Ended June 30, 1939* (Washington, DC: Government Printing Office, 1939), 30–31; Pogue, *Marshall*, 332–34; Dan Fullerton, "Bright Prospects, Bleak Realities: The US Army's Interwar Modernization Program for the Coming of the Second World War" (PhD diss., University of Kansas, December 2006), 188–89, 194–95; Odom, *After the Trenches*, 82, 99, 102, 104, 107, 200–204; and Robert Eslinger, "The Neglect of Long-Range Escort Development during the Interwar Years (1918–1943)" (Research paper, USAF Air Command and Staff College, March 1997), 16–17.

135. *ARWD/COS 1938*, p. 29.

136. For paragraph, see Odom, *After the Trenches*, 84, 102–12, 203–5, 212; Cameron, *Mobility, Shock, and Firepower*, 113–14; Green, Thomson, and Roots, *Ordnance Department*, 177–81, 195, 204–5; Johnson, *Fast Tanks*, 112–15, 203, 212; Calhoun, *McNair*, 154–55; and Weigley, *History of the US Army*, 416–17.

137. Odom, *After the Trenches*, 110.

138. Odom, 212.

139. Johnson, *Fast Tanks*, 115.

140. Green, Thomson, and Roots, *Ordnance Department*, 207.

141. For paragraph, see Odom, *After the Trenches*, 122–25, 200, 204, 223–28, 232–35; Walter Kretchik, *U.S. Army Doctrine: From the American Revolution to the War on Terror* (Lawrence: University Press of Kansas, 2011), 134–43; Michael Bonura, *Under the Shadow of Napoleon: French Influence on the American Way of Warfare from the War of 1812 to the Outbreak of World War II* (New York: New York University Press, 2012), 220–22, 229–30; and Cameron, *Mobility, Shock, and Firepower*, 109–11, 187.

142. Quoted in Hofmann, *Through Mobility*, 95–96.

143. Johnson, *Fast Tanks*, 58.

144. Kretchik, *US Army Doctrine*, 142; emphasis original.

145. Odom, *After the Trenches*, 122.

146. For paragraph, see Mahnken, *Uncovering Ways of War*, 103–7; Odom, *After the Trenches*, 184–86; Bonura, *Under the Shadow*, 223–25; Hofmann, *Through Mobility*, 198, 203–5, 210; John McLaughlin, *General Albert C. Wedemeyer, America's Unsung Strategist in World War II* (Havertown, PA: Casemate Publishers, 2012), 23–25; and Albert Wedemeyer, "The German General Staff School," report relayed by Military Attaché Berlin to MID, July 11, 1938.

147. For paragraph, see Cameron, *Mobility, Shock, and Firepower*, 139, 158, 165–67, 179, 187; Johnson, "Spanish War," 354; Odom, *After the Trenches*, 168–69, 185–86, 191–98; Green, Thomson, and Roots, *Ordnance Department*, 122; and Mahnken, *Uncovering Ways of War*, 41, 106.

148. Cameron, *Mobility, Shock, and Firepower*, 158.

149. Glantz, "Observing the Soviets," 157, 166; Zaloga and Estes, "Armor," 35; and Robert Citino, *Blitzkrieg to Desert Storm: The Evolution of Operational Warfare* (Lawrence: University Press of Kansas, 2004), 79–80.

150. Cameron, *Mobility, Shock, and Firepower*, 139.

151. Cameron, 309.

152. For paragraph, see Greenwald, "Problems of Peacetime Innovation," ii, 11, 14, 16;

Odom, *After the Trenches*, 105, 139, 165; Green, Thomson, and Roots, *Ordnance Department*, 182–83; Bolling Smith, "Antiaircraft Weapons of the Coast Artillery Corps," *Coast Defense Study Group Journal* 12, no. 2 (May 1998): 95–96, 102–4, 109; and Finney, *History of the Air Corps Tactical School*, 62.

153. For paragraph, see *ARWD/COS* 1937, p. 31, 34; *ARWD/ASOW* 1938, p. 27, 29, 33; *ARWD/COS* 1939, p. 30; Louis Johnson, Report of the Assistant Secretary of War in *Annual Reports War Department, FY Ended June 30, 1939* (Washington, DC: Government Printing Office, 1939), 16; Odom, *After the Trenches*, 111–12, 139, 164–66; Greenwald, "Problems of Peacetime Innovation," 16; Kenney, "Airplane in Modern Warfare," 22; Smith, "AA Weapons," 96–98, 108, 111; and Green, Thomson, and Roots, *Ordnance Department*, 182–83.

154. *ARWD/COS* 1937, p. 34.

155. Quoted in Green, Thomson, and Roots, *Ordnance Department*, 182–83.

156. *ARWD/COS* 1938, p. 29.

157. *ARWD/COS* 1938, p. 29.

158. For paragraph, see Harry Woodring, Report of the Secretary of War (hereafter, *ARWD/SOW* 1937), in *Annual Reports War Department, FY Ended June 30, 1937* (Washington, DC: Government Printing Office, 1937), 5–6; *ARWD/ASOW* 1938, p. 27; Fuller to MID, March 10, 1937, Fuqua to MID, June 1, 1937, and unnamed CGSS lecture, December 1, 1937, all in Cortada, *Modern Warfare*, 84, 119, 207; Noble, "Defense against Air Attack," 332–34; Griffiss to MID, August 1938, p. 8; Greenwald, "Problems of Peacetime Innovation," 11, 16, 28–29; Odom, *After the Trenches*, 164–66; and John Kreis, *Air Warfare and Air Base Air Defense* (Washington, DC: Office of Air Force History, 1988), 29–32.

159. Greenwald, "Problems of Peacetime Innovation," 16.

160. For paragraph, see *ARWD/SOW* 1937, p. 6; *ARWD/COS* 1938, p. 33–34; Odom, *After the Trenches*, 102–7, 113, 156, 204; Cameron, *Mobility, Shock, and Firepower*, 113–15; Fullerton, "Bright Prospects," 68, 145–50; Lanza, "Lessons from Spain," 192–93; John Womack, *Reorganizing for Global War: General Malin Craig and the Triangular Infantry Division, 1935–1939* (Fort Leavenworth, KS: School of Advanced Military Studies, May 2014), 4–8, 11–15, 25–29, 39; John Wilson, *Maneuver and Firepower: The Evolution of Divisions and Separate Brigades* (Honolulu: University Press of the Pacific, 2001), 125–29; and Calhoun, *McNair*, 156–62.

161. Odom, *After the Trenches*, 139.

162. Lynch, "Current Infantry Developments," 7.

163. *ARWD/COS* 1939, p. 31.

164. Fullerton, "Bright Prospects," 93.

165. For paragraph, see Futrell, *Ideas, Concepts, Doctrine*, 29, 83–84, 89; Richardson, "Development of Airpower," 16–17; Moy, *War Machines*, 7, 26–27, 59, 93–94; and Underwood, *Wings of Democracy*, 49, 51, 60, 142–43, 146.

166. Biddle, *Rhetoric and Reality*, 143.

167. Arnold, *Global Mission*, 163.

168. *ARWD/COS* 1937, p. 33.

169. For paragraph, see *ARWD/COS* 1937, p. 34–35; *ARWD/COS* 1938, p. 34–35; Dastrup, *King of Battle*, 192–95; Wilson, *Maneuver and Firepower*, 112–16, 120, 127–31; Odom, *After the Trenches*, 157–58; Calhoun, *McNair*, 158, 161–62; and Janice McKenney, *The Organizational*

History of Field Artillery, 1775–2003 (Washington, DC: US Army Center of Military History, 2007), 138, 145–48, 155.

170. For paragraph, see Wilson, *Maneuver and Firepower*, 129–33; Calhoun, *McNair*, 157, 161, 164–67, 170, 180; Womack, *Reorganizing*, 29–31, 35; Bonura, *Under the Shadow*, 225–29; *ARWD/COS* 1939, p. 28; Christopher Gabel, *Seek, Strike, and Destroy: US Army Tank Destroyer Doctrine in World War II* (Fort Leavenworth, KS: Combat Studies Institute, 1985), 7; and Odom, *After the Trenches*, 113, 157, 191–92.

171. For paragraph, see Cameron, *Mobility, Shock, and Firepower*, 137–38, 293, 301–11; Odom, *After the Trenches*, 112, 139, 149–53, 158; Green, Thomson, and Roots, *Ordnance Department*, 182–86; Gabel, *Seek, Strike, and Destroy*, 5–7; Weeks, *Men against Tanks*, 34; and Hofmann, *Through Mobility*, 226, 229, 261.

172. Lynch, "Current Infantry Developments," 7.

173. Memorandum, Chief of Staff to Chief of Ordnance, September 3, 1937, quoted in Green, Thomson, and Roots, *Ordnance Department*, 182–83.

174. Green, Thomson, and Roots, 183.

175. *ARWD/COS* 1938, p. 33.

176. Green, Thomson, and Roots, *Ordnance Department*, 184; for paragraph, see Green, Thomson, and Roots, 182–86; Odom, *After the Trenches*, 151, 153–54, 208; Johnson, *Fast Tanks*, 115; Weeks, *Men against Tanks*, 31; Hofmann, *Through Mobility*, 226; and Cameron, *Mobility, Shock, and Firepower*, 195, 295–96, 303–4.

177. Quoted in Green, Thomson, and Roots, *Ordnance Department*, 210–11.

178. Quoted in Green, Thomson, and Roots, 184.

179. For paragraph, see Cameron, *Mobility, Shock, and Firepower*, 304, 310; Odom, *After the Trenches*, 150–53; Russell Weigley, "Shaping the American Army of World War II: Mobility versus Power," *Parameters* 11, no. 3 (Autumn 1981): 16; Johnson, *Fast Tanks*, 115; Calhoun, *McNair*, 155, 180, 191; and Weeks, *Men against Tanks*, 31–32.

180. Odom, *After the Trenches*, 153.

181. Green, Thomson, and Roots, *Ordnance Department*, 184.

182. Smith, "AA Weapons," 108.

183. For paragraph, see Gabel, *Seek, Strike, and Destroy*, 5–7; Green, Thomson, and Roots, *Ordnance Department*, 182–86; Cameron, *Mobility, Shock, and Firepower*, 107, 125, 293–99, 311–12; Hofmann, *Through Mobility*, 261–62; and Johnson, *Fast Tanks*, 149–50.

184. Odom, *After the Trenches*, 151.

185. Gabel, *Seek, Strike, and Destroy*, 6.

186. Odom, *After the Trenches*, 149.

187. Calhoun, *McNair*, 191.

188. For paragraph, see Green, Thomson, and Roots, *Ordnance Department*, 189–93, 202; Cameron, *Mobility, Shock, and Firepower*, 8, 45, 76, 93, 133–34, 138, 166–67, 213–14; Odom, *After the Trenches*, 137, 144–46, 149; Johnson, *Fast Tanks*, 59, 116–18, 125–28, 134–35; and Hofmann, *Through Mobility*, 40, 87–88, 113, 151, 175, 186, 192, 223–24.

189. Odom, *After the Trenches*, 137.

190. Cameron, *Mobility, Shock, and Firepower*, 119.

191. For paragraph, see Green, Thomson, and Roots, *Ordnance Department*, 193–97, 202;

Johnson, *Fast Tanks*, 112–13, 119, 133–35; Cameron, *Mobility, Shock, and Firepower*, 74, 113–14, 133–34, 137, 200, 208; Mildred H. Gillie, *Forging the Thunderbolt: History of the US Army's Armored Forces, 1917–1945* (Mechanicsburg, PA: Stackpole, 2006), 89–91, 97; Odom, *After the Trenches*, 102, 104, 107, 144, 204; and Hofmann, *Through Mobility*, 172, 193–95, 218, 222–23, 228–29, 238.

192. Hofmann, *Through Mobility*, 218.

193. For paragraph, see Cameron, *Mobility, Shock, and Firepower*, 119, 208; Odom, *After the Trenches*, 144, 194–95; Fullerton, "Bright Prospects," 78; Johnson, *Fast Tanks*, 133–35; Hofmann, *Through Mobility*, 218–38; and Hofmann, "Tactical and Strategic Use of Attaché Information," 117, 121–26, 131, 133.

194. Lynch, "Current Infantry Developments," 5.

195. Gillie, *Forging the Thunderbolt*, 97.

196. Gillie, 96.

197. George Hofmann, "Flawed Lessons Learned: The Role of US Military Attachés in Assessing Armored Warfare during the Spanish Civil War," *Armor* 113, no. 3 (May–June 2004): 30.

198. Malin Craig, "Mechanization and Tanks," Special Statement in "General Craig's Hearing," *Army and Navy Register*, March 26, 1938, p. 4; for paragraph, see Hofmann, *Through Mobility*, 227–29, 236–37; Johnson, *Fast Tanks*, 121, 136; Odom, *After the Trenches*, 147; Cameron, *Mobility, Shock, and Firepower*, 121–23, 190, 208, 211–14, 223; and Lynch, "Current Infantry Developments," 6.

199. Gillie, *Forging the Thunderbolt*, 96.

200. Gillie, 96.

201. Zaloga, *Spanish Civil War Tanks*, 5.

202. For paragraph, see Steven Zaloga, *M3 & M5 Stuart Light Tank 1940–45* (Oxford: Osprey Publishing, 2009), 5; Cameron, *Mobility, Shock, and Firepower*, 165, 179, 213–14; Green, Thomson, and Roots, *Ordnance Department*, 122, 193–94, 212; Johnson, *Fast Tanks*, 121, 135; and Fullerton, "Bright Prospects," 93–94.

203. Green, Thomson, and Roots, *Ordnance Department*, 193–94.

204. Weigley, "Shaping the American Army," 15.

205. For paragraph, see *ARWD/SOW* 1937, p. 6; *ARWD/COS* 1937, p. 34; Cameron, *Mobility, Shock, and Firepower*, 119, 124–25, 28–29, 137, 251, 359; Gillie, *Forging the Thunderbolt*, 74, 101, 171; Green, Thomson, and Roots, *Ordnance Department*, 197, 201–2; and Johnson, *Fast Tanks*, 119–21, 133, 135, 139.

206. Lynch, "Current Infantry Developments," 5.

207. Zaloga, *M3 & M5*, 5.

208. Fullerton, "Bright Prospects," 93.

209. For paragraph, see Lynch, "Current Infantry Developments," 5–6; Green, Thomson, and Roots, *Ordnance Department*, 196–203; Cameron, *Mobility, Shock, and Firepower*, 133–38; Johnson, *Fast Tanks*, 119–24; Zaloga, *M3 & M5*, 5–6; and Hofmann, "Tactical and Strategic Use of Attaché Information," 123–32.

210. Zaloga, *M3 & M5*, 6; and Green, Thomson, and Roots, *Ordnance Department*, 197.

211. Johnson, *Fast Tanks*, 189.

212. Quoted in Gillie, *Forging the Thunderbolt*, 96.

213. For paragraph, see Hofmann, *Through Mobility*, 190, 222–23, 238, 255, 259; Kretchik, *US Army Doctrine*, 142–47, 314fn83; Cameron, *Mobility, Shock, and Firepower*, 110–12; Bonura, *Under the Shadow*, 214, 220, 229–32; Odom, *After the Trenches*, 8, 125, 131–38, 142, 148, 198, 232, 236; Hofmann, "Tactical and Strategic Use of Attaché Information," 101, 129–30; and Calhoun, *McNair*, 185–87.

214. Bonura, *Under the Shadow*, 231; and Odom, *After the Trenches*, 197.

215. Kretchik, *US Army Doctrine*, 145.

216. Odom, *After the Trenches*, 197.

217. For good discussion, see Calhoun, *McNair*, 1–25.

218. Corum, "Spanish Civil War," 332.

219. Corum, 332–33.

220. For paragraph, see Kennett, "Developments to 1939," 30, 43, 45; Futrell, *Ideas, Concepts, Doctrine*, 83, 88–89; Gary Cox, "Beyond the Battle Line: US Air Attack Theory and Doctrine, 1919–1941" (Master's thesis, USAF School of Advanced Airpower Studies, April 1996), 5–6, 28, 31; and Daniel Mortensen, *A Pattern for Joint Operations: World War II Close Air Support, North Africa* (Washington, DC: Office of Air Force History and US Army Center of Military History, 1987), 4–8.

221. Arnold, *Global Mission*, 167.

222. Finney, *History of the Air Corps Tactical School*, 73.

223. Futrell, *Ideas, Concepts, Doctrine*, 84.

224. Futrell, 84.

225. For paragraph, see Futrell, *Ideas, Concepts, Doctrine*, 85–86; Cox, "Beyond the Battle Line," 20, 30–31; Kennett, "Developments to 1939," 30, 41–42, 47, 49, 58–59; Thomas Greer, *The Development of Air Doctrine in the Army Air Arm, 1917–1941* (Washington, DC: Office of Air Force History, 1985), 87–88; Mortensen, *Pattern for Joint Operations*, 8–9; and Johnson, *Fast Tanks*, 166.

226. Futrell, *Ideas, Concepts, Doctrine*, 85.

227. Quoted in Futrell, *Ideas, Concepts, Doctrine*, 86.

228. Kennett, "Developments to 1939," 47; for paragraph, see 48–49, 52, 58–59; Cox, "Beyond the Battle Line," 20, 28, 30–31; Mortensen, *Pattern for Joint Operations*, 7–10; Hughes, *Overlord*, 55; Biddle, *Rhetoric and Reality*, 154–55; Futrell, *Ideas, Concepts, Doctrine*, 82–83, 88–89; Rein, *North African Air Campaign*, 24, 29; and Corum, "Spanish Civil War," 332.

229. Quoted in Kennett, "Developments to 1939," 48.

230. Greer, *Development*, 87.

231. Biddle, *Rhetoric and Reality*, 164.

232. For paragraph, see Odom, *After the Trenches*, 160, 162–63, 195; Corum, "Spanish Civil War," 314, 330; Smith and Hall, *Five Down*, 11, 93, 264; Calhoun, *McNair*, 189–90; Rein, *North African Air Campaign*, 31–32; and Mortensen, *Pattern for Joint Operations*, 10–12.

233. Kennett, "Developments to 1939," 58.

234. Kennett, 58.

235. Kennett, 59.

236. Odom, *After the Trenches*, 163.

237. Corum, "Spanish Civil War," 332.

238. For paragraph, see Underwood, *Wings of Democracy*, 37, 68–69, 82, 84, 87, 96–97, 105, 110; Biddle, *Rhetoric and Reality*, 146; Futrell, *Ideas, Concepts, Doctrine*, 81, 84; and Moy, *War Machines*, 73–78.

239. Arnold, *Global Mission*, 156; emphasis original.

240. Underwood, *Wings of Democracy*, 84.

241. For paragraph, see Futrell, *Ideas, Concepts, Doctrine*, 85–88; Moy, *War Machines*, 67, 94–95; and Underwood, *Wings of Democracy*, 111, 119.

242. Richard Overy, *The Bombers and the Bombed: Allied Air War over Europe, 1940–1945* (New York: Viking, 2013), 17.

243. Quoted in Futrell, *Ideas, Concepts, Doctrine*, 87.

244. Quoted in Moy, *War Machines*, 95.

245. Quoted in Moy, 95.

246. Quoted in Moy, 95.

247. For paragraph, see Moy, 95–97; Arnold, *Global Mission*, 177; Underwood, *Wings of Democracy*, 74, 77, 94, 119–22, 134–37, 144, 160, 170; Pogue, *Marshall*, 323–25, 334–35; and Ed Cray, *General of the Army: George Marshall, Soldier and Statesman* (New York: Cooper Square Press, 2000), 130–32, 135.

248. Futrell, *Ideas, Concepts, Doctrine*, 91.

249. Overy, *Bombers and the Bombed*, 17.

250. For paragraph, see Biddle, *Rhetoric and Reality*, 146, 155, 161, 164–69; Futrell, *Ideas, Concepts, Doctrine*, 64–65, 69, 81–82; Hughes, *Overlord*, 54–57; Moy, *War Machines*, 9, 31, 61–62, 65–66, 75–77, 90; Finney, *History of the Air Corps Tactical School*, 40, 68, 76–77; Johnson, *Fast Tanks*, 156, 164–66; Eslinger, "Neglect," 6, 13–18; and Underwood, *Wings of Democracy*, 36, 68–69, 82–91, 96–97, 105, 110.

251. Eslinger, "Neglect of Long-Range Escort Development," 16.

252. Quoted in Futrell, *Ideas, Concepts, Doctrine*, 82.

253. For paragraph, see Futrell, *Ideas, Concepts, Doctrine*, 80–83; Finney, *History of the Air Corps Tactical School*, 68, 78; Rein, *North African Air Campaign*, 13–14; Biddle, *Rhetoric and Reality*, 165–74; Johnson, *Fast Tanks*, 164, 204–10; and Eslinger, "Neglect of Long-Range Escort Development," 14–18.

254. Quoted in Eslinger, "Neglect of Long-Range Escort Development," 25.

255. Finney, *History of the Air Corps Tactical School*, 78.

256. Finney, 78.

257. Corum, "Spanish Civil War," 332.

258. Biddle, *Rhetoric and Reality*, 174.

259. For paragraph, see Biddle, *Rhetoric and Reality*, 173; Futrell, *Ideas, Concepts, Doctrine*, 96; Eslinger, "Neglect of Long-Range Escort Development," 23–24; and Johnson, *Fast Tanks*, 169–70, 204–10.

260. Johnson, *Fast Tanks*, 210; also see Overy, *Bombers and the Bombed*, 171–73; and David Stubbs, "A Blind Spot? The Royal Air Force and Long-Range Fighters, 1936–1944," *Journal of Military History* 78, no. 2 (April 2014): 687–88.

261. Dennis Drew, "Two Decades in the Air Power Wilderness: Do We Know Where We Are?" *Air University Review* 37, no. 6 (September–October 1986): 4.

262. Arnold, *Global Mission*, 174; emphasis added.

263. For paragraph, see Gole, *Exposing the Third Reich*, 234–36, 274; Bidwell, *History of MID*, 386; and Bonura, *Under the Shadow*, 247–48.

264. Bidwell, *History of MID*, 386.

265. Juntunen, "US Army Attachés," 1–2.

266. Corum, "Spanish Civil War," 331.

267. Juntunen, "US Army Attachés," 25; and Cortada, *Modern Warfare*, xiii, 197.

268. Green, Thomson, and Roots, *Ordnance Department*, 209–10.

269. Juntunen, "US Army Attachés," 131.

270. Odom, *After the Trenches*, 197.

271. George Hofmann, "Army Doctrine and the Christie Tank," in *Camp Colt to Desert Storm: The History of US Armored Forces*, ed. George Hofmann and Donn Starry (Lexington: University Press of Kentucky, 1999), 126.

272. Reilly, "Proving Ground," 336.

CHAPTER 4

THE YOM KIPPUR WAR
Ferocious and Fortuitous Fight

Our interest in the Arab/Israeli War, all the analyses, and all
the discussions are not just an intellectual exercise. True, it is
fascinating for soldiers, but there is a purpose to this study and
the purpose is that we want our schools, our combat developers
and those involved in training, to remember these lessons and
to relate them to our concepts.
—*Gen. William DePuy, Commanding General, US Army*
Training & Doctrine Command

By October 1973 few officers remained from the small, pre–World War II force examined in the last chapter. The American military had been a global power for over
three decades, fighting in World War II, two limited wars, and many smaller engagements. Given such experience, it would not have been surprising to ignore a less than
three-week battle among Middle Eastern nations. Yet American officers extensively
studied the Yom Kippur War, for good reason. Military historian Frederick Kagan
declares that the conflict "rocked the American defense establishment to its founda-
tions."[1] Although not all analysts would go that far, lessons from its combat contributed to the celebrated doctrinal, training, organizational, and materiel initiatives of
the subsequent decade.

Whereas Joint Chiefs of Staff (JCS) chairman Gen. Omar Bradley testified in May
1951 that escalating the Korean War to mainland China would involve the United
States "in the wrong war, at the wrong place, at the wrong time, and with the wrong
enemy," the Yom Kippur War proved for the US Army and US Air Force to be the
right war, at the right place, at the right time, and with the right enemy, according to senior American officers in early 1974.[2] Lt. Gen. Orwin Talbott, US Army
Training & Doctrine Command (TRADOC) deputy chief, stated that its study provided three benefits: (1) an unprecedented view of all-out modern conventional war;
(2) an opportunity to evaluate Soviet tactics, doctrine, and equipment; and (3) a chance
to assess the performance of US equipment against Soviet materiel.[3] Similarly, Gen.

Robert Dixon (USAF), chief of Tactical Air Command (TAC), wrote that "operations during the October War give us a glimpse into future conflicts."[4] JCS chairman Adm. Thomas Moorer declared in a congressional hearing that "no discussion of the relative military posture between the United States and USSR would be complete without an analysis of the recent conflict in the Middle East."[5]

In examining this case, I focus on the army and air force. Befitting a superpower, the US Armed Forces had expanded enormously in scale and complexity since the 1930s, including the formation of the JCS, an independent air force, and combatant commands. By March 1, 1974, Department of Defense (DOD) elements had initiated at least thirty-seven studies covering some aspect of the Yom Kippur War.[6] Concentration on army and air force lessons-learning efforts reflects service responsibility to prepare forces (e.g., doctrine, organization, training, materiel) and the critical potential of findings from the conflict to aid that process. US naval leaders generally did not regard the sea combat as significant, although unsurprisingly the Naval Electronic Systems Command scrutinized Israeli use of electronic warfare to dominate the first surface-to-surface missile battle between warships.[7] Also, I omit discussion of US Air Force (USAF) lessons from Operation Nickel Grass (the wartime transfer of critical materiel to Israel), given that such experiential learning is beyond this study's scope.

The army and air force relied on their own investigation of events as well as information collected by JCS/Office of the Secretary of Defense (OSD) initiatives. Some key documents remain classified (e.g., the army's eight-volume lessons learned study and the Weapons Systems Evaluation Group [WSEG]'s seven-volume data report[8]), but a lack of access to them does not present an insuperable problem. Senior officers' lessons and how they applied them have been well documented in open sources through published writings, available correspondence, and oral history interviews. Moreover, some important documents have been declassified—most notably, the excellent October 1974 WSEG study (*Assessment of the Weapons and Tactics Used in the October 1973 Middle East War*), whose authors drew heavily on previously completed DOD evaluations, including those referenced above. Plus, officers who have reviewed the classified material have found, as Maj. Bruce Brant (USA) notes, that the "unclassified data was very close or the same as the classified."[9]

In contrast to the first three cases, in which a major war erupted within a decade of the learning event, the US military did not engage in a large-scale conventional war for nearly twenty years after the Yom Kippur War. The American armed forces preparedness for the 1991 Persian Gulf War reflected the culmination of a protracted improvement effort that commenced after the Vietnam War. This chapter explores the contribution of lessons learning from the October 1973 fighting to that process. Although the time gap between the two Middle Eastern wars precludes attributing performance against the Iraqi military directly to findings from the earlier conflict, the subsequent discussion shows that the US Army and US Air Force generally used information obtained to facilitate a positive trajectory toward the high-level performance witnessed in 1990–91.

HOW DID THE AMERICANS ATTEMPT TO IDENTIFY LESSONS?

Even before the Yom Kippur War ended, journalists and outside commentators began characterizing it as heralding a new era, with improved antitank guided missiles (ATGMs) and surface-to-air missiles (SAMs) fundamentally altering battlefield dynamics. In a 1991 oral history, Gen. Donn Starry, USA (Ret.), recalled that "all of Washington was agog with the notion that the tank was dead; the antitank guided missile had made the tank obsolete."[10] Similarly, Brookings analyst William White wrote in 1974 that reports of significant losses of US-built aircraft to Soviet air defenses "generated widespread alarm in the American press" that tactical attack aircraft had been rendered ineffective.[11] The relatively low cost of these defensive weapons compared to modern tanks and aircraft enhanced their perceived value. Despite experienced analysts cautioning against premature judgment, Westerners generally adopted what Israeli Jehuda Wallach called "missilophobia."[12]

Although skeptical about the revolutionary nature of Arab–Israeli fighting, the US military leadership believed that it illustrated important facets of modern war. This sense, combined with the pressure generated by outside commentary, prompted commitment to identifying what really happened and preventing errant views from becoming the accepted narrative. As postmortems began appearing, Col. John Burke, USA (Ret.), warned that "the real lesson will be lost in the fog of rhetoric."[13] Critical to addressing this problem was collecting accurate data. Given uncertainty about Israeli materiel losses and frustrated by extensive Israeli Defense Forces (IDF) arms requests, the DOD, shortly after the fighting stopped, dispatched the twenty-one-man US Military Equipment Validation Team–Israel, led by Maj. Gen. Maurice Casey, USAF, to investigate Israeli needs, with a secondary tasking of conducting preliminary weapons effectiveness reviews.[14] Soon afterward they would be joined by the seventeen members of the US Military Operations Survey Team (USMOST) from the services, Joint Staff, and other DOD components. Secretary of Defense James Schlesinger established this joint group, under the direction of Brig. Gen. Lloyd Leavitt, USAF, to begin the department's focused search for military lessons.[15] Finally, the aforementioned WSEG investigation of the relative effectiveness of Soviet and US weapons, tactics, and doctrine would lead to four reports over the next year.[16] Upon designation as the senior air force representative to this JCS/OSD entity in early November 1973, Maj. Gen. Frederick "Boots" Blesse received tasking to take twenty-five army, navy, and air force personnel to Israel where, he recalled, "we evaluated everything possible."[17]

Whereas in the previous cases the combatants were either hostile or, at best, indifferent to American efforts, the US military benefited enormously from Israeli cooperation.[18] Although Casey and Leavitt reported some initial resistance and subterfuge in areas potentially affecting arms transfers, American investigators generally found their hosts to be accommodating. Blesse noted that traveling and working with Brig. Gen. Uzi Eilam of the IDF, who led a similar team, "was a delight and we became good friends in the process of accomplishing our two government missions."[19] The DOD and Israeli Ministry of Defense agreed to cooperate in (1) exploiting captured equipment; (2) collecting, organizing, and distributing data on materiel, tactics, and techniques; (3) performing joint tests and analysis of data; and (4) drawing lessons. For example, the US–Israeli Combat Vehicle Assessment Team attempted to determine what destroyed the 119 Israeli and 435 Arab tanks available for examination.[20] The Americans also found valuable survey responses from hundreds of IDF leaders on their combat experiences. US officials relished the opportunity to examine and test captured Soviet weapons that had never before been used in combat (e.g., BMP [Boyevaya Mashina Pekhoty] infantry fighting vehicle [IFV], SA-6 SAM). Based on information gathered, the Defense Intelligence Agency's Directorate for Science and Technical Intelligence released thirteen bulletins under the umbrella title "Middle East Equipment Exploitation."[21] Importantly, the cooperative effort facilitated sustained friendships between senior American and Israeli officers (e.g., Starry and IDF armor division commander Brig. Gen. Musa Peled, Dixon and Israeli Air Force [IAF] chief Maj. Gen. Benny Peled). Although Israel's de facto allied status, control of the battlefields, and perceived martial skill warranted heavy concentration on that side, the Americans eventually undertook limited investigations in Jordan and Egypt.[22] These politically useful initiatives, however, yielded minimal military insights.

Chief of Staff Gen. Creighton Abrams tasked TRADOC with leading the army's investigation.[23] While Brig. Gen. Morris Brady led a seven-month Special Readiness Study Group (SRSG), TRADOC commanding general William DePuy composed a preliminary findings memorandum in early January 1974 with the aim of quickly applying clear lessons. After Abrams registered concern that senior army officers, unlike their air force counterparts, had not visited Israel, Talbot traveled there for twelve days of meetings beginning on January 31. Abrams instructed him to find "the truth, to sort out fact from fancy, to talk to airmen, soldiers, headquarters and battalions and find out what really happened."[24] Despite receiving extensive praise for his late February trip report, Talbott's insights essentially reiterated the points in DePuy's early January 1974 memo, which would remain the basis of TRADOC's lessons. The army chief of staff also dispatched then Armor School commandant Major General Starry and XM1 tank program manager Brig. Gen. Robert Baer to Israel for an armor-focused investigation.[25] Abrams charged them with answering two questions: (1) Broadly, what should he learn from the conflict? and (2) Specifically were the XM1 requirements sound; especially, did it need a larger main gun than the planned 105 mm weapon? Starry and Baer in April 1974 spent time with leading Israeli tank expert Maj. Gen. Israel Tal, met all wartime division and most brigade and battalion commanders, examined damaged and destroyed tanks, and "walked on the ground where the battles had been fought, usually with the guys who had fought them."[26] Upon their return, these officers met with senior Army, DOD, and civilian officials, and in May and June 1974 a Talbott/Brady-led group briefed identified lessons to forward-deployed commands and key allies in Europe and Asia.[27]

Work by the SRSG, also known as the Brady Commission, continued with an emphasis on applicable findings.[28] Reflecting the core aim of "developing an action program for the Army," the group identified dozens of required "products" (e.g., tactics and techniques employed by the Israelis to suppress or degrade Arab tank tactics, changes to air defense doctrine and organization based on identified weaknesses).[29] For each assessment, the SRSG designated relevant army organizations, agencies, and schools to take the lead or provide input. In pursuit of better data, in May 1974 the service dispatched another team led by the highly regarded Dr. Joseph Sperrazza, director of the Army Materiel Systems Analysis Activity, to Israel. Col. Bruce Williams, senior army member of the WSEG team, assisted this effort and provided TRADOC senior officers with some of the hard data desired, but he warned that, unfortunately, "significant records were not accurately maintained at any level during the initial days of the war when Israeli forces were fighting to survive" and many low-level unit commanders were killed or wounded.[30] In July 1974 the SRSG submitted its eight-volume report, *Analysis of Combat Data—1973 Mideast War*, with 162 specific recommendations, mostly on tactics, training, and equipment.

The air force did not conduct an in-depth study analogous to the SRSG, but this absence did not reflect a lack of interest in the Yom Kippur War or a lack of commitment to apply perceived lessons. Aviation historian Brian Laslie points out the USAF leadership "recognized they had just come through a reckoning [the Vietnam War] and lost," yet necessary changes to address performance problems had not occurred when "the 1973 Arab-Israeli War also demonstrated to American airmen that continuing to exercise current doctrine without improvements to training and weapons systems would lead to greater failures."[31] Robert Futrell adds that since the Middle East battle involved large numbers of newly developed weapons and combat corresponded somewhat with expectations of Central European battle, it "stimulated much thought in the United States including evaluation and reaction that was perhaps keener than the evaluation and reaction to US experiences in Southeast Asia."[32] The USAF even attempted to facilitate Israeli use of its newest F-4E fighter-bomber variant with leading-edge slats, as Leavitt recalled, "for a realistic combat evaluation," by including twenty-four of them in the resupply effort.[33] Indicative of high-level attention, USMOST team leader Leavitt met with Chief of Staff Gen. George

Brown and TAC commander Dixon soon after returning from Israel in late 1973.[34] By then USAF elements had initiated several examinations of the conflict. Members of the Air Staff's Operations Directorate produced several talking papers, while TAC, the Tactical Fighter Weapons Center, and the Air Force Special Communications Center completed their own assessments.[35] Still, Maj. Gen. Harold Collins, the assistant deputy chief of staff for R&D, stated in early May 1974 that the limited existing data was a complicating factor in gauging the effectiveness of aerial weapons and systems used in the conflict.[36] In part, this difficulty resulted from a blasé attitude displayed by aviators, whether Israeli or American, toward information collection. While hundreds of IDF tank commanders replied to survey questionnaires about combat, the Israeli Air Force frustratingly did not respond to queries.[37] The lack of hard data added to the tendency to embrace sustaining lessons congruent with pre-existing preferences and downplay disruptive findings. For example, Leavitt recalled Air Staff hostility to his team's emphasis on the IAF's unanticipated difficulties with Arab integrated air defenses (IADs) given potential jeopardy for the A-X close air support (CAS) aircraft.

US military leaders appreciated that their Soviet counterparts would conduct similar investigations with potentially significant implications, but their ability to identify Russian findings and use such information was somewhat deficient. In April 1974 Dr. Malcolm Currie, DOD undersecretary of defense for research and engineering, testified to Soviet awareness about the Arab–Israeli combat and said "we should expect that they will use these lessons as a guide to modernization of current weapons or developments of new weapons."[38] Lt. Gen. Louis Wilson, commander of Pacific Command's Fleet Marine Force, asked Talbott during his June 1974 briefing stop in Hawaii, "What might the Soviets conclude to be the most important 'lessons learned' from the October War?"[39] The TRADOC deputy asked Maj. Gen. Harold Aaron, army assistant chief of staff for intelligence, who subsequently informed him that no firm evidence existed on Soviet analysis.[40] Over the next few years, the US military supported work to address that question.[41] This research revealed considerable Soviet interest, including a report that more than two hundred marshals, generals, and other key officers attended a mid-November 1974 conference "to discuss the tactical implications of the 1973 Middle East War."[42] At a second meeting two months later, the Soviet minister of defense and commander in chief of ground troops "strongly emphasized the lessons and implications of the October War."[43] The Russian armed forces applied combat data in key areas such as ATGMs and electronic warfare (EW) with major consequences for the American military, as will be discussed.[44] Still, nearly a decade after the conflict, Capt. Ronny Bragger, USA, assessed that "it is not possible, given the literature available, to develop a comprehensive view of the official Soviet lessons learned from the 1973 Middle East War."[45]

WHAT LESSONS DID THE AMERICANS IDENTIFY?

The US commenced battle in the Persian Gulf War amid widely varying forecasts from military analysts, but the Americans immediately established dominance over the Iraqis, prompting exultant and exaggerated claims of a revolution in military affairs. The most critical element for US success in the air and on the ground was the possession of unprecedented battlefield information, enabling more effective use of troops and weapons. The weapons themselves, many untested in major war, not only proved lethal but also permitted killing the enemy with less vulnerability to one's own platforms via greater range, reduced visibility, and electronic protection. Increased battle management enhanced intraservice combined arms and interservice jointness that took advantage of the relative strengths of varying assets and systems. Above all, students of the fighting considered the high-quality training of US soldiers and units as responsible for their performance. Occurring at the end of the Cold War, when the US military was still in a state of high readiness, the Persian Gulf War demonstrated the enormous progress achieved in the preceding two decades.

The Yom Kippur War, which took place at the beginning of the post-Vietnam reform effort, yielded many lessons highly relevant for the 1991 battlefield. The earlier war's shocking intensity conveyed the enormous attrition and resource consumption present in modern conventional warfare. In particular, it showed the sharply increasing lethality of combat in which, if you could see it, you could kill it. The war marked a transition point in the ever-increasing complexity of battle, especially with its extensive EW dimension. The Americans recognized that operating in such an environment required enhanced battle management as well as forces prepared to perform effectively in chaos, like the Israelis, when such battle management was not available. The war reiterated the importance of realistic training, which had enabled the IDF to prevail despite being surprised and badly outnumbered. American study of the fighting determined that the two key twentieth-century conventional warfare weapons—the tank and aircraft—remained viable with proper tactics and improved technology despite the enhanced challenge from ATGMs and SAMs. Still, the army and air force recognized they needed to make a concerted and varied effort to counter these challenges as well as bolster their own use of the defensive systems. In sum, every element central to American success in the Persian Gulf War had been a core finding available from study of Arab–Israeli combat in October 1973.

Enlightening Lessons for US Armed Forces

No revolution in military affairs. Given its allocation of extensive resources and close cooperation with the Israelis, the US military unsurprisingly identified the conflict's major lessons. Before addressing these findings, it is necessary to note the DOD appropriately rejected outside assertions that the fighting revealed a revolution in military affairs. JCS Chairman Moorer testified in late February 1974 that "time-honored strategic and tactical concepts have been underlined, reinforced and footnoted—not repealed or replaced."[46] A week later Abrams added that "we relearned some lessons, I think, from the Middle East war" related to tactics, doctrine, air–ground cooperation, and air defense.[47] Talbott and Brady began their European briefings by observing that "much, perhaps most of what we learned is not new, but it needs reemphasis, and confirms most of our own tactics and doctrine."[48] These declarations should not be taken as meaning that American military leaders dismissed the educational value of the combat, as Moorer emphasized "these footnotes to military history are, however, important and worthy of consideration."[49]

Increased lethality of the modern battlefield. The Americans identified three core findings, beginning with modern war's shocking intensity and lethality.[50] Deputy Secretary of Defense William Clements began a list of the Pentagon's lessons by citing "the heavy attrition of equipment and supplies that can result from modern, intense conventional conflict."[51] Williams, the most knowledgeable army investigator, stressed lethality above all, while Starry characterized it as "the single most impressive fact about the modern battlefield."[52] Ground officers were stunned that the Egyptians and Syrians lost more tanks in eighteen days than possessed by the entire US Seventh Army in Europe. Army officers repeatedly noted the war showed that today "anything seen on the battlefield can be hit, and anything that can be hit can be killed."[53] This reality prompted awareness of the need for techniques that reduced vulnerability as well as "affordable" weapons to ensure sufficient quantity. Beyond destroying large numbers of weapons, the vigorously contested Yom Kippur War showed modern combat consumed huge amounts of fuel, spare parts, and especially ammunition. In mid-1974 Army Materiel Command Chief Gen. Henry Miley pointed out that usage rates far exceeded US experience in Vietnam.[54] Typifying the reaction of senior officers, Dixon declared that "munitions stock levels must be realistically computed."[55]

Greater complexity of modern war. The above finding combined with other factors to produce a second general lesson—modern warfare's increased complexity.[56] USMOST team leader Leavitt explained that the ever-increasing lethality of weapons; joint service interaction; planning, communications, and intelligence requirements; and speed of new developments "all contributed to the complexity of war in October 1973."[57] Commentators focused on a few key elements of this complexity. First, the conflict showed that the challenge of integrating multiple air and ground elements had grown exponentially, especially with rapid personnel and equipment attrition. Officers accounted for 24 percent of IDF combat deaths compared to 9 percent for the US Army in the Vietnam War.[58] Williams relayed that the Israelis stressed the difficulty in understanding their battlefield environment with "the higher the echelon of command the more obscured the real situation."[59] Second, Starry briefed Abrams that, beyond the general nature of battle, command and control proved challenging "because of the numbers of Soviet-made radio-electronic combat systems employed."[60] EW had been impactful in Southeast Asia, but the Americans recognized that it played a much greater role in the Middle East. Williams argued that "secure communications are required at all maneuver unit echelons. Antijam [electronic countermeasures (ECM)] development is required."[61] Dixon averred that "crews require detailed knowledge of friendly and enemy electronic warfare capability," while Collins testified that EW was one of the war's major lessons.[62] Finally, increased night fighting contributed to the battlefield's growing complexity. Disturbingly for the Americans, the Arabs' Soviet-built equipment was generally superior to IDF materiel in the dark. In March 1974 Abrams testified that, on the basis of the Yom Kippur War, "we must give emphasis in our structure—and I think we are doing that—to the night fighting capability of all weapons systems."[63] Effectiveness required more than equipment, as Israelis showed in their superior nighttime performance despite possessing inferior materiel. Williams declared that "night training must be emphasized at all echelons by all types of units."[64] For the air force, Col. James Lindsey explained that the conflict reinforced that the lack of night air-to-ground capability "was a rather significant thing" and, "had one side or the other exploited a night capability, it could have very significantly affected the outcome, we felt."[65]

Training and leadership key to IDF superiority. Appreciating that the lethality and complexity of modern war challenged all combatants, the Americans attempted to identify why the Israelis prevailed despite being initially surprised and heavily outnumbered. Maj. Gen. Paul Gorman, TRADOC deputy chief of staff for training, observed in an influential January 1974 paper that "were we to stage a war game or maneuver to try to learn how to fight such battles, the side playing the Israelis would have lost each, and the exchange ratios would have been exactly reversed."[66] Moreover, the IDF lacked a significant qualitative advantage in materiel. Postwar exploitation of captured Soviet weapons fostered recognition, as Maj. Gen. Robert Scales later noted, that the Americans "would not be able to rely solely on superior technology to win against the quantitatively superior Soviets."[67] Rather, DePuy informed Abrams that unquantifiable factors such as "training and leadership weighed more heavily than weapons systems capabilities on the actual battlefield."[68] Talbott and Brady ended their road show by asserting that "perhaps the biggest lesson of the October Mideast war" was, rather than materiel quantity or quality, "the decisive factor was people."[69] Starry added the conflict indicated that the more intense and complex the fighting becomes, "the more men—the soldiers and their leaders, become the critical and deciding element."[70]

US officials attributed the quality of IDF training, especially its realism, as most responsible for this human advantage.[71] Clements included "the importance of trained manpower" among the Pentagon's main lessons.[72] Currie went even further, stating that "the single most important overall lesson of the war was the reminder that training is crucial."[73] In his preliminary report, DePuy observed that "perhaps the most startling aspect of weapons systems performances during the Arab-Israeli War had to do with the impact of training on battlefield results."[74] Starry pointed to the fighting, showing that the best combat units are "those that are well trained and well led and those who have trained together to a high level of excellence before battle's onset."[75] Likewise, air force officers ascribed the superior skill of Israeli pilots to their excellent training (and aircrew selection) programs. As to why Israeli training program was so effective, Gorman wrote in early January 1974 that it was not magic but conducted with more intensity and more live ammunition. Williams emphasized that the IDF obtained well-trained leaders by frequently testing them and allowing them to make and learn from mistakes.[76] He added that the US Army needed to enhance training realism with more night operations, mines, chemical/biological/radiological defenses, and camouflage. American aviators noted that the postwar IAF was "practically eliminating the limits that flying safety imposed on their training to make it more realistic."[77]

Enlightening Lessons Identified by the Army

Reaffirmation of combined-arms centrality. In transitioning to army-specific findings, the continuing importance of skilled combined-arms teams represents an appropriate place to start. The IDF had suffered from its dismissiveness of this principle, allocating over 75 percent of its defense budget to armor and aviation between the 1967 and 1973 wars.[78] In early 1974 Gorman stressed that "the Yom Kippur War underscored the soundness of the American doctrine of combined arms," while Starry wrote that "the only bit of ancient dogma that remains unscathed is the essentiality of the combined arms team."[79] Given that the Middle East fighting highlighted the coordination challenge presented by modern war, the Talbott–Brady briefing appropriately urged that "we need more and better combined arms training. This comes out loud and clear."[80]

The tank remained the primary ground weapon. While the war reinforced US officers' appreciation for combined arms, it also provided armor advocates evidence of the tank's central contribution.[81] Before the war some commentators expressed doubt about the armored vehicle's viability, given ATGMs, a position DePuy and many others rejected but without strong evidence.[82] After the Arabs and Israelis fought, the US Army determined that main battle tanks accounted for over 60 percent of the armor destroyed by both sides, over 85 percent of Arab losses. By contrast, Arab ATGMs caused only 7 percent to 24 percent of the tank kills for the vehicles examined.[83] Plus, IDF armor losses from ATGMs dropped sharply after the first few days, when the Israelis changed tactics. Thus, Starry concluded that one of the army's three core lessons should be that "the tank is the dominant land weapon system."[84] Enhancing this belief was the rarity of aircraft kills on armor protected by IADs.

Armor success a product of gunner marksmanship and tank capacity. If the tank remained king of the battlefield, what did the conflict show about effectively operating it? Analyst T. P. Schweider explained that the war's tank combat "resembled more of an Old West shoot-out, with the most *accurate* first shot often deciding the issue."[85] Senior TRADOC officers shared this understanding regarding IDF tankers' proficiency at long-range gunnery (up to three kilometers on the Sinai Peninsula) as key to their extremely favorable kill ratios.[86] Although noting the value of improved range-finders and fire control systems, the Americans believed that intensively trained IDF tank crews most accounted for the standout performance. Gorman added that the conflict provided "ample evidence that fighting masses of tanks is different from engagements involving relatively small packets," necessitating such peacetime practice.[87] Whereas the US Army assigned five tanks to a platoon, Williams reported that the Yom Kippur War reinforced the Israeli preference for three-tank platoons, which enhanced battlefield management.[88]

With its lower silhouette, excellent armor, and bigger gun, many US officers expected the Soviet T-62 to outduel the American M-60 and British Centurion, but, as Starry highlighted, the "Western tanks proved to be superior to Soviet tanks."[89] IDF soldiers touted their vehicles' advantages in speed, agility, reliability, fire control, gun elevation, and crew space. Many of these strengths resulted from Western tanks' bigger size, easing long-standing fears about this design characteristic. IDF tank commanders particularly emphasized the benefit gained from being able to carry at least sixty rounds compared to the T-62's forty-round capacity. Combat, however, revealed several deficiencies with the American M-60 tank, including the commander's exposure, a tendency for pierced hydraulic fluid lines to ignite, danger from stowing main gun shells in the turret bustle, and the coaxial machine gun's unreliability.

ATGMs essential for modern armies. Although the army concluded ATGMs had not rendered the tank obsolete, the Yom Kippur War marked the weapon's first extensive use, demonstrated its importance, and revealed tactical insights.[90] The conflict illustrated that defenders could maximize ATGM impact by canalizing tank attacks into killing zones, while advancing armor benefited from positioning friendly ATGMs in an overwatch role. IDF tank commander surveys revealed that the Arab armies launched Saggers from an average range of 1.5–2 kilometers and were particularly successful when combined with a short-range rocket-propelled grenade, the RPG-7V. The fighting also exposed the Sagger's weaknesses, especially its slow speed and a requirement for the gunner to maintain visual contact with both missile and target during flight. If the launch could be detected (the IDF eventually assigned one tank per platoon as lookout), tankers reported an 80 percent chance of being able to evade it. While disliking the US LAW (light antitank weapon) for lacking the RPG-7V's range and ruggedness, Williams reported the IDF viewed the tube-launched, optically tracked, wire-guided (TOW) ATGM in its limited combat use as "an extremely effective, accurate and easily guided *single shot system*."[91] Still, the Israelis recommended adding a night-sight, remote-firing capability like the Sagger, armor protection for the gunner, and a mobile platform.

IADs reduce CAS prospects. The war's dense IADs strongly signaled to the US Army the diminished prospects for CAS.[92] Americans took seriously former IAF commander Ezer Weizman's declaration that "the missile has bent the aircraft's wing in this war."[93] DePuy stressed to Abrams that "Army forces cannot count on CAS to substitute for artillery or antitank weapons at all times and places."[94] Similarly, Talbott and Brady argued that "we have got to base our planning on the fact that we don't have air superiority and that the troops can't get CAS every time they ask for it."[95] Culminating a year of US military study, the October 1974 WSEG report highlighted that, "for the first time, a highly skilled air force with modern aircraft was prevented from providing effective close support to their ground forces by their adversary's ground-based air defense."[96]

Increased need for artillery. The demonstrated difficulty of obtaining CAS boosted the perceived value of artillery, as did Arab exploitation of their advantage in this area.[97] The WSEG report estimated one-third of IDF casualties resulted from artillery fire and cautioned that "both the United States and the Soviet Union have artillery ordnance that is considerably more effective against personnel than those used in the October 1973 War."[98] Egyptians and Syrians possessed better counterbattery fire because of a superiority in long-range guns, effective camouflage, and use of dummy positions. The Israelis tended to expose their positions with poor communications security, while inadequately trained forward observers diminished fire accuracy. Although the Arab use of multiple rocket launchers did not have a major impact on the fighting, the Americans anticipated a growing role for such weapons given their range and rate of fire.

Emergence of close ground support. The most illuminating finding for the artillery was its potential role as a CAS enabler. Whereas historically planes supported ground units, the army discovered a requirement to assist the air force in the destruction or suppression of IADs. The Israelis exemplified this dynamic when its ground forces eliminated SAM positions west of the Suez Canal, facilitating a sharp increase in air assistance.[99] Williams conveyed to DePuy that "I would anticipate that such a mission will now be expected of artillery in order to create a survivable environment for CAS and helicopter operations."[100] The TRADOC chief agreed, writing in a 1974 concept paper that "air defense suppression in concert and collaboration with the U.S. Air Force is now one of the most important operational problems facing the ground commander."[101] Citing the Israeli experience, Air National Guard Lt. Col. William Rees provided the aviator's perspective—"our ground forces need CAS more than ever, but they must help CAS help them."[102] This requirement sparked use of the term *close ground support.*

Renewed appreciation for friendly air-defense requirement. As much as army officers worried about the implications of enemy IADs, they appreciated the need to protect their own forces. In a March 1974 congressional hearing, Abrams identified "the importance of adequate air defense" as a key finding, elaborating that "here I am not talking about a single weapon, but an envelope of weapons that covers the battle area."[103] Brig. Gen. Charles Means, SAM-D (surface-to-air missile development) program manager, concurred that Arab effectiveness resulted from "the mix of their air defense systems and numbers, mix being that they had all altitudes covered and they had redundancy in those altitude regimes."[104] Lacking sophisticated, radar-guided antiaircraft guns like the Arabs' Russian-made ZSU-23-4, IDF ground units successfully employed halftracks carrying 20 mm machine guns. The US Army had removed such weapons from most vehicles, prompting DePuy to write Abrams that "we should rethink this one."[105] The Americans found that their primary SAM, the HAWK, proved "very effective" in limited Israeli use, but analysts noted it struggled to acquire low-altitude aircraft, and a short-range air-defense missile (SHORAD) was needed.[106] Egyptian launch of twenty-six two-hundred-plus-mile Soviet Kelt cruise missiles in a suppression of enemy air-defense (SEAD) role marked the first time US-made air-defense radars had been targeted by antiradiation munitions.[107] Although only two Kelts hit their targets, detected launches prompted the Israelis to shut down their systems and signaled a growing challenge.

Benefit of forward-leaning support. The Americans recognized how much the outnumbered IDF benefited from its aggressive support and repair approach.[108] Williams and Miley stressed the wisdom of the Israelis pushing forward ammunition;

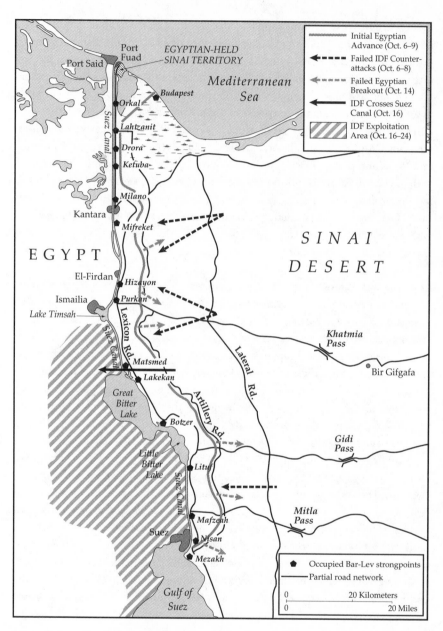

Map 4.1 Suez Canal Front, 1973

petroleum, oil, and lubricants; and spare parts. For combat service support elements to operate like the Israelis, Williams cautioned they must have the training and equipment to operate at night, conduct tactical movement, and defend themselves. The Americans praised the IDF mobile repair crews that attempted to fix disabled weapons on the spot if possible but, if not, evacuated equipment to a forward repair facility where two-thirds of the items were quickly fixed and reentered combat. Forward repair teams, as well as ammunition resupply and medevac operations, suffered significant casualties, demonstrating that such missions required armored vehicles.

Surprising chemical, biological, and radiological preparedness. The most surprising finding for army leaders was the extent to which captured equipment and prisoners of war revealed Arab preparedness to operate in a chemical, biological, and radiological (CBR) environment.[109] Abrams stated that he had been impressed "with the comprehensive CBR defense equipment in the Soviet-equipped forces of the Arab armies. . . . Our forces are not equipped in that fashion."[110] DePuy added that we "are shocked" by Soviet equipment in this area and "we have a long way to go and a lot of money may be required to catch up."[111] For example, the BMP possessed advanced seals, filters, and pressurization enabling its passage through contaminated areas without troops having to don individual protection. Based on the evidence, Williams emphasized a need for "extensive and intensive training in CBR countermeasures and decontamination."[112]

Missed or Skewed Lessons for the Army

Undiminished viability of attack helicopter. The army identified almost all of the war's key lessons, but when findings threatened highly desired weapons programs, the leadership skewed its interpretation of the evidence or simply dismissed it. The former occurred when considering what the Yom Kippur War revealed about the attack helicopter. If the robust air defenses signaled increased difficulty for the air force–provided CAS, they also cast doubt on the attack helicopter's viability. Neither side possessed such machines, but after witnessing the lethal air-defense environment, Maj. Gen. Raphael Eitan, an IDF division commander, exclaimed to Talbott that "the helicopter cannot survive. I have flown the COBRA and I know!!"[113] Although the TRADOC deputy commander included this colorful quip in his lessons presentation and some army officers concurred, Talbott and other senior American officers rejected this undesired finding. After reviewing a draft briefing for his European trip, Talbott indicated the need for a disclaimer, saying that since the Israelis did not use attack helicopters, "the October War neither proved nor disproved the effectiveness of such helicopters in mid-intensity conflict."[114] This position followed DePuy's January 1974 preliminary lessons memorandum, which contended that "unfortunately, there is too little data or experience on which to base an opinion one way or another."[115]

Downplaying IFV limitations. Given the army's strong interest in acquiring the mechanized infantry combat vehicle (MICV), American officers displayed considerable attention to the performance of the Soviet BMP IFV, whose use heralded not only its combat debut but the combat debut of a new weapon class.[116] Yet, while acknowledging the poor performance of the BMP, the army focused its comments on the inadequacy of the disliked M-113 armored personnel carrier, which it intended to replace with the MICV. The SRSG final report identified the BMP's primary advantages over the M-113 as much greater horsepower, a lower silhouette, and, most importantly, significantly more firepower, with a 73 mm smoothbore gun, four Sagger ATGMs, and a 7.62 mm coaxial machine gun. Although clearly superior to the M-113, combat showed that the BMP lacked enough armor protection to survive deployment against tanks. This finding highlighted both an enemy vulnerability that could be exploited and a significant concern given that the MICV possessed similar protection. DePuy suggested potential changes to the MICV's armament in light of the BMP's wartime record, but he continually emphasized the armored personnel carrier's obsolescence.[117] Starry added that "compared to Soviet BMPs and ATGM carriers, the M113 is a zero."[118] The Americans noted that the Israelis agreed on the need for the MICV, albeit one optimized for a standoff role.

Enlightening Lessons for the Air Force

Modern IADs severely threatened air operations. The USAF's primary takeaway was the degree to which modern IADs threatened air operations. Arab-netted ground-based air defenses accounted for at least seventy-five of the approximately one hundred downed Israeli aircraft as diversified platforms with different radar signatures and operational modes provided coverage from near ground level to sixty thousand feet.[119] An alarmed Chief of Staff Brown wrote TAC Chief Dixon in late 1973 that "I think it is apparent that surface-to-air missile defenses in the tremendous densities observed in this recent war do raise serious questions about the effectiveness of tactical air power."[120] Although maintaining that "air power is still the dominant factor in the land battle," Brown added that "the price we would have to pay with the weaponry we have in hand doing our job against a well-equipped ground force would be unacceptably high."[121] A few months later, Dixon argued that the IAF's relatively low overall loss rate showed that the Arab–Israeli War did not "signal the arrival of an era where tactical aircraft will no longer be able to survive over the battlefield," but he cautioned that "does not, in its turn, reject the effectiveness of ground-based air defenses."[122] The USAF accepted that the war showed, in the words of the chief of staff, air superiority "not only means against enemy fighters, it also means against enemy missiles."[123]

The Americans paid closest attention to the two weapons that caused the Israelis particular difficulty, the SA-6 and ZSU-23-4.[124] The mobile, medium-altitude SA-6 SAM stunned the IAF as jammers did not work against its continuous wave, semi-active guidance. Pilots reported being able to outmaneuver a SA-6 missile if detected, but detection proved problematic as it had a small exhaust signature and they lacked reliable radar identification equipment. Air Force Secretary John McLucas testified in March 1974 that its effectiveness represented the only real surprise from the war.[125] Attempts to fly under the SAMs led aircraft into danger from the highly mobile ZSU-23-4 (23 mm quad-mounted) radar-guided gun that gained renown early in the conflict after downing several planes attacking a Syrian armor column. IAF commander Peled told Leavitt that, despite regarding this weapon as formidable before the war, he had not appreciated its lethality.[126] The October 1974 WSEG report stressed that the mobile SA-6 and ZSU-23-4 "can keep pace with their armored forces, making air attacks on these forces costly."[127]

SEAD mission critical before air strikes. USAF officers believed that the IAF's failure to suppress the Arab IADs contributed significantly to their effectiveness. In a meeting shortly after the war, Leavitt recalled that "Peled rationalized that the urgent need for CAS outweighed the necessity for air defense suppression," but after subsequent discussion he "reluctantly acknowledged that failing to suppress air defenses was a serious mistake."[128] In the spring 1974 issue of *Strategic Review*, Dixon argued that IAF aircraft losses "highlight the need to suppress defenses in order to permit close air support."[129] Likewise, Maj. Gen. Robert Lukeman, assistant chief of staff for studies and analysis, attributed the unsustainable early war IAF losses to attacking without such battlefield preparation.[130] As the conflict progressed, the IAF increasingly attempted SEAD, but deficiencies with their radar-homing missiles resulted in a low hit rate, particularly against SA-6s and ZSU-23s.[131] Still, Peled regarded the launches as useful because they prompted operators to shut down radars, after which IAF aircraft bombed the air-defense batteries. For American aviators, as Joseph Doyle explains, "suppression of air defenses had been anticipated as an issue to be addressed, based in part on US experiences in Vietnam, but the Yom Kippur War had revealed this problem to be more critical than previously realized."[132]

EW proficiency vital. For the Americans, the conflict illustrated the extent to which EW proficiency had become integral to the aircraft/air-defense competition.[133] The

Israelis, overconfident because of their prior dominance, had been somewhat dismissive about EW as initially many aircraft lacked radar warning systems, chaff/ flare dispensers, and jamming pods. Once combat commenced, they quickly came to appreciate the value of ECM gear, prioritizing its delivery from the US military. Maj. Gen. Mordechai Hod, a former IAF commander, exclaimed after the war that "an ounce of ECM is worth a pound of additional aircraft, in the presence of dense, sophisticated air defense."[134] USAF officers stressed that combat showed as mandatory both ECM pods on strike aircraft and more powerful standoff jammers on other aircraft, helicopters, or drones.

Growing requirement for more accurate and longer-range munitions. The USAF also noted the growing importance of accurate, standoff weapons.[135] Based on the Israeli experience, Chief of Staff Brown identified a critical need "to hit targets from greater ranges accurately; in other words, a standoff capability so that we did not subject crews and aircraft to these dense defenses."[136] The war simply reinforced the utility of precision-guided munitions (PGMs). Although the US government refused to supply Israel with the prized laser-guided bombs, the IAF successfully used electro-optical PGMs including fifty Mavericks in the conflict's final days.[137] The IAF's comparable strike rates to the USAF in Southeast Asia impressed the Americans given that the Israelis mostly targeted vehicles whereas the USAF had primarily attacked bridges. Yet the Americans cautioned that the Israelis, facing a much-reduced air threat late in the war, had been able to close within two to three miles before releasing the Mavericks and fly multiple passes to ensure lock-on. While the more lethal air environment encouraged using standoff weapons and PGMs, it hampered obtaining the information they required. Chief of Staff Brown added "that we required the capability to locate targets with greater accuracy, day and night, and in weather."[138] Operating without such data and against dense IADs, the Israelis dropped significantly more cluster munitions than anticipated prewar.

Robust protection from aircraft shelters. The combat revealed that one type of target—planes on the ground—had become much more difficult to destroy.[139] After the IAF preemptively eliminated 370 parked aircraft in the opening hours of 1967's Six-Day War, Syria and Egypt ringed their airbases with IADs and constructed strong concrete hangerettes to safeguard planes. Based on Israeli attacks and postwar testing, Col. J. R. Brown testified that "the Arab Air Forces were almost totally protected by aircraft shelters."[140] Collins and Dixon added that the Middle East war signaled a requirement for development of an efficient anti-shelter munition.[141] Officials also noted the potential of such hangerettes, which were stronger than NATO variants, to better protect USAF aircraft in Europe.[142] Bottom line, in the future more planes would need to be destroyed in the air.

Missed or Skewed Lessons for the Air Force

Relative utility of interdiction. The air force seized on CAS difficulty in the Yom Kippur War to bolster its longtime position that interdiction provided a better way to assist ground forces.[143] The IAF's reputation for CAS excellence enhanced the potential impact of its difficulty with that mission. After severe aircraft losses in the first few days, the Israelis essentially abandoned traditional CAS until Arab IADs had been severely weakened. Ultimately, 90 percent of what was categorized as Israeli CAS strikes consisted of preplanned actions at least five kilometers behind the frontlines.[144] In briefing Mideast war lessons to the Senate Tactical Air Power Subcommittee in March 1974, Colonel Brown emphasized that Israeli planes had been unable to loiter safely above the frontline searching for targets of opportunity as occurred in the prior wars. IAF success at interdiction, especially against Syrian sustainment and follow-on forces, garnered close scrutiny from USAF officers since after the Vietnam War, as Futrell relates, "it had been fashionable to demean the significance of air attack in any so-called choking off of enemy movement toward a ground front."[145]

While emphasizing the difficulty of CAS, the US Air Force rejected data that suggested it needed to change its planned approach for what remained an air force mission.[146] A strong preexisting preference for acquisition of the durable but slow A-X (future A-10) aircraft inevitably colored the findings. When Senator Howard Cannon pointed out that the USMOST report "said that the lesson to be learned from the Mideast war was that a close-air support airplane needed to attack at high speed," Collins rejected that a "magic number" existed for safe delivery.[147] Facing pushback, he continued that the USAF view would likely correspond with the IAF if operating similar airplanes, but asserted that "our belief is that there is a tradeoff between speed and invulnerability, or relative invulnerability of the airplane, or ability to take hits."[148] The air force did accept postwar investigators' conclusion that slow-moving airborne forward air controllers would be unable to function in a Yom Kippur War–type environment. This point, however, only reinforced their questionable belief in the A-X to act as its own airborne forward air controller.

Lack of interest in air-to-air combat. Rather than prompting close attention, Israeli dominance of air-to-air engagements prompted neglect by the USAF fighter community.[149] When legislators pressed air force officers to explain why the IAF's results far exceeded the USAF's combat record in Southeast Asia despite facing similar MiGs guided by Soviet-style ground control intercept, Maj. Gen. Richard Cross and Colonel Brown from the Air Staff responded that Israeli pilots significantly outclassed their counterparts. They attributed this advantage to the quality and quantity of IAF training. The air force certainly did not dispute the value of better training; it had been the primary conclusion of the *Red Baron Reports* that examined all 625 engagements between the USAF and MiGs during the Vietnam War. Yet American aviators noted that the Israelis, who had previously prioritized air-to-air training, concluded after the Yom Kippur War that they needed to spend relatively more time conducting air-to-ground training, given the increased difficulty of that mission. Although this was the first conflict in which a majority of air-to-air kills came via missiles, the USAF had already fully embraced the need for better such missiles.

The air force leadership's most dubious position resulted from their resistance to acknowledge that IAF fighter pilots derived a significant edge from using a two-plane formation (aircraft flying abreast by up to a mile).[150] Such "loose-deuce" tactics contrasted with the Egyptian and Syrian use of the traditional four-ship "fluid-four" approach (diamond shape with a flight leader and three supporting wingmen) still employed by the USAF. Debate existed over the merit of the two approaches as the US Navy, like the IAF, had switched to two-ship formations. USAF officers testifying before the Senate Tactical Air Power Subcommittee after the Yom Kippur War appreciated that the tactics had proven superior in certain ways, but they questioned identifying two-ship formation superiority as a lesson given Israeli pilots' vast skill edge. When legislative staffers probed on the distinction between US and Israeli tactics, Colonel Brown argued that no big difference existed as flights of four readily broke up into pairs. In the face of pushback, Cross accepted that the "loose-deuce" formation worked best in small areas such as those covered by the IAF and navy MiG combat air patrols off carriers in Southeast Asia. However, he stressed that, in Vietnam, "where we had to go greater distances and were supporting larger forces, the 'fluid-four' proved to be a very effective formation."[151]

HOW DID THE ARMY APPLY ITS FINDINGS?

Of the cases examined in this book, the army in the mid-1970s offered the most favorable context for applying insights. First, it benefited from capable and generally supportive civilian and uniform leadership.[152] The July 1973 installation of Schlesinger as secretary of defense brought into office a highly confident and intelligent advocate for the military. When the actions of the tempestuous Schlesinger, who often feuded with executive and legislative officials, prompted President Gerald Ford to replace him in November 1975, the president chose the politically savvy Donald Rumsfeld. Given JCS Chairman Moorer's tendency to ignore the service chiefs, the army leadership welcomed his July 1974 replacement by the more skillful and cooperative Air Force Chief of Staff Brown. The effective and inspiring Abrams provided strong direction after becoming army chief of staff in October 1972. Upon observing the poor state of US forces in Europe, he stressed improving readiness, defined as properly trained and equipped personnel. Schlesinger shared this goal, and the resulting partnership abetted Abrams's efforts. Unfortunately, Abrams was diagnosed with terminal cancer in the spring of 1974, and he died that September; Ford then elevated Vice Chief Gen. Fred Weyand.

Abrams had closely cooperated with General DePuy, but the latter's influence remained strong after the former's tragic demise.[153] Experience as a junior officer in World War II engendered in DePuy a foundational view that battlefield performance depended heavily on sound, small-unit tactics. Senior positions in the Vietnam War reaffirmed for him the value of combined arms centered on the tank, the importance of artillery and airpower, and the utility of "overwatch." DePuy assumed command of the newly formed TRADOC in the spring of 1973 with three interrelated goals: (1) foster a training revolution, (2) produce a clearly expressed doctrine, and (3) integrate training and doctrine with combat development. Whereas previously the army looked twenty-five years ahead for planning purposes, DePuy "was chary of looking more than five years ahead."[154] He benefited from highly capable subordinates, of whom two stood out—Deputy Chief of Staff for Training Gorman and Armor School Commandant Starry. Gorman shared DePuy's belief that the army needed to place greater emphasis on "training" versus "education." Upon taking command of the Armor Center in early 1973, Starry commenced an analysis of the European battlefield that, he noted, "we had just about finished . . . to my own satisfaction when the October War came along."[155] Starry's aforementioned visit to the battlefields and interaction with IDF officers significantly affected his thinking.

Motivating senior army officers was a perception that the Red Army's relative strength in Central Europe had increased markedly.[156] Over the previous decade the Soviets had cycled through two generations of new weapons, amassed a four to one advantage in tanks, and adopted a more offensively oriented doctrine. The Americans worried that the forward location of Soviet combat units and support infrastructure enabled striking with minimal warning (a concern intensified by the recent Egyptian and Syrian attack). While the air mobility and light infantry forces cautioned against an overconcentration on Central Europe, the Yom Kippur War helped advocates for bolstering mechanized forces because it suggested that "contingency missions outside NATO were likely to pit the Army against enemies organized, trained, and equipped in the Soviet style in any case."[157] Given that US forces possessed, according to Abrams, a "marginal chance of succeeding" against the Soviets without employing tactical nuclear weapons, the army leadership had to focus on that challenge.[158]

Although Central Europe differed fundamentally from the Sinai Peninsula's open terrain and fair weather, American officers regarded the former as having considerable commonality with the Golan Heights.[159] Its topography, especially the hills, large boulders, and other obstacles in its northern half, restricted movement and visibility, as was generally true in Germany, albeit without the frequently bad weather and limited daylight in winter. The proximity of Israeli population centers to the Golan

Heights necessitated that the IDF conduct a forward defense as the Germans required of NATO. Plus, the IDF fought at a severe quantitative disadvantage, as would
US forces. Finally, Syrian use of Soviet weapons, doctrine, and tactics enhanced the
perceived relevance of the combat, even though they usually failed to make best
use of their equipment and only employed a badly caricatured version of the Soviet
approach. As Maj. George Knapp later observed, "In many ways, the battle for the
Golan Heights mirrored the U.S. Army's image of how it would have to fight a war
in Central Europe."[160]

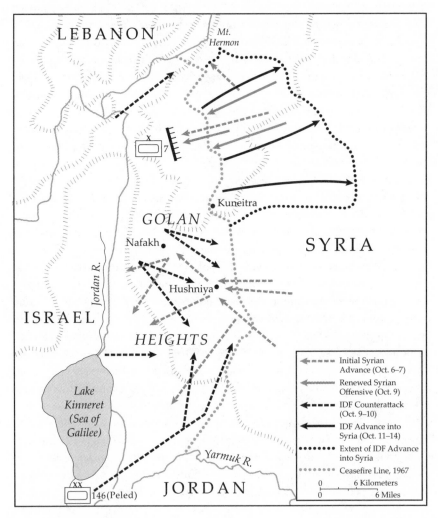

Map 4.2 Golan Heights Front, 1973

Significant personnel, materiel, and organizational transitions both complicated the army's response to the Soviet challenge and facilitated applying lessons from the Yom Kippur War.[161] Initiation of the all-volunteer force on July 1, 1973, introduced tremendous uncertainty to a service continuing to suffer from racial and gang violence and drug problems. The active force had shrunk to eleven 2/3 divisions (thirteen on paper), and the Seventh Army in Europe "was probably at the lowest state of readiness in its history."[162] Despite not being able to recruit enough soldiers to fill out existing units, Abrams lobbied aggressively for reestablishing sixteen active divisions as the minimum necessary to safeguard US interests. Schlesinger agreed, if the expanded force structure did not increase end strength (approximately 785,000 soldiers). Thus, the chief of staff directed the elimination of "every project or activity that does not contribute directly to the attainment of the required force," the shift of many support elements (e.g., logistics, civil affairs) from active to reserve status, and the rounding out of some active divisions with reserve units as a part of the so-called Total Force.[163]

In mid-1973 the army undertook its first major reorganization since 1962.[164] Service leaders appreciated that the huge Continental Army Command, as Benjamin Jensen relates, "had become a bureaucratic Gordian knot unable to manage simultaneously the competing requirements of developing future force concepts and managing military installations and personnel."[165] With the new Forces Command taking control of all US mainland combat units, a major four-star command (TRADOC) could focus exclusively on training, education, doctrine, and combat development. Although attendees at a May 1973 organizational meeting decided that TRADOC "first would sort out the doctrine for the United States Army," this proved difficult, and DePuy recalled fifteen years later that "we started out ignoring it [doctrine]" and focused on a "back to basics" training approach.[166] The army also eliminated the Combat Developments Command because, as Starry explained, it "had become divorced from the real doctrinal process, and the combat developments agencies at the schools and centers were not responsive to the center and school commanders."[167] Instead, the army shifted its Fort Leavenworth component, renamed the Combined Arms Combat Developments Activity, into TRADOC's new Combined Arms Center to facilitate integration.

The army's enhanced threat perception, relatively small size, and institutional reorganization heightened the perceived need for better weapons.[168] By the early 1970s officers regarded the M-60 tank and Cobra attack helicopter as obsolescent and watched with dismay the cancellation of their planned replacements (the MBT-70 and Cheyenne). Abrams and DePuy believed that army acquisition efforts suffered from having too many programs. Thus, the service prioritized the "Big Five" development programs—the XM1 tank, the MICV, the advanced attack helicopter (AAH), the utility tactical transport aircraft system, and the SAM-D. DePuy thought civilian support for these essential weapons would only occur if the service "could demonstrate clearly that they would improve the Army's overall combat capabilities."[169] Thus, TRADOC tried to generate supporting evidence through "scientific, objective analysis."[170] To that end, its leaders recognized that the recent Arab–Israeli combat potentially offered invaluable data.

Negatively, the political and economic environment constrained defense spending.[171] The White House hoped to reduce the military's budget given détente with the Union of Soviet Socialist Republics, while liberal and moderate legislators' preference for limiting the Pentagon's allocation dovetailed with public sentiment. Army funding suffered relative to the navy and air force in the transition from the Vietnam War. Its budget actually declined slightly in both FY74 and FY75.[172] Although the Yom Kippur War "quieted many congressional critics of defense spending," the resultant OPEC embargo produced a spike in oil prices that exacerbated the military's fiscal woes.[173] Even after reducing oil consumption by 18 percent in FY75, the army paid over 75 percent more for its fuel. Secretary of the Army Bo Callaway warned in early 1975 that rampant inflation was severely cutting into the service's procurement and R&D, and it continued to erode purchasing power for the rest of the decade even though the budget grew about 10 percent per annum.[174] Thus, the army attempted to reconstitute the force when, as Starry noted, "there were no large sums available to achieve the goal."[175]

Given this generally favorable context for applying findings, it is not surprising to discover that the Yom Kippur War had a multifaceted impact on the US Army, especially through TRADOC. Its leaders continually referenced the findings, which they briefed widely to army, DOD, and civilian decision-makers. DePuy would recall that "some of the evidence coming out of that war was awesome."[176] Starry added that before the Arab–Israeli fight TRADOC "had fussed around from June to October trying to figure out what we really ought to be doing."[177] Then combat in the Sinai Peninsula and Golan Heights laid out modern battle "for the world to see."[178] A few individuals, such as prominent RAND official Bob Komer, even expressed concern that the army was paying too much attention to the Yom Kippur War.[179]

More recently, some commentators have argued that "the historiography has inflated the war's value as a 'springboard' and understated it as an 'excuse.'"[180] That is, the findings had greater instrumental than instructional and inspirational utility as I have characterized influence throughout this work. Central to this argument, as Saul Bronfeld avers, is that insights from Arab–Israeli fighting "did not change the core ideas of Abrams, DePuy, Starry, and Gorman, which can be traced back to their experiences during World War II and afterward."[181] Roger Spiller stresses that central to the war's value was that "a new professional metaphor had been created that the

Army could employ to communicate both within and beyond itself."[182] Bronfeld adds that the conflict specifically provided DePuy with "leverage in negotiating Army budgets and to convince the infantry generals (in the field commands and TRADOC) of the need to change training methods and increase the role of armor."[183] He accurately points out that DePuy focused on lessons that aided his agenda while disregarding disruptive findings (e.g., the IAD threat to the attack helicopter).[184]

Although Bronfeld provides a valuable corrective, it is too limiting to characterize the Yom Kippur War as largely a useful resource for messaging and bureaucratic infighting given that the introduction of new weapons and tactics potentially rendered prior understandings of combat dynamics obsolete. He even acknowledges that "the actual battles of the Golan Heights, in the Sinai, and on the west bank of the Suez Canal supplied the Army with many important new data and insights."[185] Such information was inspirational as well as instructional, revealing or heightening awareness of battlefield challenges that generated some imaginative responses. Above all, study of the conflict intensified the urgency with which DePuy and other senior officers pursued change by demonstrating that the US Army was even less ready for modern conventional war than previously believed. As the TRADOC chief stated on his mid-1977 retirement, the October War "dramatized the difference between the wars that we might fight in the future and the wars we had fought in the past."[186] While preliminary findings exerted a myriad of influences from the beginning of 1974 with the FY74 Supplemental and FY75 budget processes, officials from the command met in August of that year to consider how to implement the 162 recommendations in the SRSG's recently completed final report.[187] TRADOC'S FY75 Annual Report of Major Activities stated that "the implications of the October War for US Army training and doctrine were so great that the historical record of TRADOC for the fiscal year 1975, can best be illuminated by beginning with this subject."[188]

Beneficial but Initially Incomplete Application for the Army

Two-stage doctrinal renaissance. Implementing the SRSG's recommendations resulted in many beneficial changes, but any assessment of how the army applied lessons must begin with the overarching subject of doctrinal reform that was so critical to the army's readiness for the Central European battlefield. This process culminated a decade after the Yom Kippur War with adoption of the much-praised AirLand Battle, but arriving at this understanding was a two-step process in which findings from the Arab–Israeli fighting exerted distinct influences on each phase. This example is noteworthy for both involving all three basic types of influence—instructional, instrumental, and inspirational—as well as showing how returning to the foreign war at a later date in a different context can yield previously unappreciated benefits.

Senior officers had long recognized the need for revision of the Operations Field Manual (FM100-5), which had not undergone significant change since 1962, but the Arab–Israeli combat created a sense of urgency and reframed the problem.[189] DePuy stressed that it showed the next war in Central Europe "will be largely settled in weeks with the forces and weapons on hand at the outset," a disturbing finding given the Americans had struggled at the outset of almost every prior conflict.[190] Thus, as the first page of the new doctrine declared, "the US Army must, above all else, *prepare to win the first battle of the next war.*"[191]

TRADOC used findings from the Yom Kippur War to devise and sell a defense-oriented approach to stop the Soviets.[192] Study of the Arab–Israeli fighting combined with a February 1975 Force Ratio Study revealed that current battlefield dynamics favored a defender against an attacker three times as strong, while an attacker possessing inferior weapons required a six to one edge to be confident of success. Given the extent of its numerical inferiority, the US Army, as DePuy stressed, "must know where the attack is coming from and concentrate forces at that point."[193] Thus, TRADOC, in designing a flexible tactical defense scheme, emphasized that the "first and most important" question was how to move in combat.[194] DePuy explained that, based on the Middle East data, "in order to move on the battlefield in the face of weapons with high lethality, enemy weapons must be suppressed. You suppress by a combined arms team."[195] Starry added that the fighting showed that "ATGMs promised to provide forward-deployed forces a new dimension in defense."[196] Given the modern battlefield's demonstrated complexity, the army understandably elevated the doctrinal importance attached to EW. Jensen sums up that "the suppress-to-move, move-to-concentrate concept, as a responsive repertoire, defined the way the Army should adapt to the configuration of modern warfare," and was based on what occurred in October 1973.[197] In particular, as Bronfeld points out, the outstanding Golan defensive battle of Lt. Col. Avigdor Kahalani's tank battalion (the 77th of the 7th Armored Brigade) during the war's first days served as "the model that DePuy presented to American forces in Western Europe."[198]

The collected data indisputably aided DePuy in overcoming internal opposition to this approach.[199] Despite the TRADOC chief prioritizing doctrinal reform from early 1974, progress initially proved slow with no designated lead agency and a growing schism between Starry, pushing an armor-centric doctrine, and Maj. Gen. Thomas Tarpley, head of the Infantry School, who remained enamored with the air mobility concept. Despite his infantry background, DePuy unmistakably and unsurprisingly favored the Armor Center. In July Starry emphasized to him that "we have to have a groundswell *for* us, and my guess is we haven't much time to get it swollen."[200] Toward that end, Starry added that "while I believe that what we're about needed to be done anyway, it is nonetheless convenient for a number of reasons to tie it at least loosely to the October War."[201] The late July distribution of a draft concept marked

DePuy's assumption of a direct role to enable rapid progress. Although known in army lore as the "pot of soup" letter because the TRADOC chief conveyed that doctrine development should be like a "pot of soup" to which anyone could contribute an ingredient, DePuy "carefully patrolled his kitchen."[202] Spiller characterizes this document as "a refined version of the briefing on the implications on the Middle East war he had been giving for several months."[203] In response to pressure from infantry and air mobile officers, TRADOC organized an early October 1974 senior-level conference ostensibly to evaluate small-unit tactics in light of the Yom Kippur War. Its real purpose, however, was to sell TRADOC's scheme. Attendees' acceptance or at least lack of explicit opposition spurred DePuy's efforts. By then the TRADOC chief had used the briefings on the war's lessons to garner support from top army, DOD, and government officials. Complaints led to some modifications to mollify air mobility / airborne practitioners as well as the addition of chapters on chemical and tactical nuclear weapons, but TRADOC kept focus on a battlefield "fought similarly to the October War."[204]

The army's new FM100-5 guidance, subsequently referred to as Active Defense, became operative on July 1, 1976.[205] Given the infantry community's concern about the proposed reforms and an army leadership largely composed of Vietnam War veterans, Kevin Sheehan contends that "the real question must be how did DePuy obtain the autonomy to change Army operational and tactical doctrine *unilaterally* in the manner he saw fit?"[206] He cites the Yom Kippur War as the most important factor.[207] TRADOC's control of the army's lessons-learning process and its core finding in support for the tank's centrality on the modern battlefield certainly facilitated the success. The command leadership used the Israelis as well as the Germans and even the USAF to validate the approach and tamp down internal resistance. In talking points provided to Weyand, DePuy noted given that the army lacked the type of battlefield experience needed, FM100-5 "derives much of its substance through prolonged study of the Arab/Israeli War and continuing close, professional collaboration with the Israeli Army."[208]

Conceptual concerns and implementing experiences sparked vigorous criticism and calls for change.[209] Although some commentators endorsed Active Defense as a step forward after the lost years of the Vietnam era, a sizable majority of the almost eighty articles that appeared within four years of its issuance in the Command General Staff College's journal *Military Review* sharply disparaged it. Exacerbating hostile reaction was the perception of it as "DePuy's doctrine" given the insular development process. A myriad of condemnations emerged, some of which had support from neglected aspects of the Yom Kippur War. For example, a frequently expressed objection was that the doctrine's formulaic focus on firepower and force ratios undervalued the psychological/human dimension of warfare. As Paul Herbert points out, "FM100-5 devoted an entire chapter to weapons but less than a page to leadership."[210] Given that studies of Arab–Israeli combat emphasized soldier proficiency and initiative-taking as vital to battlefield success, this neglect was disconcerting. Plus, although the October War had impressed on US officers the complexity of modern battle, especially with the increased EW dimension, commanders following the new guidance discovered, as Sheehan relates, that it "called for a degree of synchronization that would be difficult to achieve in training and, arguably, impossible to achieve amid the 'friction' of war."[211] Many critics charged the doctrine with overemphasizing firepower at the expense of maneuver, which ran counter to army tradition and what many viewed had been essential to the IDF success. TRADOC countered that FM100-5 did not neglect maneuver, which it regarded as essential to combined arms and massing firepower where needed. Such a response, however, did not ameliorate concern that the new field manual at a minimum represented a dangerous shift in emphasis.

Given that DePuy and Starry had relied extensively on Yom Kippur War lessons to design and validate the new doctrine, TRADOC's failure to account for Soviet reaction to that same war was particularly troubling.[212] DePuy maintained the traditional belief that the Red Army would launch mass armor thrusts on narrow fronts to create breakthroughs, but, as Jensen notes, the Soviets "had initiated their own tactical revolution in response to the 1973 Arab-Israeli War."[213] Although a debate exists among scholars whether the conflict served as inspiration or validation for this new approach, the Soviets now emphasized multipronged attacks to probe for and exploit weak spots. In the May–June 1978 issue of *Infantry Journal*, army captains Gregory Fontenot and Matthew Roberts stressed that the doctrine's assumption that the Soviets would attack as expected (mass for breakthrough) represented a severe weakness.[214] Similarly, in an October 1978 report for OSD, defense consultant Steven Canby cautioned that the new "ex post and opportunistic" Soviet operational maneuver meant serious consequences for the FM100-5's approach, which lacked flexibility.[215] Within a few years the army leadership recognized that these criticisms and others made the document untenable.

The TAC–TRADOC "era of good feelings." Before turning to the Starry-led response, I need to address how study of the Yom Kippur War contributed to the blossoming TAC–TRADOC relationship, which would ultimately assist introduction of a more expansive army operational concept.[216] Abrams and Air Force Chief of Staff Brown, who had worked together effectively during the Vietnam War, sought to improve peacetime cooperation. On October 5, 1973, the day before Egypt and Syria attacked, Abrams expressed to DePuy that "it is absolutely essential that a close relationship exist, at all levels, between the two services."[217] He wanted the TRADOC commander to commence discussions based on "mutual interests" with Dixon, who had become TAC chief four days earlier. Before Dixon headed to his new assignment,

Brown similarly conveyed the importance of this initiative. Thus, the TAC–TRA-DOC relationship would have developed without the Yom Kippur War, but lessons from that conflict intensified its perceived need and created a sense of urgency.

Understanding the importance of this stimulus requires appreciating the obstacles to interservice cooperation.[218] As Dixon later observed, the Abrams–Brown experience in Southeast Asia typified wartime ad hoc partnerships, but the return of peace prompted the army and air force to retreat inward.[219] Much of the USAF leadership still consisted of strategic bombing generals who treasured independence. Army pursuit of the fast Cheyenne attack helicopter had upset aviators, who criticized it as redundant to the new CAS plane. A belief that this charge contributed to the Cheyenne's August 1972 termination alienated many ground officers, especially with their continuing doubts about receiving adequate CAS. Talbott's reaction to a mid-January 1974 speech by the air force chief of staff exemplifies suspicion that the air force would hijack the Yom Kippur War lessons narrative. In a copy of Brown's remarks, where it read "Israel's airpower achieved the expectations which were held for it," Talbott added "unfortunately for Israel this was *not* true."[220] When the text elaborated on why the IAF was the critical factor in preventing defeat, the TRADOC deputy jotted down, "a very inaccurate description of what happened."[221]

Yet, despite initial concerns by each service that the other would manipulate their findings from the Arab–Israeli combat, the army and air force quickly came to appreciate that the conflict overwhelmingly demonstrated an increased need to work together.[222] John Romjue, Susan Canedy, and Anne Chapman highlight that "the great materiel-lethality lesson of that war was sobering for pilots and tankers alike . . . encouraging greater U.S. Air Force–Army cooperation."[223] After reading Talbott's Israel trip report, Gen. Donald Bennett, head of US Army Pacific Command, wrote that effective CAS must be available "from the *first* day of combat. We can't afford the luxury of redeveloping the system *after* the war has started."[224] Dixon concurred, writing that "tactical air suppliers have to know exactly what the Army wants, and the Army must know what can—and cannot—be done."[225] In their Yom Kippur War assessments, the services attempted to avoid alienating each other when discussing sensitive subjects. For example, Talbott informed Abrams that the CAS section of his trip report "has been re-edited several times. . . . As now written, it accurately describes what happened in close air support but should not exacerbate the interservice problem."[226]

The ten-mile distance between TRADOC and TAC, along with their separation from the Pentagon, aided what would become known as "the era of good feelings."[227] By July 1975 increasing interaction prompted establishment of a joint office to oversee seven working groups: airspace management, reconnaissance/surveillance, air-defense suppression, EW, forward air controller / forward observer, air base defense, and air logistics. Attention to most of these areas had been generated or heightened by study of Arab–Israeli combat, especially the critical needs for SEAD cooperation. On November 1, 1976, the services published a joint manual on airspace management, which, as Futrell notes, the two Chiefs of Staff hailed "a harbinger of the solution of air-land problems."[228] Still, progress should not be overstated as it related largely to procedures, avoiding potentially inflammatory subjects such as doctrine and requirements. Endeavoring to expand the "symbiotic relationship," Dixon in late 1978 penned an enthusiastic and somewhat overstated characterization of how the TAC–TRADOC dialogue had expanded in its five years. Still, he correctly predicted that "joint participation will be invaluable in maximizing Army and Air Force capabilities," and the improved relationship proved a significant asset as TRADOC worked to fix the army's doctrinal problem.[229]

AirLand Battle replaces Active Defense. Inspired by his experience as the commander of V Corps and a reexamination of the Yom Kippur War, Starry assumed command of TRADOC on July 1, 1977, with priority on correcting Active Defense's flaws.[230] After conducting months of evaluations with his subordinates in Europe, Starry came to appreciate that problematically "we tackled the tactical problem up forward [but] we kind of brushed aside the operational level considerations, the theater-level considerations."[231] Then, in February 1977, while he was still in Germany, an armored division of the Soviet 8th Guards Combined Arms Army rapidly advanced undetected several hundred kilometers to the border along the Fulda Gap, dramatizing "the scope of the corps commander's problem" with follow-on echelons. The lieutenant general accepted an invitation from a visiting Musa Peled to return to the Golan Heights and review the October 1973 war for potential insights. In a June 1995 letter to army historian Richard Swain, Starry recalled that "listening to the Israeli description of echeloned Syrian forces on the Golan Heights, seeing the ground, understanding the flow of battle there, all served to illuminate the follow-on echelon problem."[232] As a well-versed historian of the Yom Kippur War commented, Starry's ability to extrapolate from the Golan Heights to Central Europe reveals an imaginative brilliance given what he recalled as the Israelis describing the Syrians attacking with "echelon after echelon after echelon" was actually at best a poorly executed, two-echelon attack.[233]

It is notable how Starry's focus shifted from the tactical, three years earlier, to the operational level of war.[234] In a 1981 TRADOC oral history interview he acknowledged that "I must confess that at the time we wrote that [Active Defense], which was 1974 or 1975, I frankly did not understand the second echelon or the follow-on echelon problem."[235] In 1977, with his attention shifted to that challenge, Starry concentrated on the October 8 flanking counterattack by Peled's reserve armored division. The American believed this effort best exemplified how to win outnumbered, given that "instead of deploying his reinforcing division piecemeal to plug gaps in the line,

[Peled] insisted on taking the initiative, attacking onto the flank of the overwhelming Syrian force."[236] Starry attempted to transpose Peled's description of events "onto V Corps terrain east from the Vogelsburg to the Thuringerwald in East Germany, with German weather, German visibility, German foliage, with German elevations superimposed."[237] Even Bronfeld, who stresses the insights Starry gained from his long service before the Yom Kippur War, acknowledges that the Arab–Israeli conflict "had an important influence on the cognitive process" by which the TRADOC chief developed the new operational doctrine.[238]

Starry arrived at his new command incorrectly believing that FM100-5 (1976) could be modified to address follow-on echelons. The growing recognition that the Soviets would not attack with massed armor thrusts meant that the army's design to counter the initial attack on narrow fronts was also flawed.[239] Realizing that the existing doctrine could not be adapted, TRADOC began working on a replacement. The conceptual solution evolved under different names in the late 1970s and early 1980s until becoming comprehensively known as AirLand Battle, but it remained based on the simultaneous, not sequential, engagement of Soviet frontline and follow-on forces. In responding to the latter challenge, as Starry recalled, revisiting the Golan Heights "led to a concept for extending the battlefield in time (the campaign) and distance (the theater of operations)."[240] A TRADOC pamphlet explained that US forces would "destroy the integrity of the enemy operational scheme, forcing him to break off the attack or risk resounding defeat."[241] Although not expecting the Russians to collapse like the Syrians, Starry and others believed them more vulnerable to such an approach than an attrition-based effort. Adopting this concept meant embracing the more human elements of the IDF's standout performance that had been neglected in Active Defense even though US Army study of the Arab–Israeli fighting showed that "modern electronic countermeasures would severely disrupt effective command control, placing a premium on the initiative of subordinate commanders."[242] Starry stressed that, rather than force ratios "in the end, the side that somehow, at some time, somewhere in the course of battle seizes the initiative and holds it to the end, will be the side that wins."[243] As Walter Kretchik points out, in contrast to the prior doctrine's attempt to "regulate the chaos of war through technology," AirLand Battle "restored the soldier to prominence," incorporating Auftragstaktik (mission orders).[244] That is, junior and midlevel officers were told the objective but not how to achieve it.

Although appealing conceptually, TRADOC had to address whether extant technology enabled AirLand Battle's execution.[245] Conversations with the Israelis facilitated Starry's recognition that reaching far beyond the front lines required two basic capabilities: (1) reconnaissance and surveillance to identify key targets and (2) attack platforms able to destroy them. As he put it, "we must see deep and attack deep."[246] Unfortunately, as he outlined to the deputy chief of staff for operations and plans in December 1978, after evaluating Soviet maneuvers and "from analysis of Syrian and Egyptian versions of Soviet echelonment of forces in the Yom Kippur War," the army could not satisfy either requirement with conventional weapons.[247] TRA-DOC leaders recognized that implementation required USAF target-acquisition and weapons-delivery capabilities, prompting intensified cooperation with TAC now under a cooperative Gen. William Creech. The Active Defense doctrine actually had a chapter titled "Air-Land Battle," which declared that *the Army cannot win the land battle without the Air Force,*" but its focus on frontline Soviet forces narrowly defined the air force role.[248] Now the deep battle component "made air interdiction a fundamental concern of Army commanders in ways it had not been previously" and led to formal articulation of the battlefield air interdiction mission.[249] In May 1981 the air force and army agreed on an offensive air support approach, with CAS and battlefield air interdiction as critical force multipliers, although Starry believed that the US Army could not be as reliant as the IDF on airpower to address follow-on echelons given the much larger ground forces.

AirLand Battle, which became official army doctrine in August 1982, garnered widespread acclaim in contrast to the severe criticism of Active Defense. Given the influence of Yom Kippur War on both documents, what do these contrasting results say about applying lessons? As Romjue stresses, the 1976 FM100-5 "reflected the immediacy and importance for its authors of the 1973 Arab-Israeli War, whose tactical lessons it fully embodied."[250] Yet, given that its discussed shortcomings at the operational level quickly doomed it, does Starry deserve credit for better use of combat data? Whereas DePuy concentrated on the Yom Kippur War's contribution in solving what he had already identified as the problem, Starry gave more attention to what the conflict revealed about the nature of the problem the army faced and suggested potential answers. Of course, as noted previously, using lessons from a foreign war to fuel imagination represents a high form of application but one fraught with danger when employed by a less skilled practitioner than Starry. Moreover, comparing DePuy in the mid-1970s and Starry in the late 1970s, as Bronfeld does, is somewhat unfair. Although Starry deserves full praise for his development of an offensive-oriented, maneuver concept that became AirLand Battle, R. Zach Alessi-Friedlander correctly points out that in the mid-1970s "the Army was not ready for the more advanced forms of warfare to which it aspired."[251] Starry, who initially possessed views similar to DePuy, evolved his understanding as the limitations of FM100-5 became clear from personal experience and he reexamined the Yom Kippur War. This changed perspective propelled a growing divergence with DePuy, as reflected in the retired general's 1981 complaint that the new guidance failed to give appropriate weight to "the great benefits that flow from synchronizing in time, space, and task."[252] Above all, Starry demonstrated the potential utility from reexamining a foreign conflict when the service's context changes to identify previously unappreciated or underappreciated lessons.

Other Constructively Applied Lessons

Restructured heavy divisions. Ideally, doctrinal change would precede organizational, training, and materiel decisions, but application of information from the Yom Kippur War occurred simultaneously. I first consider the war's influence on army organization, given that it was the dimension most closely aligned with the emerging doctrine and most positively impacted by absorbing Arab–Israeli combat data.[253] Concern about the division structure, which dated from the early 1960s, had prompted the army to explore modifications before the October War. Soon afterward it adopted "selective improvements," such as transitioning the engineer construction battalions to heavy combat battalions and introducing target-acquisition batteries.[254] More fundamentally, the Middle East battles "vividly demonstrated" to the army that the requirements for mission success had changed, after which it "placed new emphasis upon mechanized and armored divisions with increased mobility and fire-power."[255] Still, before reacting to cues, senior officers wanted to validate findings and evaluate their appropriateness for the US service. As Starry explained, "We couldn't just say, 'Well, here it is . . . we saw it in the deserts in the Yom Kippur War, so it's got to be right for us.'"[256] Thus, in early 1976 the army tasked TRADOC with forming a division restructuring study (DRS) group to determine the Heavy Division's optimum size, mix, and organization. Romjue observes that "DePuy and the DRS planners had entertained a supreme concern for the 'new lethality' that the Yom Kippur War had demonstrated. There was no diminution of this in Starry's approach (Division 86)" adopted after he took over TRADOC.[257] The structure ultimately approved in mid-1980 reflected many of the findings from the Arab–Israeli combat—improved command and control with smaller companies and platoons (decreasing junior leaders' span of control), augmented antitank capability, integration of shooters and jammers, increased fire support, organic EW and chemical defense units, and enhanced support battalions that aimed to "arm, feed, fix, and feed forward." Where the army retreated from applying lessons, it was done largely for practical reasons. For example, it abandoned the DRS recommended division air-defense brigade because of personnel constraints and equipment deficiencies.

Modified tank units. In addressing a critical question of this reorganization—the structure of smaller tank units—the army investigated but did not emulate Israeli practice.[258] Information about the wartime effectiveness of the IDF's three-tank platoons in the demanding command-and-control environment exacerbated doubts among American officers about its five-tank platoons. The DRS recommended three tanks per platoon, eleven per company (instead of seventeen), and thirty-six per battalion (instead of fifty-four). In September 1978 the retired DePuy endorsed this position, as "the Israelis have demonstrated the high-performance of such a tactical system" and army testing validated its superiority.[259] Although initially in favor, Starry came to believe that the three-tank platoon, as Romjue notes, "had high costs not previously analyzed," especially a concerning requirement for 100 percent readiness, given doubts about the new XM1's reliability.[260] Thus, the army's Division 86 had four-tank platoons, fourteen-tank companies, and fifty-eight-tank battalions. In this case, a foreign war lesson influenced the discussion about and experimentation with tank unit size, but the US Army embraced a modified approach that best suited its needs.

Introduced CEWI battalions. An excellent example of how combat data can inspire change occurred in the area of electronic warfare.[261] As Lt. Col. Don Gordon, actively involved in this effort, observed, the army's analysis of the Middle East War "indicated that a revival of military intelligence and electronic warfare was desperately needed."[262] Abrams, in December 1973, established this objective as a top priority, and the following year his successor, Weyand, formed the Intelligence Organization and Stationing Study to identify a way forward. Highly critical of the army's compartmentalized approach, the panel's recommendations "led to the most sweeping reorganization of military intelligence in a generation."[263] Among the reforms adopted by the army was the Combat Electronic Warfare Intelligence (CEWI) unit, with a plan to assign a battalion to each division and a group to each corps. The decision to assign, not attach, these units reflected how the CEWI concept "removed the veil and introduced requirements for both the army and the intelligence service to understand each other."[264] The army, in late 1976, placed the first CEWI battalion in the Second Armored Division, followed in mid-1977 by one in the Eighty-Second Airborne Division to allow concept exploration for both heavy and light divisions.

This effort seems a textbook application of a foreign war finding, but progress occurred slowly amid limited budgets, competing priorities, technical difficulties, and lingering concerns about integration from both intelligence specialists and combat commanders. In March 1975 Secretary Callaway stated that, among the priority projects accelerated as a result of lessons from the Yom Kippur War, "we are striving to field a new family of telecommunications devices to provide commanders better means of combat command and control."[265] He added, "We are also seeking ways to expand our capability in the complex area of electronic warfare."[266] Yet quick results did not follow, as Gordon complained in 1980 that the army "needs a lot of better CEWI equipment."[267] Despite the general enthusiasm for realistic training, many field commanders resisted having a strong EW component "for fear of wrecking the exercises' value for the infantry and tanks."[268] Writing in the early 1990s, Maj. Patrick Kelly lamented that the army failed to optimize the CEWI's utility as it suffered from "antiquated equipment, severe personnel shortages, and an absence of doctrine."[269]

Improved fire-support approach. An ultimately more impactful organizational change inspired by problems revealed in the Yom Kippur War was a new fire-support approach.[270] The conflict showed the impracticality of using standard airborne direction, given IADs as well as the inadequacy of the current forward ground observer teams on the expanded battlefield. Thus, the army formed the Close Support Study Group to identify how best to enhance forward observation. Although acknowledging technology offered long-term possibilities, the Close Support Study Group focused on organizational reforms with the establishment of FIST (fire-support teams) at the company level as well as similar fire-support sections at the battalion and brigade levels. Many gunners feared that placing observers under infantry and armor officers would prevent effective, massed fire. Rebuking this parochial view, FIST proponents argued that it would increase combined-arms proficiency. The army approved the concept in 1977, which artillery historian Boyd Dastrup observes "revolutionized fire support."[271]

Renewed attention to chemical weapons defense. Whereas postwar study significantly enhanced preexisting appreciation of EW and fire-support challenges, it caused the army to reverse its deemphasis of chemical warfare (CW).[272] Previously, senior officers' view of chemical weapons as superfluous, combined with civilian antipathy, prompted the diminution of army CW capabilities, including the mid-1973 closure of the Chemical School and the request that Congress abolish the Chemical Corps. Less than a year later, however, Abrams stated "how impressed we were with the comprehensive CBR defense equipment in the Soviet-equipped forces of the Arab armies. . . . I think we will have to do more on defense."[273] As CW expert Jonathan Tucker explains, "by transforming U.S. perceptions of the chemical warfare threat," the Yom Kippur War "gave the Army Chemical Corps a new lease on life."[274] The service initiated a comprehensive CW review, which identified substantial organizational, materiel, and training deficiencies. In 1977 the army activated the 68th Chemical Company, with plans to add such a unit to every division. The Division 86 structure expanded the size of this unit, which became a nuclear-biological-chemical company. These organizational changes, along with issuing better gear to soldiers and increasing CW training, improved preparedness, but it took the failure of CW treaty talks, the collapse of détente, and the alleged communist CW use in the late 1970s for the service to obtain needed resources and authority to meet this challenge.

Mixed response to support cases. Bureaucratic inertia, fiscal challenges, and even contradictory findings from the Yom Kippur War limited the application of the conflict's lessons regarding logistics.[275] Although the intensity of modern war demonstrated in the Middle East heightened American appreciation of voracious supply demands, that same intensity encouraged maximizing frontline combat strength. Ultimately, the latter understanding, along with high threat perception, domestic and allied pressure, and the Nunn Amendment, prompted the army to shift personnel from support to combat positions (thirty thousand in Europe and sixty thousand total). This action enabled forty-eight additional combat battalions, but Gen. James Polk, USA (Ret.), warned in mid-1975 that, for the US Army in Europe, "the impending changes in the 'teeth to tail' ratio reduce self-sufficiency and flexibility while adding very little to on-the-ground combat power."[276] Acknowledging that "much of this so-called new strategy derives from the events of the Yom Kippur War of 1973," Polk emphasized that it was clear from the same conflict that "our planning factors for resupply of men and materiel, granted over a shorter period of time, will have to be revised upwards rather drastically."[277] Senior civilian and military officials' concern about deficient support capability in the active force grew as exercises highlighted the problem. As the army's FY79 history pointed out, "virtually no base existed that could sustain combat troops beyond the first few weeks of a war."[278] Still, TRADOC historian Romjue almost parrots specific army support lessons from the Yom Kippur War in describing how the final Division 86 structure "provided for battle damage repair as far forward as possible by maintenance teams whose work would be aided by built-in test equipment and maximal replacement by component and through cannibalization. Prompt recovery and removal for repair of damaged major weapon systems were stressed. Fuel resupply emphasized timely forecasting of needs and rapid response by a flexible system."[279]

Conduct of more realistic training. Attributing the IDF's combat effectiveness to its superior officers and soldiers reinforced the army's prewar prioritization of training and drove the pursuit of greater realism going forward.[280] A study of prior wars perplexingly revealed that more training did not diminish the likelihood of high casualties in a unit's first combat. The failing resulted, as Chapman explains, because "field training exercises and maneuvers, especially those involving multiple companies or battalions, had always lacked realism."[281] In January 1974 Gorman observed in an influential paper ("How to Win Outnumbered") that the recent Middle East combat showed armor units needed to combine gunnery and tactical movement training instead of static range practice. That same month Gen. Walter Kerwin, Forces Command chief, noted that the war demonstrated a need to shoot well, and he complained about the training of his tank units.[282] In response, DePuy and Kerwin initiated a program to identify, train, and deploy "master gunners." In a second January paper Gorman urged "scrapping conventional infantry training approaches in favor of force-on-force training with TES [Tactical Engagement Simulation]."[283] Concern existed that such simulation would reduce live-fire training budgets, but Gorman successfully argued the former's value for addressing combat-revealed requirements, especially combined arms and nighttime proficiency. In March 1974, after receiving multiple briefings on the Arab–Israeli fighting, Abrams stated that in the desire for safety, training realism had been excessively sacrificed and the army was taking steps to rectify this mistake.[284] Soon the training establishment "was being bombarded" with new circulars meant to convert instructors to DePuy's understanding of modern war.[285] The common refrain from TRADOC leaders when assessing training the rest of the decade was a need for more realism. Beyond providing insights into how to train, DePuy emphasized that the Yom Kippur War "helped us argue for more training within the Army establishment" at a time when the high price of fuel created strong pressures to reduce the number and scope of exercises.[286]

National Training Center established. Perhaps most importantly, the combat data led to the formation of the National Training Center (NTC). TRADOC's 1975 adoption of the Army Training and Evaluation Program as "the principal vehicle for measuring training readiness among companies, battalions, and brigades" enhanced the perceived need for better exercise facilities, especially given the increasing range and complexity of modern battles as indicated by Arab–Israeli fighting.[287] Thus, Gorman began developing the NTC concept "where a total combat environment could be simulated for training heavy battalion task forces."[288] Regarding this initiative as essential to replicating the IDF's ability to win outnumbered, TRADOC leaders were vociferous advocates for this joint project with Forces Command. After army attendees lauded the initial USAF Red Flag exercise (a program encouraged by the Yom Kippur War, as will be discussed), Gorman complained in November 1976 that "we are five years behind or more" in providing realistic training.[289] Although the army leadership signed off on the NTC in April 1977 at Fort Irwin (near Red Flag), politics and cost concerns delayed its establishment until August 1979 and exercises until 1981. It would prove the service's most expensive peacetime training initiative ever and critics remained, given the cost, but the NTC significantly boosted preparedness. A proud Gorman recalled many years later that his early January 1974 memorandum produced after studying Arab–Israeli combat "led directly to the actions that culminated in the National Training Center."[290]

Enhanced Weapons/Equipment Programs for the Army

The army mostly attempted to apply Yom Kippur War data to weapons programs, but it did so in distinct ways and with varying degrees of success. Attributing past acquisition struggles in part due to civilian contractors and the Army Materiel Command pulling equipment R&D away from operational considerations, DePuy sought to better integrate systems with doctrine, training, and combat development.[291] Information from Arab–Israeli combat advanced this process, although not without resistance from arms manufacturers and materiel developers. A disgruntled Starry complained that they "simply don't accept gracefully having anyone raise even the shadow of a doubt about their programs, despite lessons of the October War."[292] Yet, as shown below, DePuy, Starry, and other officers exhibited similar behavior when a finding threatened to delay or delegitimize a highly desired weapon. Regardless, the army usually at least considered combat signals, beginning with the need for more weapons, given the unexpected attrition. As Army Secretary Callaway testified in early 1975, this finding, combined with the Soviet threat, necessitated that the army "move more aggressively toward its materiel objectives than it has been able to in the past."[293] Defense Secretary Schlesinger proposed that year reallocating $5 billion ($23.3 billion in constant dollars) from FY77–FY81 strategic programs to conventional forces.[294] Although his successor, Rumsfeld, concurred with spending more on conventional forces, money remained a limiting factor, as did bureaucratic, political, and cultural considerations.

Of the three beneficial ways in which the army used findings, revelation of an unmet requirement and demonstration of a severe flaw with a current system were particularly valuable, given the unlikelihood of such information emerging from tests and exercises.

MLRS as long-range support. The best example of this application was the acquisition of a conventionally armed, rapid-fire unguided rocket system.[295] The US field artillery had traditionally focused on tube guns and nuclear-armed missiles when the Arab–Israeli fighting contributed significantly to a reevaluation. Facing an enemy in Central Europe who, like the Egyptians and Syrians in October 1973, possessed a large quantitative edge in artillery and strong IADs, the army, as Dastrup relates, "decided in 1975 to develop a multiple rocket launcher for counterbattery work and suppression of enemy air defenses."[296] In discussing rapid development of the tracked General Support Rocket System, the Department of the Army's FY79 Historical Summary highlighted its potential to satisfy the "close ground support" (SEAD) requirement, which had emerged from the Yom Kippur War.[297] When the army finalized the structure of its new heavy division in 1980, the field artillery brigade included a battery (nine launchers) of the renamed MLRS (multiple launch rocket system). It became such an integral component of army operations that decades later this weapon was sometimes mistakenly characterized as being one of the "Big Five" programs.[298]

Replacement of flammable hydraulic fluid. A simple but meaningful correction occurred after Israeli reports revealed an unexpected vulnerability.[299] When Arab shells penetrated tank turret hulls and ruptured hydraulic lines, the fluid ignited with catastrophic consequences for crews. Army R&D personnel reiterated that the hydraulic fluid was not flammable, prompting concerned Armor School officers to invite the lab official in charge to visit. After he demonstrated that hydraulic fluid in a pan would not ignite, the tankers showed that pricking a highly pressurized line and lighting a match resulted in the fluid acting like a flamethrower. Abrams reported in March 1974 that the US Army had not previously encountered this problem and was hard at work on a nonflammable substitute.[300] The army resolved the problem quickly, reducing American tankers' danger from a vehicle fire.

Arab–Israeli fighting also generated recognition of a need for significant modifications to some weapon programs.

Extensively altered infantry fighting vehicle. Major changes to the MICV, the most vulnerable Big Five program, exemplify this type of influence.[301] After failed attempts in the 1960s to develop an IFV, the army commenced the MICV's development in late 1972 so "foot soldiers" could operate closely with friendly tanks. When a congressional staffer in March 1974 inquired about MICV survivability as a result of the Middle East War's lethality, Abrams responded coyly "that is, a very good question, sir. We are really working on that right now."[302] After evaluating the BMP's performance and testing captured vehicles, American officers disconcertingly appreciated, as Starry observed, "that neither the BMP nor MICV can stand *mixed in* with tanks in the central battle and survive."[303] Overlapping with the IFV question was how to satisfy the demonstrated need for a better scout vehicle.[304] Prior recognition of the M-114's deficiencies had precipitated the armored reconnaissance scout vehicle program. Yet concern about the combustible M-114 was so great after the Yom Kippur War that the army leadership sought almost one thousand of the much-maligned diesel-powered M-113A1s in FY74 Supplemental Budget as a stopgap for the scouting role. Legislators rejected this request as the service possessed over eleven thousand M-113s, while the TRADOC leadership got the disliked armored reconnaissance scout vehicle canceled to ensure focus on the higher priority MICV. Instead, given that, as Starry later acknowledged, "all our studies, including those of the Yom Kippur War, validate the need for the cavalry mission," the army merged the armored reconnaissance scout vehicle program and the MICV program.[305]

The demonstrated vulnerability, however, prompted a major evolution in the resulting vehicle's design and combat role because "to survive they all had to stand off—on flanks, overwatching or wherever, especially in the attack."[306] While findings from the conflict prompted the army to bolster procurement of its new medium (Dragon) and heavy (TOW) ATGM systems, losses suffered by infantry employing such weapons convinced the army to develop a TOW-equipped M-113 (the improved-TOW vehicle). Although agreement also existed on arming the MICV's scout variant with TOWs, concern existed about adding them to the infantry model. As Starry wrote in May 1976, "If the infantry is in the right place, then the TOWs are in the wrong place," and vice versa.[307] Two months later the army initiated a program review, led by Brig. Gen. Richard Larkin, amid concern that Congress would end support especially given reports of Soviet post–Yom Kippur War doubt about the BMP. Weighing heavily the Middle East fighting, the task force recommended and the army approved that both infantry and cavalry versions should be equipped with twin-TOW launchers despite having to cut space for two infantrymen.

Although the TOW-equipped MICV would give "mechanized infantry units a remarkable density of antitank firepower," support grew for an armored or heavy infantry fighting vehicle (HIFV) capable of operating with tanks to perform the MICV's initial mission.[308] After the Yom Kippur War, the IDF modified small numbers of Centurion and T-55 tanks to be HIFVs, and the US Army initiated preliminary studies. In 1977 the logic for the HIFV prompted senators Sam Nunn and Gary Hart to mandate another review of the MICV (now designated the IFV). This group in mid-April 1978 reaffirmed the IFV requirement, rejecting the HIFV given technical and cost risks. Although noting that "the HIFV makes sense," Starry concurred that, above all, "we need the IFV."[309] The army's repeated rejection of alternatives to the IFV, eventually named the Bradley, resulted in its funding despite continuing outside doubts. Throughout the IFV's tortured development process involving multiple reviews and major design changes, the Yom Kippur War served as a reference point. The fundamental problem was that the conflict signaled the need for two types of vehicles—a forward-positioned HIFV and a standoff ATGM-equipped MICV—and the army could not afford both. Still, as the fighting showed, the latter was the more pressing requirement, and without Arab–Israeli combat data, the service's prospects for procuring such a system seem low.

Corroboration of existing and developmental programs with minor adjustments was the third type of influence. Collected information indicated the appropriateness of system characteristics as well as providing compelling evidence with which to lobby executive and legislative officials. Of course, recognition of this potential benefit encouraged program managers to assert such support. Noting that everyone drew their best examples from the Yom Kippur War, Starry complained that "listening carefully, one wonders if in October of 1973 there were several wars or just one."[310] Although such efforts at times proved frustrating to the army leadership, they did not undermine the net gain from this use of combat data.

Validation of tank need and XM1 design. Most significantly, senior officers seized on the conflict's evidence that "the tank is the dominant land weapon system."[311] After DOD and congressional skeptics killed the first two M-60 replacements, Abrams in 1972 initiated a third effort (the XM1). In mid-1974 the army established the Tank Special Study Group to review the XM1's design in light of Middle East combat data. This effort had instructional value to ensure the XM1 satisfied the modern battlefield's requirements as well as instrumental utility by being able to demonstrate to legislators that they had seriously considered this recent experience, especially evidence about the ATGM threat. Lt. Gen. Howard Cooksey, deputy chief of staff for research, development, and acquisition, reported in March 1975 that the Tank Special Study Group found that "the major XM1 design parameters are sound and should not be modified."[312] Program manager Baer added that its enhanced composite armor, lower silhouette, improved agility, and especially compartmentalization of crew and ordnance would "drastically reduce disasters such as those experienced by tanks in the Yom Kippur War."[313] The demonstrated need to shoot at long range, on the move, in close battlespace, and at night validated the XM1's expensive, computerized fire control system. Findings did prompt some recommended changes. Most notably, the army decided against replacing the .50 caliber coaxial machine gun with the 25 mm Bushmaster cannon. Israeli tankers opposed such a switch, given that their inability to distinguish between lightly armored vehicles and main battle tanks on the chaotic modern battlefield had resulted in firing the main gun at all targets. Plus, the fighting showed a continuing need for the tank's secondary weapons to be capable of high-volume antipersonnel and antiair fire. Other suggested modifications (e.g., concentrating ammunition below the turret ring and altering the suspension to provide better protection against mines) were, according to Starry, "considered too far removed from traditional US tank design philosophy."[314]

The most pressing question was the sufficiency of the XM1's 105 mm rifled gun.[315] Abrams had primarily dispatched Starry and Baer to answer whether "we need a larger gun based on tank-on-tank experience in Israel."[316] With new German and French tanks adopting larger, smoothbore cannons like that used on Soviet armor and with the OSD urging the army to adopt a common "NATO gun," service leaders faced pressure to embrace the German 120 mm cannon even though it risked significantly delaying M1 production. Baer testified in March 1975 that based on Arab–Israeli combat and testing, the 105 mm gun with underway improvements "could meet the operational requirements of the U.S. Army at that time."[317] Above all, the Baer–Starry trip led to enhanced ammunition, especially long-rod or kinetic-energy penetrators, that would sufficiently pierce enemy tank armor. Besides not delaying production, use of the smaller 105 mm gun allowed stowage of six to ten more rounds, a notable benefit, given IDF reporting on the value of large ammunition loads. Army leaders won DOD approval to commence production of a 105 mm–armed M1 with the understanding that the follow-on variant would substitute the German smoothbore 120 mm gun. Israeli tank performance combined with increased Soviet threat perception to increase legislative support as the army acquired over three thousand M1s before shifting to M1A1 production in 1985. The wisdom of sticking with the 105 mm gun never faced a battlefield judgment as the army tanks that excelled in the 1991 advance north into Iraq were 120 mm–equipped M1A1s.

The conflict also spurred the army to improve the quality and quantity of its existing tank force.[318] Reflective of the importance attached to this effort, the first four slides of TRADOC's mid-August 1974 briefing on implementing the Brady study recommendations addressed actions taken to enhance the M-60 tank series, especially the new A3 variant.[319]

SAM-D program revitalized. Another Big Five program that received a much needed boost was the SAM-D.[320] Although the service leadership had for many years strongly supported this program to replace the medium- (HAWK) and high-altitude (Nike Hercules) air defenses, it suffered from technical difficulties and DOD skepticism about army possession of such an extended-range missile. A month before the Middle East conflict, Schlesinger informed the program manager that it should be terminated. Arab–Israeli combat, however, enhanced army and DOD officials' appreciation of the SAM-D requirement, especially given its ability to operate in a dense EW environment and engage multiple targets. In January 1974, instead of killing the program, the defense secretary required proof of principle testing for its troubled track-via-missile guidance system before full development resumed. Not only had the Middle East War bolstered the SAM-D's perceived value, Currie testified in April 1974 that its lessons would result in modifications "to improve the system's low altitude capability, mobility, utility of launchers, and interface with our airborne systems."[321] A series of successful mid-1970s test firings put the now-named Patriot program back on track, with it entering limited production in 1980.

Improved artillery capability. In some cases, the validation was not so much for a particular weapon but an area of warfare as occurred with the field artillery.[322] Dastrup explains in a branch history that, "prodded by the threat's strength in Europe and the recent Yom Kippur War of October 1973, the field artillery initiated an ambitious modernization program."[323] This effort began with the 1974 Fire Support Mission Area Study, which identified requirements and solutions especially for destroying tanks. Task force members concluded that obtaining such capability as well as reducing the time from request of fire to first round on target required computerization. Thus, although the troubled development of the complex Tactical Fire Direction System began in the 1960s, it now received greater priority as did improved mortar (TPQ-36) and artillery (TPQ-37) locating radars. Beyond promoting faster and more accurate fire direction, the Arab–Israeli combat led to pursuit of better ammunition (e.g., scatterable mines, prolonged duration white phosphorous smoke rounds, and PGMs). Reflective of the army's application of this general lesson, one-third of the forty-eight new combat battalions formed in the mid-1970s were field artillery, more than any other type.

Enthusiastic Application without Result

Struggle to upgrade air defenses. Although the aforementioned boost to the SAM-D program represented a positive reaction to the demonstrated importance of air defense, the army struggled to implement the two broader findings—the key to effectiveness was an integrated network of systems, and it had particularly neglected the lower end of the spectrum. Air Defense Center commandant Maj. Gen. C. J. LeVan stressed that "the Mideast war of 1973 validated the criticality of air defense and showed vividly that it is required as an integrated member of the combined arms team."[324] Given the perceived need, Norman Augustine, assistant secretary of the army for research and development, added that "we are dead serious in our intent to squeeze every last ounce of performance from existing systems [I-HAWK, Chaparral, and Vulcan] by product improvement."[325] Still, regarding such efforts as insufficient, the army initiated two major initiatives.

First, although a study group had already been formed in early 1973 to evaluate European SHORAD systems, forward progress would likely have languished without the war graphically illustrating a priority requirement for forward, short-range, all-weather protection.[326] Moving quickly, the army in July 1974 solicited bids and in January 1975 selected an American version of the French/German Roland II. The plan to deploy it initially to protect airbases and logistical complexes rather than forward combat forces seems at odds with the Middle East experience, but LeVan explained that rear-area targets faced greater threat of all-weather attack, warranting priority coverage and allowing use of a cheaper wheeled variant instead of the French/German tracked vehicle. Responsive to Arab–Israeli combat data, the Americanized Roland had a more powerful tracking radar and enhanced electronic counter-countermeasures capability. While the army obtained DOD permission for expedited development given its priority, technical difficulty and funding constraints prompted service and congressional sentiment to shift gradually to continued reliance on the "more cost effective" I-Chaparral. The Roland program died in 1981.

With the SHORAD system initially intended to protect rear areas, the army attempted to safeguard frontline combat forces by acquiring a mobile, radar-controlled AA gun analogous to the Soviet ZSU-23-4 that performed so well against the Israelis.[327] The Air Defense Center generated "requirements for an air-defense gun system based on observations of the Yom Kippur War."[328] Then the army established a formal requirement for a medium caliber, all-weather, radar-guided division air-defense gun that could keep pace with armor and mechanized forces while also introducing modest upgrades to the severely deficient Vulcan 20 mm self-propelled gun.[329] Although users and the R&D community strongly supported the new AA gun, army system analysts opposed it as too costly given greater manpower requirements compared to

missiles.[330] Service leaders, regarding it as a priority, pushed for expedited development. The desire for quick results, however, led to an effort to kludge together existing components from disparate weapons (e.g., M-48 tank hull, F-16 radar, and AA
gun), which unsurprisingly proved problematic. The technical difficulties, combined
with continued disagreement between gun and missile advocates, hampered development and drove up costs until the 1985 cancellation of the division air-defense
gun (the M247 Sergeant York). Difficulties with the Roland II and the Sergeant York
programs elevated the importance of the Stinger man-portable air-defense system,
which garnered wide acclaim in the mid-1980s after successful use in Afghanistan. By
then over a decade had passed since the Yom Kippur War, and the army deserved a
middling, if not poor, grade for its attempt to apply the conflict's air-defense lessons
to obtain markedly better, networked capability. Positively, it reserved scarce space
for air-defense equipment on early airlift flights to the Arabian Peninsula in 1990.
Lt. Col. Frank Caravella points out that such behavior was "a relatively new phenomenon, the origin of which can be largely traced to an earlier confrontation [the 1973
War] that took place in the same sun-bleached corner of the world."[331]

Misapplied or Ignored Conflict Information

Preserved commitment to the ATGM attack helicopter. In sharp contrast to the
eagerly applied lessons in the preceding paragraphs, army leaders focused on eliminating the perceived danger from the Yom Kippur War to one of their most prized
programs—the AAH.[332] Service enthusiasm for an ATGM-armed attack helicopter
had been buoyed by spring 1972 trials in Germany involving Cobras simulating TOW
launches and jury-rigged Hueys firing TOWs at North Vietnamese armor during the
Easter Offensive. While continuing to develop the TOW-equipped Cobra, the army
prioritized the AAH, which it designed to be more survivable and lethal than the Cobra but less complex and costly than the canceled Cheyenne. Reports from the Middle East conflict, however, generated doubts about the attack helicopter's viability.
In March 1974 Abrams acknowledged that "there were some environments in that
war that you would not be able to stick the AAH into."[333] A year later *New York Times*
military correspondent Drew Middleton observed that the army's evaluation of the
Yom Kippur War "ends the love affair between the generals and the helicopters."[334]

Yet key officers maintained faith in the attack helicopter, either minimizing the
generalizability of the Arab–Israeli experience or citing it as justification for acquiring the more-capable AAH.[335] When legislators questioned why the army still
wanted them, Abrams, at the same hearing at which he provided the above quote
acknowledging their limitations, downplayed the war's applicability given terrain
and weather differences between the Middle East and Central Europe. Dismissing

Israeli doubts, he asserted that "it may sound arrogant, but I must also say that there is no one in the world who has had more experience in using helicopters in difficult circumstances and in a high antiaircraft environment, than the U.S. Army."[336] DePuy simply declared that "the Arab/Israeli War did not reveal much about Army aviation."[337] Maj. Gen. William Maddox, Army Aviation Center commanding general, argued that the fighting actually validated the AAH's design and concept of operations as its use at night with nap-of-the-Earth tactics and better ECM would enable survivability. Proceeding as aggressively as possible, the army in 1976 first deployed TOW-equipped Cobras to Europe and selected the YAH-64 as the AAH (Apache). Importantly for the attack helicopter's survivability and effectiveness, information from the Middle East enhanced support for development of the Hellfire ATGM, which doubled the TOW's range and used laser guidance. Proponents cite the Hellfire-equipped Apache's laudatory career as vindication, but skeptics point out that it never had to engage in combat against the density of IADs experienced by the IDF in October 1973, let alone what would have occurred in a Central European war with the Soviets.

HOW DID THE AIR FORCE APPLY ITS FINDINGS?

Although somewhat evident from the preceding TRADOC-TAC discussion, a brief articulation of the USAF's decision context is necessary to understand its responses to the Yom Kippur War.[338] Soaring fuel costs and the associated inflationary pressure presented a particularly acute budgetary challenge for the air force. Secretary McLucas emphasized this point by noting that, despite reducing FY75 fuel consumption by 27 percent from the FY73 level, its fuel costs increased 133 percent.[339] The air force chief of staff in February 1975 added, "I would judge that the impact of inflation on defense buying power represents a greater and more immediate threat to our military capability than any other single factor."[340] Like the army, the tactical air force prioritized the Soviet threat in Central Europe. Exacerbating concern, the service possessed fewer aircraft, personnel, and bases than at any time since before the Korean War.

Fortunately, the USAF had strong, capable leadership. In August 1973 aviation generalist Gen. George Brown replaced Gen. John Ryan, who "personified the SAC [Strategic Air Command] mold."[341] Wanting commanders able to operate on the modern battlefield, Brown directed his personnel chief to identify officers "for early promotion to facilitate the youth movement" to eclipse the bomber-dominant World War II generation.[342] Brown so impressed Nixon and Schlesinger that they promoted him chairman of the Joint Chiefs effective July 1974. His replacement, Gen. David Jones, was another generalist whom colleagues characterized "as intelligent, hardworking, and a confident, independent thinker."[343] Although Brown and Jones did not emerge from the fighter ranks, their tenures witnessed TAC's raising influence after SAC dominated the USAF's first twenty-five years. In particular, Dixon's assumption of command one week before the Yom Kippur War marked "the most significant date in the development of the Air Force culture change."[344] A few years later he observed that "a key influence in reshaping TAC force employment and training is the lessons learned by the IAF during the October 1973 war—lessons that are generally applicable to high-threat environments."[345]

Two long-standing aspects of USAF culture—love of advanced technology and embrace of flying safety—would shape and be shaped by attempts to apply Yom Kippur War findings. First, the air force had always sought to solve problems with better aircraft.[346] Struggles in the Vietnam War and growing Soviet numerical advantages intensified the USAF's commitment to technology as a force multiplier. Yet, by the mid-1970s, service leaders recognized that aircraft cost had to be an acquisition consideration lest the communists attain an unmanageable quantitative edge. For example, Brig. Gen. John Ralph, director of doctrine, concepts, and objectives, argued in early 1975 that "we must ensure not only that emerging technologies are relevant to the future needs of operating forces, but also that they are fiscally procurable."[347] This appreciation, however, should not be taken as detracting from a strong institutional preference for possessing the best machines possible. When a vocal group of outside critics, including retired colonels John Boyd and Everest Riccioni, advocated for low-tech planes that could be purchased in large numbers, USAF leaders responded that simple, short-range fighters (e.g., F-104; F-5) had performed poorly in Vietnam. As RAND scholar Carl Builder observed two decades later, "for the Air Force aerodynamic performance and technological quality of its aircraft have always been of higher priority than the number."[348]

A flying safe culture had emerged in the 1950s out of SAC leaders' abhorrence for losing expensive long-range bombers.[349] As strategic bombing generals obtained senior commands throughout the service, including TAC, they mandated a flying safe culture despite its debilitating effect on fighter pilot skills. Although the outbreak of Vietnam War freed tactical aviators in Southeast Asia, Col. Marshall Michel, USAF (Ret.), points out that, with the November 1968 cessation of Rolling Thunder, "the combat culture began to change from 'get the job done' to 'don't lose airplanes.'"[350] Col. Dawson O'Neill, USAF (Ret.), recalled that in 1970 "there was pressure to water down every training profile to the least risk."[351] The end of the war threatened to exacerbate this situation, prompting fighter pilots, especially at the Tactical Fighter Weapons Center and the Air Staff's Tactical Fighter Division, to maneuver for more realistic training.

Arab–Israeli combat data would be filtered through the Vietnam War experience in which poor results "severely compromised airpower theories and many of the justifications for airpower that had become so prominent in the nuclear era."[352] The Americans highlighted three core lessons from their most recent combat. First, based on a flawed belief that any aviator could be proficient with any type of aircraft after six months of training, the Universal Pilot program had inadequately prepared pilots. This deficiency combined with flawed tactics and inadequate equipment to produce an air-to-air kill ratio far below World War II and the Korean War rates. Second, improved ground-based air defenses presented a much greater challenge to aircraft survivability and operational effectiveness. Concern about the SA-2, which claimed its first victim over Vietnam in July 1965, encouraged low-altitude approaches, but aviators quickly discovered that "flying at altitudes below 3000 feet was virtual suicide" given intense AAA.[353] Third, although large support packages reduced losses, attack aircraft usually missed their target. Thus, the USAF in June 1967 intensified development of precision-guidance munitions.

Of particular relevance for decision-making were the 1972 Linebacker operations during which the USAF introduced new technologies and techniques developed in the three and half years since the end of Rolling Thunder.[354] Despite facing a much improved air-defense network in North Vietnam, enhanced ECM gear, upgraded navigation systems, and better Wild Weasel (SAM killer) teams limited air force losses. Signaling a new era, in mid-May aircrews used Pave Knife laser-guided bomb (LGB) designators to drop several spans of the Paul Doumer Bridge and the main span of the Thanh Hóa Bridge, a target of hundreds of failed attacks between 1965 and 1968. The term *surgical strike* soon emerged as the air force and the public became enamored with the LGB.[355] Compared to an approximately 5 percent direct-hit rate for munitions delivered by F-105s between 1965 and 1968, USAF aircraft registered 47.5 percent direct hits with LGBs and an even better 53.5 percent with electro-optical guided bombs such as the AGM-65A (Maverick).[356] The air force leadership celebrated its progress in the air-to-ground area, especially given the frustrating air-to-air competition, where fighter losses to MiGs remained high (especially compared to the navy). Still, the new PGM technology only worked in daytime, clear-weather environments.

Amid this reform-favoring context, lessons from the Yom Kippur War meaningfully aided progress in each of the three areas airpower analyst Benjamin Lambeth identifies as key to the USAF's lauded transformation—aircrew proficiency, equipment performance, and operational concepts.[357] In spring 1974 congressional testimony, senior DOD and air force officials repeatedly referenced how the Arab–Israeli conflict demonstrated factors critical for US tactical aviation to flourish. Given that the Yom Kippur War's aerial dimension represented an intensification of the Southeast Asian experience, the USAF moved quickly to apply these findings. While the service leadership used them to inform the FY74 Supplemental and FY75 budget requests broadly, Chief of Staff Brown tasked the Air Staff, TAC, and Air Force Systems Command to work together to address problems demonstrated by the Arab–Israeli combat. In briefing the results of that investigation, which included reviewing 112 R&D efforts, Colonel Lindsey explained in March 1974 that "we tried to look at what came out of that war, and what we should do to enhance tactical force capabilities."[358]

Systematic Application to Air Force R&D Programs

Initiation of the Pave Strike Program. The air force leadership selected 11 R&D programs for increased emphasis.[359] Lindsey explained that the initiative aims "to get them in the inventory as fast as we can and make sure that they are not slowed up for the lack of resources, facilities, and personnel."[360] He stressed that, above all, it "is to get us a night and adverse weather capability."[361] For these projects, the air force wanted to nearly double the allocated FY74 funds in the supplemental budget as well as obtain substantially more money in subsequent years. When legislators questioned the appropriateness of including R&D efforts in a supplemental spending bill, Major General Collins argued, as Futrell relates, that although the program "would not be immediately fruitful . . . it was important for long-term security to spark the technology it required."[362] Despite the legislators rejecting this funding request on philosophical grounds, the air force leadership maintained the Pave Strike initiatives "to assure their expeditious entry into the operational force."[363]

USAF officials usually grouped the eleven projects around three key objectives: (1) detect, locate, and acquire hostile emitters; (2) protect the strike force; and (3) deliver munitions with greater accuracy and range.[364] The first category included the Tactical Advanced Location and Strike System and the Precision Emitter Location Strike System (PELSS), which were being developed given the difficulty in ascertaining electronic emitters during the Vietnam War. In justifying the steep expense of these systems, especially the more advanced PELSS, Brigadier General Ralph observed that the requirements to identify radar sites "have become increasingly important as a result of the Mid-East War and are likely to receive higher priority in the future."[365] Among the most highly valued Pave Strike projects were two efforts to enhance strike force protection. After the January 1968 loss of an EB-66 standoff jammer over North Vietnam forced the withdrawal of these planes to safer airspace, the air force sought to convert F-111As to operate as jammers in high-threat environments. The unprecedented EW in October 1973 underscored the need for this system. The USAF had introduced specially modified aircraft and antiradiation missiles to target SAMs in Vietnam, but mixed results from the Wild Weasel program led TAC to seek a more capable system in a modified F-4E. The October 1973 war prompted the air force to not only include the Advanced Wild Weasel in Pave Strike but seek further upgrades as well as increase support for the navy-led effort to develop a better anti-radiation missile.[366] The lethality of the wartime skies also motivated the inclusion of the multimission remotely piloted vehicle to conduct EW, reconnaissance, and weapons-delivery missions "in extremely high-threat areas."[367] Finally, the USAF appreciated the indicated need for munitions able to strike in poor visibility and at longer ranges (e.g., a laser-guided Maverick, a low-altitude version of the electro-optical glide bomb, or EOGB, and a long-range variant of the modular guided glide bomb, or MGGB).

Some of the Pave Strike initiatives matured into valuable assets, while others failed to result in operational capabilities.[368] Forty-two EF-111As, carrying three tons of EW gear above fifty thousand feet, provided the air force with an effective, survivable standoff jammer. Another positive outcome was the Advanced Wild Weasel (F-4G), although its performance would initially be limited by the slow development of the HARM (high-speed antiradiation missile). Additional program successes included the EOGB-II munition, the Pave Tack target designator, and the imaging IR seeker. The air force terminated the expensive and complicated planar-wing MGGB-II for lack of performance. Although it alternatively modified a small number of the nuclear air-launched cruise missiles to carry conventional warheads, Gen. John Vogt, USAF (Ret.), observed in the mid-1980s that, with regard to long-range, conventional weapons, "here's where the Air Force, in my judgment, has really dropped the ball," despite the Yom Kippur War impetus.[369] Enthusiasm for the multimission remotely piloted vehicle quickly diminished amid sharply escalating costs and technical difficulties. The air force leadership retained its commitment to the expensive and technically challenging PELSS because of a lack of alternatives, but the service ultimately canceled the system a decade later for being only "marginally effective."[370] The mixed record for Pave Strike projects was the inevitable outcome of a series of R&D initiatives attempting to tackle demanding battlefield tasks, but this result suggests that the "special management emphasis" touted by air force leaders did not yield significant benefit.

Other Constructive Applications

Beyond Pave Strike, the USAF responded to data on IAF challenges and Israeli adjustments with training initiatives, materiel modifications, and tactical reforms. As with the army, the air force benefited instrumentally, instructionally, and inspirationally.

Embrace of realistic training, including the Red Flag program. Although the Vietnam War clearly demonstrated the inadequacy of air force training, limited improvement had been achieved prior to the Yom Kippur War, elevating sensitivity to this critical deficiency.[371] Col. C. R. Anderegg, USAF (Ret.), points out that few USAF aviators in the Vietnam era "had ever trained against a dissimilar adversary, a fighter of different performance, size, and armament flown by a pilot with different tactics and temperament."[372] Dissimilar air combat training was especially valuable given the contrast between the USAF's radar-equipped, big-engined fighters, optimized for longer-range engagements, and the small, maneuverable MiGs, which excelled at dogfighting. Despite establishing the 64th Fighter Weapons Squadron with T-38s to serve as MiG proxies in October 1972, the air force leadership did not require wing commanders, who feared accidents and exposing pilot incompetence, to train with this unit. The first successful effort only occurred in mid-1973, but positive feedback, combined with study of the Yom Kippur War, prompted the USAF to embrace dissimilar air combat training. In March 1974 TAC also ordered the Tactical Fighter Weapons Center to initiate more realistic air-to-ground training based on the October War experiences. In general, Dixon and Chief of Staff Jones concluded that IAF wartime effectiveness illustrated the "overriding requirement" for highly prepared aircrews and ground personnel to maximize aircraft potential.[373] To facilitate that objective, the TAC chief in May 1975 dispatched a group of Israeli F-4 pilots to assess American operations. The visitors, drawing on their recent combat experience, were highly critical of flight restrictions that compromised realistic training. Emboldened by this evaluation, Dixon used his authority, as Michel relates, "to abolish the 'fly safe' culture in TAC, replacing it with a culture that emphasized realism, flexibility, and local control."[374]

Establishment of the much-lauded Red Flag program represented the most significant manifestation of the realistic training approach.[375] The October War "added urgency" to reformers' pursuit of large, demanding exercises given a fear that the United States could not prevail in the foreshadowed type of battle.[376] Whereas new pilots in prior conflicts initially flew low-risk sorties, expectation that a NATO / Warsaw Pact fight would be at least as intense as the Arab–Israeli combat precluded such on-the-job training. Red Flag offered a way to obtain an aircrew's "first ten combat missions" during peacetime. With safety and especially cost concerns blocking this initiative on the Air Staff, Col. Richard "Moody" Suter briefed it to Dixon, who immediately recognized the potential and brushed aside difficulties to enable the November 1975 inaugural exercise. Flight operations began with blue forces practicing ECM against actual Soviet radars, followed by air-to-air missions and culminating with a series of attacks against well-protected targets and at least one live ordnance drop. The TAC chief appreciated that Red Flag's "realism" would largely determine its value. Noting that the Israelis tolerated mishaps as the cost of preparedness, Dixon convinced Jones that Red Flag required accepting greater risk. As a result, exercises in 1976 produced 4.6 times the command's average number of accidents and 11.4 times the rate for the entire air force.[377] News of these losses brought pressure from the chief of staff, but Dixon successfully resisted reducing exercise difficulty. Despite the accident rate remaining high throughout the 1970s, the shift from a flying safe culture to the realistic training culture occurred rapidly as aviators witnessed the benefits. Red Flag almost certainly would have happened without the Yom Kippur War, but comprehension of its lessons accelerated the process, enhanced the severity of the challenge provided to aircrews, and sustained commitment to that severity despite resultant losses.

Given its success, Dixon and his successor, Creech, expanded Red Flag and introduced other colored flag exercises over the next decade (e.g., Blue, command and control; Copper, air defense) to improve and diversify training.[378] Two efforts stand out. First, recognizing Israeli combat effectiveness was not simply a product of aircrew proficiency; the USAF moved to bolster ground operations. Michel notes that Dixon "was extremely interested in the high sortie rates the Israeli Air Force regularly generated and how they were able to 'surge' in the 1973 Middle East War."[379] Although optimizing aircraft use was just as essential for the USAF given the Warsaw Pact's numerical superiority, the Americans had not developed such proficiency. After consulting with Peled, Dixon established Black Flag, which tested ground crews' ability to sustain two days of max sortie rates. Second, Creech, who had been strongly impressed by the EW challenge experienced by the Israelis in the Yom Kippur War, initiated in early 1981 an annual, dedicated six-week electronic warfare exercise known as Green Flag. After the first iteration confirmed his concern about a lack of EW preparedness, the TAC chief ordered more training and improved equipment. Ultimately, as Laslie sums up, "the creation of the training exercise Red Flag in 1975 and subsequent exercises were the most important steps in achieving the later battlefield success of the 1990s."[380]

Development of a stealth aircraft. Skill alone was insufficient to prevail in modern combat, and lessons from the Yom Kippur War helped foster development and acquisition of required weapons. While its impact most broadly occurred through validating existing programs with indicated enhancements, Arab–Israeli combat inspired some important innovations. Most notably, the air force pursued a radical alternative to suppressing IADs—an aircraft capable of avoiding detection.[381] In November 1973 the USAF Scientific Advisory Board and TAC personnel considered the alarming evidence on aircraft survivability. Similarly, the Defense Science Board's 1974 Summer Study examining European war scenarios "was heavily influenced" by the Middle East fighting and concluded that US attack aircraft would likely suffer unsustainable losses even with improved SEAD.[382] Later that year DOD research director, Currie, who frequently referred to the IAF's air-defense challenge in October 1973, asked air force and DOD scientists if a manned aircraft could be built with a radar signature as small as the mini-RPVs then under investigation. The Defense Advanced Research Projects Agency established a program to develop a low-observable aircraft, which led to Lockheed building two prototypes. Despite much skepticism and limited funding, the initial flight in December 1977 revealed that Lockheed "had indeed accomplished a fundamental breakthrough."[383] The first F-117 flew in June 1981 and entered service a little over two years later, giving the USAF a unique, albeit very expensive, capability ten years after the Yom Kippur War.

Impetus for JSTARS. The daunting complexity of the October 1973 battlefield sparked another ambitious program, the joint surveillance target attack radar system (JSTARS).[384] As Kenneth Werrell points out, it was no coincidence that the same month as the conflict Currie "ordered the Air Force and the Army to look into systems that could detect, locate, and attack enemy armor that moved behind enemy lines."[385] In 1975 the USAF Scientific Advisory Board identified a requirement for such an aircraft, and the Defense Advanced Research Projects Agency commenced funding two years later. Unfortunately, the army and air force possessed distinct operational concepts for the JSTARS, which resulted in technical and bureaucratic difficulties that significantly delayed the program. The performance of two prototypes in the Persian Gulf War, however, showed its potential value.

Improved aerial battle management. While inspiring JSTARS, the Yom Kippur War's battlefield complexity importantly validated for USAF leaders the expensive airborne warning and control system (AWACS).[386] The service had used a series of EC-121 Rivet Top variants to collect and distribute real-time information during the Vietnam War, but it had been developing the far more capable AWACS since 1963. Initially viewed as an Air Defense Command asset, the DOD determined in August 1973 that it would be of greater value in a tactical role. When testifying to the merit of this decision in mid-1974, Currie highlighted that "the events of the October Middle East war have amply demonstrated the advantages of a central command and control system."[387] The following year the USAF characterized the program as its top priority for general purpose forces.[388] The October war's intense EW competition, however, fueled outside concern that the AWACS radar would be susceptible to jamming. Although the USAF dismissed such vulnerability, worried legislators refused to authorize production until an outside panel of EW experts supported the air force position. In the interim, the air force, after study of the Arab–Israeli combat data, initiated enhancements to the AWACS's core configuration to enable more effective operations in a high-intensity environment. For decades, beginning in 1977, this plane would prove of immense aid to aviators.

Bolstered EW capabilities. The Yom Kippur War's impact was even more pronounced on EW as the subject "took on an air of immediacy" after the shocking early war IAF losses.[389] Chief of Staff Jones stressed in early 1975 that Middle East War assessments combined with USAF experience in Vietnam to "underscore the need for effective tactical electronic warfare systems."[390] In addition to the already discussed EF-111 standoff jammer, the air force focused on ECM pods, which were introduced early in the Vietnam War. IAF struggles with the SA-6 indicated a need for pods that jammed "electrical impulses over a broad spectrum of wave bands" and particularly justified the first programmable system (ALQ-131) then in development.[391] The air force sought significant additional funding to conduct R&D, update the existing inventory, and procure new ECM pods. Information, especially Israeli success at jamming Syrian communications, also incentivized pursuit of a capability to block transmissions. American officers had long appreciated the potential disruptive value of such means, given the Red Air Force's reliance on ground control intercept. The USAF now developed the EC-130 Compass Call aircraft to "break up the integrated defense systems into bite-sized chunks" that jamming pods, EF-111s and Wild Weasel aircraft could defeat.[392] General Creech regarded the EC-130, along with the EF-111 and F-4G, as a "must-have" SEAD platform, and it entered service in the early 1980s.[393] The high cost of EW capability made obtaining adequate support during peacetime difficult both within the air force and from Congress. In somewhat ameliorating that challenge for TAC, the Yom Kippur War exerted a valuable instrumental influence as well as shaping understanding of the required capabilities.

Belated fighter formation shift. Finally, combat data contributed to an overdue change in basic USAF air-to-air tactics.[394] As noted, fighter squadrons had flown the "fluid-four" formation, with a flight lead and three protective wingmen, since World War II, but modern aircraft and missiles favored two planes flying abreast so that "all aircraft were freed to be shooters, with none wasted as mere lookouts for the leader."[395] Lambeth notes that, "not surprisingly, air force fighter aircrews at the unit level were keenly sensitive to this deficiency of the fluid-four approach," but the service leadership and its tactical guidance elements retained belief in the traditional method.[396] The IAF, which, like the US Navy but not the Egyptians and Syrians, had adopted looser two-ship formations, provided further evidence of its superiority during the Yom Kippur War and pushed the USAF in that direction. Although Air Staff officers attempted to deny or downplay claims of the two-ship formation's superiority, Colonel Brown in March 1974 testimony responded to persistent questions about whether the air force planned to switch by stating that "this is being evaluated at our Fighter Weapons School."[397] The growing weight of evidence finally precipitated a shift to two-ship formations in the mid-1970s, with early Red Flag exercises validating this change.

CHAPTER 4

Conflicting Signals Complicate Application

As occurred in the other cases, air force decision-makers found themselves in possession of findings that encouraged opposing choices, necessitating either compromise,
neglect of lessons, or embrace of competing approaches.

High-low aircraft compromise. For its tactical aircraft inventory, the Yom Kippur
War productively contributed to USAF leaders accepting a high/low mix that ran
counter to their instincts.[398] In the early 1970s, while a budget-motivated OSD pushed
for a combination of expensive, advanced aircraft and less costly planes, the air force
emphasized ensuring a qualitative edge. TAC had placed top priority on obtaining an
all-weather air-to-air fighter since the mid-1960s, when combat in Southeast Asia revealed significant deficiencies with the dual-purpose fighter-bombers then in service.
The resulting single-seat, two-engine F-X (future F-15) demonstrated "outstanding
potential" from its first flight in 1972. Initially the Middle East conflict reinforced
USAF sentiment for an F-15 concentration. The leadership argued, as Dixon explained, that deploying an effective force "becomes more difficult as the sophistication of Soviet weapon systems—demonstrated so dramatically during the Yom
Kippur War—increases at a rapid rate."[399] Moreover, as Colonel Brown pointed out
in March 1974 congressional testimony, the protection provided by aircraft shelters
in Egypt indicated that more planes would have to be destroyed in the air, reiterating
the requirement for superior aircraft.[400] Still, senior officers could not deny that the
level of attrition experienced revealed a need for sufficient numbers to absorb inevitable losses. Whereas Defense Secretary Schlesinger in July 1973 failed to convince
the air force hierarchy to support acquisition of the relatively inexpensive lightweight
fighter (LWF), the Arab–Israeli combat, combined with fiscal realities, led the USAF
to reverse its position. When the chief of staff in March 1974 formed the Tactical
Fighter Modernization Group to assess how to replace the F-4, the air force included
cost as a decision criteria, ensuring that the LWF would be part of the recommended
tactical aviation mix. Ultimately, as Futrell points out, the Yom Kippur War "gave
impetus to the acquisition of more sophisticated weapons and also larger quantities
of less costly but still usable weapons."[401]

If the air force had to accept the LWF, its officers reimagined the aircraft as a capable fighter-bomber.[402] With the IAF wartime experience demonstrating the increased
vulnerability of attack aircraft and the need for more such planes, Schlesinger in
April 1974 reclassified the LWF as the multirole air combat fighter. After selecting the
F-16 over the F-17, the air force initiated several changes that significantly enhanced
its strike capability (e.g., adding a simple but highly capable pulse Doppler radar
and more pylons on enlarged wings). These changes, especially the radar, outraged
early LWF proponents. One of them, Pierre Sprey, argued that the Yom Kippur War

242

showed that tactical aircraft did not need radars as almost all Israeli air-to-air kills came from older Mirage IIIs with guns and heat-seeking missiles, not radar-equipped F-4s.[403] Yet, as Michel points out, this assertion epitomizes distortion of a foreign war experience to suit one's advocacy. The IAF largely assigned its F-4s to conduct ground attacks, but they dominated Arab fighters when participating in air-to-air engagements. Although more expensive and complex, the still-affordable F-16 possessed the power and agility to be an excellent dogfighter as well as the computer-aided bomb system to deliver munitions accurately.

Sustained debate over optimal air-to-ground approach. While conflicting Yom Kippur War cues precipitated a productive compromise for tactical aircraft procurement, they fueled on extended debate over the best strike approach against targets protected by dense IADs. Advocates of "go low" and "roll back" methods both cited Arab–Israeli combat data to support their position. Improved SEAD assisted both approaches contributing to broad support for the development of such capabilities and its establishment as an important service mission.[404] As Doyle points out, whereas the term *suppression* rarely appears in USAF budget requests in the early 1970s before the Yom Kippur War, it is mentioned nearly thirty times in the comparable mid-1970s budget requests.[405] Still, considerable doubt existed to whether the Americans could adequately suppress Soviet IADs, especially in the near term. Thus, following Israeli pilots, a clear majority of attack aviators in the mid-1970s pushed for "going low" under radar coverage when attacking protected targets.[406] American aircrews in Southeast Asia had experience flying such approaches and popping up at the last minute to drop munitions, but IAF pilots reported that the SA-6 missile envelope required attacking at extremely low levels. Dixon directed that "go low" tactics be employed at Red Flag, and TAC initiated development of an LGB that worked for a low-level flight profile. After F-4s in December 1978 successfully demonstrated this new LGB with the Pave Spike target designator, Anderegg relates that "most doubts about the viability" of low-level PGM strikes vanished.[407] Above all, "go low" proponents stressed that the IAF showed that aircrews required frequent and realistic training to maintain the necessary proficiency with this demanding flight profile.

Creech, however, took over TAC in May 1978 with a firm belief that the Yom Kippur War signaled a need to move away from the "go low" approach.[408] He recalled that as USAF Europe's director of operations and intelligence in the mid-1970s, Israeli pilots had told him of the futility of attempting to fly under the SA-6s and radar-guided AAA. He argued that information from the Arab–Israeli conflict, combined with intelligence on the latest Soviet SAMs, indicated that the only viable response was an "all-weather, rollback" approach (suppression/destruction of SAMs enabling aircraft to launch PGMs at medium altitudes). Although Creech referred to the "Go Low disease" and regarded it as unrealistic, he allowed continued training as skills had to be preserved while the USAF developed the technology to defeat air defenses. Much of that technology had been inspired or encouraged by the Yom Kippur War, as discussed above, but Creech ensured the appropriation of greater funding. Critics pushed back, citing not only the enormous cost and technical difficulty of the "roll back" approach but also doubt over whether NATO's ground forces could survive a surprise attack without immediate air support. Thus, aviators would be forced to strike ground targets without SEAD in a repeat of the IAF's predicament on October 6, 1973. The debate between "go low" and "roll back" proponents persisted until combat during the Persian Gulf War demonstrated the superiority of the latter.

Nonapplication

Unwavering commitment to the A-10. Although the USAF lacked enthusiasm for CAS, it remained a mission in need of a new aircraft.[409] Gen. William Momyer, TAC chief, stressed in May 1973 that CAS in Europe "is a different way of life than what our forces saw in Vietnam."[410] The following month, the USAF, attaching particular importance to killing tanks, chose the A-10 for full-scale development with its lethal 30 mm GAU Gatling gun, titanium "bathtub" cockpit, and engines positioned to reduce SAM vulnerability. Members of the specially formed Senate Subcommittee on Close Air Support, however, doubted the A-10's viability and demanded a fly-off against the A-7, the only pure strike aircraft then in the USAF inventory. Before the fly-off could be conducted, the Yom Kippur War occurred. As noted in the lessons section, potential danger to the A-10 program significantly affected how air force officials interpreted the Middle East fighting. When Senator Cannon, in a March 1974 hearing, referenced the USMOST report that the Israelis now believed CAS had to be conducted at high speed, Collins rejected this conclusion. Eventually the air force, similar to the army and the AAH, evolved from rejecting the Arab–Israeli combat to claiming it actually supported adopting the desired platform. For example, in June 1974 Lukeman declared that not only did Central Europe's bad weather particularly advantage the A-10 as the A-7's speed would be of far less value than in the clear visibility of the Middle East, but the A-10's superior ECM carrying capacity addressed a key Yom Kippur War lesson.[411] Regardless, USAF commitment to the A-10 remained firm, and after prevailing in the fly-off it became an integral part of the USAF's tactical aviation mix.

CONCLUSION

Although the US military undertook several military operations during the remainder of the 1970s and the 1980s, its next major conflict occurred almost twenty years after the Yom Kippur War. Army and air force units designed to defeat the Warsaw

Pact in Central Europe with better doctrine, improved organization, new weapons, and more realistic training fought Iraqi forces in the Persian Gulf War. In a six-week campaign, the air force excelled at night operations, SEAD, and precision munitions delivery, although operating in adverse weather remained a problem. In the climactic one-hundred-hour ground phase, the army's Big Five weapon systems and its AirLand Battle doctrine garnered extensive praise as units rapidly advanced, overwhelming the enemy and suffering few casualties. Enhancing the US military's dominance was "absolute control over the electromagnetic spectrum."[412] After the war, Jack Krings, former director of DOD's Operational Test and Evaluation, gleefully noted that "the high/low-tech debate is over," with the former investment vindicated.[413] The US military's performance generated much celebration as validation of the reform efforts initiated in the 1970s, even if the adversary was of a lower caliber than the Cold War–era Soviets. In a postwar Senate hearing, Maj. Gen. Barry McCaffrey (USA) responded to a question about the victory's speed by exclaiming that "this war didn't take 100 hours to win, it took 15 years."[414]

Lessons learned from the Yom Kippur War contributed to this extended effort with their instrumental, instructional, and inspirational influences, but the degree of that influence is difficult to gauge. As Kagan points out, although the 1970s "marked a true watershed in the history of the military art," the delayed battlefield demonstration of their effects until 1991 meant that "certain expansions and new ideas had entered into the equation, blurring the importance of the 1970s changes themselves."[415] Still, commentary after the Persian Gulf War frequently referenced insights from that earlier conflict. In discussing new systems with long development periods (e.g., JSTARS, Army Tactical Missile System) that showed great promise, Starry noted, "All the things that flowed from that train of thought out of the 1973 War went into the front end of the Gulf and came out the back a success."[416] James Kitfield adds that the 1st Brigade of the 24th Mechanized Infantry Division's advance into the Euphrates River Valley "was exactly the kind of swift, deep flanking attack that retired general Don Starry had once envisioned from the Golan Heights as his mind was helping concoct AirLand Battle."[417] Similarly for the air force, the stealth F-117s, inspired by the threat of dense IADs demonstrated in the Middle East, shined in safely and successfully bombing targets in Iraq's well-defended capital. While Operation Desert Storm air campaign chief Lt. Gen. Chuck Horner had participated in the Air Staff's post–Yom Kippur War evaluation, Brig. Gen. Larry Henry, architect of the EW component, "specifically credited Israeli experience [1973 and 1982] as having inspired his concept of operations."[418] Finally, the Arab–Israeli conflict helped spark the training revolution that most accounted for the Persian Gulf War effectiveness. As former USAF chief of staff Gen. Larry Welch emphasized in 1992, "Today, the quality and focus of training raises soldiers, sailors, airmen, and marines to the performance levels of 'combat veteran' before actual combat begins."[419]

By multiple metrics—money allocated, personnel assigned, time committed, material produced—the Yom Kippur War was the most extensive investigation of a foreign war ever undertaken by the US Armed Forces. The army effort particularly stands out. Israeli Maj. Gen. Abraham "Bren" Adan noted upon his arrival in Washington as military attaché in August 1974,

> I found that the American army had dozens of officers engaged in learning the lessons of the Yom Kippur War. Tens of thick volumes were produced; tactics, organizational structure of units, changes required in weapons arsenals—all of these were examined. I could not help making the comparison with our own methods. With the Americans, there is a scientific process of data collecting and an effort to adopt an objective approach. . . . To the Americans' credit it must be said that this admiration did not prevent them from analyzing the facts meticulously, pinpointing weak points and leveling criticism at several past and present IDF conceptions. I was very impressed by their intellectual openness and their scientific approach in eliciting lessons.[420]

The basis of Adan's praise stems from his comparison of the Americans' structured enterprise to an ad hoc Israeli approach. Is that praise warranted? As discussed, the investigation started slowly. In lobbying for a study of Israel's Peace for Galilee campaign in Lebanon, Starry in November 1982 complained that the army's initial fumbling "is so alarmingly reminiscent of our 1974 fumbling while trying to get lined up to learn about the Yom Kippur War."[421]

In particular, one can question the "scientific process" of these undertakings, given that the army, as well as the air force, by January 1974 had drawn their basic lessons from the Yom Kippur War. Much of the army's subsequent work seems like a search for evidence to support these conclusions versus a truly open investigation, even if it appeared that way to Adan. Senior TRADOC officers continued pressing Williams and other collectors for hard data throughout the first half of 1974 to facilitate the generation of supported recommendations. Twenty-five years later, Starry, upon reflection, criticized that "all too often the height and breadth of data and information could be measured in kilometers, the depth of analysis in millimeters."[422] Yet the potential value of such analysis for him is questionable as suggested by his follow-on statement that "in the end nothing changed significantly the conclusions we had drawn early on from walking the battlegrounds with those who had fought, listening to their descriptions of what had happened, and availing ourselves of the penetrating operational analysis."[423]

The air force did not even conduct an extensive data-intensive evaluation. The USAF approach was somewhat understandable given that the Yom Kippur War's aerial dimension represented an intensification of the Vietnam War rather than a departure as true for the ground combat. Moreover, it, like the IAF, possessed a culture less enamored with the pursuit of detailed information to guide behavior. Offsetting the risk of this neglect, many air force personnel, including leaders of the USMETVI, USMOST, and WSEG investigations, were present in Israel after the conflict and had ample opportunity to identify useful insights. The growing bond between American and Israeli aviators afforded the former the opportunity to benefit from the latter's experiences. Nonetheless, this philosophy made them more vulnerable to developments that countered initial expectations. Fortunately, preliminary judgments about the Middle East combat by the US Army and US Air Force proved fundamentally correct.

Importantly, the Yom Kippur War provided a sense of the modern conventional battlefield precisely when the US military refocused on it. In terms of core findings, American officers expressed surprise at what probably should have been the least surprising lesson. For the fourth time in the four wars studied, investigators emphasized the increased lethality of combat. This "discovery" says something about the nature of man's ability to devise weapons of ever greater destructiveness but also perhaps how—even for veterans—the violence of war exceeds imagination and memory. The conflict's other primary takeaway—including the increasing complexity of warfare, the growing significance of EW, and the expanding danger of IADs—contributed to an expectation that future fights would be short, intense, chaotic affairs in which forces needed to be ready at the outset. The Israelis' ability to prevail in such an environment despite suffering strategic surprise and numerical inferiority highlighted the critical need for well-trained personnel.

The most contentious assessments were army and air force findings that ATGMs and SAMs had not rendered the tank and aircraft obsolete. Investigation of the Arab–Israeli combat in conjunction with the Israelis marshaled evidence that supported these judgments. The analysis was especially valuable for the tank, given that a growing number of advocates in the defense community favored a move away from armor's lead role in ground forces. For example, at a March 1975 Senate hearing, Senator John Culver asked why the army's analysis of high kills by tanks in the Yom Kippur War "does not appear to hold up in any recent war game scenarios in NATO where the tank and other antitank weaponry are considered."[424] Army officers responded authoritatively that the conclusions from an actual intense war are "factually determined from physical examination of the tanks" compared to war games, which focus on only a small slice of simulated combat.[425] The USAF appreciated that the IAF, like Israeli ground forces, sharply reduced the loss rate suffered in the war's first days by altering tactics. Bottom line, although the services acknowledged the ATGMs and SAMs used in the Arab–Israeli fighting demonstrated a growing battlefield impact that needed to be addressed, they did not undermine the central role of tanks and aircraft.

When evidence from the Yom Kippur War threatened programs, however, the army and air force tended to display far less willingness to acknowledge available information. The most notable case was with the attack helicopter's viability. When the Israelis who had fought the war were adamant that helicopters would not be able to survive a battlefield with robust IADs, the Americans shrugged off this disruptive insight, citing their own unmatched "experience in using helicopters in difficult circumstances and in a high antiaircraft environment."[426] Some even asserted that the highly lethal battlefield demonstrated the need for a better antitank helicopter (the AAH) flown by well-trained aircrews with better tactics. Likewise, although the increased danger of IADs represented one of the air force's most basic lessons, aviators rejected that this challenge precluded the employment of a relatively slow, sturdy CAS aircraft (i.e., the A-10). Rather, aviators focused on elements that shaped the lesson in a way to favor their position. In this case, lethal air defense demonstrated that airborne FACs could not operate in modern combat, necessitating an attack aircraft able to perform this role itself.

In identifying and assessing the application of lessons, it is necessary to recognize that the army and air force used the conflict in three basic ways. First, officers employed information obtained from investigation of the Arab–Israeli combat *instructionally* for planning what to do or what is needed on the modern battlefield and how to prioritize efforts to satisfy service requirements. Collected data prompted numerous small but valuable changes that enhanced the US military's preparedness for future war (e.g., introduction of nonflammable hydraulic fluid, restored attention to chemical weapon defenses, increased war reserve stockpiles). Appreciation of requirements that had previously been unrecognized (e.g., ground-based SEAD), neglected (e.g., forward area air defense), or lacking urgency (e.g., standoff suppression, EW) led to notable responses. The army crafted a range of intensified or new initiatives (e.g., more realistic training, CEWI battalions, MLRS). At a minimum, Arab–Israeli combat provided evidence that the Active Defense and subsequent AirLand Battle approaches had merit and at maximum it guided how the ground forces planned to fight. Uniquely among the cases studied in this book, the USAF established an umbrella program (Pave Strike) of eleven existing R&D initiatives warranting acceleration based on findings. Beyond Pave Strike, the air force applied information to embrace a high/low tactical aviation mix of F-15s and F-16s as well as pursue support systems that enhanced battle management and EW capability.

Second, not surprisingly given that much of the data from the Arab–Israeli fighting validated prior understandings, the USA and USAF leaderships used the lessons *instrumentally* to overcome internal opposition, JCS and OSD interference, and White House and Congress obstruction to adopt already identified requirements. This type of influence usually receives less attention, but Yom Kippur War–derived evidence proved immensely useful leverage for senior officers, especially TRADOC (DePuy,

Starry) and TAC (Dixon, Creech) commanders. The demonstrated nature and lethality of combat justified a push for system upgrades and increased numbers of existing weapons (e.g., M-60 tanks, TOW ATGMs, ECM pods, Sidewinder missiles) to reduce the growing gap with Soviet forces. Even more importantly, the performance of newer Soviet weapons facilitated the development and ultimately acquisition of more advanced equipment (e.g., M1 tanks, Patriot SAMs, F-15s, AWACs), about which executive and legislative officials possessed reservations on cost and performance grounds. Additionally, the TRADOC leadership emphasized its application of Yom Kippur War lessons throughout the two-plus-year development of the new operations doctrine (FM100-5 [1976]) to steamroll opposition.

Critically, the conclusion that the IDF prevailed because of its superior officers and soldiers facilitated efforts to enhance training (e.g., introduce greater realism, construct better facilities, and increase simulator use). Given that high-quality, realistic training engendered opposition especially for large-scale initiatives (e.g., National Training Center, Red Flag) due to its significant costs and risks, army and air force advocates seized on the Middle East conflict to show the necessity of such activity. Technical and resource limitations did slow some aspects of the training revolution, but the Israeli example as well as positive results from the initial steps sustained momentum. Ultimately, the US Armed Forces obtained much improved tactical and operational proficiency from the better training. As Kagan concludes, this was especially true for the army, with DePuy, Gorman, and Starry creating "an American military able for the first time in its history to take the field on very short notice with a superb standard of training and a good deal of experience in highly realistic simulated combat."[427] Appropriately, some veterans from the time and scholars subsequently note that this success came at a cost, as it produced a force less able to adapt when engaged in other types of missions or facing unanticipated developments.[428]

Finally, beyond applying findings from what transpired, the Americans used study of the war *inspirationally* to imagine the future battlefield and pursue development of new solutions to prepare for it. As noted in prior chapters, such application entails risk, as it can be abused by officers wanting to project an environment that fits their preferred version of tomorrow. Yet, when done effectively, fueling imagination can be a highly productive way to use a foreign war. The air force and defense science community provided an excellent example of being inspired to respond to a clearly demonstrated problem of intense IADs with development of a stealth aircraft (the F-117) to operate undetected by enemy radars. In contrast to study of the war revealing a problem to be "solved," Starry, in the spring of 1977, had a problem to be solved for which his response was inspired by reexamination of the Yom Kippur War. He extrapolated from the Syrian multiphase advance and Peled's divisional counterattack to conceptualize about how to defeat Soviet follow-on echelons. This insight ultimately led to the highly praised AirLand Battle doctrine. A more questionable example was the potential for ATGM-equipped attack helicopters to operate effectively in high-threat areas as undertaken by Maddox, DePuy, and other senior officers. Starry later recalled that despite the absence of large number of armed helicopters in the Arab–Israeli fighting, "it was not difficult to foresee their introduction, postulate their effect on the battle, and analyze their impact on other factors that we could examine firsthand."[429] The Apache has served the army extremely well for decades, but it never had to fly against IADs of the density present in the Yom Kippur War, let alone that which would have been encountered in Central Europe.

The case study provides notable examples of the struggle to choose between lessons signaling contrary courses of action. The most basic such tension resulted from the highly lethal combat of the Yom Kippur War highlighting both the difficulty of defeating the initial attack as well as adequately supplying combat forces in modern war. How did the army with a force size capped at approximately 785,000 soldiers address this dilemma? Its leadership focused on the former, shifting personnel from support to combat positions. This choice enabled forty-eight more combat battalions, but by the October 1978 Nifty Nugget exercise, recognition existed of the cost in logistical capabilities, as only a few weeks of war could be supported. Did the army's behavior represent a misapplication of lessons? One could answer yes, as more balanced consideration would have preserved better distribution of personnel, but their actions were understandable given the extremely high threat perception of an initial Red Army advance in the mid-1970s. Alternatively, the air force leadership actually benefited from the Yom Kippur War, signaling the need for both technically cutting-edge F-15s to dominate improved Soviet weapons and cheaper but capable F-16s to keep the ratio of forces within a manageable level, as OSD had been pushing. Senior aviators accepted the necessity for a high/low tactical aviation mix, which worked out extremely well, especially given that the F-16 after modification turned out to be an effective fighter-bomber.

The inability to apply lessons fully due to a lack of resources is an understandable constraint that has hampered every case studied, but the army leadership's failure to account for how the Soviet response to its own lessons about the fighting would alter the challenge in Central Europe was a self-inflicted and dangerous failing. Most notably, the US Army concept adopted in 1976 was based on a faulty assumption that the Red Army would attack with concentrated thrusts, entailing greater risk as the communists shifted to a more decentralized, opportunistic approach. As Kretchik observed, problematically the new "doctrine had addressed lessons from the 1973 Arab-Israeli War, but the Soviets had also changed their precepts" out of recognition of modern weapons' lethality, especially ATGMs.[430] One can understand army leaders, especially DePuy, being driven by high threat perception and a desire for swift remedial action despite at least some awareness of changing Soviet views. Yet, with the new doctrine stressing the importance of understanding the enemy, ultimate judgment of the architects of FM100-5 (1976) must be critical because they based their approach on a flawed assessment of their opponent. Capturing the dynamic nature of war preparation in which militaries are simultaneously applying lessons ("learning from the learners") is a difficult challenge, especially as practitioners seek to maximize the information's political value before interest dissipates. Senior officers, however, must be cognizant of this challenge and consider its implications.

Ultimately, the oft-repeated characterization of the Yom Kippur War as "fortuitous" by key military reformers in the 1970s aptly captures the conflict from the American perspective. Study of its lessons contributed to the radical improvement in capability achieved by both the army and air force in the subsequent decade. One of the most critical benefits was motivating TRADOC and TAC to boost peacetime cooperation. Each of the earlier foreign wars examined had also shown the value of interservice cooperation, but that lesson had not been translated into improved partnerships (army–navy relations actually worsened as a result of applied findings in the Russo-Japanese War case). This time the urgency and importance of working together signaled by Arab–Israeli combat prompted concrete progress in key areas such as command and control and SEAD. The positive results are not surprising, given a highly favorable context with the US military coming out of a failed war and possessing an extremely high threat perception. If learning from a foreign war did not occur in this case, it would be unlikely to ever be a significant factor. Nonetheless, one must end on a cautionary note, given that much of the information from the conflict validated what army and air force officers already wanted to do. When the data jeopardized highly valued programs and approaches, as noted, they showed no reluctance to reject evidence as irrelevant or distort it to serve desired objectives.

NOTES

Epigraph: William DePuy, "Implications of the Middle East War on U.S. Army Tactics, Doctrine, and Systems," in *Selected Papers of General William E. DePuy*, comp. Richard Swain (Fort Leavenworth, KS: Combat Studies Institute, 1994), 111.

1. Frederick Kagan, *Finding the Target: Transformation of American Military Policy* (New York: Encounter, 2007), 19.

2. *Military Situation in the Far East: Hearings before the Committee on Armed Services and the Committee on Foreign Relations, United States Senate*, 82nd Congress, 1st session, part 2 (Washington, DC: Government Printing Office, 1951), May 15, p. 732.

3. Orwin Talbott, "1973 Mideast War Briefing," Box 1, Folder: List of Slides, Orwin Talbott Papers, US Army Heritage and Education Center at Carlisle Barracks, p. 19.

4. Robert Dixon, "The Range of Tactical Air Operations," *Strategic Review* 2 (Spring 1974): 24.

5. *Department of Defense Appropriations for Fiscal Year 1975*, part 1: *Hearing before a House Subcommittee of the Committee on Appropriations*, 93rd Congress (Washington, DC: Government Printing Office, 1974), February 27, p. 448.

6. JCS, Operations Directorate, *Middle East Crisis 1973 Lessons Learned Abstract* (Washington, DC: Joint Chiefs of Staff, March 1, 1974).

7. For good general discussions of naval lessons learned, see the declassified WSEG Report 249, *Assessment of the Weapons and Tactics Used in the October 1973 Middle East War*, October 1974, p. 22–26, 99–111 (accessed electronically via the CIA's FOIA Reading Room, http://www.cia.gov); and Benyamin Telem, "Naval Lessons of the Yom Kippur War," in *Military Aspects of the Israeli–Arab Conflict*, ed. Louis Williams (Tel Aviv: University Publishing Projects, 1975), 228–37.

8. (U) CACDA Report, *Analysis of Combat Data—1973 Mideast War*, vol. I–VIII, June–July 1974, SECRET NOFORN; and (U) WSEG Report 237, *Data from the October 1973 Middle East War*, vol. I–VII, October–November 1974, SECRET NOFORN (Except Israel).

9. Bruce Brant, "Battlefield Air Interdiction in the 1973 Middle East War and Its Significance to NATO Air Operations" (Master's thesis, Command and General Staff College, 1986), 12; also email exchange with Maj. R. Zach Alessi-Friedlander (USA), July 6, 2017.

10. Donn Starry, "Desert Storm Lessons Learned," September 18, 1991, oral history interview in *Press On! Selected Works of General Donn A. Starry*, vol. 2, ed. Lewis Sorley (Fort Leavenworth, KS: Combat Studies Institute Press, 2009), 1226.

11. William White, *US Tactical Air Power: Missions, Forces, and Costs* (Washington, DC: Brookings Institution, 1974), 69n10.

12. Jehuda Wallach, "The Yom Kippur War: A Review of the Main Battles in Retrospect—and Their Lessons," in *Military Aspects of the Israeli–Arab Conflict*, ed. Louis Williams (Tel Aviv: University Publishing Projects, 1975), 227.

13. John Burke, "Precision Weaponry: The Changing Nature of Modern Warfare," *Army* 24 (March 1974): 13.

14. Maurice F. Casey, *Oral History Interview* (Fairfax, VA: Air Force Public Affairs Alumni Association, 1995), 47–48; Walter Poole, *The Joint Chiefs of Staff and National Policy, 1973–1976* (Washington, DC: Office of the Chairman of the Joint Chiefs of Staff, 2015), 178; and Joseph Doyle, *The Yom Kippur War and the Shaping of the United States Air Force* (Maxwell AFB, AL: Air University Press, 2019), 18–19.

15. Lloyd R. Leavitt, *Following the Flag: An Air Force Officer Provides an Eyewitness View of Major Events and Policies during the Cold War* (Maxwell AFB, AL: Air University Press, 2010), 485–89; Doyle, *Yom Kippur War and Shaping of USAF*, 17–19; and Poole, *JCS*, 170.

16. John Ponturo, *Analytical Support for the Joint Chiefs of Staff: The WSEG Experience, 1948–1976* (Arlington, VA: Institute for Defense Analysis, July 1979), 320, 328; and R. Z. Alessi-Friedlander, "Learning to Win When Fighting Outnumbered: Operational Risk in the US Army, 1973–1982, and the Influence of the 1973 Arab-Israeli War" (Master's thesis, Command and General Staff College, 2016), 95.

17. Frederick C. Blesse, *Check Six: A Fighter Pilot Looks Back* (Mesa, AZ: Champlin Fighter Museum Press, 1987), 164.

18. For paragraph, see Leavitt, *Following the Flag*, 486–87, 495; Casey, *Oral History Interview*, 47–48; WSEG Report 249, p. ix, 2, 6, 8, 47–49, 52; Talbott to Maj. Gen. Howard Cooksey, February 14, 1974, Talbott to Maj. Gen. John Cushman, March 4, 1974, and Maj. Gen. Harold Aaron to Talbott, April 9, 1974, all Box 1, Folder: Messages, Orwin Talbott Papers; Donn Starry, "TRADOC's Analysis of the Yom Kippur War," March 16, 1999, speech in *Press On! Selected Works of General Donn A. Starry*, vol. 1, ed. Lewis Sorley (Fort Leavenworth, KS: Combat Studies Institute Press, 2009), 223; Marshall Michel III, "The Revolt of the Majors: How the Air Force Changed after Vietnam" (PhD diss., Auburn University, December 2006), 7, 186, 407–8; Doyle, *Yom Kippur War and Shaping of USAF*, 18–20; and Glenmore S. Trenear-Harvey, *Historical Dictionary of Air Intelligence* (Lanham, MD: Scarecrow, 2009), 67.

19. Blesse, *Check Six*, 164.

20. WSEG Report 249, p. 6, 47–48.

21. See Abstract 1-2, Defense Intelligence Agency, "Middle East Equipment Exploitation," Technical Intelligence Bulletin Series, in King, *Middle East Crisis 1973 Lessons Learned Abstracts*.

22. US MOIST Team Visit to Jordan Trip Report, May 31, 1974, Box 1, Folder: Cover Letters and Attached Trip Report; and US Military Visit to Egypt Trip Report, July 31, 1974, Box 2, Folder: Report on the US Military Visit to Egypt, July 14–23, 1974, Orwin Talbott Papers.

23. For paragraph see Brig. Gen. Morris Brady memorandum, February 26, 1974, Box 1, Folder: Collection and Exploitation of Information on the Israeli-Arab War; Lt. Gen. Elmer Almquist to DePuy, January 23, 1974, Box 1, Folder: Messages; Abrams to Talbott, March 25, 1974, Box 1, Folder: Correspondence, all in Orwin Talbott Papers; DePuy, January 14, 1974, letter to Abrams in *Selected Papers of General William E. DePuy*, 69, 74; Paul Herbert, *Deciding What Has to Be Done: General William E. DePuy and the 1976 Edition of FM100-5* (Fort Leavenworth, KS: Combat Studies Institute, July 1988), 30; and John Cushman, *Fort Leavenworth—A Memoir*, part 2, *1973–1976* (self-published, September 2001), 34, http://www.west-point.org/publications/cushman/6aVolumeSix.pdf.

24. Talbott, "1973 Mideast War Briefing," 1.

25. Donn A. Starry, "October 1973 Mideast War," May 12, 1975, Box 59, Folder 3, Donn Starry Papers, US Army Heritage and Education Center at Carlisle Barracks; Starry, "Reminiscences of General Creighton Abrams," December 14, 1976, oral history interview in *Press On!*, 2:1194; and Starry, "Desert Storm Lessons Learned," 2:1225, 1232–33.

26. Starry, "Desert Storm Lessons Learned," 2:1225.

27. Abrams memorandum, April 1, 1974, Box 1, Folder: Briefings on October War—Europe, and Talbott to Weyand, June 19, 1974, Box 1, Folder: Briefings on October War in Far East, both in Orwin Talbott Papers.

28. For paragraph, see Brady memorandum, February 26, 1974; Herbert, *Deciding What Has to Be Done*, 30; Charles Shrader, *History of Operations Research in the US Army*, vol. 3: *1973–1995* (Washington, DC: Center of Military History, 2009), 127; Maj. Gen. Robert McAlister to Talbott, July 12, 1974, Box 1, Folder: Correspondence, Orwin Talbott Papers; Alessi-Friedlander, "Learning to Win," 94–98; and DePuy, "Implications of the Middle East War," 104–5.

29. Brady memorandum, February 26, 1974; Maj. Gen. John Cushman to Talbott, March 26, 1974, Box 1, Folder: Correspondence, Orwin Talbott Papers.

30. Williams to Talbott, June 24, 1974, p. 1, and attached handwritten note from DePuy to Talbott, Box 1, Folder: Letter by Col. Bruce I. Williams (with enclosures) about the Mid-East War and Lessons Learned, Orwin Talbott Papers; see also McAlister to Talbott, July 12, 1974, and Williams to DePuy, August 22, 1974, Box 1, Folder: Correspondence February–August 1974, Orwin Talbott Papers.

31. Brian Laslie, *The Air Force Way of War: US Tactics and Training after Vietnam* (Lexington: University Press of Kentucky, 2015), 34.

32. Robert Futrell, *Ideas, Concepts, Doctrine*, vol. 2: *Basic Thinking in the United States Air Force, 1961–1984* (Maxwell AFB, AL: Air University Press, 1989), 484.

33. Leavitt, *Following the Flag*, 477; see also *Military Procurement Supplemental, Fiscal Year 1974: Hearing before the Senate Committee on Armed Services*, 93rd Congress (Washington, DC: Government Printing Office, 1974), March 12, p. 38.

34. Leavitt, *Following the Flag*, 498–501.

35. *Department of Defense Authorization for Fiscal Year 1975*, part 8: *Hearing before the Senate Tactical Air Power Subcommittee of the Committee on Armed Services*, 93rd Congress (Washington, DC: Government Printing Office, 1974), March 20, p. 4448–50; Abstract 4-1, Deputy Chief of Staff, USAF, Plans and Operations, "Implications of the 1973 Middle East War," January 18, 1974, and Abstract 4-2, Air Force Special Communications Center, Electronic Warfare Evaluation of Middle East War, October 1973, both in King, *Middle East Crisis 1973 Lessons Learned Abstracts*; Talbott to Dixon, February 25, 1974, Box 1, Folder: Correspondence, Orwin Talbott Papers; and Doyle, *Yom Kippur War and Shaping of USAF*, 19–20.

36. *Department of Defense Appropriations for Fiscal Year 1975*, part 4: *Department of the Air Force, Hearing before DOD Subcommittee of the Senate Committee on Appropriations*, 93rd Congress (Washington, DC: Government Printing Office, 1974), May 2, p. 585.

37. WSEG Report 249, p. 75; Williams to Talbott, June 24, 1974, Inclosure 3: Organization of the Tank Platoon and Battalion Company, 1-3.

38. *Department of Defense Appropriations for Fiscal Year 1975*, part 4: *Research, Development, Test, and Evaluation, Hearing before a House Subcommittee of the Committee on Appropriations*, 93rd Congress (Washington, DC: Government Printing Office, 1974), April 29, p. 467.

39. Quoted in Talbott to Aaron, June 25, 1974, p. 2, Box 1, Folder: Briefing on October War in Far East, Orwin Talbott Papers.

40. Talbott to Aaron, June 25, 1974, and Aaron to Talbott, June 27, 1974, Box 1, Folder: Briefing on October War in Far East, Orwin Talbott Papers.

41. Alessi-Friedlander, "Learning to Win," 102.

42. Phillip Karber, "The Soviet Anti-Tank Debate," *Survival* 18, no. 3 (May–June 1976): 105.

43. Karber, 105.

44. Karber, 105–11; and Neil Munro, *The Quick and the Dead: Electronic Combat and Modern Warfare* (New York: St. Martin's, 1991), 123–31, 179–80.

45. Ronny Bragger, "Lessons Learned: 1973 Middle East War A Soviet Perspective" (Student research report, US Army Russian Institute, 1981), 2.

46. *DOD Appropriations FY75*, part 1, February 27, 1974, p. 450.

47. *DOD Appropriations FY75*, March 6, p. 610.

48. Talbott, "1973 Mideast War Briefing," 1.

49. *DOD Appropriations FY75*, part 1, February 27, 1974, p. 450.

50. For paragraph, see DePuy, "Implications of the Middle East War," 85; *DOD Appropriations FY75*, part 1, February 27, 1974, p. 452, and April 29, 1974, p. 466; Joint Chiefs of Staff, *Logistics Lessons Learned 1973 Middle East War*, November 27, 1974, appendix E (Washington, DC: Joint Chiefs of Staff, 1975); WSEG Report 249, p. 27, 49, A3; Williams to Talbott, June 24, 1974, Inclosure 4: Combat Service Support; Henry Miley Jr. "Mid-East War Logistics," *Army Logistician* 6, no. 4 (July–August 1974): 2–5; and Doyle, *Yom Kippur War and Shaping of USAF*, 25–26.

51. *Military Procurement Supplemental, FY74*, March 12, 1974, p. 81.

52. Donn Starry, "Armor Conference Keynote Address," *Armor* (November–December 1975), in *Press On!*, 1:152.

53. Starry, "October 1973 Mideast War," 2–6.

54. Miley, "Mid-East War Logistics," 3.

55. Dixon, "Range of Tactical Operations," 23–24.

56. For paragraph, Williams to Talbott, June 24, 1974; WSEG Report 249, p. 13, 18, 63–64, 67–68, 84; Starry, "TRADOC's Analysis of the Yom Kippur War," 1:222–23; Alessi-Friedlander, "Learning to Win," 89–98; Antoine Bousquet, *The Scientific Way of Warfare: Order and Chaos on the Battlefields of Modernity* (New York: Columbia University Press, 2009), 128–30, 161; William Richardson, "Trip to Israel by Assistant Commandant, US Army Infantry School, 29 July–5 August, 1974," Box 1, Folder: Messages, Orwin Talbott Papers; and *Military Procurement Supplemental, FY74*, March 12, 1974, p. 6.

57. Leavitt, *Following the Flag*, 489.

58. "Israel's Officer Casualties Soar," *Armed Forces Journal* 111, no. 7 (March 1974): 18.

59. Williams to Talbott, June 24, 1974, p. 3.

60. Starry, "Desert Storm Lessons Learned," 2:1226.

61. Williams to Talbott, June 24, 1974, Inclosure 8: General Notes, 1.

62. Dixon, "Range of Tactical Air Operations," 24; and *DOD Appropriations FY75*, May 2, 1974, p. 585.

63. *DOD Appropriations FY75*, March 6, 1974, p. 611.

64. Williams to Talbott, June 24, 1974, Inclosure 8: General Notes, 1.

65. *DOD Authorization FY75*, March 20, 1974, p. 4449–50.

66. Paul Gorman, "How to Win Outnumbered," January 8, 1974, in *Strategy and Tactics for Learning: The Papers of General Paul F. Gorman* (Fort Leavenworth, KS: Combat Studies Institute Press, 2011), 6.

67. Robert Scales, *Certain Victory: The US Army in the Gulf War* (Washington, DC: Potomac, 2006), 10; also see *DOD Appropriations FY75*, April 29, 1974, p. 466.

68. DePuy letter to Abrams, January 14, 1974, p. 73.

69. Talbott, "1973 Mideast War Briefing," 21.

70. Starry, "American Military Thought: A Perspective," January 17, 1989, speech in *Press On!*, 1:436.

71. For paragraph, see *Department of Defense Authorization for Fiscal Year 1975*, part 8: *Military Procurement, Hearing before the Senate Tactical Air Power Subcommittee of the Committee on Armed Services*, 93rd Congress (Washington, DC: Government Printing Office, 1974), March 13, p. 4244, 4249–50; Gorman, "How to Win Outnumbered," 6–7; WSEG Report 249, p. 21, 48,

92–94, A2–3; and Williams to Talbott, June 24, 1974, p. 3–4, Inclosure 8: General Notes.

72. *Military Procurement Supplemental, FY74*, March 12, 1974, p. 83.

73. *DOD Appropriations FY75*, April 29, 1974, p. 467.

74. DePuy letter to Abrams, January 14, 1974, p. 73.

75. Starry, "TRADOC's Analysis of the Yom Kippur War," 1:223.

76. Williams to Talbott, June 24, 1974, p. 3–4.

77. Michel, "Revolt of the Majors," 185.

78. Edward Luttwak and Daniel Horowitz, *The Israeli Army, 1948–1973* (Cambridge, MA: Abt Books, 1983), 327–36.

79. Paul Gorman, "Infantry in Mid-Intensity Battle," January 22, 1974, in *Strategy and Tactics for Learning*, 8; and Starry, "Observations on the Tank-Antitank Battlefield," *Armor* (January–February 1974), in *Press On!*, 1:229.

80. Talbott, "1973 Mideast War Briefing," 20.

81. For paragraph, see Starry, "October 1973 Mideast War," 2-6 to 2-7; WSEG Report 249, p. 9–10, 18–19, 56, 85–86; William DePuy letter to John Culver, May 12, 1975, in *Selected Papers of General William E. DePuy*, 167; Starry, "Tanks Forever," *Armor* (July–August 1975), in *Press On!*, 1:49; and Saul Bronfeld, "Fighting Outnumbered: The Impact of the Yom Kippur War on the US Army," *Journal of Military History* 71, no. 2 (April 2007): 471–72.

82. Warren Lennon, "The Death of the Tank," *ARMOR* 81, no. 1 (January–February 1972): 4–20; and Kagan, *Finding the Target*, 37.

83. The Combat Vehicle Assessment Team found that 8 out of 119 IDF tanks examined were exclusively hit by Sagger ATGMs, while another 3 were hit by Saggers and other antitank munitions, and 18 hits were from unknown antitank munitions (possibly Saggers). Thus, ATGMs accounted for 8 (7 percent) to 29 (24 percent) of the 119 tanks examined. Analysts cautioned that up to 200 Israeli tanks remained in Egyptian-controlled territory and thus not included in the study, many of which were destroyed or disabled early in the war during a period of greater ATGM effectiveness. WSEG Report 249, p. 10, 56.

84. Starry, "October 1973 Mideast War," 2-1.

85. T. P. Schweider, *The Main Battle Tanks of the Yom Kippur War* (San Diego: Simulation Design Corporation, 1975), 26; emphasis original.

86. DePuy letter to Abrams, January 14, 1974, p. 71–72; Starry, "October 1973 Mideast War," 2-8; and Gorman, "How to Win Outnumbered," 6.

87. Gorman, "How to Win Outnumbered," 7.

88. Williams to Talbott, June 24, 1974, Inclosure 3: Organization of the Tank Platoon and Battalion Company, 1–3.

89. Starry, "October 1973 Mideast War," 2–13; for paragraph, see DePuy, "Implications of the Middle East War," 82, 104–5; WSEG Report 249, p. 6–7, 46–49; and Williams to Talbott, June 24, 1974, Inclosure 2: Tank Main Gun Ammunition Requirements, 4-5, and Inclosure 7: Anti-Tank Guided Missiles, 1.

90. For paragraph, see WSEG Report 249, p. 8–10, 52–56; Starry, "Observations on the Tank-Antitank Battlefield," 1:229; *TRADOC Bulletin 2—Soviet ATGM's: Capabilities and Countermeasures*, February 1975, p. 3, 6–13, 18–19, 23–25, http://www.apps.dtic.mil; and DePuy, "Implications of the Middle East War," 81, 85.

91. Williams to Talbott, June 24, 1974, Inclosure 7: Anti-Tank Guided Missiles, 1 (emphasis original).

92. For paragraph, see *DOD Appropriations FY75*, February 27, 1974, p. 451; and Starry, "October 1973 Mideast War," 2-7.

93. Quoted in Shmuel Gordon, "The Air Force and the Yom Kippur War: New Lessons," *Israel Affairs* 6, no. 1 (1999): 222.

94. DePuy letter to Abrams, January 14, 1974, p. 71.

95. Talbott, "1973 Mideast War Briefing," 20.

96. WSEG Report 249, p. 13.

97. For paragraph, see WSEG Report 249, p. 10–11, 56–62, A1; Miley, "Mid-East War Logistics," 4; and Boyd Dastrup, *King of Battle: A Branch History of the US Army's Field Artillery* (Fort Monroe, VA: TRADOC, 1992), 290, 294.

98. WSEG Report 249, p. 11.

99. John Kreis, *Air Warfare and Air Base Air Defense, 1914–1973* (Washington, DC: Office of Air Force History, 1988), 328, 337.

100. Williams to DePuy, August 22, 1974, p. 3.

101. Quoted in Benjamin Jensen, *Forging the Sword: Doctrinal Change in the US Army* (Stanford, CA: Stanford University Press, 2016), 37.

102. William Rees, "TAC AIR: Member of the Team," *Infantry* 66, no. 3 (May–June 1976): 20; see also Donald Alberts, "A Call from the Wilderness," *Air University Review* 27, no. 6 (November–December 1976): 38.

103. *DOD Appropriations FY75*, March 6, 1974, p. 610; see also Talbott, "1973 Mideast War Briefing," 20.

104. *Fiscal Year 1976 and July–September 1976 Transition Period DOD Authorization*, part 6, *Hearing before the Senate R&D Subcommittee of the Committee of Armed Services*, 94th Congress (Washington, DC: Government Printing Office, 1975), March 25, p. 3562.

105. DePuy letter to Abrams, January 14, 1974, p. 71.

106. WSEG Report 249, p. 69.

107. WSEG Report 249, p. 74; and Kreis, *Air Warfare*, 334.

108. For paragraph, see Williams to Talbott, June 24, 1974, Inclosure 4: Combat Service Support, 1-3; Miley, "Mideast War Logistics," 4–5; and WSEG Report 249, p. 7, 49, 51, A3.

109. For paragraph, see WSEG Report 249, p. 66–67; and Jonathan Tucker, *War of Nerves: Chemical Warfare from World War I to Al-Qaeda* (New York: Anchor, 2006), 227–30.

110. *DOD Appropriations for FY 1975*, March 5, p. 648.

111. DePuy, "Implications of the Middle East War," 105.

112. Williams to Talbott, June 24, 1974, Inclosure 8: General Notes, 1.

113. Quoted in Talbott to Raphael Eitan, March 5, 1974, p. 1, Box 1, Folder: Correspondence, Orwin Talbott Papers.

114. Talbott to Col. John Prillaman, May 19, 1974, p. 2–3, Box 1, Folder: Briefings on October War—Europe, Orwin Talbott Papers.

115. DePuy letter to Abrams, January 14, 1974, p. 73.

116. For paragraph, see DePuy letter to Abrams, January 14, 1974, p. 72–73; Gorman,

"Infantry in Mid-Intensity Battle," 6, 11; Starry, "October 1973 Mideast War," 2-4 to 2-7; and WSEG Report 249, p. 7–8, 11, 28, 51–52, 56, 60.

117. William DePuy, "Letter to R. W. Komer, the RAND Corporation," April 24, 1975, in *Selected Papers of General William E. DePuy*, 158.

118. Starry, "The Central Battle," April 24, 1978, speech in *Press On!*, 1:315.

119. *DOD Authorization FY75*, March 20, 1974, p. 4449; WSEG Report 249, p. 13, 77–79; Kreis, *Air Warfare*, 336–37; and Doyle, *Yom Kippur War and Shaping of USAF*, 4–6, 22–24.

120. Quoted in Laslie, *Air Force Way of War*, 38.

121. Quoted in Laslie, 38.

122. Dixon, "Range of Tactical Air Operations," 23.

123. Quoted in Futrell, *Ideas, Concepts, Doctrine*, 487.

124. For paragraph, see WSEG Report 249, p. 14, 70–74, 79; *Department of Defense Appropriations for Fiscal Year 1975*, part 9, *Hearing before the House Subcommittee on DOD Appropriations of the Committee on Appropriations*, 93rd Congress (Washington, DC: Government Printing Office, 1974), June 26, p. 281; *Military Procurement FY 1975*, part 8, *Hearing before the Senate Subcommittee on Tactical Air Power of the Committee on Armed Services*, 93rd Congress (Washington, DC: Government Printing Office, 1974), March 14, p. 4310–11; and Kenneth P. Werrell, *Archie, Flak, AAA, and SAM: A Short Operational History of Ground-Based Air Defense* (Maxwell AFB, AL: Air University Press, 1988), 140–43.

125. *Department of Defense Appropriations for Fiscal Year 1975*, Part 4: *Hearing before the Senate Subcommittee on DOD Appropriations of the Committee on Appropriations*, 93rd Congress (Washington, DC: Government Printing Office, 1974), March 7, p. 4–5.

126. Leavitt, *Following the Flag*, 493–94.

127. WSEG Report 249, p. 71.

128. Leavitt, *Following the Flag*, 494–95; also see Doyle, *Yom Kippur War and Shaping of USAF*, 24–25, 42–46.

129. Dixon, "Range of Tactical Air Operations," 23.

130. *DOD Appropriations FY75*, June 26, 1974, p. 285.

131. WSEG Report 249, p. 73–74; Futrell, *Ideas, Concepts, Doctrine*, 488; and Kreis, *Air Warfare*, 331, 337.

132. Doyle, *Yom Kippur War and Shaping of USAF*, 31.

133. For paragraph, see WSEG Report 249, p. 22, 73–74, 88, 97–98; *DOD Authorization FY75*, March 20, 1974, p. 4449; Leavitt, *Following the Flag*, 474, 494; "Yom Kippur Fighting Underscores EW Importance," *Electronic Warfare* 6 (January 1974): 24, 36; Werrell, *Archie*, 143–44; and Doyle, *Yom Kippur War and Shaping of USAF*, 24.

134. Quoted in Edgar O'Ballance, *No Victor, No Vanquished: The Yom Kippur War* (San Rafael, CA: Presidio, 1978), 306.

135. For paragraph, see *DOD Authorization FY75*, March 14, 1974, p. 4316; *DOD Authorization FY75*, March 20, 1974, p. 4448; Dixon, "Range of Tactical Air Operations," 23; and WSEG Report 249, p. 16–21, 80–89, 94–96.

136. *Department of Defense Appropriations for Fiscal Year 1975*, part 2: *Department of the Air Force, Hearing before a House Subcommittee of the Committee on Appropriations*, 93rd Congress (Washington, DC: Government Printing Office, 1974), April 1, p. 272.

137. *DOD Appropriations FY75*, May 2, 1974, p. 585.

138. *DOD Appropriations FY75*, April 1, 1974, p. 272.

139. For paragraph, see WSEG Report 249, p. 20, 89–90; and "DOD Military Team Visit to Egypt Trip Report," July 31, 1974, Appendix E, Part IV, Box 2, Folder: Report on the US Military Visit to Egypt, July 14–23, 1974, Orwin Talbott Papers.

140. *DOD Authorization FY75*, March 13, 1974, p. 4244.

141. *DOD Appropriations FY75*, May 2, 1974, p. 585; and Dixon, "Range of Tactical Air Operations," 24.

142. *DOD Authorization FY75*, March 14, 1974, p. 4315.

143. For paragraph, see *DOD Authorization FY75*, March 14, 1974, p. 4308–17; and WSEG Report 249, p. 13, 17–19, 28, 33, 82–86.

144. Brant, "Battlefield Air Interdiction," 76–77.

145. Futrell, *Ideas, Concepts, Doctrine*, 547.

146. For paragraph, see *DOD Appropriations FY75*, June 26, 1974, p. 280–82, 285; and WSEG Report 249, p. 17–18, 83–84.

147. *DOD Authorization FY75*, March 14, 1974, p. 4312.

148. *DOD Authorization FY75*, March 14, 1974, p. 4312.

149. For paragraph see *DOD Authorization FY75*, March 13, 1974, p. 4241–52; WSEG Report 249, p. 20–21, 90–94; and Michel, "Revolt of the Majors," 155–57.

150. For paragraph, see Lon Nordeen, *Air Warfare in the Missile Age*, 2nd ed. (Washington, DC: Smithsonian Books, 2010), 148; Laslie, *Air Force Way of War*, 49–50; and *DOD Authorization FY75*, March 13, 1974, p. 4249–51.

151. *DOD Authorization FY75*, March 13, 1974, p. 4251.

152. For paragraph, see Poole, *JCS*, 4–10, 28; Michel, "Revolt of the Majors," 174–75, 247; and Lewis Sorley, *Thunderbolt: From the Battle of the Bulge to Vietnam and Beyond: General Creighton Abrams and the Army of His Times* (New York: Simon & Schuster, 1992), 333–35, 345–52, 360–63.

153. For paragraph, see William E. DePuy, *Changing an Army: An Oral History of General William E. DePuy, USA Retired*, Romie Brownlee and William Mullen, interviewers (Carlisle, PA: Military History Institute Senior Officer Oral History Program, 1979), 171–73, 180–84; Roger Spiller, "In the Shadow of the Dragon: Doctrine and the US Army after Vietnam," *RUSI Journal* 142, no. 6 (December 1997): 44–45; John Romjue, Susan Canedy, and Anne Chapman, *Prepare the Army for War: A Historical Overview of the Army Training and Doctrine Command, 1973–1993* (Washington, DC: TRADOC, 1993), 9–10; and Herbert, *Deciding What Has to Be Done*, 7, 15–16, 21–23.

154. Starry, "TRADOC Organization and Rationale," February 5, 1982, letter in *Press On!*, 1:936.

155. Starry, "Reminiscences," 2:1193.

156. For paragraph, see *Fiscal Year 1976 and July–September 1976 Transition Period Authorization*, part 2: *Hearing before the Senate Committee on Armed Services*, 94th Congress (Washington, DC: Government Printing Office, 1975), February 7, p. 403, 452–53; *Research and Development, Fiscal Year 1976 and 1976 Transition*, part 6: *Hearing before the Research and Development Subcommittee of the Committee on Armed Services*, 94th Congress (Washington, DC: Government Printing

Office, 1975), March 17, p. 3168, 3205, 3219; Kevin Sheehan, "Preparing for an Imaginary War? Examining Peacetime Functions and Changes of Army Doctrine" (PhD diss., Harvard University Press, 1988), 151–53; and Philmon Erickson, "The '73 War: Implications for US Army Forces in NATO" (Master's thesis, Command and General Staff College, 1978), 139–43.

157. Herbert, *Deciding What Has to Be Done*, 9.

158. Quoted in Kagan, *Finding the Target*, 20.

159. For paragraph, see Bronfeld, "Fighting Outnumbered," 473–74; and Richard Swain, "AirLand Battle," in *Camp Colt to Desert Storm: The History of US Armored Forces*, ed. George Hofmann and Donn Starry (Lexington: University Press of Kentucky, 1999), 368.

160. George Knapp, "Antiarmor Operations on the Golan Heights, October 1973," in *Combined Arms in Battle since 1939*, ed. Roger Spiller (Fort Leavenworth, KS: Command and General Staff College, 1992), 27.

161. For paragraph, see Richard Stewart, gen. ed., *American Military History*, vol. 2: *The United States Army in a Global Era, 1917–2008*, 2nd ed. (Washington, DC: Center of Military History, 2010), 373, 376, 379–81; Scales, *Certain Victory*, 6–8; Starry, "Force Structure Issues," November 30, 1989, speech, in *Press On!*, 1:472; *DOD Appropriations FY75*, March 5, 1974, p. 610, 617, 644; and *DOD Authorization FY76*, February 7, 1975, p. 370–73, 401, 416, 473–75.

162. Herbert, *Deciding What Has to Be Done*, 5.

163. Quoted in Sheehan, "Preparing for an Imaginary War," 169.

164. For paragraph, see William Gardner Bell and Karl Cocke, eds., *Department of the Army Historical Summary, Fiscal Year 1973* [hereafter, *DAHS FY73*] (Washington, DC: Center of Military History, 1977), 6, 45–46; Romjue, Canedy, and Chapman, *Prepare the Army*, 5–10; and John Cushman, *ORAL HISTORY: Lieutenant General John H. Cushman, US Army, Retired*, vol. 5: *Leavenworth, Korea, and Reflections on a Career* (self-published, 2014), http://www.west-point.org/publications/5-VolumeFive.pdf, 21-1 to 21-3.

165. Jensen, *Forging the Sword*, 31.

166. Col. Edwin Scribner, quoted in Sheehan, "Preparing for an Imaginary War," 167; William DePuy, "Presentation to the TRADOC Commanders' Vision '91 Conference," October 5, 1988, in *Selected Papers of General William E. DePuy*, 431.

167. Starry, "Development of Doctrine," March 19, 1993, oral history interview in *Press On!*, 2:1261.

168. For paragraph, see Kagan, *Finding the Target*, 36, 40–41; David Trybula, *Big Five: Lessons for Today and Tomorrow* (Alexandria, VA: Institute for Defense Analyses, May 2012), 67; and Romjue, Canedy, & Chapman, *Prepare the Army*, 44.

169. Herbert, *Deciding What Has to Be Done*, 77.

170. William DePuy, "The Further Work of the TRADOC," May 25, 1977 speech, in *Selected Papers of General William E. DePuy*, 256.

171. For paragraph, see *DAHS FY73*; *DOD Authorization FY76*, February 7, 1975, p. 380; and *Department of Defense Appropriations for Fiscal Year 1976*, part 2: *Army, Hearing before a Senate Subcommittee of the Committee on Appropriations*, 94th Congress (Washington, DC: Government Printing Office, 1975), March 12, p. 23, 37–40, 48–49.

172. *DAHS FY73*, p. 105–7; Karl Cocke, ed., *Department of the Army Historical Summary, Fiscal Year 1974* [hereafter, *DAHS FY74*] (Washington, DC: Center of Military History, 1978), 83–85;

and Karl Cocke, ed., *Department of the Army Historical Summary, Fiscal Year 1975* [hereafter, *DAHS FY75*] (Washington, DC: Center of Military History, 1978), 70–71.

173. Poole, *JCS*, 29.

174. *DOD Authorization FY76*, February 7, 1975, p. 377–78; DOD *Authorization FY76*, March 12, 1975, p. 23.

175. Starry, "Modernization," April 10, 1980, speech in *Press On!*, 1:674.

176. DePuy, *Changing an Army*, 190.

177. Starry, "Desert Storm Lessons Learned," 2:1225.

178. Starry, 2:1225.

179. DePuy letter to Komer, April 24, 1975, p. 158.

180. Bronfeld, "Fighting Outnumbered," 468.

181. Bronfeld, 496.

182. Spiller, "Shadow of Dragon," 47.

183. Bronfeld, "Fighting Outnumbered," 468.

184. Bronfeld, 468, 481–82.

185. Bronfeld, 472.

186. Quoted in Henry Gole, *General William E. DePuy: Preparing the Army for Modern War* (Lexington: University Press of Kentucky, 2008), 240.

187. Alessi-Friedlander, "Learning to Win," 99.

188. Quoted in Bronfeld, "Fighting Outnumbered," 466.

189. DePuy letter to Weyand, February 18, 1976, p. 179–80; and Sheehan, "Preparing for an Imaginary War," 154, 169, 173.

190. William DePuy, "Modern Battle Tactics," August 17, 1974, in *Selected Papers of General William E. DePuy*, 138.

191. Headquarters, Department of the Army, *Field Manual 100-5: Operations*, July 1, 1976, http://www.cgsc.contentdm.oclc.org; emphasis original.

192. For paragraph, see Alessi-Friedlander, "Learning to Win," 102, 110–13; Bronfeld, "Fighting Outnumbered," 483; Jensen, *Forging the Sword*, 42–46; and John Romjue, *From Active Defense to AirLand Battle: The Development of Army Doctrine, 1973–1982* (Fort Monroe, VA: TRADOC Historical Office, 1984), 4–5.

193. DePuy, "Implications of the Middle East War," 94.

194. Starry, "Armor Conference Keynote Address," 1:154.

195. DePuy, "Implications of the Middle East War," 77.

196. Donn Starry, "Reflections," in *Camp Colt to Desert Storm: The History of U.S. Armored Forces*, ed. George Hofmann and Donn Starry (Lexington: University Press of Kentucky, 1999), 550.

197. Jensen, *Forging the Sword*, 42.

198. Bronfeld, "Fighting Outnumbered," 483; also see Starry, "Active Defense," Letter to Maj. Gen. C. P. Benedict, 1st Infantry Division (Mech), March 13, 1978, in *Press On!*, 1:301.

199. For paragraph, see DePuy letter to Weyand, August 18, 1976, p. 180; Herbert, *Deciding What Has to Be Done*, 39–48, 53–59, 80–82, 90–92; Spiller, "Shadow of Dragon," 47–50; Sheehan, "Preparing for an Imaginary War," 173–88, 191, 194–95; and Starry, "Life and Career of General Donn A. Starry," February 1986, oral history interviews in *Press On!*, 2:1110–15, 1125–26.

200. Starry to William DePuy letter, July 8, 1974, in *Press On!*, 1:272; emphasis original.

201. Starry to DePuy, July 8, 1974, in *Press On!*, 1:272.

202. Adam Joyce, "The Politics of 'the Army You Have': Change and Continuity in the US Military, 1972–2008" (PhD diss., New School for Social Research, 2012), 200.

203. Spiller, "Shadow of Dragon," 48.

204. Herbert, *Deciding What Has to Be Done*, 90.

205. For paragraph, see Herbert, *Deciding What Has to Be Done*, 85, 93; DePuy letter to Weyand, August 18, 1976, p. 181–82; Spiller, "Shadow of Dragon," 49–51; and Bronfeld, "Fighting Outnumbered," 488–89, 497.

206. Sheehan, "Preparing for an Imaginary War," 195; emphasis original.

207. Sheehan, 197–98.

208. William DePuy, "Talking Paper on Field Manual, 100-5, Operations," July 8, 1976, in *Selected Papers of General William E. DePuy*, 194.

209. For paragraph, see Spiller, "Shadow of Dragon," 51–52; Romjue, *Active Defense to Air-Land Battle*, 13–21; Sheehan, "Preparing for an Imaginary War," 199–203, 216–17; and Herbert, *Deciding What Has to Be Done*, 96–105.

210. Herbert, *Deciding What Has to Be Done*, 100.

211. Sheehan, "Preparing for an Imaginary War," 212.

212. For paragraph, see Phillip Karber, "The Tactical Revolution in Soviet Military Doctrine, Part I," *Military Review* 57, no. 11 (November 1977): 83–85; Shimon Naveh, *In Pursuit of Military Excellence: The Evolution of Operational Theory* (New York: Frank Cass, 1997), 272–73; and Sheehan, "Preparing for an Imaginary War," 213–17.

213. Jensen, *Forging the Sword*, 61.

214. Gregory Fontenot and Matthew Roberts, "Plugging Holes and Mending Fences," *Infantry* 68, no. 3 (May–June 1978): 34–36; see also Donald Griffin, "If the Soviets Don't Mass," *Military Review* 59, no. 2 (February 1979): 2–13.

215. Quoted in Romjue, *Active Defense to AirLand Battle*, 17.

216. For paragraph, see Robert J. Dixon, "TAC-TRADOC Dialogue," *Strategy Review* 6, no. 1 (Winter 1978): 45–46; Herbert, *Deciding What Has to Be Done*, 68–72; and Futrell, *Ideas, Concepts, Doctrine*, 530, 539–42.

217. Quoted in Laslie, *Air Force Way of War*, 101.

218. For paragraph, see Futrell, *Ideas, Concepts, Doctrine*, 521–27; and Trybula, *Big Five*, 39.

219. Dixon, "TAC-TRADOC Dialogue," 45–46.

220. Talbott to Weyand, February 27, 1974, with attached marked copy of a January 11, 1974, speech by USAF Chief of Staff Gen. George S. Brown, 9, Box 1, Folder: Correspondence, Orwin Talbott Papers; emphasis original.

221. Talbott to Weyand, February 27, 1974, p. 9.

222. For paragraph, see Laslie, *Air Force Way of War*, 101; Benjamin Lambeth, *The Transformation of American Air Power* (Ithaca, NY: Cornell University Press, 2000), 83–85; Herbert, *Deciding What Has to Be Done*, 69; and Harold Winton, "Partnership and Tension: The Army and Air Force between Vietnam and Desert Shield," *Parameters* 26, no. 1 (Spring 1996): 102–4.

223. Romjue, Canedy, and Chapman, *Prepare the Army*, 66.

224. Gen. D. V. Bennett to Talbott, March 15, 1974, p. 1, Box 1, Folder: Correspondence, Orwin Talbott Papers; emphasis original.

225. Dixon, "Range of Tactical Air Operations," 24.

226. Talbott to Abrams, February 28, 1974, Box 1, Folder: Correspondence, Orwin Talbott Papers.

227. Swain, "AirLand Battle," 388; for paragraph, see Dixon, "TAC-TRADOC Dialogue," 45–49; Herbert, *Deciding What Has to Be Done*, 69–72; Futrell, *Ideas, Concepts, Doctrine*, 530–31, 539–42; and Winton, "Partnership and Tension," 102–4.

228. Futrell, *Ideas, Concepts, Doctrine*, 541.

229. Dixon, "TAC-TRADOC Dialogue," 45.

230. For paragraph, see Starry, "Air Force: AirLand Battle," May 13, 1995, oral history interview in *Press On!*, 2:1285; Alessi-Friedlander, "Learning to Win," 153–58; and Starry, "Reflections," 551–52.

231. Quoted in Herbert, *Deciding What Has to Be Done*, 97.

232. Quoted in Bronfeld, "Fighting Outnumbered," 492.

233. Email exchange with Kenneth Pollack, July 17, 2019; and Starry, "Air Force: AirLand Battle," 2:1285.

234. For paragraph, see Starry, "Reflections," 551–53; and Alessi-Friedlander, "Learning to Win," 60–62, 82, 133, 157.

235. Starry, "Experiences as a Commander," July 29, 1981, oral history interview in *Press On!*, 2:1202.

236. Quoted in R. Z. Alessi-Friedlander, "Learning to Win While Fighting Outnumbered: General Donn A. Starry and the Challenge of Institutional Leadership during a Period of Reform and Modernization," *Military Review*, online exclusive article, April 2017, p. 8n26.

237. Quoted in Alessi-Friedlander, "Learning to Win," thesis, 157.

238. Bronfeld, "Fighting Outnumbered," 491.

239. For paragraph, see Starry, "Letter to General E. C. Meyer," chief of staff, June 26, 1979, in *Press On!*, 1:343–44; Starry, "AirLand Battle I," Message to Multiple Addresses, January 29, 1981, in *Press On!*, 1:365; Romjue, *Active Defense to AirLand Battle*, 23–36, 42–47, 65–72; Jensen, *Forging the Sword*, 59–62, 68–79; Alessi-Friedlander, "Learning to Win," thesis, 152–64, 167–78, 181; Clinton Ancker III, "The Evolution of Mission Command in US Army Doctrine 1905 to the Present," *Military Review* 93, no. 2 (March–April 2013): 46–48; and Sheehan, "Preparing for an Imaginary War," 219–21.

240. Starry, "Reflections," 551.

241. TRADOC Pamphlet 525-5, *Operational Concept for the AirLand Battle and Corps Operations-1986* (Fort Eustis, VA: TRADOC, 1981), 2, 7, quoted in Alessi-Friedlander, "Learning to Win," thesis, 164.

242. Romjue, *Active Defense to AirLand Battle*, 67.

243. Starry, "TRADOC's Analysis of the Yom Kippur War," 1:222.

244. Walter Kretchik, *US Army Doctrine: From the American Revolution to the War on Terror* (Lawrence: University Press of Kansas, 2011), 202, 205.

245. For paragraph, see Bronfeld, "Fighting Outnumbered," 491–94; Jensen, *Forging the*

Sword, 71–74; Starry, "Air Force: AirLand Battle," 2:1278–79, 1284, 1287; Romjue, *Active Defense to AirLand Battle*, 32–39, 41, 50, 62–65; Starry, "Letter to General Frederick Kroesen, CG, US Army Europe and 7th Army," July 23, 1981, in *Press On!*, 1:10; Winton, "Partnership and Tension," 105–9; and Futrell, *Ideas, Concepts, Doctrine*, 542–55.

246. Starry, "Army of the Future," February 14, 1980, speech in *Press On!*, 1:670.

247. Starry, "Tactical Nuclear Weapons Employment," Message to E. C. Meyer, Deputy Chief of Staff for Operations, December 28, 1978, *Press On!*, 1:731.

248. *FM100-5: Operations* (Washington: Department of the Army, 1976), 8-1; emphasis original.

249. James Slife, *Creech Blue: General Bill Creech and the Reformation of the Tactical Air Force, 1978–1984* (Maxwell AFB, AL: Air University Press, 2004), 34.

250. Romjue, *Active Defense to AirLand Battle*, 72; see also Bronfeld, "Fighting Outnumbered," 474; and Alessi-Friedlander, "Learning to Win," thesis, 122.

251. Alessi-Friedlander, "Learning to Win," thesis, 133.

252. Quoted in Alessi-Friedlander, "Learning to Win," thesis, 181.

253. For paragraph, see Karl Cocke, ed., *Department of the Army Historical Summary, Fiscal Year 1976* [hereafter, *DAHS FY76*] (Washington, DC: Center of Military History, 1977), 6; Karl Cocke and Rae T. Panella, eds., *Department of the Army Historical Summary, Fiscal Year 1977* [hereafter, *DAHS FY77*] (Washington, DC: Center of Military History, 1979), 6, 16–17; Karl Cocke, ed., *Department of the Army Historical Summary, Fiscal Year 1978* [hereafter, *DAHS FY78*] (Washington, DC: Center of Military History, 1980), 20–21; Karl Cocke, ed., *Department of the Army Historical Summary, Fiscal Year 1979* [hereafter, *DAHS FY79*] (Washington, DC: Center of Military History, 1982), 15–16; John Wilson, *Maneuver and Firepower: The Evolution of Divisions and Separate Brigades* (Washington, DC: Center of Military History, 1998), 354–59, 379–83, 389; John Romjue, *A History of Army 86*, vol. 1: *Division 86: The Development of the Heavy Division, September 1978–October 1979* (Fort Monroe, VA: Historical Office, TRADOC, June 1982), 1–10, 32–33, 43, 55–56, 74, 80, 100, 107, 128; John Romjue, *A History of Army 86*, vol. 2: *The Development of the Light Division, The Corps, and Echelons above Corps, November 1979–December 1980* (Fort Monroe, VA: TRADOC Historical Office, 1982), 11–16, 23; and William DePuy, "Are We Ready for the Future?," *Army* 28, no. 9 (September 1978), in *Selected Papers of General William E. DePuy*, 269–70, 274–75.

254. Wilson, *Maneuver and Firepower*, 383.

255. *DAHS FY76*, p. 3.

256. Starry, "Development of Doctrine," 2:1256.

257. Romjue, *History of Army 86*, 1:13.

258. For paragraph, see Starry, "Development of Doctrine," 2:1256–58; Williams to Talbott, June 24, 1974, Inclosure 3: Organization of the Tank Platoon and Battalion Company, 3–4; Romjue, *History of Army 86*, 1:9–11, 43, 49–50, 74–76, 111, 128; and DePuy, "Are We Ready," 269–74.

259. DePuy, "Are We Ready," 269.

260. Romjue, *History of Army 86*, 1:10.

261. For paragraph, see *DAHS FY76*, p. 25; *DAHS FY77*, p. 29–30; Don Gordon, "The CEWI Battalion: A Tactical Concept That Works," *Military Review* 60, no. 1 (January 1980): 2–12; John Finnegan, *The Military Intelligence Story*, 2nd ed. (Fort Belvoir, VA: Intelligence and Security

Command, 1998), 35, 48, 53, 80; and Richard Sheridan, "CEWI: From Concept to Reality," *Military Intelligence* 6, no. 4 (October–December 1980): 6–7, 94.

262. Gordon, "CEWI Battalion," 6.

263. Finnegan, *Military Intelligence*, 35.

264. Patrick Kelly, "The Electronic Pivot of Maneuver: The Military Intelligence Battalion (Combat Electronic Warfare Intelligence)" (Research paper, School of Advanced Military Studies, 1993), 1.

265. *DOD Appropriation FY76*, March 12, 1975, p. 19; also see *DAHS FY76*, p. 20–21.

266. *DOD Appropriation FY76*, March 12, 1975, p. 19.

267. Gordon, "CEWI Battalion," 11.

268. Munro, *Quick and the Dead*, 214.

269. Kelly, "Electronic Pivot of Maneuver," 13.

270. For paragraph, see Dastrup, *King of Battle*, 294–97; *DAHS FY77*, p. 20; and Romjue, *History of Army 86*, 1:43.

271. Dastrup, *King of Battle*, 297.

272. For paragraph, see Amoretta Hoeber and Joseph Douglass Jr., "The Neglected Threat of Chemical Warfare," *International Security* 3, no. 1 (Summer 1978): 55, 60–62, 65, 71, 73; *DAHS FY73*, p. 33; *DAHS FY74*, p. 11; *DAHS FY75*, p. 14; *DAHS FY76*, p. 6, 15; Karl Cocke, ed., *Department of the Army Historical Summary, Fiscal Year 1980* [hereafter, *DAHS FY80*] (Washington, DC: Center of Military History, 1983), 14–15, 39; Tucker, *War of Nerves*, 223–29, 239–42; Romjue, *History of Army 86*, 2:15; and Romjue, Canedy, and Chapman, *Prepare the Army*, 101–2.

273. *DOD Appropriations FY75*, March 5, 1974, p. 648–49; also see *DOD Authorization FY76*, February 7, 1975, p. 443.

274. Tucker, *War of Nerves*, 226.

275. For paragraph, see *DOD Appropriations FY75*, March 5, 1974, p. 642–43, 686; *DOD Authorization FY76*, February 7, 1975, p. 370, 374, 383, 390–91; *DAHS FY74*, p. 3, 39; *DAHS FY75*, p. 5–6; Wilson, *Maneuver and Firepower*, 366–67; and Kagan, *Finding the Target*, 20–23.

276. James Polk, "The New Short War Strategy," *Strategic Review* 3 (Summer 1975): 52.

277. Polk, 52–53.

278. *DAHS FY79*, p. 5.

279. Romjue, *History of Army 86*, 1:32.

280. For paragraph, see *DAHS FY73*, p. 32–33; DePuy, *Changing an Army*, 186–87, 191; Herbert, *Deciding What Has to Be Done*, 26–27, 37, 52, 80; Kagan, *Finding the Target*, 47–48; Alessi-Friedlander, "Learning to Win," thesis, 100–101, 131–39; Gorman, "How to Win Outnumbered," 3–6, 10–15; and Gorman, "Infantry in Mid-Intensity Battle," 11–13.

281. Anne Chapman, *The Origins and Development of the National Training Center, 1976–1984* (Fort Monroe, VA: TRADOC, 1992), 69.

282. Quoted in Alessi-Friedlander, "Learning to Win," 134–35.

283. Paul Gorman, *The Secret of Future Victories* (Alexandria, VA: Institute for Defense Analyses, February 1992), III-36.

284. *DOD Appropriations FY75*, March 5, 1974, p. 620.

285. Spiller, "Shadow of the Dragon," 48.

286. DePuy, *Changing an Army*, 191.

287. Scales, *Certain Victory*, 12; for paragraph, see Chapman, *Origins and Development of the NTC*, 1–2, 7–17, 21–28, 33–37, 41, 84–87, 142; and Starry, "National Training Center," Message to Vice Chief of Staff Kerwin, April 19, 1978, in *Press On!*, 1:790–91.

288. Chapman, *Origins and Development of the NTC*, 23.

289. Quoted in Chapman, 16.

290. Gorman, *Secret of Future Victories*, III-33.

291. Paul Herbert, "Toward the Best Available Thought: The Writing of Field Manual 100-5, Operations by the United States Army, 1973–1976" (PhD diss., Ohio State University, 1985), 60; Starry, "Life and Career," 2:1115–18; DePuy, January 8, 1975, draft memo to Weyand in *Selected Papers of General William E. DePuy*, 143–46; and Romjue, Canedy, and Chapman, *Prepare the Army*, 42–43.

292. Starry, March 18, 1974, letter to Talbott, in *Press On!*, 1:271.

293. *DOD Appropriations FY76*, March 12, 1975, p. 40.

294. Poole, *JCS*, 35–37.

295. For paragraph, see Dastrup, *King of Battle*, 293–94, 300; and Romjue, *History of Army 86*, 1:78–79, 116.

296. Dastrup, *King of Battle*, 293.

297. *DAHS FY79*, p. 188.

298. Trybula, *Big Five*, 5.

299. Starry, "Development of Doctrine," 2:1262–63.

300. *DOD Appropriations FY75*, March 5, 1974, p. 661–62.

301. For paragraph, see W. Blair Haworth Jr., "Moving Target: The US Army Infantry Fighting Vehicle Program in the 1970s," in *Providing the Means of War*, ed. Shannon Brown (Washington, DC: USA Center of Military History, 2005), 183–84; and Steven Zaloga, *M2/M3 Bradley: Infantry Fighting Vehicle, 1983–1995* (London: Osprey, 1995), 4–9.

302. *DOD Appropriations FY75*, March 5, 1974, p. 663.

303. Starry, "Heavy Infantry Fighting Vehicle," Message to Multiple Addresses, November 16, 1977, in *Press On!*, 1:238 (emphasis original).

304. *Military Procurement Supplemental, FY74*, March 12, 1974, p. 72–73, 123, 126–27; *Military Procurement Supplemental, FY74*, Armed Services Committee Report, April 9, 1974, p. 24; *DOD Appropriations FY75*, March 5, 1974, p. 664; and *Military Procurement—Fiscal Year 1976*, part 7: *Hearing before the Senate Committee on Armed Services*, 94th Congress (Washington, DC: Government Printing Office, 1975), March 12, p. 3829, 3868, 3898.

305. Starry, "Wheeled Reconnaissance Vehicles," Letter to General Bernard Rogers, January 19, 1979, in *Press On!*, 1:71.

306. Starry, "Heavy Infantry Fighting Vehicle," 1:238; for paragraph, see *DOD Appropriations FY75*, March 5, 1974, p. 664–65; DePuy, "Letter to General Frederick Weyand, Chief of Staff," April 29, 1975, in *Selected Papers of General William E. DePuy*, 161–62; *DAHS FY74*, p. 137; *DAHS FY80*, p. 234; Haworth, "Moving Target," 184–88; Starry, March 7, 1980, letter to Meyer in *Press On!*, 1:82; and Trybula, *Big Five*, 27–29.

307. Starry, "Letter to MG Willard Latham, 18 May 1976," in *Press On!*, 1:232.

308. Haworth, "Moving Target," 185; for paragraph, see 188–92; Zaloga, *M2/M3 Bradley*, 13–15; Starry, "Heavy Infantry Fighting Vehicle," 1:236–39; and Starry, "Reflections," 554.

309. Starry, "Heavy Infantry Fighting Vehicle," 1:239.

310. Starry, "Combined Arms," *Armor*, September–October 1978, in *Press On!*, 1:243.

311. Starry, "October 1973 Mideast War," 2–7; for paragraph, see Robert Sunell, "The Abrams Tank System," in *Camp Colt to Desert Storm: The History of US. Armored Forces*, ed. George Hofmann and Donn Starry (Lexington: University Press of Kentucky, 1999), 433–35, 438–39, 445–47; DePuy, "Implications of the Middle East War," 82, 106–7; *DOD Authorization FY76*, March 17, 1975, p. 3168–74; 3187–94, 3207–11, 3217–20; Starry, "Armor/Antiarmor in the Future of Land Combat," October 6, 1988, in *Press On!*, 1:127–28; and Williams to Talbott, July 16, 1974, "The Requirements for a Combat Vehicle Rapid Fire Cannon," Box 2, Folder: US Military Visit to Egypt, Orwin Talbott Papers.

312. *DOD Authorization FY76*, March 17, 1975, p. 3218.

313. *DOD Authorization FY76*, March 17, 1975, p. 3173.

314. Starry, "TRADOC's Analysis of the Yom Kippur War," 1:224.

315. For paragraph, see Sunell, "Abrams Tank System," 439, 442–47; Starry, "Reminiscences," 2:1194; *DOD Authorization FY76*, March 17, 1975, p. 3181–89, 3224–25; *Military Procurement—Fiscal Year 1977, Research, Development, Test and Evaluation: Hearing before the Senate Subcommittee on Research and Development of the Committee on Armed Services*, 94th Congress (Washington, DC: Government Printing Office, 1976), April 6, p. 6989, 7014–20, 7023, 7039; *DAHS FY75*, p. 117–21; *DAHS FY77*, p. 136–39; *DAHS FY78*, p. 20; *DAHS FY79*, p. 192; *DAHS FY80*, p. 229; Starry, "Message to General Walter Kerwin, Vice Chief of Staff, 16 January 1978," in *Press On!*, 1:68; and Kagan, *Finding the Target*, 37–38.

316. Quoted in Sunell, "Abrams Tank System," 439.

317. *DOD Authorization FY76*, March 17, 1975, p. 3181.

318. *DOD Appropriations FY76*, March 12, 1975, p. 19–20, 41, 85–86; *DOD Authorization FY76*, March 12, 1975, p. 3828–29, 3831, 3872–73, 3891–92; *DOD Authorization FY76*, March 17, 1975, p. 3199–203, 3216; and *DOD Authorization FY77*, April 6, 1976, p. 6996–7005, 7027–29, 7040.

319. Alessi-Friedlander, "Learning to Win," thesis, 100.

320. For paragraph, see *DOD Appropriations FY75*, March 5, 1974, p. 631–32; *DOD Appropriations FY76*, March 12, 1975, p. 18, 44, 93; *DOD Authorization FY76*, March 25, 1975, p. 3513–20, 3524, 3533–36, 3541–47, 3553, 3572–75; and Trybula, *Big Five*, 57–62, 67.

321. *DOD Appropriations FY75*, April 29, 1974, p. 473.

322. For paragraph, see *DOD Appropriations FY75*, March 5, 1974, p. 666; *DOD Authorization FY76*, February 7, 1975, p. 390–91; Dastrup, *King of Battle*, 290–99; *DAHS FY73*, p. 30, 165–66; *DAHS FY74*, p. 131–32; *DAHS FY75*, p. 113, 118–19; *DAHS FY76*, p. 21, 133; and DePuy, "Implications of the Middle East War," 108–9.

323. Dastrup, *King of Battle*, 290.

324. *Department of Defense Authorization for Fiscal Year 1976*, part 9: *Tactical Air Power, Hearing before the Senate Tactical Air Power Subcommittee of the Committee on Armed Services*, 94th Congress (Washington, DC: Government Printing Office, 1975), March 13, p. 4477.

325. *DOD Authorization FY76*, March 13, 1975, p. 4420.

326. For paragraph, see DePuy letter to Abrams, January 14, 1974, p. 71; *DAHS FY73*, p. 39–40, 172; *DAHS FY75*, p. 119–20; *DAHS FY76*, p. 135; *DAHS FY77*, p. 129, 137; *DAHS FY78*, p. 160; *DAHS FY79*, p. 187–88; *DAHS FY80*, p. 231; *DOD Authorization FY76*, March 13, 1975,

p. 4485–86, 4489–96, 4516–23; and *DOD Authorization FY76*, March 17, 1975, p. 3115–21, 3127–32, 3154–56.

327. For paragraph, see *DAHS FY78*, p. 160; *DAHS FY79*, p. 188; *Military Procurement Supplemental, FY74*, March 12, 1974, p. 25; *DOD Authorization FY76*, March 12, 1975, p. 3856; *DOD Authorization FY76*, March 13, 1975, p. 4481–88, 4529–44; DePuy, "Implications of the Middle East War," 89, 101, 109–10; Starry, "Life and Career," 2:1119; Romjue, *History of Army 86*, 1:7, 40, 55–56, 80–81, 119; and Erickson, "The '73 War," 152.

328. Starry, "Reflections," 555.

329. *DAHS FY76*, p. 136.

330. *DOD Authorization FY76*, March 13, 1975, p. 4484.

331. Frank J. Caravella, *First to Fire* (Fort Bliss, TX: Air Defense Artillery School, 1995), 85.

332. For paragraph, see *DOD Appropriations FY75*, March 5, 1974, p. 652–56; *DOD Authorization FY76*, March 13, 1975, p. 4430–31; *DAHS FY73*, p. 40–41, 166–67; *DAHS FY74*, 135; Trybula, *Big Five*, 37–43; and Nordeen, *Air Warfare*, 42.

333. *DOD Appropriations FY75*, March 5, 1974, p. 656.

334. Drew Middleton, "US Alters Military Stance as Deadlier Arms Spread," *New York Times*, July 9, 1975.

335. For paragraph, see *DOD Appropriations FY75*, March 5, 1974, p. 653–56; *DOD Appropriations FY75*, April 29, 1974, p. 471; *DOD Appropriations FY76*, March 12, 1975, p. 43–44; *DOD Authorization FY76*, March 13, 1975, p. 4420–23, 4427, 4431, 4437, 4440, 4451, 4466; *DAHS FY73*, p. 40–41; *DAHS FY76*, p. 133; *DAHS FY77*, p. 133; *DAHS FY78*, p. 164; and Chris Bishop, *Apache AH-64 Boeing (McDonnell Douglas) 1976–2005* (Oxford: Osprey, 2005), 7.

336. *DOD Appropriations FY75*, March 5, 1974, p. 656.

337. DePuy, "Implications of the Middle East War," 111.

338. For paragraph, see *Military Procurement Supplemental, FY74*, March 12, 1974, p. 21; *Department of Defense Appropriations for Fiscal Year 1976*, part 4: *Department of the Air Force: Hearing before a Senate Subcommittee of the Committee on Appropriations*, 94th Congress (Washington, DC: Government Printing Office, 1975), February 26, p. 3, 50–51, 102, 207; Michel, "Revolt of the Majors," 173–76, 245–46, 323–25; White, *Tactical Air Power*, 39–42; and Dennis Drew, "Two Decades in the Air Power Wilderness: Do We Know Where We Are?," *Air University Review* 37, no. 5 (September–October 1986): 8–11.

339. *DOD Appropriations FY76*, February 26, 1975, p. 3.

340. *DOD Appropriations FY76*, February 26, 1975, p. 83.

341. Mike Worden, *Rise of the Fighter Generals: The Problem of Air Force Leadership, 1945–1982* (Maxwell AFB, AL: Air University Press, 1988), 194.

342. Worden, 223.

343. Worden, 215.

344. Michel, "Revolt of the Majors," 182.

345. Edgar Ulsamer, "TAC's Focus Is on 'Lean and Lethal,'" *Air Force Magazine* 58, no. 3 (March 1975): 30.

346. For paragraph, see Kenneth Werrell, *Chasing the Silver Bullet: U.S. Air Force Weapons Development from Vietnam to Desert Storm* (Washington, DC: Smithsonian Books, 2003), 4–5, 15, 58; Michel, "Revolt of the Majors," 8–9, 14n8, 20–21, 80–83, 132–33, 165; John Ralph, "Tactical

Air Systems and the New Technologies," in *Other Arms Race: New Technologies and Non-Nuclear Conflict*, ed. Geoffrey Kemp, Robert Pfaltzgraff, and Uri Ra'anan (Lexington, MA: Lexington, 1975), 18–22; and Slife, *Creech Blue*, 65–68.

347. Ralph, "Tactical Air Systems," 18.

348. Carl Builder, *The Icarus Syndrome: The Role of Air Power Theory in the Evolution and Fate of the U.S. Air Force* (New Brunswick, NJ: Transaction, 2009), 156.

349. For paragraph, see C. R. Anderegg, *Sierra Hotel: Flying Air Force Fighters in the Decade after Vietnam* (Washington, DC: Air Force History and Museums Program, 2001), 89; Michel, "Revolt of the Majors," 6, 13fn2, 22–25, 45, 48, 103–5, 112, 157–68, 191–95; and Donald Mrozek, *The USAF after Vietnam: Postwar Challenges and Potential for Responses* (Maxwell AFB, AL: Air University Press, 1988), 15–17.

350. Michel, "Revolt of the Majors," 95.

351. Dawson R. O'Neill, "How the Aggressors Began—I Think," *Daedalus Flyer* 38, no. 1 (Spring 1998): 12.

352. Kagan, *Finding the Target*, 25; for paragraph, see Anderegg, *Sierra Hotel*, 17, 26, 39–40, 76; Nordeen, *Air Warfare*, 7, 10, 13, 15, 26–28, 50, 57–59; Lambeth, *Transformation of American Air Power*, 13, 18, 27, 35, 49; and Werrell, *Chasing the Silver Bullet*, 39–40, 139, 144–45, 148–49.

353. Nordeen, *Air Warfare*, 28.

354. For paragraph, see Worden, *Rise of Fighter Generals*, 189, 196–203; Lambeth, *Transformation of American Air Power*, 26, 39, 48, 53; Werrell, *Chasing the Silver Bullet*, 53, 145–46, 150–52; Nordeen, *Air Warfare*, 43, 48, 50, 58–59; Werrell, *Archie*, 115–18, 120–24, 127; and Anderegg, *Sierra Hotel*, 8, 25, 29, 31, 122–23, 135–36.

355. Anderegg, *Sierra Hotel*, 126.

356. Werrell, *Chasing the Silver Bullet*, 152.

357. Lambeth, *Transformation of American Air Power*, 56; for paragraph, see *DOD Appropriations FY75*, February 27, 1974, p. 451; *DOD Authorization FY75*, March 14, 1974, p. 4306–18; *DOD Appropriations FY75*, May 2, 1974, p. 526; Futrell, *Ideas, Concepts, Doctrine*, 489–90; and Doyle, *Yom Kippur War and Shaping of USAF*, 38–42, 48–49, 70.

358. *DOD Authorization FY75*, March 20, 1974, p. 4449.

359. For paragraph, especially see *DOD Authorization FY75*, March 20, 1974, p. 4448–72; *Military Procurement Supplemental, FY74*, March 12, 1974, p. 7–8; *Military Procurement Supplemental, FY74*, Armed Services Committee report, April 9, 1974, p. 3, 27–28; *DOD Appropriation FY75*, May 2, 1974, p. 526; and *Department of Defense Appropriations for Fiscal Year 1976*, part 4: *Department of the Air Force: Hearing before a Senate Subcommittee of the Committee on Appropriations*, 94th Congress (Washington, DC: Government Printing Office, 1975), March 19, p. 416–18.

360. *DOD Authorization hearing FY75*, March 20, 1974, p. 4466.

361. *DOD Authorization hearing FY75*, March 20, 1974, p. 4464.

362. Futrell, *Ideas, Concepts, Doctrine*, 489.

363. *DOD Appropriations FY76*, February 26, 1975, p. 26.

364. For paragraph, see *Military Procurement Supplemental, FY74*, March 12, 1974, p. 26–31, 82–83; *DOD Authorization FY75*, March 20, 1974, p. 4451–62; *DOD Appropriations FY75*, May 2, 1974, p. 51–52, 579, 607–8; *Department of Defense Authorization for Fiscal Year 1976*, part 8: *Hearing before the Senate Tactical Air Power Subcommittee of the Committee on Armed Services*, 94th

Congress (Washington, DC: Government Printing Office, 1975), March 11, p. 4294–304, 4322–31; *DOD Authorization FY76*, March 12, 1975, p. 4341–81, 4397–406; Dixon, "Range of Tactical Air Operations," 23; Futrell, *Ideas, Concepts, Doctrine*, 480–82, 489, 542, 559–60; Ralph, "Tactical Air Systems," 23–27; Werrell, *Archie*, 108–9, 116; Werrell, *Chasing the Silver Bullet*, 51–52, 139, 144–49, 154–55; Thomas Ehrhard, *Air Force UAVs: The Secret History* (Arlington, VA: Mitchell Institute for Airpower Studies, July 2010), 23–31, 34–35; Anderegg, *Sierra Hotel*, 127–28, 136–37, 140, 219; and Doyle, *Yom Kippur War and Shaping of USAF*, 27–28.

365. Ralph, "Tactical Air Systems," 26.

366. Navy leadership of the AGM-88 high-speed antiradiation missile's development precluded its inclusion in Pave Strike, but combat data from the Yom Kippur War prompted enhanced USAF funding. *Military Procurement Supplemental, FY74*, March 12, 1974, p. 26, 83; *Department of Defense Authorization for Fiscal Year 1976: Hearing before the Senate Subcommittee on Tactical Air Power of the Committee on Armed Services*, 94th Congress (Washington, DC: Government Printing Office, 1975), March 18, p. 4950–53, 4963; and Doyle, *Yom Kippur War and Shaping of USAF*, 41.

367. *DOD Appropriations FY75*, May 2, 1974, p. 579.

368. For paragraph, see Futrell, *Ideas, Concepts, Doctrine*, 512, 544–46, 560–62; Anderegg, *Sierra Hotel*, 134, 140–41; Michel, "Revolt of the Majors," 310–11, 344; Andreas Parsch, "AGM-112," *Directory of U.S. Military Rockets and Missiles*, http://www.designation-systems.net /dusrm/m-112.html; Ehrhard, *Air Force UAVs*, 29–40; and Bill Gunston, *The Illustrated Encyclopedia of the World's Rockets and Missiles* (London: Leisure, 1979), 129.

369. Quoted in Richard Kohn and Joseph Harahan, eds., *Air Interdiction in World War II, Korea, and Vietnam: An Interview with General Earle E. Partridge, General Jacob E. Smart, and General John W. Vogt Jr.* (Washington, DC: Office of Air Force History, 1986), 92.

370. Quoted in Slife, *Creech Blue*, 59.

371. For paragraph, see *DOD Authorization FY76*, March 11, 1975, p. 4190–200, 4247–55; O'Neill, "How the Aggressors," 12–16; Michel, "Revolt of the Majors," 6, 100–104, 154–55, 186–88, 196–98; Doyle, *Yom Kippur War and Shaping of USAF*, 49–50; and Laslie, *Air Force Way of War*, 8–9, 23, 33–51.

372. Anderegg, *Sierra Hotel*, 71.

373. *DOD Appropriations FY76*, February 26, 1975, p. 109; and Ulsamer, "TAC's Focus," 30.

374. Michel, "Revolt of the Majors," 7.

375. For paragraph, see Laslie, *Air Force Way of War*, 55–67; Michel, "Revolt of the Majors," 7, 222, 228–31; and Anderegg, *Sierra Hotel*, 93–100.

376. Michel, "Revolt of the Majors," 202.

377. Michel, 220.

378. For rest of paragraph, see Lambeth, *Transformation of American Air Power*, 61–65, 80–81; Slife, *Creech Blue*, 51–55; Michel, "Revolt of the Majors," 234–38, 281–82; Laslie, *Air Force Way of War*, 72–81; and *DOD Appropriations FY76*, February 26, 1975, p. 109.

379. Michel, "Revolt of the Majors," 236.

380. Laslie, *Air Force Way of War*, 55.

381. For paragraph, see Werrell, *Chasing the Silver Bullet*, 125–34; Doyle, *Yom Kippur War and Shaping of USAF*, 46–48; Bill Sweetman, *Lockheed Stealth* (St. Paul, MN: Zenith, 2004), 21–33; and Laslie, *Air Force Way of War*, 92–96.

382. Sweetman, *Lockheed Stealth*, 21.

383. Lambeth, *Transformation of American Air Power*, 74.

384. For paragraph, see Werrell, *Chasing the Silver Bullet*, 199–205; Winton, "Partnership and Tension," 107–8; and Starry, "Desert Storm Lessons Learned," 2:1229.

385. Werrell, *Chasing the Silver Bullet*, 200.

386. For paragraph, see *Department of Defense Authorization for Fiscal Year 1976: Hearing before the Senate Tactical Air Power Subcommittee of the Committee on Armed Services*, 94th Congress (Washington, DC: Government Printing Office, 1975), March 6, p. 4031–38, 4048–65; *DOD Appropriations FY76*, February 26, 1975, p. 35–36, 63–69, 104–5, 118, 197, 211–12; and Werrell, *Chasing the Silver Bullet*, 189–99.

387. *Department of Defense Appropriations for Fiscal Year 1975: Hearing before a Senate Subcommittee of the Committee on Appropriations*, 93rd Congress (Washington, DC: Government Printing Office, 1974), June 25, p. 182.

388. *DOD Appropriations FY76*, February 26, 1975, p. 118.

389. Robert Jensik, "The Evolution of Electronic Combat Doctrine" (Research Report, Air War College, Maxwell AFB, April 1994), 2; for paragraph, see Jensik, 10–11; *DOD Appropriations FY75*, March 7, 1974, p. 5; Edgar Ulsamer, "Needed: A New Family of EW Systems," *Air Force Magazine* 59, no. 2 (February 1976): 28–30; *Military Procurement Supplemental, FY74*, March 12, 1974, p. 31, 136–37; *DOD Authorization FY76*, March 11, 1975, p. 4274–80, 4288–92; Futrell, *Ideas, Concepts, Doctrine*, 555; Ralph, "Tactical Air Systems," 25; Doyle, *Yom Kippur War and Shaping of USAF*, 41–42, 45–46; Slife, *Creech Blue*, 17, 51–59; and "Yom Kippur Fighting Underscores EW Importance," 30, 36.

390. *DOD Appropriations FY76*, February 26, 1975, p. 108.

391. Geoffrey Kemp and Robert Pfaltzgraff, "New Technologies and the Emerging Geo-Strategic Environment," in *Other Arms Race: New Technologies and Non-Nuclear Conflict*, ed. Geoffrey Kemp, Robert Pfaltzgraff, and Uri Ra'anan (Lexington, MA: Lexington, 1975), 133–34.

392. Munro, *Quick and the Dead*, 223.

393. Slife, *Creech Blue*, 57; see also Doyle, *Yom Kippur War and Shaping of USAF*, 45–46.

394. For paragraph, see Laslie, *Air Force Way of War*, 49–51; Anderegg, *Sierra Hotel*, 20–21, 34–35, 59, 83–85; Nordeen, *Air Warfare*, 50, 58–59, 148; and David Gish, "F-4 Air-to-Air Training," *Fighter Weapons Review* (Fall 1975): 2–5.

395. Lambeth, *Transformation of American Air Power*, 66.

396. Lambeth, 47.

397. *DOD Authorization FY75*, March 13, 1974, p. 4251.

398. For paragraph, see *DOD Appropriations FY75*, May 2, 1974, p. 585; *DOD Appropriations FY76*, February 26, 1975, p. 33–34, 72–73; Futrell, *Ideas, Concepts, Doctrine*, 490, 502–3, 556–58; Ralph, "Tactical Air Systems," 31–32; White, *Tactical Air Power*, 27, 31, 42–43, 50–51, 58–59, 72; Werrell, *Chasing the Silver Bullet*, 59–73, 79–93; Anderegg, *Sierra Hotel*, 149–53, 164, 173; Michel, "Revolt of the Majors," 134, 137, 176–80; Doyle, *Yom Kippur War and Shaping of USAF*, 40–41; and Poole, *JCS*, 28–33.

399. Ulsamer, "Tac's Focus," 32.

400. *DOD Authorization FY75*, March 13, 1974, p. 4247.

401. Futrell, *Ideas, Concepts, Doctrine*, 490.

402. For paragraph, see Werrell, *Chasing the Silver Bullet*, 93–98; Michel, "Revolt of the Majors," 180–82; *DOD Appropriations FY76*, February 26 and March 19, 1975, p. 224, 441–42; and Futrell, *Ideas, Concepts, Doctrine*, 502–3, 562–63.

403. Michel, "Revolt of the Majors," 336–38.

404. Dixon, "Range of Tactical Air Operations," 23; Alberts, "Call from the Wilderness," 42; and Doyle, *Yom Kippur War and Shaping of USAF*, 42–46.

405. Doyle, 44.

406. Anderegg, *Sierra Hotel*, 60–65, 129–33, 138–42; Doyle, *Yom Kippur War and Shaping of USAF*, 52–53; Lambeth, *Transformation of American Air Power*, 69–70; and Werrell, *Chasing the Silver Bullet*, 153–55.

407. Anderegg, *Sierra Hotel*, 133.

408. For paragraph, see Laslie, *Air Force Way of War*, 69–70; Slife, *Creech Blue*, 27–33; Michel, "Revolt of the Majors," 278–84, 304; and Doyle, *Yom Kippur War and Shaping of USAF*, 53.

409. For paragraph, see Werrell, *Chasing the Silver Bullet*, 106–19; Futrell, *Ideas, Concepts, Doctrine*, 519–31; Doyle, *Yom Kippur War and Shaping of USAF*, 28; *DOD Authorization FY75*, March 14, 1974, p. 4312–13, 4318–22; and *DOD Appropriations FY76*, February 26, 1975, p. 34, 72, 108, 278–79.

410. Quoted in Brant, "Battlefield Air Interdiction," 78.

411. *DOD Appropriations FY75*, June 26, 1974, p. 280–81.

412. Jensik, "Electronic Combat Doctrine," 16.

413. Quoted in Michel, "Revolt of the Majors," 399.

414. Quoted in Scales, *Certain Victory*, 35.

415. Kagan, *Finding the Target*, 66.

416. Starry, "Desert Storm Lessons Learned," 2:1229.

417. James Kitfield, *Prodigal Soldiers: How the Generation of Officers Born of Vietnam Revolutionized the American Style of War* (New York: Simon & Schuster, 1995), 402.

418. Doyle, *Yom Kippur War and Shaping of USAF*, 67–68.

419. Foreword to Gorman, *Secret of Future Victories*, iii.

420. Avraham Adan, *On the Banks of the Suez: An Israeli General's Personal Account of the Yom Kippur War* (New York City: Presidio, 1980), 466–67.

421. Starry, "Situations in Germany and Israel," November 30, 1982, letter to Gen. E. C. Meyer, in *Press On!*, 1:945.

422. Starry, "TRADOC's Analysis of the Yom Kippur War," 1:223.

423. Starry, 1:223.

424. *Research and Development FY 1976*, March 17, 1975, p. 3227.

425. *Research and Development FY 1976*, March 17, 1975, p. 3228.

426. *DOD Appropriations FY75*, March 5, 1974, p. 656.

427. Kagan, *Finding the Target*, 52.

428. Cushman, *Oral History*, 21-7; and Kagan, *Finding the Target*, 52.

429. Starry, "TRADOC's Analysis of the Yom Kippur War," 1:222.

430. Kretchik, *US Army Doctrine*, 201.

CONCLUSION

A soldier . . . in peacetime is like a sailor navigating by dead reckoning.
You have left the terra firma of the last war and are extrapolating from
the experiences of that war. The greater the distance from the last
war, the greater became the chances of error in this extrapolation.
Occasionally there is a break in the clouds: a small-scale conflict occurs
somewhere and gives you a "fix" by showing whether certain weapons
and techniques are effective or not; but it is always a doubtful fix.
—*Michael Howard*

The doubt described by Michael Howard, above, in part reflects that there is no single path for future combat but a range of potential uses of force. Yet scrutiny of foreign wars helps map out this martial spectrum and identify the requirements for effectiveness in different areas. In this way even extremely experienced armed forces, such as the twenty-first-century US military, can benefit, especially given that its heavy concentration on counterinsurgency, counterterrorism, and aerial bombardment in permissive environments has prompted questions about a lack of activity on other missions. Such worry generated considerable interest from the US Army and Air Force about the Second Lebanon War (2006), which seemed like a cautionary tale as the highly regarded Israeli Defense Forces, after many years occupied with essentially policing, struggled against a Hezbollah force that combined irregular soldiers with missile systems.[1] Nearly a decade later some investigators contended that the battle for control in the Eastern Ukraine, particularly given Russian participation, offered another important example of hybrid warfare as "emerging military technology and concepts were employed in a nascent form but pointed the way toward a disruptive future."[2] Belief that the Department of Defense should better take advantage of the educational opportunities presented by foreign wars has led to calls for a return to the use of military observers.[3]

The practicality of individual proposals aside, what can be said about learning from such conflicts based on the cases investigated in this book? I address this overarching question by answering four subordinate inquiries. What changed about the conduct of such efforts between the first and last cases examined? Despite such changes, what impediments to learning lessons recurred? Do other relevant experiences offer guidance on how to address these obstacles or reiterate the difficulty they impose? Would a broader orientation in contrast to the task-oriented, narrow, relevance-guided approach usually employed produce a more profitable return from investigating other people's wars?

CONTEXTUAL CHANGE AND IMPROVED LEARNING

As a first step to understanding and improving lessons learning from foreign wars, one must ask what changed and what did not in conducting such efforts from the first to the last case. Technological developments enabled much faster conveyance of personnel, materiel, and information. Whereas the Delafield commissioners engaged in a long, arduous journey to reach Sebastopol and exchanged messages with the secretary of war via slow-moving post, investigators after the October War could reach Israel on the day of their departure from the United States and possessed instantaneous communications capability. Additionally, the educational level and professionalization of the officer corps rose markedly, establishing an increasingly sophisticated foundation of military knowledge. The expanding scope and complexity of warfare necessitated such professionalization as well as the military's institutional growth and specialization. Most notably, the army, in the early twentieth century, introduced a series of advanced schools including the General Service and Staff College and the Army War College. By the early 1970s it had also established an array of analytical organizations such as the Combined Arms Combat Developments Activity and Army Materiel Systems Analysis Activity.

These changes improved the services' capability at each stage of the lessons-learning process (acquisition, evaluation, dissemination, and application), but they especially enhanced the evaluation phase. The introduction of educational and analytical organizations with the purpose, expertise, and time to study observations, insights, and lessons enabled a much fuller examination of the combat. Lacking such investigatory resources, the mid-nineteenth-century army and navy almost exclusively used findings from the Crimean War *instructionally* (e.g., army adoption of the innovative 12-pound French field artillery piece) and *instrumentally* (e.g., navy proponents overcoming internal resistance to placing large Dahlgren guns on board its warships). All the cases contain examples when such informational uses provided benefits to the applying service, but they increasingly gained *inspirationally* as the military's capacity to examine problems and develop responses improved. Exemplifying this development after the Yom Kippur War, the army's diverse schools and analytical entities analyzed emergent issues, while particularly salient challenges prompted the establishment of dedicated investigatory bodies. For example, the Close Support Study Group considered how to provide artillery assistance on the increasingly lethal battlefield, and the Intelligence Organization and Stationing Study searched for how to better address the growing electronic warfare dimension of combat. Among the results from these inquiries were the innovative FIST (fire-support team) and combat electronic warfare intelligence battalion. For the Air Force, the demonstrated danger of dense Egyptian and Syrian integrated air defenses sparked a range of responses, most imaginatively a successful effort, in conjunction with the Defense Advanced Research Projects Agency, to develop a stealth aircraft to avoid detection (the future F-117).

RECURRING PITFALLS TO LEARNING FROM OTHER PEOPLE'S WARS

Nonetheless, neither these technological nor institutional advancements enabled practitioners to avoid persistent hazards that reduced gains from studying foreign conflicts and even resulted in some counterproductive applications. This section identifies the seven most salient pitfalls based on the case studies. Some of these are always present; others are context dependent. Some of these primarily impede accurate information gathering, while others mainly interfere with effective application of findings. Any attempt to improve the utility of lessons-learning efforts needs to address these obstacles, avoiding or at least minimizing their impact.

Preexisting Preferences Exerting Harmful Influence

It is appropriate to begin with contamination resulting from officers' preexisting preferences given this pernicious influence shapes every aspect of the process—what data to pursue, how to interpret information identified, and whether such findings are generalizable and relevant. While some scholars attempt to differentiate between the relative bureaucratic, cultural, and ideational effects on such preferences, the cases suggest a synergy among them, which produces a strong tendency to skew information collection and analysis, especially against disruptive developments (indications of the need for unwanted institutional changes). That is, a proclivity exists for what is known as confirmation bias, in which investigators seek information that validates existing views rather than searching for data that would falsify them. The crux of the problem is that officers, branches, components, and even services appreciate the potential of foreign war data to be used as a weapon for advancing policy as well as an instrument for understanding modern combat.[4] Thus, they seek to control the narrative. For example, Naval War College professor Alfred Thayer Mahan and Lt. Cdr. William Sims presented sharply contrasting characterizations of the May 1905 Battle of Tsushima and its lessons because they emphasized distinct metrics, ones best suited to reinforcing their prewar predilections. The potential for bias-motivated divergence increases as focus shifts from the tactical to the operational to the strategic. This outcome should not be surprising, as Thomas Mahnken explains: "Research in the field of cognitive psychology has demonstrated that preconceptions have a particularly pervasive influence on the analysis of ambiguous

275

information."[5] Ultimately, it is easy to understand why a frustrated army general, Donn Starry, complained in 1978 that "listening carefully, one wonders if in October of 1973 there were several wars or just one."[6]

Failure to Accurately Identify What Happened

Obviously, the failure to accurately determine what happened is more than a pitfall; it undermines the entire process. The cases showed that the Americans were able to identify with fidelity a considerable amount of what occurred from Madrid to Port Arthur, but investigatory realities (e.g., limited number of collectors, lack of cooperation from belligerents, political sensitivity of the conflict, and short-war duration) contributed to an inability to capture other salient events. Examiners displayed an understandable but nonetheless potentially problematic inclination to stress directly witnessed happenings even if not representative of the overall combat. Observers in the Russo-Japanese War who viewed fighting at different stages, different battles, and even the same battle from different vantage points filed conflicting reports. Best exemplifying this danger, Capt. John Morrison, present early in the war and witness to a few instances of poor Russian gunnery against Japanese attacks, downplayed the growing importance of fire support. Although other Americans highlighted that Russian field artillery improved markedly and gunners for both sides significantly impacted battles, the influential Morrison retained confidence in his findings. Similarly, one or two battles in a war may receive outsize weight because of their perceived revelatory value, impact on the war's outcome, or validation of preexisting expectations. Illustrating this phenomenon, the prominent, well-covered 1937 battles of Guadalajara and Brunete, Spain, during which motorized and mechanized forces suffered severe losses, resonated with senior army leaders and foot soldiers given their infantry-centric view of combined arms. Historians, however, have criticized these early Spanish Civil War fights as misleading not only about future infantry–armor interaction but also about other combat during the war.[7] Limited resources and access encouraged collecting information from other external witnesses, but such secondhand data, although at times valuable, often suffered from the above challenges with the added filter of the source military's own bias. For some noteworthy developments, such as innovative Russian casualty treatment in the Crimean War and Luftwaffe fighter tactics in the Spanish Civil War, investigators simply lacked any awareness about them.

Application of Disputed "Lessons"

Accurately identifying what happened on a foreign battlefield is a necessary but not sufficient condition for beneficial learning. As noted in the introduction, the organizational learning cycle requires agreement on what happened, its significance, and what should be done.[8] The case studies showed many examples of this dynamic resulting in the adoption, modification, and development of better weapons, organizational schemes, training initiatives, and tactics, techniques, and procedures. Perhaps even more valuable than the embrace of what worked was the exposure of flawed current practice that galvanized correction. After study of how Japanese control of the hills surrounding Port Arthur led to its December 1904 capture, the US Army became concerned about the similar terrain around Subig Bay in the Philippines and abandoned its previous deference to the navy on this location being the main American maritime base in the Pacific. When criticized about the army's new stance, which proved decisive, the General Staff "maintained that it was only applying the 'lessons of the Manchurian War,'" which showed the position was indefensible from landside attack.[9]

The process of applying accurately identified, agreed-upon, relevant lessons, however, was at times tainted by efforts to manufacture an artificial consensus or impose a disputed finding through exercise of bureaucratic power. The possibility for such action expands with proponents' control of the foreign war lesson narrative. For instance, senior officials including the Delafield commissioners, chief engineer Col. Joseph Totten, and Secretary of War Jefferson Davis vigorously touted the Crimean War "insight" of masonry fortifications' continuing viability after criticism of such works in the prior decade. This finding guided army policy despite some junior engineers arguing that the strength of the earthworks defending Sebastopol's landside showed their superior resistance against modern firepower. When senior officers disagreed among themselves or adopted a passive attitude, other figures could significantly influence the process. The aforementioned Russo-Japanese War observer Morrison returned from Manchuria and became the army's leading tactics instructor at Fort Leavenworth, confidently passing along his infantry-centric, retrograde interpretation of the fighting. Unsurprisingly, Morrison's view resonated with the infantry, which retained faith in the viability of frontal attacks and downplayed requirements for field artillery and machine-gun support despite ample evidence of their growing requirement from other observers.

Inappropriate Rejection of Lesson Generalizability

While applying disputed "lessons" has proved problematic, so has dismissing disruptive findings because of unfounded rejections of generalizability. A JCS study after the Yom Kippur War appropriately warned, "care must be taken to consider the environment in which the conflict took place and any unique conditions that existed which may have a qualifying effect on the lessons learned."[10] Yet, instead of exercising such due caution, service branches and components fearful of a foreign war's implications have instead attempted to ignore the conflict. Reflective of this behavior, the horse cavalry after the Russo-Japanese War and the mechanized cavalry after the Spanish Civil War stressed soldier incompetence, an insufficient number of engagements, and unfavorable terrain among the reasons to disregard the fighting. The US Army Air Corps essentially declared the combat in Spain irrelevant for the United States because the belligerents primarily conducted "air cooperation missions" (striking ground troops and equipment) instead of "air force missions" (bombing strategic targets). As a result, the air corps even neglected available insights (e.g., the requirement for long-range fighter escorts to accompany strategic bombers) that would have facilitated execution of its preferred way of war. This propensity is not exclusive to disaffected service elements, as evidenced by the willingness of Chief of Staff Gen. Creighton Abrams and Gen. William DePuy, although generally strong advocates for applying Yom Kippur War lessons, to dismiss the combat's generalizability when the effectiveness of integrated air defenses threatened the high-priority advanced attack helicopter program.

Confident Embrace of Misleading Information

Practitioners have also erred by expecting accurate observations to be reflective of the future battlefield when they instead quickly became obsolete. A danger always exists that a highly effective weapon, organization, or tactic emerges to invalidate combat-generated lessons, but particularly concerning is how preparedness at times suffered because service leaders ignored the potential for measures taken by other militaries in response to the same cues to undermine applied US findings. This deficiency occurred when the army used insights from the October 1973 war to restructure its central European defense concept to maximize stopping power against concentrated Soviet armor thrusts. The Russians, however, reacted to the same experience by accelerating an already underway shift to a less concentrated, more opportunistic approach, which meant the new US doctrine entailed considerable risk. The introduction of successful weapons often generated enthusiasm for obtaining such capabilities even though militaries "almost invariably produce an antidote which nullifies or reduces their effectiveness."[11] While the US Army moved expeditiously in the late 1930s to adopt essentially a copy of the German 37 mm Pak 36 antitank gun, which had proved deadly early in the Spanish Civil War, the European militaries responded to the same combat by increasing tank armor and armament, rendering the 37 mm antitank gun obsolete. This case is a particularly egregious example as the service leadership prevented the Ordnance Department from developing larger caliber antitank guns, apparently to enhance the 37 mm gun's acquisition prospects. Alternatively, a weapon's failed combat debut on occasion led to its mistaken dismissal, despite the potential for subsequent design corrections and better tactics. Seven years after the disappointing performance of the highly touted British Lancaster rifled artillery in the Crimean War, Union troops used such a weapon to so quickly and thoroughly penetrate Fort Pulaski's defenses that in effect "all of the Third System coastal forts in the United States were rendered obsolete," to the shock of Jefferson Davis and other students of the earlier conflict.[12]

Identification of Findings with Contradictory Guidance

A less apparent but surprisingly frequent dilemma is the discovery of two valid and relevant lessons that signal contradictory behavior. In such circumstances, decision-makers, if unable to pursue a delicate balance, must choose an inherently risky course of action by ignoring one finding or both. After the Russo-Japanese War illustrated the increasing complexity and scale of modern war, the army leadership recognized it needed to bolster the combined-arms training of active-duty soldiers and the basic skills of National Guard troops. Summer maneuvers offered the best opportunity to do both, but attempting one interfered with the other. Similarly, the intense, lethal October 1973 battlefield encouraged shifting the tooth-to-tail ratio to obtain more frontline combat power as well as boosting logistics capability given the sharply increased rates of resource consumption. In both examples, the army prioritized the cue that synced with legislator sentiment (National Guard training and combat force expansion, respectively), enhancing its political support. Although an understandable response, in both cases field exercises later revealed debilitating consequences. By contrast, the Air Force after the Yom Kippur War benefited from being able to adopt a balanced response to tactical aircraft lessons. With the deadly aerial combat indicating a requirement for both technologically advanced aircraft to counter improved Soviet equipment as well as affordable planes to sustain fighting, USAF leaders finally embraced the secretary of defense's push for a high-low mix of F-15 air superiority fighters and F-16 fighter-bombers.

Failure to Sustain Support for a Valuable Lesson

Although the theoretical literature on innovation and adaptation usually focuses on adoption of the initial change, the case studies show the limitation of this perspective for evaluating whether lessons are truly learned. Development of proficiency with a newly employed system tends to be challenging, especially if the precipitating factor for this change is a lesson from a foreign war. The impact of such insight fades as decision-makers lose interest with the passage of time, particularly if they regard the initial reforms as sufficient implementation of a lesson. Such neglect may be appropriate given the emergence of new information or other considerations, but in some circumstances this behavior severely erodes an applied finding's warranted change. The consequences are evident from one of the seemingly best responses to foreign war stimuli in the cases examined. After the Russo-Japanese War, the army instituted a number of positive and significant reforms to its field artillery (e.g., shift to indirect fire as its primary tactic, establishment of battalions and regiments to mass fire, and separation from the coastal artillery to better address its unique needs). Yet these rapidly adopted steps (1905–7) were not followed with the requisite education, funding, and training to enable officers and troops to gain proficiency with indirect fire and combined arms. As a result the American Expeditionary Force that arrived in France in 1917 disappointingly, but not surprisingly, struggled at these critical elements of modern battle.

NO EASY REMEDIES—THE DIFFICULTY OF RELATED EFFORTS

There is no procedural scheme or organizational structure that will ensure avoidance of these pitfalls. Learning lessons from foreign war in a way that maximizes future military effectiveness is hard. The case studies provide ample evidence of this bottom line, but a brief consideration of related efforts amplifies this conclusion. First, the US military has found it difficult to benefit sufficiently from its own combat experiences despite heavy investment in what is a less challenging task than learning from foreign wars. Second, the German army, the most accomplished martial learning institution of the industrial age, struggled when attempting to absorb information from external conflicts.

American forces since the nation's founding have attempted to improve when at war, but a dedicated institutional commitment to lessons learning commenced with the army in World War I.[13] A series of factors make such an enterprise less demanding than a foreign war investigation.[14] First, and above all, the more compelling motivation of poor battlefield performance drives learning from one's own experience versus curiosity amid peacetime uncertainty generating attention to other people's combat. Second, a military has access to significantly more data from its own experiences with soldiers, sailors, marines, and airmen ("collectors") present at the source working in bottom-up fashion unlike a limited number of wartime observers or postwar investigators operating as interlopers in a foreign conflict. Third, the decentralization of authority necessitated by the rapid dynamics of fighting facilitates greater information flow and abets implementation of identified best practices and potential solutions to problems. Finally, the ongoing combat offers opportunities for immediate feedback on instituted changes and subsequent refinements. Such an iterative process is not available when applying lessons identified from foreign wars.

Yet, despite these advantages, the US military has at best amassed a mixed record in learning from its own experiences. Correctly identifying events often proves difficult for participants amid the intensity and chaos of battle.[15] Institutional preferences and bias do not disappear with the onset of war and remain influential especially when interpreting murky information from the front. As evidenced by American Expeditionary Force senior officers' interference in learning during World War I, the attitude of military leaders has proven a critical variable in the appreciation of discovered knowledge, especially disruptive data. In the past century, the US military has continually instituted more sophisticated processes and organizations to improve battlefield learning. In particular, progress occurred in the 1980s with the introduction of the Center for Army Lessons Learned and the JCS Joint Lessons Learned Program.[16] Still, JCS and service efforts did not produce the desired level of learning, as dissatisfaction in the early years of Operation Enduring Freedom and Operation Iraqi Freedom led to additional measures. These improvements, for example, contributed to notable adaptation and innovation by army and marine corps units in Iraq between 2005 and 2007, and the DOD has continued to introduce refinements, especially through the web-based Joint Lessons Learned Information System, to better share lessons as well as support the field commander.[17]

While the US military has become more technically proficient at the collection, dissemination, and archiving of information, organizational learning remains highly dependent on what leaders deem to be germane to the institution's core mission.[18] Exemplifying the potentially harmful consequences of this condition was the US Army's neglect of lessons from the Bosnia and Herzegovina Implementation Force (1995–96) and Stabilization Force (1996–2004). Col. Pat Proctor, USA (Ret.), points out that officers during these deployments, schooled in high-intensity conflict, "struggled to meet the intellectual challenge of operating in an environment where mission success required dealing with civilians, establishing civil governance, practicing the 'art of street diplomacy' and exercising a nuanced application of force under strict rules of engagement."[19] As a result of these experiences, the army had the opportunity to better prepare for low-intensity activities. But it neglected information on operating in human environments and instead focused on revealed lessons about force deployability, which had consequences for high-intensity conflict. The resultant development of the interim brigade combat team was clearly a positive for the army, but overlooking low-intensity conflict findings left the service unnecessarily unprepared for the challenges of Operation Enduring Freedom and Operation Iraqi Freedom. The 1995–96 Russian action in Chechnya offered some of the same lessons as Bosnia about operating in urban environments, but even reinforcing cues from its own and other experiences produced no significant traction, largely because of flawed predictions of future requirements and a cultural dislike of such activities.[20]

The potential for such synergistic insights is particularly pronounced for a military frequently engaged in the use of force like the US military. First, findings from a foreign war may supplement or intensify lessons from contemporaneous or recent American experience, as occurred for the USAF with the Yom Kippur War and Vietnam War. Even if not providing much new information, similar findings in a different context boost confidence about the validity of insights. A foreign war may also provide complementary information by presenting aspects not covered by recent US military activity to facilitate a fuller picture of preparedness considerations. Whereas the danger from improvised explosive devices in Afghanistan and Iraq prompted the development of V-shaped lightly armored vehicles to protect their bottom and sides, Russian precision fire with specialized warheads in the Eastern Ukraine demonstrated the increased threat from above.[21] Danger, however, exists if the military or service uses a foreign war to dismiss its own experiences. The long-standing dislike of conducting counterinsurgency and stabilization operations has discouraged learning and retaining lessons from such activities after their completion. The US Army after the Vietnam War showed this perspective with its almost exclusive concentration on insights based on the Yom Kippur War and neglect of the Vietnam War experiences.

The Prussian/German army, the military institution that best learned from its own experiences during the industrial age, struggled to translate this prowess into productive outcomes when considering other people's wars, highlighting the difficulty of this task. Although gaining significant benefits from study of the Spanish Civil War burnished its learning reputation at the tactical and operational levels, this case, unlike for the United States, counts as a direct experience given its active support of the Nationalists and explicit experimentation with weapons and tactics.[22] In the other three foreign wars examined, the Germans were motivated outsiders attempting to learn from the foreign conflict. One can find notable examples of the Germans outperforming the Americans in identifying lessons and using such findings productively. For example, after investigating the Russo-Japanese combat, Daniel Kenda points out the Imperial German Army was "probably the most perceptive about how the machine gun affected the conduct of land warfare" and subsequently developed better capabilities and tactics for this indispensable element of modern war.[23] The Germans also responded more aggressively to the Yom Kippur War's lethality. While the US Army interpreted the evidence as largely validating its XM1 tank design, including retention of the 105 mm gun, the Germans increased the Leopard II's maximum weight limit by almost 20 percent to enable strengthened protection features and the use of a 120 mm smoothbore gun.[24]

Yet examples of German failures also exist. Whereas American, British, and French observers pointed out that the Imperial Japanese Army in 1904–5 had increased the spacing of attacking infantry to reduce vulnerability, the Germans reported their continued use of the tightly controlled German tactical model.[25] This error reflects the German tendency to suffer from the same key pitfall as the Americans in allowing preexisting preferences to shape their interpretation of events. Allan Millett and Williamson Murray attribute German success at experiential learning to their open and honest composition and consideration of after-action reports, but such practices did not generally translate to the study of foreign wars.[26] Without such an informational foundation, the service's ability to enhance military effectiveness suffered.

Given that the Americans are criticized for their tendency to neglect the operational level, it is of particular interest that the German army's operational emphasis did not yield significantly better outcomes, as best exemplified by the study of the Russo-Japanese War.[27] Reflective of their prewar beliefs, the Germans zeroed in on Japanese flanking maneuvers, especially at the Battle of Liaoyang, as responsible not only for their operational success but also the war's favorable outcome. When events did not follow expectations, the Germans criticized Japanese or Russian senior officers for acting incompetently rather than seriously considering if the facts on the ground precluded predicted results. Closer scrutiny of the combat's tactical dimensions of battle, especially when maneuver was not possible (e.g., the five-month siege of Port Arthur), would have aided appreciation of the challenges that could not be overcome simply with aggressive commanders. Moreover, the Germans' regard of operations as decisive contributed significantly to their neglect of the war's strategic dimensions, particularly the crucial role of naval power. Although investigation of the Russo-Japanese fighting enhanced senior German officers' appreciation of modern war's lethality, the conflict reinforced their overriding faith that attacking via envelopment was the optimal way to prosecute war rather than giving them pause to consider difficulties with this operational concept. Rather than any particular level of war being the most fruitful source of lessons, it is the interconnectedness between the levels that needs to be understood. Exacerbating this demanding requirement is that all the military great powers attempting to learn from foreign wars suffered from the aforementioned pitfalls that bedeviled American efforts.

WAY FORWARD—A BROADER ORIENTATION?

Given the challenges of learning from other people's wars, the US military, especially the army, has understandably attempted to maximize concrete benefits by adopting a narrow, pragmatic approach. As historian Maureen O'Connor notes, this orientation has occurred since the mid-nineteenth-century start of such efforts as governments wanted "a return from their investment in foreign learning" rather than a dispassionate analysis of events.[28] Enhancing prospects of satisfying this goal, the services tasked investigators with a lengthy list of subjects of interest and questions to answer. In particular, leaders sought hard (quantitative) data to validate judgments often reached quickly by senior officers to facilitate responding to cues before interest in the event faded. The US military has especially looked to combat-derived information to indicate the correct course of action for core activities among theoretically debated alternatives. This perspective only grew stronger in the twentieth century, culminating with the army leadership forming its basic insights from the Yom Kippur War by early January 1974 and structuring its formal review to amass supporting quantitative data and generate actionable recommendations (162 in all).[29] As the cases show, this approach has yielded a wide array of tangible benefits accounting for its repeated employment.

Yet the cases also reveal that this approach entails deleterious consequences and needs to be modified to maximize gains from studying foreign conflicts. What is the problem? Rather than hard data functioning as a neutral fulcrum between debated approaches, leaders with preexisting preferences frequently form snap judgments about the fighting and seek information to undergird their beliefs. Moreover, concentration on the more measurable aspects of battle encourages attention to the individual weapon performance and tactics. As a result, it diminishes the likelihood of capturing developments at the operational and strategic levels. Appreciating what happened at these levels is far less quantifiable and less generalizable, but neglecting these dimensions means forgoing a rare opportunity to examine subjects for which it is particularly difficult to structure realistic exercises and prepare officers.[30] Moreover, the authority of quantitative combat data tends to promote a false precision about weapon performance and tactical engagements. For example, the US Army after the Yom Kippur War placed considerable significance on the cause of Israeli armor losses. Examination of accessible destroyed tanks led to the frequently cited statistic that ATGMs accounted for only 7 percent to 24 percent of the total.[31] The study, however, could not include the many IDF tanks that remained in Arab territory, vehicles largely lost early in the war when ATGMs were most dangerous. This limitation should have introduced some caution about the finding that enemy tanks represented the far greater threat, but that conclusion reflected the outcome desired by the army leadership and was enthusiastically embraced. Finally, focus on quantitative data tends to discourage appreciation of the dynamism of the learning process as others respond to the same stimulus, an aspect that cannot be captured in the same way.

Can the benefits of past practice be obtained without suffering the negative consequences of that approach? Again, no specific procedural scheme or organizational structure would achieve this goal. Rather, what is needed is a shift away from narrowly constructed investigations and limited consideration of findings to a broader orientation. As I elaborate in the recommendations below, this more expansive concept involves four dimensions—what to collect, what to disseminate, what to include, and how to judge the worthiness of knowledge acquired. I want to be clear that I am not advocating forgoing the potential benefits from the high-profile, immediate postwar context, which requires some quick judgments. The approach, however, should not be optimized toward such gains, given the resultant risk to generating more comprehensive and dynamic insights.

PRINCIPLE 1: Compile a Complete and Accurate History

At first blush, such an objective seems uncontroversial, but it runs counter to the way practitioners have conceptualized these lessons-learning efforts. As Millett and Murray observed thirty years ago, the challenge is "how does the analyst put the historical experience to work for policymakers without doing violent damage to the facts and interpretations of past experience?"[32] Most pointedly, how much direction should be given to observers and investigators? Reflective of conventional wisdom, Lt. Gen. Paul Newton, then commander of the British Army's Force Development and Training Command, stated nearly a decade ago that "the key is to 'hunt' not 'gather' lessons."[33] Such an approach might be sensible when involved in an ongoing war and trying to benefit from one's own experiences, but information collection from a foreign war requires both hunting and gathering. That is, although the exclusion of tasking is bureaucratically unrealistic and substantively unwise, given a need to ensure coverage of critical subjects, such guidance should be minimized to avoid canalizing the investigation and promoting confirmation bias. In particular, a need exists to abet the capture of nontechnical/tactical findings. As a recent IDA report on insights from the Eastern Ukraine argues, "projecting these lessons into the future and more importantly, into conflicts of a different character from the one being examined, requires a different approach."[34] In the cases studied, the best outcomes resulted from the endeavors of stalwart soldiers such as Peyton March, Townsend Griffiss, and Donn Starry displaying curiosity, rigor, and even-handedness in contrast to observers such as John Morrison and Stephen Fuqua, who employed a harmful, albeit well-intentioned, focus on data that reaffirmed their retrograde views. Given that combatants attempt to apply their own battlefield lessons as a conflict progresses, capturing this evolution needs to be an explicit part of the information-gathering process to not only discover what happened but reinforce the dynamism of war.

PRINCIPLE 2: Maximize Information Dissemination

Obtaining as accurate and complete a history as possible provides a foundation for discovery, but taking full advantage of the collected material requires maximizing its exposure to soldiers, sailors, aviators, and marines. Although in sum the contextual changes between the 1850s and 1970s enhanced the learning process, one negative was the increasing restriction on information gathered. While the War Department withheld some sensitive data from the Crimean and Russo-Japanese War observer reports, most of their accounts received publication, greatly aiding officers' consideration of the experience. The changing collection modalities for the latter two cases, along with the military's growing complexity, meant that increasing amounts of data became controlled on "national security" grounds. Practically, such constraint impedes examination, especially if researchers, educators, and combat developers lack access to the supporting raw data. Although considerations of secrecy are necessary, the military needs to minimize classification restrictions as much as possible. As Anthony Dibella observes, "If there is one common trait of learning organizations, it is that information and knowledge flows freely up, down, and across."[35] The mechanisms of applying this recommendation are not difficult given the extensive development of institutions (e.g., Center for Army Lessons Learned) and web-based platforms (e.g., Joint Lessons Learned Information System), which greatly abet the flow and storage of accessible data about the US military's own experiences.[36] Observations, insights, and lessons from foreign wars should be treated in the same way, especially given the potential benefit from reassessment of the experience at a later date when it might be of more use. Availability of data is particularly important for progress when considering combat in noncore areas for which the institutional leadership is less likely to direct attention, even if they represent subjects of potential greatest gain given their prior neglect.

PRINCIPLE 3: Learn from the Learners

Expanding the scope of the investigation and the availability of collected information are imperative steps to capturing available insights, but the potential for the effort to enhance military effectiveness also requires identification of other militaries' interpretation of and reaction to the same combat. First, awareness of the lessons generated by potential adversaries may enhance one's own understanding. Findings, when in accord with US conclusions, function as reinforcement while divergent views should prompt scrutiny of one's conclusions, reducing the possibility of confirmation bias. These efforts may also reveal useful data about subjects neglected by US investigators, helping correct damaging oversights. Second and more significantly, knowledge of other militaries' understanding of events and how they apply such information to their forces is critical for future preparedness. As noted in discussion of one pitfall ("confident embrace of misleading information"), each case study had examples of harmful actions from neglecting such impacts when engaged in competition with rivals. Even when leaders have acknowledged the importance of such awareness, as exemplified by the declarations of army leaders about the Red

Army in the mid-1970s, past practice has shown a tendency to not follow through as all the relevant data may not exist for some time after the precipitating event. While such attention might be thought of as simply sound intelligence collection, making it an explicit component of the lesson-learning effort should increase appreciation for the dynamic nature of learning and the need to reassess periodically the continuing viability of one's own applied lessons.

PRINCIPLE 4: Consider Lessons beyond Current Priorities

Adoption of this perspective may generate the most resistance given the normal modus operandi of military institutions, but I believe it is essential to better use the fortuitous educational opportunities provided by other people's wars. In every case, civil and military decision-makers understandably emphasized relevance when considering whether the services should respond to a finding. As Starry emphasized, "we couldn't just say, 'Well here it is . . . we saw it in the deserts in the Yom Kippur War, so it's got to be right for us.'"[37] For the US military, relevance usually consists of two components. First, does the information abet accomplishing the service's core mission(s)? Concentrating on commerce protection, the navy in the late 1850s dismissed the salience of the armored floating battery's impressive debut in the Crimean War. As Secretary Isaac Toucey declared, "It is universally admitted to be inexpedient to endeavor to compete with other great commercial powers in the magnitude of their naval preparations."[38] Thus, while the British and French navies engaged in an ironclad arms race, the Americans did not even construct a test ship. Second, is the finding compatible with how an institution prefers to accomplish its tasks given resources and culture? Rather than follow the three-tank platoons that provided the IDF superior command and control on the chaotic Yom Kippur War battlefield, the army opted to shift from five-tank to four-tank platoons in part because the smaller three-tank formation required essentially 100 percent readiness. Satisfying this demand concerned senior American officers, given their experience and doubt about the new M1's reliability.

Employing this traditional conception of "relevance" is problematic when evaluating lessons from foreign wars given frequently mistaken presumptions about what will be germane. Only a few years after the Navy Department's dismissal of the floating battery's relevance, the US Civil War erupted, with both sides scrambling to construct ironclads. The United States would have been at an unnecessarily steep and potentially dangerous disadvantage if the British and French fleets had entered the conflict at the outset, as was distinctly possible. Not surprisingly, potentially important areas of warfare deemed irrelevant or low priority are usually much less understood. In 1974, after the Yom Kippur War, the USAF provided one of the more direct applications of findings with the Pave Strike program (accelerating eleven R&D

projects to facilitate air-to-ground strikes on targets with robust air defense protection). Yet all these initiatives already existed because their need had been recognized from the USAF's own difficulties in Southeast Asia. While data from the dramatic Arab–Israeli fighting had informational and political value, the potential benefit from a foreign war is far greater for what it signals about neglected areas of future combat. Although the secretary of the navy's 1905 Annual Report noted the growing role of mine warfare as an important lesson from the Russo-Japanese War, the battleship-fixated service did not seriously consider this culturally unappealing maritime activity.[39] As a result, the navy's knowledge and capability improved only marginally in the decade before US entry into World War I, during which it struggled in this area, including construction of the massive North Sea Mine Barrage. Moreover, the case studies showed that the probability for avoiding corrupted lessons is higher for new or previously ignored subjects (e.g., mines in the 1850s and 1900s and close ground support in the mid-1970s) than issues of preexisting dispute (e.g., battleship design in the 1900s and infantry–tank relationship in the late 1930s).

Taking full advantage of other people's wars requires not only bolstering core capabilities but enabling a more adaptive force. Although armed forces must develop and prioritize core competencies, the key is doing so without sacrificing flexibility, given that future wars rarely occur as anticipated. As Gen. James Polk, USA (Ret.), stated after the Yom Kippur War, "the prudent war-planner . . . wants to have a force that is flexible and adaptable, and has no glaring weaknesses apparent to the enemy."[40] Foreign war investigations facilitate this objective since, as O'Connor points out, they "can give an idea of the range of strategic and tactical possibilities, establishing certain parameters within which the patterns of the next big war will probably fall."[41] This benefit can be particularly useful for a military like that of the United States, with extensive battlefield experience concentrated on particular activities and thus prone to tunnel vision. Adopting this perspective will not be easy for military leaders, as the very combat examined often creates a sense of urgency about current threats and revealed deficiencies that encourages focus on near-term initiatives to bolster deterrence and defense. The primary objection to expanding the parameters of what makes something relevant is the diminished availability of resources for established priorities. Yet, rather than generating expensive ready capabilities, responding to cues about neglected areas only requires robust exploration (e.g., conceptualizing ideas, conducting R&D, and experimenting with organizations and tactics) to enhance understanding and lay a foundation, should they become necessary. Satisfying such application should be achievable without compromising the readiness in areas of seemingly greater importance. Applying concrete findings to current priorities is an essential component of learning lessons, but so is the proper consideration of the broader questions engendered and challenges revealed by foreign conflicts.

NOTES

Epigraph: Michael Howard, "Military Science in an Age of Peace," *Journal of the RUSI for Defence Studies* 119, no. 1 (March 1974): 4.

1. For example, see William Arkin, *Divining Victory: Airpower in the 2006 Israel-Hezbollah War* (Montgomery, AL: Air University Press, 2007); Matt Matthews, *We Were Caught Unprepared: The 2006 Hezbollah-Israel War* (Fort Leavenworth, KS: Combat Studies Institute Press, 2008); Stephen Biddle and Jeffrey Friedman, *The 2006 Lebanon Campaign and the Future of Warfare: Implications for Army and Defense Policy* (Carlisle, PA: Strategic Studies Institute, 2008); Scott Farquhar, ed., *Back to Basics: A Study of the Second Lebanon War and Operation Cast Lead* (Fort Leavenworth, KS: Combat Studies Institute Press, 2009); and David Johnson, *Hard Fighting: Israel in Lebanon and Gaza* (Washington, DC: RAND Press, 2011).

2. Robert Angevine, et al., "Learning Lessons from the Ukraine Conflict" (Alexandria, VA: Institute for Defense Analyses, document NS D-10367, May 2019), 1. For other examples, see John Garcia, et al., "Ukraine Lessons Learned: News from the Front" (Fort Leavenworth, KS: US Army Combined Arms Center, November 2015); Mary Ellen Connell and Ryan Evans, *Russia's Ambiguous Warfare and Implications for the US Marine Corps* (Alexandria, VA: Center for Naval Analyses, 2016); Amos Fox, *Hybrid Warfare: The 21st Century Russian Way of Warfare* (Fort Leavenworth, KS: US Army School for Advanced Military Studies, 2017); and Michael Kofman, Katya Migacheva, Brian Nichiporuk, Andrew Radin, Olesya Tkacheva, and Jenny Oberholtzer, *Lessons from Russia's Operations in Crimea and Eastern Ukraine* (Santa Monica, CA: RAND, 2017).

3. Rick Chersicla, "Special Forces as Military Observers in Modern Combat" (Modern War Institute at West Point, September 18, 2016); John Nutt, "Joint Conflict Observer Team: An Old Concept Redefined" (Research paper, Naval War College, February 3, 2003); and Kelly Alexander, "The Marine Corps Combat Observer Program: 'Messengers of Warfighting in the 21st Century'" (Master's thesis, USMC Command and Staff College, Marine Corps University, April 18, 2002).

4. Donald Mrozek, *The US Air Force after Vietnam: Postwar Challenges and Potential for Responses* (Maxwell AFB, AL: Air University Press, 1988), 6–7; and William Vacca, "Learning about Military Effectiveness: Examining Theories of Learning during the Russo-Japanese War" (PhD diss., Rutgers University, 2009), 276–78, 288, 293, 385.

5. Thomas Mahnken, *Uncovering Ways of War: US Intelligence and Foreign Military Innovation, 1918–1941* (Ithaca, NY: Cornell University Press, 2009), 6.

6. Donn Starry, "Combined Arms," *Armor Magazine*, September–October 1978, in *Press On! Selected Works of General Donn A. Starry*, vol. 1, ed. Lewis Sorley (Fort Leavenworth, KS: Combat Studies Institute Press, 2009), 243.

7. Steven Zaloga, *Spanish Civil War Tanks: The Proving Ground for Blitzkrieg* (Oxford: Osprey, 2010), 28, 40; and George Hofmann, "Flawed Lessons Learned: The Role of US Military Attachés in Assessing Armored Warfare during the Spanish Civil War," *Armor* 113, no. 3 (May–June 2004): 30.

8. Janine Davidson, *Lifting the Fog of Peace, How Americans Learned to Fight Modern War* (Ann Arbor: University of Michigan Press, 2010), 23.

9. Richard Challener, *Admirals, Generals, and American Foreign Policy, 1898–1914* (Princeton, NJ: Princeton University Press, 1973), 241.

10. Appendix E, "Combat Consumption Rates for Weapons Systems," in Joint Chiefs of Staff, Logistics Directorate, *Logistic Lessons Learned 1973 Middle East War*, November 27, 1974 (Washington, DC: Joint Chiefs of Staff, 1975), 1.

11. C. N. Barclay, "Learning the Hard Way: Lessons from the October War," *Army* 24, no. 3 (March 1974): 28–29.

12. Angus Konstam, *American Civil War Fortifications (1): Coastal Brick and Stone Forts* (New York: Osprey, 2003), 48.

13. Dennis Vetock, *Lessons Learned: A History of US Army Lesson Learning* (Carlisle Barracks, PA: US Army Military History Institute, 1988), 37–54; and Michael Shurkin, "How the US Military Learned to Learn in World War I: Lessons from the American Expeditionary Forces," *War on the Rocks*, August 22, 2018.

14. Robert Foley, Stuart Griffin, and Helen McCartney, "'Transformation in Contact': Learning the Lessons of Modern War," *International Affairs* 87, no. 2 (2011): 269–70; James Russell, *Innovation, Transformation, and War: Counterinsurgency Operations in Anbar and Ninewa Provinces, Iraq, 2005–2007* (Stanford, CA: Stanford University Press, 2011), 31, 200; Tom Dyson, *Organization Learning and the Modern Army: A New Model for Lessons-Learned Processes* (London: Routledge, 2020), 1–4, 23–24; Anthony Dibella, "Can the Army Become A *Learning Organization?* A Question Reexamined," *Joint Forces Quarterly* 56, no. 1 (2010): 119–22; and Robert Foley, "Dumb Donkeys or Cunning Foxes? Learning in the British and German Armies during the Great War," *International Affairs* 90, no. 2 (March 2014): 22–24.

15. Allan Millett and Williamson Murray, "Lessons of War," *National Interest* 14 (Winter 1988–89): 89–90.

16. Vetock, *Lessons Learned*, 124–25; Foley et al., "'Transformation in Contact'," 256–59; Dibella, "Can the Army Become a *Learning Organization?*," 117–18; and Jon Thomas and Douglas Shultz, "Lessons about Lessons: Growing the Joint Lessons Learned Program," *Joint Forces Quarterly* 79, no. 4 (October 2015): 113–19.

17. Thomas and Shultz, "Lessons about Lessons," 118–19; Dibella, "Can the Army Become a *Learning Organization?*," 117–18; and Russell, *Innovation*, 196–200.

18. For paragraph, see Pat Proctor, "Lessons Unlearned: Army Transformation and Low-Intensity Conflict," *Parameters* 47, no. 4 (Winter 2017–18): 33–45.

19. Proctor, 38.

20. Stephen Blank and Earl Tilford, *Russia's Invasion of Chechnya: A Preliminary Assessment* (Carlisle Barracks, PA: Strategic Studies Institute, 1995), 12.

21. Angevine et al., "Learning Lessons," 9.

22. Williamson Murray, "Comparative Approaches to Interwar Innovation," *Joint Forces Quarterly* 25 (Summer 2000): 84; James Corum, "The Luftwaffe and Lessons Learned in the Spanish Civil War," in *Air Power History: Turning Points from Kitty Hawk to Kosovo*, ed. Sebastian Cox and Peter Gray (New York: Frank Cass, 2005), 68, 77, 83–85; and Steven Zaloga and Kenneth Estes, "Armor: Was the Spanish Civil War a Testing Ground for the Military Use of Tanks?," in *History in Dispute*, vol. 18: *The Spanish Civil War*, ed. Kenneth Estes and Daniel

Kowalsky (Detroit: St. James Press, 2005), 259–62; Williamson Murray, "Thoughts on Lessons Learned in the Past," in *Learning the Lessons of Modern War*, ed. Thomas Mahnken (Stanford, CA: Stanford University Press, 2020), 28, 31–32; and Foley, "Dumb Donkeys or Cunning Foxes?," 11–16, 23–24.

23. Daniel Kenda, "Lessons Learned from the Use of the Machine Gun during the Russo-Japanese War and the Application of Those Lessons by the Protagonists of World War I" (Master's thesis, Command and General Staff College, 2005), 56.

24. Leo Daugherty III, "'The Tip of the Spear': The Bundeswehr, Soviet Force Restructuring and Development of West Germany's Armored Forces, 1951–1986," *Journal of Slavic Military Studies* 25, no. 4 (October 2012): 477–78; and Rolf Hilmes, "Modern German Tank Development, 1956–2000," *Armor* 110, no. 1 (January–February 2001): 18–19.

25. Vacca, "Learning," 148, 161, 360.

26. Millett and Murray, "Lessons of War," 89; see also Foley, "Dumb Donkeys or Cunning Foxes?," 5, 11–16.

27. For paragraph, see Vacca, "Learning," 183–84, 247–48, 274–75, 286–87, 335–55, 360–62; and Keir Lieber, "The New History of World War I and What It Means for International Relations Theory," *International Security* 32, no. 2 (Fall 2007): 179–83.

28. Maureen P. O'Connor, "In the Eye of the Beholder: Western Military Observers from Buena Vista to Plevna" (PhD diss., Harvard University, 1996), 378.

29. R. Z. Alessi-Friedlander, "Learning to Win When Fighting Outnumbered: Operational Risk in the US Army, 1973–1982, and the Influence of the 1973 Arab-Israeli War" (Master's thesis, Command and General Staff College, 2016), 99.

30. Murray, "Thoughts on Lessons Learned," 25, 43.

31. Declassified WSEG Report 249, *Assessment of the Weapons and Tactics Used in the October 1973 Middle East War*, October 1974, p. 22–26, 99–111 (accessed electronically via the CIA's FOIA Reading Room); William DePuy, letter to Senator John Culver, May 12, 1975, in *Selected Papers of General William E. DePuy*, comp. Richard Swain (Fort Leavenworth, KS: Combat Studies Institute, 1994), 167; and Donn Starry, "October 1973 Mideast War," May 12, 1975, Box 59, Folder 3, Donn Starry Papers, US Army Heritage and Education Center at Carlisle Barracks, 2–6.

32. Millett and Murray, "Lessons of War," 84; see also Frank Hoffman, "Learning Large Lessons from Small Wars," *War on the Rocks*, February 5, 2014.

33. Foley et al., "Transformation," 262–63.

34. Angevine et al., "Learning Lessons," 1.

35. Dibella, "Can the Army Become a *Learning Organization?*," 121.

36. Foley et al., "Transformation," 258–59, 268–69; Vacca, "Learning," 389, 407; Russell, *Innovation*, 200–201, 203; and Thomas and Schultz, "Lessons about Lessons," 117–19.

37. Donn Starry, "Development of Doctrine," March 19, 1993, oral history interview in *Press On! Selected Works of General Donn A. Starry*, vol. 2, ed. Lewis Sorley (Fort Leavenworth, KS: Combat Studies Institute Press, 2009), 1256.

38. Quoted in Kenneth Hagan, *This People's Navy: The Making of American Sea Power* (New York: Free Press, 1991), 140.

39. Charles Bonaparte, Report of the Secretary of the Navy, December 4, 1905, in *Annual Reports of the Navy Department for the Year 1905* (Washington, DC: Government Printing Office, 1906), 19–20.

40. James Polk, "The New Short War Strategy," *Strategic Review* 3 (Summer 1975): 56; see also Michael Evans, "Learning Lessons: The Value of a Contemporary Approach to History," in *Learning the Lessons of Modern War*, ed. Thomas Mahnken (Stanford, CA: Stanford University Press, 2020), 17–18.

41. O'Connor, "In the Eye of the Beholder," 396.

SELECTED BIBLIOGRAPHY

PRIMARY SOURCES

Crimean War

Crist, Lynda, and Mary Dix, eds. *Papers of Jefferson Davis*, Vol. 5: *1853–1855*. Baton Rouge: Louisiana State University Press, 1985.

———. *Papers of Jefferson Davis*, Vol. 6: *1856–1860*. Baton Rouge: Louisiana State University Press, 1989.

Dahlgren, John. *Shells and Shell-Guns*. Philadelphia: King & Baird, 1856.

Davis, Jefferson, *Report of the Secretary of War*, December 1, 1853. Washington, DC: Beverly Tucker, 1853.

———. *Report of the Secretary of War*, December 4, 1854. Washington, DC: A.O.P. Nicholson, 1854.

———. *Report of the Secretary of War*, December 3, 1855. Washington, DC: Cornelius Wendell, 1855.

———. *Report of the Secretary of War*, December 1, 1856. Washington, DC: Cornelius Wendell, 1856.

Delafield, Richard. *Report on the Art of War in Europe in 1854, 1855, and 1856*. Washington, DC: George W. Bowman, 1860.

Dobbin, James. *Report of the Secretary of Navy*, December 4, 1854. Washington, DC: A.O.P. Nicholson, 1854.

———. *Report of the Secretary of Navy*, December 3, 1855. Washington, DC: Cornelius Wendell, 1855.

———. *Report of the Secretary of Navy*, December 1, 1856. Washington, DC: Cornelius Wendell, 1856.

Floyd, John. *Report of the Secretary of War*, December 5, 1857. Washington, DC: Cornelius Wendell, 1857.

———. *Report of the Secretary of War*, December 6, 1858. Washington, DC: William A. Harris, 1858.

———. *Report of the Secretary of War*, December 1, 1859. Washington, DC: George W. Bowman, 1859.

Halleck, Henry. *Elements of Military Art and Science*. 2nd ed. New York: D. Appleton, 1859.

Hayes, J. D., ed. *Samuel Francis Du Pont: Selection from His Civil War Letters*, Vol. 1: *The Mission: 1860–1862*. Ithaca, NY: Cornell University Press, 1969.

———. *Samuel Francis Du Pont: Selection from His Civil War Letters*, Vol. 2: *The Blockade: 1862–1863*. Ithaca, NY: Cornell University Press, 1969.

———. *Samuel Francis Du Pont: Selection from His Civil War Letters*, Vol. 3: *The Repulse: 1863–1865*. Ithaca, NY: Cornell University Press, 1969.

McClellan, George. *Report of the Secretary of War: Communicating the Report of Captain George B. McClellan, One of the Officers Sent to the Seat of War in Europe in 1855 and 1856*. Washington, DC: A.O.P. Nicholson, 1857.

Mordecai, Alfred. *The Military Commission to Europe in 1855 and 1856: The Report of Major Alfred Mordecai*. Washington, DC: George W. Bowman, 1860.

Rowland, Dunbar, ed. *Jefferson Davis, Constitutionalist*, Vol. 2: *His Letters, Papers, and Speeches*. Jackson: Mississippi Department of Archives and History, 1923.

Toucey, Isaac. *Report of the Secretary of Navy*, December 3, 1857. Washington, DC: Cornelius Wendell, 1857.

Russo-Japanese War

Archives
Theodore Roosevelt Center Digital Library, Dickinson State University (TRCDL).

Government Reports
Annual Reports of the Navy Department for the Year 1904. Washington, DC: Government Printing Office, 1904.
    Report of the Secretary of the Navy
Annual Reports of the Navy Department for the Year 1905. Washington, DC: Government Printing Office, 1906.
    Report of the Secretary of the Navy
    Report of the Chief of the Bureau of Navigation
    Report of the Chief of Bureau of Ordnance
    Report of the Surgeon-General
Annual Reports of the Navy Department for the Year 1906. Washington, DC: Government Printing Office, 1907.
    Report of the Secretary of the Navy
Annual Reports of the Navy Department for the Year 1907. Washington, DC: Government Printing Office, 1908.
    Report of the Secretary of the Navy
Annual Reports of the War Department for the Fiscal Year Ended June 30, 1904. Washington, DC: Government Printing Office, 1904.

Volume 1: Overview

Report of the Secretary of War

Volume 2: Armament, Transportation, and Supply

Report of the Chief of Ordnance

Report of the Chief of Artillery

Report of Chief of Engineers, Military Affairs

Report of the Quartermaster-General

Annual Reports of the War Department for the Fiscal Year Ended June 30, 1905. Washington, DC: Government Printing Office, 1905.

Volume 1: Overview

Report of the Secretary of War

Report of the Chief of Staff

Volume 2: Armament, Transportation, and Supply

Report of the Chief of Artillery

Report of the Board of Ordnance and Fortification

Report of the Commissary-General

Report of the Chief Signal Officer

Volume 4: Militia Affairs, Military Schools and Colleges

Report of the School of Submarine Defense

Volume 9: Chief of Ordnance

Report of Chief of Ordnance, Appendix

Annual Reports of the War Department for the Year Ended June 30, 1906. Washington, DC: Government Printing Office, 1906.

Volume 1: Overview

Report of the Secretary of War

Report of the Chief of Staff

Volume 2: Armament, Transportation, and Supply

Report of the Board of Ordnance and Fortification

Report of the Chief of Artillery

Report of the Quartermaster-General

Report of the Commissary-General

Report of the Chief Signal Officer

Report of Surgeon-General

Volume 3: Division and Department Commanders

Report of Department of the East

Report of the Philippines Division

Volume 4: Militia Affairs, Military Schools and Colleges

Report of the Engineer School

Volume 6: Chief of Ordnance

Report of the Chief of Ordnance

Annual Reports of the War Department, 1909. Washington, DC: Government Printing Office, 1909.

  Volume 6: Chief of Ordnance

   Report of the Chief of Ordnance

Annual Reports of the War Department, 1910. Washington, DC: Government Printing Office, 1910.

  Volume 1: Overview

   Report of the Chief of Staff

  Volume 6: Chief of Ordnance

   Report of the Chief of Ordnance

1920 Secretary of War Annual Report. Washington, DC: Government Printing Office, 1921.

Reports of Military Observers Attached to the Armies in Manchuria during the Russo-Japanese War, Part 1: *Captain Peyton March, Captain John Morrison, Captain Carl Reichmann and Lieutenant Colonel Walter Schuyler.* Washington, DC: Government Printing Office, 1906.

Reports of Military Observers Attached to the Armies in Manchuria during the Russo-Japanese War, Part 2: *Colonel Valery Havard and Colonel John Van R. Hoff.* Washington, DC: Government Printing Office, 1906.

Reports of Military Observers Attached to the Armies in Manchuria during the Russo-Japanese War, Part 3: *Major Joseph Kuhn.* Washington, DC: Government Printing Office, 1906.

Reports of Military Observers Attached to the Armies in Manchuria during the Russo-Japanese War, Part 4: *Major Charles Lynch.* Washington, DC: Government Printing Office, 1907.

Reports of Military Observers Attached to the Armies in Manchuria during the Russo-Japanese War, Part 5: *Captain William Judson and Lieutenant Colonel Edward McClernand.* Washington, DC: Government Printing Office, 1907.

War Department, U.S.A. Annual Reports, 1907. Washington, DC: Government Printing Office, 1907.

  Volume 1: Overview

   Report of the Chief of Staff

   Report of the Secretary of War

  Volume 2: Armament, Transportation, and Supply

   Report of the Board of Ordnance and Fortification

   Report of the Chief of Artillery

   Report of Quarter-Master General

  Volume 4: Militia Affairs, Military Schools and Colleges

   Report of the Infantry and Cavalry School

Volume 6: Chief of Ordnance
 Report of the Chief of Ordnance
War Department Annual Reports, 1908. Washington, DC: Government Printing Office, 1908.
 Volume 1: Overview
 Report of the Secretary of War
 Report of the Chief of Staff
 Volume 2: Armament, Transportation, and Supply
 Report of the Chief of Coastal Artillery

Publications

Cotten, Lyman. "The Naval Strategy of the Russo-Japanese War." US Naval Institute *Proceedings* 36, no. 1 (March 1910): 41–60.

Ferrand, M. C. "Torpedo and Mine Effects in the Russo-Japanese War." Translated by Philip Alger. US Naval Institute *Proceedings* 33, no. 4 (December 1907): 1479–86.

Fiske, Bradley. "Compromiseless Ships." US Naval Institute *Proceedings* 31, no. 3 (September 1905): 36,550–53.

———. "Why Togo Won." US Naval Institute *Proceedings* 31, no. 4 (December 1905): 807–9.

Horn, Tiemann. "Present Method and Lessons in Regard to Field Artillery Taught by the Russo-Japanese War." *Journal of the US Artillery Association* 30, no. 3 (November–December 1908): 251–62.

Kuhn, Joseph. "From Port Arthur to Mukden with Nogi." *Journal of the US Infantry Association* 2, no. 4 (April 1906): 34–47.

Macomb, Montgomery. "Attack and Defense of an Experimental Redoubt." *Journal of the US Infantry Association* 5, no. 3 (November 1908): 358–68.

———. "Machine Guns in the Russian Army." *Journal of the US Infantry Association* 3, no. 3 (January 1907): 3–21.

———. "Notes on the Russian Infantry Soldier." *Journal of the US Infantry Association* 2, no. 4 (April 1906): 3–33.

Mahan, Alfred Thayer. *Naval Administration and Warfare: Some General Principles*. Boston: Little, Brown, 1918.

———. "Reflections, Historic and Other, Suggested by the Battle of the Sea of Japan." US Naval Institute *Proceedings* 32, no. 2 (June 1906): 447–71.

McCully, Newton. *The McCully Report: The Russo-Japanese War, 1904–1905*. Annapolis, MD: Naval Institute Press, 1977.

Morison, Elting, ed. *The Letters of Theodore Roosevelt*, Vol. 4: *The Square Deal, 1903–1905*. Cambridge, MA: Harvard University Press, 1951.

———. *The Letters of Theodore Roosevelt*, Vol. 5: *The Big Stick, 1905–1907*. Cambridge, MA: Harvard University Press, 1952.

———. *The Letters of Theodore Roosevelt,* Vol. 6: *The Big Stick, 1907–1909.* Cambridge, MA: Harvard University Press, 1952.

Reichmann, Carl. "Chances in War." *Journal of the US Infantry* 3, no. 1 (July 1906): 3–29.

———. "Chances in War—Concluded." *Journal of the US Infantry* 3, no. 2 (October 1906): 3–21.

Schroeder, Seaton. "Gleanings from the Sea of Japan." US Naval Institute *Proceedings* 32, no. 1 (March 1906): 47–93.

Schulz, Edward. "Land Defense of Seacoast Fortifications." *Journal of the Military Services Institution of the United States* 36, no. 133 (January–February 1905): 88–103.

Sims, William. "The Inherent Tactical Qualities of the All-Big-Gun, One-Caliber Battleships of High Speed, Large Displacement, and Gun-Power." US Naval Institute *Proceedings* 32, no. 4 (December 1906): 1337–66.

White, R. D. "With the Baltic Fleet at Tsushima." US Naval Institute *Proceedings* 32, no. 2 (June 1906): 597–620.

Spanish Civil War

Annual Reports of the War Department for the FY Ended June 30, 1937. Washington, DC: Government Printing Office, 1937.
> Volume 1: Overview
>> Report of the Secretary of War
>> Report of the Chief of Staff

Annual Reports of the War Department for the FY Ended June 30, 1938. Washington, DC: Government Printing Office, 1938.
> Volume 1: Overview
>> Report of the Chief of Staff
>> Report of the Assistant Secretary of War

Annual Reports of the War Department for the FY Ended June 30, 1939. Washington, DC: Government Printing Office, 1939.
> Volume 1: Overview
>> Report of the Secretary of War
>> Report of the Assistant Secretary of War
>> Report of the Chief of Staff

Canevari, Emilio. "Forecasts from the War in Spain: Lessons Based on Technical and Tactical Experience." *Army Ordnance* 18, no. 107 (March–April 1938): 273–80.

Cortada, James, ed. *Modern Warfare in Spain: American Military Observations on the Spanish Civil War, 1936–1939.* Washington, DC: Potomac, 2012.

Fuller, J.F.C. "The Spanish War." *Army Ordnance* 19, no. 111 (November–December 1938): 139–43.

———. "The Tank in Spain." *Army Ordnance* 19, no. 109 (July–August 1938): 24–27.

Greene, Joseph. "The Case for Antitank." *Infantry Journal* 45, no. 3 (May–June 1938): 213–22.

Johnson, Wendell. "Spain: A Year and a Half of Modern War." *Infantry Journal* 45, no. 2 (March–April 1938): 133–40.

———. "Spanish War: A Review of the Best Foreign Opinion." *Infantry Journal* 45, no. 4 (July–August 1938): 351–56.

Jones, Byron Q., comp. *Spanish War: Reports and Articles*, Vol. 1: *September 1, 1936 to August 17, 1937*. Carlisle Barracks, PA: Army War College, 1937.

———. *Spanish War: Reports and Articles*, Vol. 2: *August 17, 1937 to September 1, 1938*. Carlisle Barracks, PA: Army War College, 1938.

Kenney, George. "The Airplane in Modern Warfare." *US Air Services* (July 1938): 17–22, 36.

Lanza, Conrad. "Lessons from Spain." *Field Artillery Journal* 28, no. 3 (May–June 1938): 183–96.

Liddell Hart, Basil. "Lessons from Spain." In *Europe in Arms*. Rev. ed. New York: Random House, 1937.

———. "Lessons of the Spanish War." *Army Ordnance* 18, no. 106 (January–February 1938): 201–4.

Lynch, George. "Current Infantry Developments." *Infantry Journal* 45, no. 1 (January–February 1938): 3–9.

Mackin, Robert. "Airplanes Can Be Stopped." *Coast Artillery Journal* 80, no. 5 (September–October 1937): 396–401.

Merten, Fred. "Cavalry in the War in Spain." *Cavalry Journal* 47, no. 6 (November–December 1938): 47.

Noble, Charles. "Defense against Air Attack." *Cavalry Journal* 47, no. 4 (July–August 1938): 332–34.

Phillips, Thomas. "Air Power and Troop Movement." *Infantry Journal* 81, no. 3 (May–June 1938): 195–97.

Reilly, Henry. "Attack in Spain." *Field Artillery Journal* 29, no. 4 (July–August 1939): 331–35.

———. "Proving Ground in Spain." *Army Ordnance* 19, no. 114 (May–June 1939): 333–36.

Rudolph, Jack. "Guadalajara: An Aerial Counter-Attack." *Infantry Journal* 45, no. 2 (March–April 1938): 109–14.

Usera, Vincent. "Some Lessons from the Spanish War." *Field Artillery Journal* 29, no. 5 (September–October 1939): 406–16.

Yom Kippur War

Bell, William Gardner, and Karl Cocke, eds. *Department of the Army Historical Summary, Fiscal Year 1973*. Washington, DC: Center of Military History, 1977.

Brownlee, Romie, and William Mullen III, interviewers. *Changing an Army: An Oral History of General William E. DePuy.* Carlisle Barracks, PA: US Army Military History Institute, Senior Officer Oral History Program, 1979.

Casey, Maurice. *Oral History Interview.* Fairfax, VA: Air Force Public Affairs Alumni Association, 1995.

Cocke, Karl, ed. *Department of the Army Historical Summary, Fiscal Year 1974.* Washington, DC: Center of Military History, 1978.

———. *Department of the Army Historical Summary, Fiscal Year 1975.* Washington, DC: Center of Military History, 1978.

Cocke, Karl, et al., eds. *Department of the Army Historical Summary, Fiscal Year 1976.* Washington, DC: Center of Military History, 1977.

———. *Department of the Army Historical Summary, Fiscal Year 1977.* Washington, DC: Center of Military History, 1979.

———. *Department of the Army Historical Summary, Fiscal Year 1978.* Washington, DC: Center of Military History, 1980.

———. *Department of the Army Historical Summary, Fiscal Year 1979.* Washington, DC: Center of Military History, 1982.

Cushman, John. *Fort Leavenworth—A Memoir, Part Two, 1973–1976.* Self-published, 2013. http://www.west-point.org/publications/cushman/6aVolumeSix.pdf.

———. *Oral History; Lieutenant General John H. Cushman, US Army, Retired,* Vol. 5: *Leavenworth, Korea, and Reflections on a Career.* Self-published, 2014. http://www.2ndbde.org/brigade_commanders/ltg_jack_cushman/5-VolumeFive.pdf.

Dixon, Robert. "The Range of Tactical Air Operations." *Strategic Review* 2, no. 2 (Spring 1974): 21–26.

———. "TAC-TRADOC Dialogue." *Strategic Review* 6, no. 1 (Winter 1978): 45–54.

Gorman, Paul F. *Strategy and Tactics for Learning: The Papers of General Paul F. Gorman.* Fort Leavenworth, KS: Combat Studies Institute Press, 2011.

Joint Chiefs of Staff, Logistics Directorate. *Logistic Lessons Learned 1973 Middle East War.* Washington, DC: Joint Chief of Staff, 1975.

Joint Chiefs of Staff, Operations Directorate. *Middle East Crisis 1973 Lessons Learned Abstracts.* Washington, DC: Joint Chiefs of Staff, 1974.

Leavitt, Lloyd R. *Following the Flag: An Air Force Officer Provides an Eyewitness View of Major Events and Policies during the Cold War.* Maxwell AFB, AL: Air University Press, 2010.

Miley, Henry. "Mid-East War Logistics." *Army Logistician* 6, no. 4 (July–August 1974): 2–5.

Orwin Talbott Papers, US Army Heritage and Education Center at Carlisle Barracks.
Box 1, Folder: Briefings on October War—Europe.
Box 1, Folder: Briefings on October War in Far East.
Box 1, Folder: Collection and Exploitation of Information on the Israeli-Arab War.

Box 1, Folder: Correspondence, February–August 1974.

Box 1, Folder: Cover Letters and Attached Trip Report, US MOIST Team Visit to Jordan, May 1974.

Box 1, Folder: Letter by Bruce I. Williams about the Mid-East War and Lessons Learned.

Box 1, Folder: List of Slides, 1973 Mideast War Briefing.

Box 1, Folder: Messages (most concerning the Arab-Israeli War).

Box 2, Folder: Report on the US Military Visit to Egypt, July 14–July 23, 1974.

Sorley, Lewis, ed. *Press On! Selected Works of General Donn A. Starry*, Vol. 1. Fort Leavenworth, KS: Combat Studies Institute Press, 2009.

———. *Press On! Selected Works of General Donn A. Starry*, Vol. 2. Fort Leavenworth, KS: Combat Studies Institute Press, 2009.

Starry, Donn. "October 1973 Mideast War," May 12, 1975, Box 59, Folder 3, Donn Starry Papers, US Army Heritage and Education Center at Carlisle Barracks.

Swain, Richard, comp. *Selected Papers of General William E. DePuy*. Fort Leavenworth, KS: Combat Studies Institute, 1994.

US House of Representatives, Hearings before the DOD Subcommittee of the Appropriations Committee.

DOD Appropriations for FY75, Part 1 (February 27, March 5 and 6, 1974).

DOD Appropriations for FY75, Part 2 (April 1, 1974).

DOD Appropriations for FY75, Part 4 (April 29, 1974).

DOD Appropriations for FY75, Part 9 (June 26, 1974).

US Senate, Hearings before the DOD Subcommittee of the Appropriations Committee.

DOD Appropriations for FY75, Part 4 (March 7 and May 2, 1974).

DOD Appropriations for FY75 (June 25, 1974).

DOD Appropriations for FY76, Part 4 (February 26 and March 19, 1975).

DOD Appropriations for FY76, Part 2 (March 12, 1975).

US Senate, Hearings before the Armed Services Committee.

Military Procurement Supplemental, FY74 (March 12, 1974).

DOD Authorization, Part 2 (February 7, 1975).

Military Procurement FY76, Part 7 (March 12, 1975).

US Senate, Hearings before the R&D Subcommittee of the Armed Services Committee.

DOD R&D, FY76, Part 6 (March 17 and 25, 1975).

Military Procurement FY77, RDT&E (April 6, 1976).

US Senate, Hearings before the Tactical Air Power Subcommittee of the Armed Services Committee.

Military Procurement FY75, Part 8 (March 13, 14, and 20, 1974).

Military Procurement FY76, Parts 8 (March 6 and 11, 1975).

Military Procurement FY76, Part 9 (March 13 and 18, 1975).

Weapons Systems Evaluation Group Report 249, *Assessment of the Weapons and Tactics Used in the October 1973 Middle East War*, October 1974. Document is now declassified. Accessed electronically via the CIA's FOIA Reading Room.

SECONDARY SOURCES

Alessi-Friedlander, R. Z. "Learning to Win When Fighting Outnumbered: Operational Risk in the U.S. Army, 1973–1982 and the Influence of the 1973 Arab-Israeli War." Master's thesis, Command and General Staff College, 2016.

Arcangelis, Mario de. *Electronic Warfare: From the Battle of Tsushima to the Falklands and Lebanon Conflicts*. Poole, UK: Blandford, 1985.

Armstrong, David. *Bullets and Bureaucrats: The Machine Gun and the United States Army, 1861–1916*. Westport, CT: Greenwood, 1982.

Biddle, Tami Davis. *Rhetoric and Reality in Air Warfare: Evolution of British and American Ideas about Strategic Bombing, 1914–1945*. Princeton, NJ: Princeton University Press, 2004.

Bidwell, Brian. *History of the Military Intelligence Division, Department of the Army General Staff, 1775–1941*. Frederick, MD: University Publications of America, 1986.

Bonura, Michael. *Under the Shadow of Napoleon: French Influence on the American Way of Warfare from the War of 1812 to the Outbreak of World War II*. New York: New York University Press, 2012.

Braisted, William. *The US Navy in the Pacific, 1897–1909*. Annapolis, MD: Naval Institute Press, 2008.

Bronfeld, Saul. "Fighting Outnumbered: The Impact of the Yom Kippur War on the U.S. Army." *Journal of Military History* 71, no. 2 (April 2007): 465–98.

Cameron, Robert. *Mobility, Shock, and Firepower: The Emergence of U.S. Army's Armor Branch, 1917–1945*. Washington, DC: US Army Center of Military History, 2008.

Challener, Richard D. *Admirals, Generals, and American Foreign Policy, 1898–1914*. Princeton, NJ: Princeton University Press, 1973.

Chapman, Anne. *The Army's Training Revolution, 1973–1990: An Overview*. Washington, DC: Center of Military History, 1994.

Clark, J. P. *Preparing for War: The Emergence of the Modern U.S. Army, 1815–1917*. Cambridge, MA: Harvard University Press, 2017.

Coffman, Edward. *The Old Army: A Portrait of the American Army in Peacetime, 1784–1898*. New York: Oxford University Press, 1986.

———. *The Regulars: The American Army, 1898–1941*. Cambridge, MA: Harvard University Press, 2007.

Dastrup, Boyd. *King of Battle: A Branch History of the U.S. Army's Field Artillery.* Fort Monroe, VA: US Army Training and Doctrine Command, 1992.

Davidson, Janine. *Lifting the Fog of Peace, How Americans Learned to Fight Modern War.* Ann Arbor: University of Michigan Press, 2010.

Davis, Russell. *The Challenge of Adaptation: The US Army in the Aftermath of Conflict, 1953–2000.* Fort Leavenworth, KS: Combat Studies Institute Press, 2008.

Dibella, Anthony. "Can the Army Become a *Learning Organization?* A Question Re-examined." *Joint Forces Quarterly* 56, no. 1 (2010): 117–22.

Doyle, Joseph. *The Yom Kippur War and the Shaping of the United States Air Force.* Maxwell AFB, AL: Air University Press, 2019.

Dyson, Tom. *Organizational Learning and the Modern Army: A New Model for Lessons-Learned Processes.* London: Routledge, 2020.

Eslinger, Robert. *The Neglect of Long-Range Escort Development during the Interwar Years (1918–1943).* Research paper, USAF Air Command and Staff College, March 1997.

Estes, Kenneth, and Daniel Kowalsky, eds. *History in Dispute,* Vol. 18: *The Spanish Civil War.* Detroit: St. James, 2005.

Falk, Stanley. "Soldier-Technologist, Major Alfred Mordecai and the Beginnings of Science in the US Army." PhD diss., Georgetown University, 1959.

Finney, Robert. *History of the Air Corps Tactical School, 1920–1940.* Maxwell AFB, AL: Research Studies Institute, USAF Historical Division, 1955.

Foley, Robert. "Dumb Donkeys or Cunning Foxes? Learning in the British and German Armies during the Great War." *International Affairs* 90, no. 2 (March 2014): 279–98.

Frame, Arthur. "U.S. Military Commission to Crimean War and Influence on the U.S. Army before the American Civil War." PhD diss., University of Kansas, 1993.

Futrell, Robert. *Ideas, Concepts, Doctrine: Basic Thinking in the United States Air Force, 1907–1960,* Vol. 1. Washington, DC: Ross & Perry, 2002.

———. *Ideas, Concepts, Doctrine: Basic Thinking in the United States Air Force, 1961–1984,* Vol. 2. Maxwell AFB, AL: Air University Press, 1989.

Gillie, M. H. *Forging the Thunderbolt: History of the U.S. Army's Armored Forces, 1917–1945.* Mechanicsburg, PA: Stackpole Books, 2006.

Gole, Henry. *Exposing the Third Reich: Colonel Truman Smith in Hitler's Germany.* Lexington: University Press of Kentucky, 2013.

Green, Constance McLaughlin, Harry Thomson, and Peter Roots. *The Ordnance Department: Planning Munitions for War.* Washington, DC: US Army Center of Military History, 1990.

Greenwood, John. "The American Military Observers of the Russo-Japanese War (1904–1905)." PhD diss., Kansas State University, 1971.

Hagan, Kenneth. *This People's Navy: The Making of American Sea Power.* New York: Free Press, 1991.

Herbert, Paul. *Deciding What Has to Be Done: General William E. DePuy and the 1976 Edition of FM100–5*. Fort Leavenworth, KS: Combat Studies Institute, July 1988.

Hofmann, George. "The Tactical and Strategic Use of Attaché Intelligence: The Spanish Civil War and the U.S. Army's Misguided Quest for a Modern Tank Doctrine." *Journal Military History* 62, no. 1 (January 1998): 101–33.

———. *Through Mobility We Conquer: The Mechanization of U.S. Cavalry*. Lexington: University Press of Kentucky, 2006.

Hofmann, George, and Donn Starry, eds. *Camp Colt to Desert Storm: The History of U.S. Armored Forces*. Lexington: University Press of Kentucky, 1999.

Hone, Trent. *Learning War: The Evolution of Fighting Doctrine in the U.S. Navy, 1898–1945*. Annapolis, MD: Naval Institute Press, 2018.

Hope, Ian. *A Scientific Way of War: Antebellum Military Science, West Point, and the Origins of American Military Thought*. Lincoln: University of Nebraska Press, 2015.

Hsieh, Wayne. *West Pointers and the Civil War: The Old Army in War and Peace*. Chapel Hill: University of North Carolina Press, 2009.

Jensen, Benjamin. *Forging the Sword: Doctrinal Change in the U.S. Army*. Stanford, CA: Stanford University Press, 2016.

Johnson, David. *Fast Tanks and Heavy Bombers: Innovations in the U.S. Army, 1917–1945*. Ithaca, NY: Cornell University Press, 2003.

Juntunen, Kim. "U.S. Army Attachés and the Spanish Civil War, 1936–1939: Gathering of Technical and Tactical Intelligence." Master's thesis, Temple University, May 1990.

Kretchik, Walter. *U.S. Army Doctrine: From the American Revolution to the War on Terror*. Lawrence: University Press of Kansas, 2011.

Laslie, Brian. *The Air Force Way of War: U.S. Tactics and Training after Vietnam*. Lexington: University Press of Kentucky, 2015.

Linn, Brian McAllister. *The Echo of Battle: The Army's Way of War*. Cambridge, MA: Harvard University Press, 2007.

Mahnken, Thomas, ed. *Learning the Lessons of Modern War*. Stanford, CA: Stanford University Press, 2020.

———. *Uncovering Ways of War: U.S. Intelligence and Foreign Military Innovation, 1918–1941*. Ithaca, NY: Cornell University Press, 2009.

McBride, William. *Technological Change and the United States Navy, 1865–1945*. Baltimore: Johns Hopkins University Press, 2000.

McKenney, Janice. *The Organizational History of Field Artillery, 1775–2003*. Washington, DC: US Army Center of Military History, 2007.

Michel, Marshall. "The Revolt of the Majors: How the Air Force Changed after Vietnam." PhD diss., Auburn University, 2006.

Moten, Matthew. *The Delafield Commission and the American Military Profession*. College Station: Texas A&M University Press, 2000.

Murray, Williamson, and Allan Millett, eds. *Military Innovation in the Interwar Period.* New York: Cambridge University Press, 1996.

Nenninger, Timothy. *The Leavenworth Schools and the Old Army: Education, Professionalism, and the Officer Corps of the United States Army, 1881–1918.* Westport, CT: Greenwood Press, 1978.

Nesmith, Vardell. "Quiet Paradigm Change: Evolution of the Field Artillery Doctrine of United States Army, 1861–1905." PhD diss., Duke University, 1977.

O'Connell, Robert. *Sacred Vessels: Cult of the Battleship and the Rise of the US Navy.* New York: Oxford University Press, 1993.

O'Connor, Maureen. "In the Eye of the Beholder: Western Military Observers from Buena Vista to Plevna." PhD diss., Harvard University, 1996.

Odom, William. *After the Trenches: The Transformation of the U.S. Army, 1918–1939.* College Station: Texas A&M University Press, 1999.

Oyos, Matthew. *In Command: Theodore Roosevelt and the American Military.* Lincoln, NE: Potomac, 2018.

Pershing, John J. *My Life before the World War, 1860–1917.* Lexington: University of Kentucky Press, 2013.

Raines, Edgar. "Major General J. Franklin Bell and Military Reform: The Chief of Staff Years, 1906–1910." PhD diss., University of Wisconsin–Madison, 1976.

Reardon, Carol. *Soldiers and Scholars: The U.S. Army and the Uses of Military History, 1865–1920.* Lawrence: University Press of Kansas, 1990.

Romjue, John. *From Active Defense to AirLand Battle: The Development of Army Doctrine, 1973–1982.* Fort Monroe, VA: TRADOC, 1984.

———. *A History of Army 86, Vol. 1: Division 86: The Development of the Heavy Division, September 1978–October 1979.* Fort Monroe, VA: Historical Office, TRADOC, June 1982.

Romjue, John, Susan Canedy, and Anne Chapman. *Prepare the Army for War: A Historical Overview of the Army Training and Doctrine Command, 1973–1993.* Washington, DC: TRADOC, 1993.

Schneller, Robert. *A Quest for Glory: Biography of Rear Admiral John A. Dahlgren.* Annapolis, MD: Naval Institute Press, 1996.

Sheehan, Kevin. "Preparing for an Imaginary War? Examining Peacetime Functions and Changes of Army Doctrine." PhD diss., Harvard University, 1988.

Skelton, William. *American Profession of Arms: The Army Officer Corps, 1784–1861.* Lawrence: University Press of Kansas, 1992.

Stebbins, Steven. "Indirect Fire: The Challenge and Response in the U.S. Army, 1907–1917." Master's thesis, University of North Carolina–Chapel Hill, 1993.

Vacca, William. "Learning about Military Effectiveness: Examining Theories of Learning During the Russo-Japanese War." PhD diss., Rutgers University, 2009.

Vetock, Dennis. *Lessons Learned: A History of US Army Lesson Learning*. Carlisle Barracks, PA: US Army Military History Institute, 1988.

Werrell, Kenneth. *Chasing the Silver Bullet: U.S. Air Force Weapons from Vietnam to Desert Storm*. Washington, DC: Smithsonian Institution Scholarly Press, 2003.

Wilson, John. *Maneuver and Firepower: The Evolution of Divisions and Separate Brigades*. Honolulu, HI: University Press of the Pacific, 2001.

INDEX

Note: Figures are indicated by page numbers in *italics*.

Welles, Gideon, 41, 42
Werrell, Kenneth, 240
Wesson, Charles, 154
Westover, Oscar, 150, 168
West Point, 18, 28–29, 32, 34, 98
Weyand, Fred, 209, 215
Weyland, Otto, 149
White, R.D., 63, 75
White, William, 191
Wilcox, Cadmus, 18, 35
Wild Weasel SAM Killer, 235–237, 241
Williams, Bruce, 193, 196, 197–203, 246
Williams, John Sharp, 79
Wilson, Louis, 194
Winslow, Cameron, 75
Wood, Leonard, 79, 80, 89, 94, 96–97, 102
Wood, Oliver, 138
Woodring, Harry, 153
Woodruff, J. A., 90
World War I, 63–64, 73, 88, 89, 91, 103,
    109–10, 114, 138, 143, 154, 280–81
World War II, 141, 157, 158–59, 161, 164–65,
    166, 167, 170–71, 173, 235
Wright, Luke, 96
WSEG (Weapons Systems Evaluation
    Group), 190, 191, 193, 200, 205, 247

XM-1 (and M1) tank, 156, 192–93, 211, 222,
    228–29, 247, 249, 282, 287

Yashima, Japanese Navy, 76
Yom Kippur War, 7, 277, 279, 282, 287;
    aircraft shelters in, 206; air-to-air

combat, 207, 241; anti-aircraft artillery.
201, 231–32; antitank guided missiles
in, 199–200; application of findings
in, 208–44; bombing in, 217, 234–36;
chemical warfare preparedness, 203,
223; close air support in, 200, 207, 217,
244; combined-arms approach in, 198,
223, 226; complexity of battle, 196–97,
240; electronic warfare in, 195, 197,
205–6, 222, 236, 241; enlightening lessons,
198–203, 204–6; field artillery in, 200–1,
223, 226, 230; forward-leaning support
in, 201–3; Golan Heights in, *210*; gunner
marksmanship in, 199; helicopters in,
203–4, 232–33; identification of lessons
from, 191–208; impact on doctrine, 213–
216, 218–220; infantry fighting vehicles in,
192, 204, 227–28; integrated air defenses
in, 194, 199, 200, 201, 204–5, 230–31,
239, 243; leadership in, 197–98; lethality
in, 196, 223–24; machine guns in, 199,
204, 217, 229, 236–37; missed or skewed
lessons, 203, 207–8; precision guided
munitions, 206, 237; Suez Canal front,
202; suppression of enemy air defenses
in, 201, 205; tanks in, 198–99, 221–22,
228–30, 247, 256n83; training in, 197–98,
199, 224–25. 238–39; warships in, 190

Zaloga, Steven, 148, 163, 164
ZSU-23-4 AAA, 201, 205, 231

ABOUT THE AUTHOR

Brent L. Sterling is an adjunct professor at the Walsh School of Foreign Service, Georgetown University. He is the author of *Do Good Fences Make Good Neighbors? What History Teaches Us about Strategic Barriers and International Security* (Georgetown University Press, 2009). He has spent the past thirty years as a defense analyst, including positions at the Central Intelligence Agency and consulting firms.